MW01489110

ISBN
Hardcover: ISBN-13: 979-8879959673
Paperback: ISBN-13: 979-8332485923

Library of Congress Control Number: 2024916338

This book is dedicated to Charles and Roseann Asztalos, who married on October 9, 1948—two ordinary people who lived extraordinary lives. It is also dedicated to Vincent Robert Hicks, Cate, Rosey, Elle and Hank Asztalos who will make the next chapters of this story.

Index

The Invisible Highway
Prologue

The lives of Charles and Roseann Asztalos are classic American melting pot stories. Their parents and grandparents immigrated to the United States in the late 1800s and early 1900s as part of a wave of Europeans looking for a new life in the Promised Land. The adults who raised them began their lives in villages on the European continent and were shaped by the horrors of World War I. They risked the arduous voyage for a new life in America. Charles and Roseann's generation had their youth interrupted by the Great Depression, and they came of age to serve our country in its darkest hours during World War II. The war forever changed them in ways they could never guess when they began to experience life in the 1930s.

Charles and Roseann fulfilled their older family members' dreams of creating an American family. They blended four European families and produced four children without allegiance to the old world or--for that matter-- to the old immigrant neighborhoods from which they were born. Their three sons and one daughter scattered across the four corners of this country and married outside their parents' tight-knit communities. Charles and Roseann's grandchildren are even further removed from this legacy as they carry the heritages from each parent's side of the family.

Charles and Roseann were indeed part of a generational engine that produces Americans.

Chapter 1
We Came to America

S.S. Pennsylvania from the Norway Heritage collection

Welké Kapussany, Austro-Hungarian Empire
May 10, 1863

As the Civil War raged in the United States (U.S.), Juliánna Köllösÿ and her husband Janos Asztalos gave birth to a son in a village within the Austro-Hungarian Empire called Welké Kapussany. He was promptly baptized into the Hungarian Orthodox Church.

That village today is called Veľké Kapušany (Hungarian: Nagykapos). It is a small town on the eastern plains of current-day Slovakia, less than five miles from the Ukrainian border. Since it was traditionally part of Hungary proper, the area has a large Hungarian population.

The name "Kapušany" is likely derived from the Latin word Copus, meaning "gate." This area's earliest settlers go back to the Neolithic period, and from the second half of the tenth century until 1918, it was part of the Kingdom of Hungary. The first written references to the settlement span back to 1211, and it was awarded town status in 1430. The area frequently served as a way station for Germans, Russians, Poles, and Hungarians emigrating from the east to the west. When Janos and Juliánna lived in Welké Kapussany, it had about 268 residents. Today it is a large town with nearly 10,000 inhabitants.

Janos and Juliánna named their baby Sandor. "Sandor" and "Asztalos" are relatively common names among Hungarians. In the Hungarian language, "asztalos" means "cabinet maker" or "carpenter" and is as ordinary as the name "Carpenter" is among English-speaking people. Additionally, the Hungarian church lists people taking that name back to its earliest recordings. Therefore, one could suspect that a person somewhere in Sandor's family lineage made furniture.

Sandor grew up working on a farm. Although Austria-Hungary had a scattering of regions with industrialization, almost two-thirds of the population were subsistence farmers. Wealth was concentrated in a small landowning aristocracy that possessed nearly half of the arable land. Feudalism forced the Asztalos family and other Hungarians to exist in a perpetual state just above starvation with no ability to improve their lives. Additionally, during the mid-1870s, heavier-than-normal rains and flooding ravaged their fields, further threatening their tenuous existence.

It is easy to see why villagers from Welké Kapussany and other Hungarians began a wave of immigration where they risked everything for a new life in the U.S. In the late 1870s and 1880s, villagers with last names Eszterhai, Esterhauzi, Kisch, Kovacs, and Asztalos, some related to Sandor, began to immigrate to the U.S. at the cusp of what would become the largest wave of Hungarian exodus to the New World. In 1880, Passaic, New Jersey, Pittsburg, Pennsylvania, and Youngtown, Ohio, had clusters of less than 100 Hungarians who lived and worked together. These pioneers planted the seeds for large Hungarian communities that still exist today.

There were several waves of Hungarian immigrants to the U.S. dating back to the 1850s. However, the 1870 to 1914 wave of Hungarian immigrants--labeled the turn-of-the-century "economic immigrants"— was the largest. They came to the U.S. for work opportunities that did not exist in Europe. Peasants and unskilled workers were attracted to the steel mills, coal mines, and factories, primarily in the Ohio Valley. Nearly two million immigrants came from Hungary during the four decades leading up to World War I.

As pioneers from the village left for the U.S., Sandor married, grew a family, and farmed in Welké Kapussany. In April 1887, János and Mária Köblös arranged for their daughter Mária to marry twenty-four-year-old Sandor. She was four years younger than him. In Hungary, they had three children: Amelia, born in 1889, Marie in 1892, and Alex.

Sandor's emigration story was typical of the millions of other Hungarians who left the Old World's feudal agriculture existence to find a new life in the mines and mills of industrial America.

Sandor's story begins with letters from his sister-in-law, Zsuzsanna Eszterhay, living in Painesville, Ohio, and Mária's relative, Erzsi Köblös in Passaic. These pioneers invited their relatives over with tales of their journey, jobs, and life in boarding houses.

Zsuzsanna and Erzsi vividly described their long ocean voyage on board a sailing ship with cramped and uncomfortable conditions. They described how their group from Welké Kapussany, along with all the other passengers and crew, filled every space on deck and in the ship's rigging as it slowly made its way into New York Harbor. It moved past Liberty Island, with the Statue of Liberty under construction. Finally, the buildings of New York came into view. Then they saw the gleam of a white fort called Castle Garden, whose guarded gateway they had to pass. Even though they traveled through some of Europe's grandest cities to meet their ship, they could only cry as they marveled at the grandeur of New York Harbor.

As the passengers disembarked the ship, they became part of the tens of thousands of immigrants who would pass through Castle Garden on the southern tip of Manhattan each year. Established by New York State on August 1, 1855, this open area served as the county's first organized immigration portal and the main entry point for immigrants into the U.S. It was closed in 1892, with the nation's first federal immigration station opening on Ellis Island.

The letters went on about how they were met by fellow countrymen, relief workers, missionaries, con artists, and agents looking for laborers. One of the many horse-drawn carriages that carted the immigrants to their fellow countrymen's neighborhoods in Manhattan took Zsuzsanna, Erzsi, and their companions to the Hungarian section located from 75th

Street to 83rd Street between Third and Lexington Avenues. There they found boarding, familiar food, and support.

Agents for mills in Pennsylvania, Ohio, and New Jersey told them that there were jobs at the end of a train ride. So, after a short recuperation, Zsuzsanna trekked across several states to arrive in Painesville while Erzsi crossed the river to Passaic. Both trips required navigating a new country where they did not speak the language or know the customs. However, it was all possible due to the assistance of fellow Hungarians who came before them.

The letters concluded that you could achieve your dreams in America through hard work. Both offered to help Sandor's family by providing an end address to use for the transit, the promise of a job and living quarters, and, more importantly, the knowledge that there is a Hungarian community waiting to help them establish their lives in America.

The decision for Sandor to leave was difficult. He had to leave all that was familiar to him in pursuit of a better livelihood. Although life was hard on the farm, he was surrounded by family. His village roots went back to at least his grandfather living there since the beginning of the century. In addition to his wife and young children, his parents, sister Juliánna, and extended family members, including his Uncles Karoly and Ferentz, and Aunt Maria, were part of his support network.

It was also prohibitively expensive to travel to America, even under the cheapest and most austere conditions. Sandor would have to travel over one thousand miles by train, foot, or other ground transit to one of the major ports like Hamburg, Cherbourg, or Antwerp. He would need to pay for the food, board, and transportation incurred during the overland transit, then thirty dollars for a steerage class ticket aboard a steamer or sailing ship. Sandor also had to have several dollars in his pocket upon arrival in the U.S., so he was not labeled a "pauper" and returned to Europe. Lastly, he needed to pay his way from the dock in the New World to his ultimate destination. It is all but impossible for a subsistence farmer to save enough money on his own to afford the voyage.

To overcome these obstacles, emigrants traveled in groups from the same village, where several young men and women agreed to support each other on the arduous voyage. Sandor and eleven other villagers, both relatives and neighbors, planned their passage. The group consisted of nine men and three women. They ranged in age from thirty-eight to fifteen, and each had someone in the U.S. assisting them. Their families pooled their funds and sold what they could to scrape together enough money for the transit. Their relatives in the U.S. prepaid their thirty-dollar third-class tickets, which included an ocean crossing and train fare from Philadelphia, PA., to any location along the Pennsylvania Railroad Line. Thirty dollars was a sizable expense for the new Americans considering that the average unskilled worker only earned between $500 and $600 per year.

Because of the cost and difficult travel conditions, Sandor (and the five other married villagers in the group) made the voyage without his wife and young children. Mária would stay back and care for their children until Sandor could earn enough money to pay her way. Grandparents and cousins would also help raise the children.

In early 1895, the day arrived when Sandor's group assembled in the village square to begin their trek. Sandor and the following men: Erzsebet Kes, age 15; Erzsebet Asztalos, 17; Zsegmund Capp, 31; Gaspar Cziaki, 17; János Szabo, 34; Mihaly Danji, 26; János Köblös, 38; and Emmerich Berties, 24 joined the following women: Juliana Eszterhay, 35; Juliana Vekso, 19; and Eszti Köblös, 17 to hug their families goodbye. They clutched bags with as much food, clothing, and bedding as they could carry. They planned to travel 1,000 miles across Austria-Hungary, Germany, France, and Belgium to the Dutch port of Antwerp. There they would board a steamship to Philadelphia. Once they arrived in the U.S., five would travel to Passaic, five to Painesville, and two to the Pittsburg area.

The group arrived at Antwerp on March 20 and presented their tickets to an American Line representative. Their third-class ticket provided them a space in one of the S.S. Pennsylvania's "steerage" compartments.

The Pennsylvania was a passenger-cargo steamship built in Philadelphia in 1872. She was explicitly constructed to move people and goods between Europe and the Port of Philadelphia. Three years before the

Welké Kapussany group's arrival, she began an exclusive route between Antwerp and Philadelphia, transporting European laborers for Philadelphia's booming industries. Along with holds of cargo, she carried between two and three hundred immigrants on each voyage.

Before boarding their ship, the group took baths and were "de-loused." Single men were assigned to the forward compartment, and women were back aft. Between them was a compartment berthing families. The travelers were pleased to find that most of the passengers were Hungarian, with many recruited by American companies from towns throughout the Empire. Once all 248 passengers and cargo were on board, Captain Thomas ordered the crew to pull in the lines, and the Pennsylvania began her crossing of the Invisible Highway.

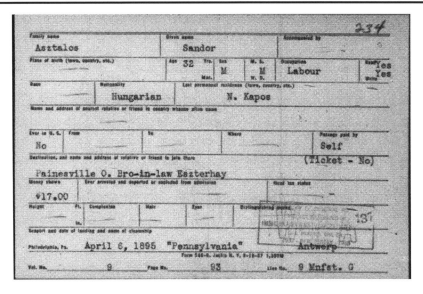

Delaware Bay, United States
April 4, 1895

The seventeen-day crossing was uneventful, except for an outbreak of cholera infantum among the family steerage compartment's children. Two-year-old Anna Valyks died while crossing the ocean, and all the passengers stood silent for her burial at sea. Late Thursday, April 4, the weary passengers ran topside as they heard shouts of "land-ho." The passengers caught their first glimpse of their new country on either side of the ship as the vessel slipped past Cape May, NJ. Once inside

Delaware Bay, Pennsylvania began the slow and dangerous eighty-seven-mile journey up the Delaware River to Pier 53 in Philadelphia. The river had narrow channels and dangerous shallows. In the eight months before the Pennsylvania's arrival, including April, thirty-two ships ran aground on shoals. Half the groundings were steamships. The Pennsylvania ran up upon Dan Baker shoals earlier in the year and was aground for seventeen hours, where she blocked the channel and essentially shut down all ship traffic.

Sadly, a second child, three-year-old Joseph Zacek, died as the ship traversed the river. The passengers prayed that the disease would not prevent them from docking in the New World.

About seven miles south of their berth in Philadelphia, the ship slowed as it approached the Lazaretto Quarantine Station located on the Delaware River's western bank in Tinicum Township (adjacent to what is now Philadelphia International Airport). The Station screened and, if necessary, quarantined all shipboard personnel for communicable diseases before arriving in Philadelphia. In addition, the complex included a hospital capable of housing 500 patients. It was built in response to Philadelphians who blamed immigrants for the devastating outbreaks of cholera, yellow fever, scarlet fever, smallpox, and other communicable diseases in the 1700s and 1800s.

The lookout in the Station's watchtower rang the bell, which alerted the bargeman and medical staff of the approaching Pennsylvania. A barge transported a physician and quarantine captain alongside the ship to inspect the crew, cargo, and passengers for any signs of disease or contamination. With the death of two children from cholera infantum, the station physician transferred all the passengers and crew to the quarantine station for an in-depth examination. After several hours, the medical staff gave all the passengers a clean bill of health and cleared the Pennsylvania to sail the final last miles of its voyage. Passengers wept with relief as the ship's anchor raised and the propeller began to turn.

On Saturday, April 6, the passengers ascended on deck to view Philadelphia and celebrate their successful crossing of the Invisible

Highway. It was overcast with intermittent rain, but they could see the city's distinct skyline as the crew inched the ship up to Pier 53.

Once the ship was secured to the dock adjacent to the Washington Avenue Immigration Station, customs agents and employees of the Pennsylvania Railroad ushered Sandor and the other passengers down a gangplank into the Station's upper level. Disheveled from their voyage, the group from Welké Kapussany shuffled through the customs and immigration process. In 1895, the U.S. had an open immigration policy without visas or extensive governmental entry processes to navigate. Having completed their health screening in Lazaretto, all Sandor and his fellow travelers had to do was clear a cursory screening, and they could proceed inland.

Using the ship's manifest, an immigration official recorded their name, age, marital status, former residence, and destination. Though he left his homeland, Sandor was proud of his name and heritage. Upon arrival in the U.S., many names were "Americanized" through morphing or shortening. For example, many people now bear the last name of "Astalos," where either immigration officials or the shipping clerks who produced the ships' manifests removed the "z." The official recorded Sandor's last name minus his "z." Incensed by the name change and to the horror of his fellow travelers, he objected to this desecration and held up the process until the official restored the "z" and accurately reflected that "Sandor Asztalos" had crossed the ocean and landed in America.

The twelve Welké Kapussany passengers, with their railroad tickets in hand, proceeded through a large lobby, then down a stairwell to the lower level, where they collectively exchanged their Austro-Hungarian Krones for 161 U.S. dollars. The next stop was a comfort station that offered them a chance to clean up, then to the Pennsylvania Railroad ticket booths, where they split into two groups. They hugged each other, not knowing if they would ever see one another again, and said goodbye. Eszti, both Erzsebets, and Julianas boarded a train to Passaic while Janos, Emmerich, Gaspar, Zsegmund, and Sandor, heading to Painesville, joined Mihaly and János Köblös for an initial train ride to Pittsburg. As they awaited their trains, the group rested on large benches. They watched their fellow passengers, with no planned destination, get recruited by locals to work in the factories of Philadelphia. They could purchase sandwiches, coffee, and cigars. Even though Sandor felt like a strong coffee, he resisted spending any money because each penny spent meant he would have to wait longer to be with Mária.

Sandor eventually settled in Youngstown, Ohio, approximately 65 miles south of Painesville. He took up employment as a laborer in one of its mills or coal mines, which enthusiastically recruited Hungarians and other immigrants to feed their growing demand for workers. Earlier in the century, several factors allowed Youngstown to become an industrial hub for the adolescent nation. First, iron ore and coal deposits were discovered nearby. That discovery was followed by digging the Youngstown branch of the Pennsylvania and Ohio Canal, then completing several major railway lines, including the Baltimore & Ohio, the Erie Lackawanna, the New York Central, and the Pennsylvania Railroad. These natural resources and transportation to move finished goods made Youngstown and other cities in the Mahoning Valley one of the nation's significant iron and steel-producing areas.

Sandor joined a community of around 15,000 Hungarians living in Youngstown. He watched new steel mills, like Youngstown Sheet and Tube and Republic Steel, expand and recruit more immigrants to the community, including Poles, Italians, and his fellow Hungarians. Sandor initially lived in a boarding house or barracks-type housing provided by his employer on the lower East Side, near the steel mills. Not long after he arrived, he sent for Mária, who followed the same route.

Sandor and Mária "Americanized" their names to Alex and Mary and joined Youngstown's newly established First Reformed Church. They spent much of the next fourteen years in Youngstown and areas in eastern Ohio and western Pennsylvania. During that time, their family enjoyed the Old World's customs within that area's thriving Hungarian population while trying to fit into their new American homeland.

On Saturday, July 10, 1897, the Mahoning Valley economy had ground to a crawl due to a nationwide strike by coal miners. It was also caught in the grip of a heatwave. The Pittsburg Post-Gazette warned that babies were especially susceptible to the dangerous heat. Thirteen miles south of Pittsburg in McKeesport, Mária and Sandor had a boy whom they named Karoly. He was baptized into the First Reform Church by Pastor Frederick Mayer, with his godparents János Kosztyo and Erzsi Banese looking on. Karoly only attended school until the sixth grade then likely worked in a mill to help support the family. This was common for children as it was years before Congress enacted the first child labor laws.

Pietro Iozzia in Santa Croce Camerina, Italy

Santa Croce Camerina, Sicily, Kingdom of Italy
1904

While Sandor was working in an American mill, a young man in a small village on the southern coast of Sicily stared out over the Mediterranean Sea, planning a new life in that land far over the horizon. Twenty-one-year-old Pietro Iozzia had been at odds with his parents, Gaetano and Rose Paci-Iozzia, over a girl they forbade him to marry. His frustration grew such that he plotted to leave his bucolic village of Santa Croce Camerina and cast a new life for the two of them.

Santa Croce Camerina is a picturesque spot with its gently rolling landscape nestled on a plain just south of the Iblean Mountains. Not far from the town square are wide expansive beaches on the Mediterranean Sea. It has always been an agricultural town, with many villagers cultivating early fruits in the greenhouses surrounding the town. It is also known for its beautiful flowers, which are exported across Italy.

Santa Croce Camerina also has a rich history, with the earliest records dating back to the Bronze Age. Its architecture reflects its early Christian roots. The town has several frescoes to Elena with the Holy Cross. Tradition has it that these frescos give the town its name, as Santa Croce is Italian for "Holy Cross." It had been invaded and occupied multiple times throughout its history. Conquerors include the Romans, Arabs, Nazi Germans, and Allied Armies in World War II. Its population in 1901 was only 6,081, with many of those inhabitants being members of the Iozzia and the Blundo families, the latter being the family of Pietro's future wife.

Pietro was born into a peasant family on March 11, 1883, and attended school until second grade. Like his father and the generations before him, he left school then because he was "old enough" to work on the farm. Moreover, he was expected to work the soil until he devolved into an old man.

Another villager, Giuseppina Blundo, was the daughter of a well-off shop owner and wore custom-made clothes with expensive jewelry. Though the village was small, Pietro and Giuseppina lived in different circles. Pietro toiled and lived life in the fields around the village, and Giuseppina grew up in an upscale intown house playing with other children of businessmen and professionals. Along the way, the rich girl and farmhand fell for each other. Despite their parents' objections, they secretly met, and their attraction grew. Eventually, they fell in love and asked permission to start a life together. However, their parents forbid marriage, unable to see beyond the village's history of planned marriages and caste system.

Pietro's escape to the New World was like Sandor's, where the journey was paved by those who came before him. Like Sandor, he was not the first to emigrate from his village, but he was at the front of a wave that would continue until well after World War II.

At the turn of the 20th century, Santa Croce Camerina emigrants arrived by boat to work in the factories and mills clustered in Paterson and Hackensack, NJ. Former villagers now living in the New World lent one another a hand with jobs and language. They gathered regularly for dinner, holidays, and to play soccer. On October 8, 1916, the unofficial gatherings formalized to create what today is the San Giuseppe Santa Croce Camerina Society. Pietro did not know it, sitting on the beach overlooking the Mediterranean Sea, but he would be an active member of that organization one day.

Pietro's grandson Robert at the entrance to Santa Croce Camerina in 1980.

In 1904, twenty-five-year-old Giuseppe De Martino returned to Santa Croce Camerina after working for two years in Hackensack. Back in his Sicilian village, he shared stories about life in the New World and recruited villagers to accompany him on a return trip. Pietro listened to him describe life in the New World, where there was an opportunity to live, work, and, more importantly, marry in ways that did not exist in Santa Croce Camerina. It appealed to him as he thought about his life.

Pietro was twenty-one years old, not in a good relationship with his parents, a peasant who could not read or write, forbidden from being with the woman he loved, and sensing the only future the village could offer him was a lifetime of more of the same. Over the years, he heard about others who started new lives in New Jersey. Now it was his opportunity to take that same journey.

In February 1905, fourteen travelers, including Giuseppe De Martino, gathered in the town square to begin their journey to New Jersey. All the travelers identified someone in Paterson or Hackensack who would take them in once they arrived. They all had as much cash in their pockets as they and their families could muster together. The money would go toward ground transportation to the port, a third-class ticket to America, and some money in their pocket to clear U.S. Immigration without being turned back as a pauper.

With little money, some food, and their family members' well wishes, the group headed north out of town toward the Italian mainland. Pietro was the exception. He had to raise the money for the voyage and provisions himself because his parents forbid him to leave.

The ages of the fourteen travelers were between 22 and 37, with Pietro being the youngest. He was a handsome solid-built man with a healthy physique who stood at five feet four inches and weighed 130 pounds. He had a fair complexion and thick black hair. Pietro had a look that would put people at ease. His health was good, and he was physically and mentally ready for the arduous voyage ahead.

The names and ages of the other twelve travelers with Pietro and Giuseppe were Ferdinando Iozzia, 25; Salvatore Librio, 37; Giovanni Brancato, 24; Emmanuelle Fciofassi, 24; Giovanni Venzarbino, 27; Guglielmo Mandara, 24; Giuseppe Lessandrello, 29; Guglielmo Gulino, 35; Giambattista Lallieri, 28; Jicbeo Tisa, 23; Antonio Natiso, 31; and Fabatous Trofamo, 28. The group made their way over the mountainous interior of Sicily, across the Straits of Messina, and up the Southern Italian coast to Naples, where they purchased third-class tickets for the S.S. Citta Di Torino, a ship of the La Veloce Line whose primary mission was to feed the ever-expanding American economy with Italian immigrants.

The ship departed Genoa on May 9 for the 435-mile trip to Naples with emigrant passengers from Northern Italy. Two days later, tied to the Naples docks, it awaited another load of emigrants to fill every bit of space on board. Pietro and the group looked at the tired and rusted ship with a red star--the symbol for La Veloce Line--on its single cream-colored smokestack.

The Citta Di Torino was built by N. Odero & Company in Genoa and went into service in 1898. She had a single funnel and two masts, one on its bow and the other on its stern. The ship had a single propeller and could make twelve knots, taking seventeen or eighteen days to cross the Atlantic Ocean. She primarily sailed a roundtrip route from Italian ports to North and South America.

On May 11, Pietro and the thirteen other travelers merged into a crowd and crossed the gangplank onto the ship. The ship loaded 1,536 passengers, with forty in second class and the remaining to fill the 1,496 third class berths. The steamer's remaining holds were filled with lemons and oranges from southern Italy.

Once aboard the ship, Pietro was interviewed by a crewmember to ensure he could pass U.S. Immigration and be added to the ship's manifest. He told the crewmember that he worked on a farm and, thus, his occupation was recorded as "countryman." He had the equivalent of ten dollars in his possession (but departed the ship with eleven dollars after picking up one dollar during the crossing). He stated he was never in prison, an institution for treating the insane, or on charity, and he was neither a polygamist nor an anarchist. His destination was joining his friend Matteo Deodato who resided at 208 Market Street in Paterson, though he did not have a train ticket from New York City to Paterson. Matteo was related to Giuseppina, Pietro's future wife.

A medical examination on the Citta di Torino found Pietro in good mental and physical health without deformed or crippling conditions. That finding allowed him to receive a medical certificate from Doctor Rossi Agostino, an Italian physician who was the ship's surgeon, and he sailed with it on the crossing. Passengers who failed to answer the questions correctly or failed the medical examination were sent ashore. Once all the passengers who passed their examination were on board, the cargo holds full of citrus, and the manifest complete, the Citta Di Torino cast its lines from the dock and set out on an eighteen-day, 4,395-mile voyage to the Port of New York.

According to Heritage Ezine, an online publication focusing on Italy's heritage, third-class accommodations aboard immigrant ships were grueling and sometimes fatal. Immigrants berthed *"in poor hygienic condition, squatting on the deck, near the stairs, with a plate between their legs and a piece of bread between the feet... To be able to sleep, the emigrant lay down completely dressed, on his storage of bundles and suitcases, amid the smells of urine, feces, vomit...."*

Just because Pietro could board the ship, departing the gangplank in New York was not guaranteed. Shipwrecks with heavy loss of life were common due to poor maintenance of the ships. Pietro also risked boarding a *"ghost ship."* Immigration ships did not have a sickbay, pharmacy, or other medical care for the immigrants crammed in unsanitary conditions. The conditions were ripe for contagious diseases to spread among the passengers. According to Heritage Ezine: *"It was common that ships with sick passengers, dozens of deaths during the voyage, and epidemics were rejected and sailed again in search of another port."*

Pietro's ship was not immune from the horrors that plagued other immigrant ships. According to Heritage Ezine's article entitled *"The horror of emigration ships,"* a diary of the Citta Di Torino in November 1905 (six months after Pietro's crossing) states, *"Until now among the 600 passengers there have been forty-five deaths of which twenty for typhoid fever, ten for bronchopulmonary disease, seven measles, five influenza, three accidents on deck."*

On May 28, the day before arriving in New York, the ship's captain completed the paperwork to allow Pietro and the other immigrants to enter the U.S. He completed multiple affidavits stating:

> *"I Captain Emanuele of the CITTA DI TORINO from Napoli, do solemnly, sincerely, and truly that I have caused the surgeon of said vessel sailing therewith, or the surgeon employed by the owners thereof, to make a physical and oral examination of each and all of the aliens named in the forgoing Lists or Manifest*

Sheets, in number, and that from the report of said surgeon and from my own investigation, I believe that no one of said aliens is an idiot, or insane person, or a pauper, or is likely to become a public charge, or is suffering from a loathsome or a dangerous contagious disease, or is a person who has been convicted of a felony or other crime or misdemeanor involving moral turpitude, or a polygamist, or an anarchist, or under promise or agreement, expressed or implied, to perform labor in the United States, or a prostitute..."

He signed and dated the documents. Then Doctor Rossi Agostino signed a second affidavit stating he had examined the alien passengers and concurred with the captain's affidavit.

The following day, Monday, May 29, the Citta Di Torino steamed into New York Harbor. Most passengers packed in the ship's bowels were sick from eighteen days of unsanitary living and poor diet. Just when Pietro and the other travelers felt like they were going to die, word spread that the ship was entering the harbor. Hundreds of immigrants, including the fourteen Santa Croce Camerina travelers, ascended from their dark and smelly quarters onto the deck. It was a beautiful day in New York--sunny, clear blue skies with a temperature of seventy degrees Fahrenheit. The sight of land, paired with the cool air and hot sun on Pietro's face, let him know that, at last, the voyage was over!

After some cheering and smiles, the crowd grew silent as they all stared at a large woman with spikes on her head, holding a lamp high in her right hand. Pietro whispered to his fellow travelers, *"She is like a goddess that represents the big powerful country that will be our new home."*

The ship tied up to the pier in New York Harbor, and although he was unaware, the first steps of Pietro's new country recognizing him began. Inspectors from New York's quarantine authorities checked the ship for contagious diseases such as cholera, smallpox, typhus, yellow fever, or plague. Accompanying them was a medical officer from the Public Health and Marine Hospital Service who also inspected the ship. Captain Emanuele presented immigration officials with the signed ship's manifest, each page containing extensive information on about thirty passengers. With all the ship's documents in order, the forty second-class passengers skipped Ellis Island and disembarked directly to the U.S. The remaining passengers boarded a ferry for a short ride to the Immigrant Inspection Station on Ellis Island.

Like most days, Ellis Island was packed with long lines and groups of immigrants making their way through the process of becoming Americans. In addition to the Citta Di Torino, five other ships: the Tuscarora from London, Fontebelle from Saint Thomas, Armenia from Hamburg, Caledonia from Glasgow, and the Patria, also from Naples, discharged their passengers to the Station that day. It was common for the 850 staff to receive up to ten thousand people in a single day.

Pietro walked off the ferry with a label on his jacket that read, "Pietro Iozzia, Citta Di Torino." In addition to his luggage, he had an immigrant inspection card in his hand. The first person the group met was an Italian-speaking interpreter assigned to help guide them through the process. The average interpreter working on Ellis Island spoke six languages, with some speaking as many as twelve.

The weary travelers from Santa Croce Camerina proceeded into the main building through the baggage room, where Pietro--like everyone else--left his luggage to be claimed after completing the immigration process. Pietro then climbed a steep stairway as doctors watched him and other immigrants ascend and walk into the Great Hall of the Registry Room. Along the stairs and pathway, doctors looked for any obvious signs of illness or disability. When they saw a symptom or problem, they marked the immigrant's coat lapel or shirt with letters in colored chalk to indicate the problem. Examples are "H" for heart problems, "K" for hernias, "Sc" for scalp problems, "X" for mental disability, or "Pg." for pregnant. Pietro did not understand why these uninformed individuals marked other travelers, but he was happy nobody wrote on his clothes because marked individuals were sent into another line.

Pietro and the other Santa Croce Camerina immigrants huddled together through the process. They were then placed in single-file rows for examination by doctors for any physical defects. When Pietro arrived at the front of the line, he walked about fifteen feet to a uniformed doctor. The doctor quickly examined him, then directed him to walk thirty feet to a second doctor. Just before getting to the second doctor, Pietro made a right turn. During Pietro's walk, the doctor's eyes closely watched him as he examined his feet, gait, and body up to his eyes, checking if he had to adjust his vision after making the turn. Because he was healthy, the staff directed Pietro to the next step in the process.

The Santa Croce Camerina travelers and the other passengers on Pietro's thirty-person manifest page were grouped in the Registry Room. First, William Alexander, an immigration inspector and interpreter, verified the manifest's information. Then, he asked Pietro some of the following questions:

1. *"What is your name?*
2. *How old are you?*
3. *Are you male or female?*
4. *Are you married or single?*
5. *What is your occupation?*
6. *Are you able to read and write?*
7. *What country are you from?*
8. *What is your race?*
9. *What is the name and address of a relative from your native country?*
10. *What is your final destination in America?*
11. *Who paid for your passage?*
12. *How much money do you have with you?*
13. *Have you been to America before?*
14. *Are you meeting a relative here in America? Who?*
15. *Have you been in a prison, almshouse, or institution for the care of the insane?*
16. *Are you a polygamist? Are you an anarchist?*
17. *Are you coming to America for a job? Where will you work?*
18. *What is the condition of your health?*
19. *Are you deformed or crippled?*
20. *How tall are you?*
21. *What color are your eyes and hair?*
22. *Do you have any identifying marks?*
23. *Where were you born?*
24. *Who was the first President of America?*

25. *What are the colors of our flag?*
26. *How many stripes are on our flag? How many stars?*
27. *What is the Fourth of July?*
28. *What is the Constitution?*
29. *What are the three branches in our government?*
30. *Which President freed the slaves?*
31. *Can you name the thirteen original colonies?*
32. *Who signs bills into law?*
33. *Who is the current President of the United States?*
34. *What is America's national anthem called?"*

Pietro provided enough satisfactory answers that William Alexander signed off on his card granting Pietro entry into the U.S. He directed Pietro down the "Stairs of Separation," where he said goodbye to many other Citta Di Torino passengers and reclaimed his luggage from the Baggage Room.

Pietro and his fellow thirteen travelers cleared Immigration, but that was not the case for all the Citta Di Torino passengers. One-hundred-and-fifty-one passengers received the dreaded "LPC" label, which stood for "Likely Public Charge." This label came from the section of law which excluded anyone who might become a burden on the public. The main reasons noted for holding these passengers were "been in prison," "convict," or "medical certificate." Other reasons included "no address to go to," "incomplete address," or "single parent." Many of these passengers were deported back to Italy. Seven passengers were transferred to the immigration hospital to either be cured or deported once able to travel.

With the immigration approval process behind them, Pietro and his fellow travelers needed to get to Market Street in Paterson. They exchanged the Italian liras in their pockets for U.S. dollars. The fourteen travelers then boarded a ferry to New Jersey. As the group crossed the Hudson River, they could see the Citta Di Torino and said a prayer that they survived the crossing and were in the New World. With a total of $160.00 among them, Guglielmo Mandara and Giuseppe Martino headed to Hackensack, where Guglielmo was meeting his friend Angelo Corba, and Giuseppe was rejoining his brother-in-law at 59 Main Street.

The other twelve voyagers were on their way to 208 Market Street in Paterson.

Upon arriving in Paterson, Pietro started to plan how to bring Giuseppina across the Invisible Highway. He settled in a boarding house in the section of Paterson inhabited by others from his village. He worked a string of jobs, including a laborer with Public Service Electric and Gas, established two years before his arrival.

After three and one-half years of working long hours and sacrificing to save every penny he could, Pietro mailed twenty-five-year-old Giuseppina enough money to follow his path. Giuseppina left Santa Croce Camerina with a 29-year-old friend from the Fazio family. They traveled to Syracuse, Italy, then on to Naples. On August 7, 1909, they boarded the S.S. America and, after a 12-day voyage, arrived in New York City on August 19. One month after her arrival, Pietro and Giuseppina were married in a ceremony performed by Father Cisicci at Saint Michaels Roman Catholic Church in Paterson.

Pietro liked to fix, make, or tinker with things, so he always wore work clothes. The number of times he wore a tuxedo can be counted on one hand, and the number of suits and ties on two. While it was out of his character, he was a handsome groom in a long black tuxedo, stiff-collared tuxedo shirt, white bow tie, and gloves. Giuseppina wore a lace gown midway down her shin, lace gloves, and a lace and pearl headpiece. She carried a bouquet of a dozen roses. She did not smile for her wedding picture; instead, she held her head up proudly and stared straight into the camera. That would be her signature look for whatever life was going to throw at the newlywed couple.

Like Sandor and his family, Pietro and Giuseppina Americanized their names to become Peter and Josephine. Pietro worked hard and learned to read, write, and speak English. They saved his money to pay cash for a house at 73 Beckwith Avenue in Paterson and started a family. Ten months after their marriage, in July 1910, Giuseppina gave birth to their first child, Thomas. Next came Carmen in 1912 and Anthony two years later.

Giuseppina was the perfect mate for Pietro. Born October 12, 1884, to Carmelo and Carmela Diodato Blundo, she had four siblings, of which two came to New Jersey and two did not. Giuseppina was short in stature, standing at five feet and one inch. She had a fair complexion with thick black hair. She usually carried a serious look on her face and came across as determined and meant business, which accurately described her nature. Though she came from a well-off family, she knew the value of earning and saving money. While dedicated to being a good provider, Pietro was always planning the next adventure. Giuseppina was the rock of frugalness and kept regimental stability in the marriage. While she had a kind heart, she rarely smiled, and she was the glue that held the family together through the Great Depression and two world wars. Finally, with Pietro, the conscientious provider, they began to eke out their part of the American dream.

However, once settled, the boy who ran to America to escape his family saw his New World family grow with new and old family members.

Pietro and Giuseppina's wedding party

Welké Kapussany, Austro-Hungarian Empire
1904

Amelia, Marie, and Alex continued to grow up in Welké Kapussany. The oldest daughter, Amelia, turned fifteen in 1904, and even though

Sandor and Mária continued to work and save in Youngstown, they planned her marriage. Letters between Mária and Sandor with Agnes and Stephen Kisch arranged for a nuptial between Amelia and their son Lajos. Agnes was an Esterhauzi and related to Mária.

Lajos was eight years older than Amelia. He was from the same village as her and worked as a blacksmith. The two shared a dream to live in America and give their children an American life. Amelia got an opportunity to join Lajos' sister Lizzie and brother-in-law Janos Gaczy, living in Passaic, and shortly after traveled across the Invisible Highway to earn enough money to bring Lajos over. Janos had earlier immigrated to Passaic in 1896, and Lizzie joined him the following year. He worked in a mill. Janos and Lizzie would earn enough money to start a family, have a daughter named Lizzie, and rent their own house.

Amelia worked as a millhand and initially lived in a boarding house with twelve other boarders at 223 Fourth Street in Passaic. It was a block from Janos and Lizzie's house and next to the Hungarian Reform Church. Two years after Amelia emigrated, Lajos completed his voyage to be with her. He made his way to the French port of Le Havre, boarded the S.S. La Touraine on Wednesday, January 20, 1906, and arrived on Ellis Island eight days later. Amelia, Janos, and Lizzie greeted him after he cleared Immigration and brought him to Passaic.

Lajos Americanized his name to "Louis Kish" and formally married Amelia on December 30, 1907, at the Hungarian Reform church next to her boarding house. The Reverend Elemer Huthy performed the service with Janos as the best man. While it was not until this day that they "officially" became man and wife, they would always consider their "real" wedding to be back in Hungary in 1904. They then moved to Duquesne, Pennsylvania, where they rented a house at 404 Third Beach Alley. Moving allowed Amelia to be closer to her parents and her "American" brother Karoly.

Lajos became a laborer in a steel mill where he and Amelia would live the American dream. He would work his way to a boilermaker position at the Carnegie Steel Company. He and Amelia became American citizens, bought a house at 160 South Sixth Street, and raised seven children. Unfortunately, two of their children, Ernest, and Carl, were killed while serving in the U.S. Army during World War II. Amelia passed away in 1951, and Lajos lived to the ripe old age of 81, dying on March 4, 1962, in the same house he and Amelia bought in 1919.

Youngstown, Ohio
1910

While American life was better than that offered by the Hungarian economy, it was still highly toilsome for miners and steelworkers, who were considered expendable by their employers. Sandor and other workers were required to perform exhausting work twelve hours a day, seven days a week. There were no days off or sick leave. Safety standards were virtually non-existent. Newspapers reported near-daily casualties from mine cave-ins, steel mill explosions, and industrial accidents. Many of those killed and maimed were immigrant workers. Foremen, who were German, English, or Irish, administered harsh discipline to Slav and Hungarian workers.

Worker strikes for better wages and working conditions were met with violence from anti-immigrant law enforcement and employee-hired thugs masquerading as security details. Shiploads of naive Hungarians and other Eastern European workers were, unknown to them, brought in by the steel and mining companies to break these strikes. Their appearance led to further resentment and discrimination against any non-English speaking and non-white people in the community, including Hungarians. Sandor and other Hungarian immigrants were despised because they took the lowest paying jobs and lived on next to nothing, saving everything to return to, or bring family over from their native land.

It was also an arduous place for Mária to raise Karoly. Steel-mill towns, composed of dirty buildings, were drab, gritty, and covered with a suffocating smoke that constantly belched out of factories. Prejudice, anti-immigrant violence, and the desire to live with compatriots forced Hungarians and other immigrants to settle in enclaves in the least desirable parts of towns. These run-down sections reeked from overcrowded exhausted workers, suffering from poor hygiene and living in filthy housing. They were filled with rowdy bars and brothels frequented by single men seeking relief from their cramped and dilapidated boarding houses.

Sandor dreamed he could work less time, plant a garden, raise a couple hundred chickens, and better know his family. At get-togethers with other Hungarians, he sang songs, including the following:

Szénpor szárítja fel könnyeinket,
Füstbe fullad kacagásunk,
Kis falunkba hazatérni vágyunk,
Hol minden fűszál ért magyarul.

(The coal powder absorbs our tears,
Our laughter is drowned in smoke,
We yearn to return to our little village
Where every blade of grass understood Hungarian.)

In 1910, Sandor took his family back to Welké Kapussany, where he again took up farming. Like other Hungarians who returned to their home country, he likely based that enormous decision on news from back home that Hungary's economy was relatively flourishing and conditions for those working its land had improved. Additionally, he saved enough money to return and purchase a small farm.

Four years after arriving, his family's world was jolted by the start of World War I, a bloody conflict that engulfed the entire European continent.

Chapter 2
The First World War

Kingdom of Italy
1914-1918

World War I was marked by catastrophic diplomatic and military failures resulting in thirty-eight million military and civilian casualties (seventeen million dead and twenty million wounded). Because generals executed outdated military tactics against modern weaponry and forced the troops to endure extreme living conditions, eleven million military personnel were slaughtered or lost their lives to diseases or injuries.

In addition to a horrendous death toll, the war had other long-lasting effects that impacted populations on a macro and micro level, including the Asztalos and Iozzia-Blundo families.

Before 1914, Italy had aligned itself with the Central Powers countries of Germany and Austria-Hungary. However, when hostilities began, Italy chose a wait-and-see approach. This stand divided the country and caused enormous social discontent. On April 26, 1915, the Italian government finally entered the war on the Triple Entente side, with Britain, France, and Russia, against its former ally, Germany.

The U.S. declared war on Germany and its allies on April 6, 1917, and Congress authorized a draft in June. Immigrants who had filed their "first papers" declaring their intention to become U.S. citizens were eligible to join the military, and thousands of Italians served. Since Italy was an ally against Germany, Italian Americans were also given a choice to return and fight in the Italian military. Many Italians enlisted in the U.S. military, while others chose to return home and fight. The Iozzia/Blundo family showed that same diversity of service.

Pietro's brother-in-law (Giuseppina's sister's husband), Consolato Foti, chose to travel the Invisible Highway back to Italy and serve in its Navy. On December 4, 1895, he was born in Gallina, Italy, a beautiful seaside community less than fifty miles from Santa Croce Camerina. He immigrated to the U.S. as a young man. Living in Pennsylvania but not yet an American citizen when Italy joined the Triple Entente, he volunteered for service in the Italian Navy and served with distinction on a ship in the Mediterranean Sea. In typical veteran fashion, Consolato rarely spoke about his service in the war. He only told funny stories like how the ship went to General Quarters upon sighting what looked like a submarine's periscope. He helped fire the ship's guns at what turned out to be a pipe sticking out of the water. In January 1920, with his military service complete, he sailed from Naples to New York aboard the S.S. America to resume his New World life.

It would take the Italian government fifty years to recognize Consolato for his service. In 1968 the Italian Parliament responded to its aging World War I veterans and passed a statute creating a military decoration called the Order of Vittorio Veneto. The medal was authorized that March by the fifth President of the Republic of Italy to honor all servicemen of World War I who had already earned or were qualified for, due to their brave deeds, a Medaglia e Croce di Guerra al Valor Militare Medal (Cross of War for Military Valor) and served at least six months between 1915 and 1918 or in earlier conflicts. Consolato applied and was approved, along with 600,000 other veterans, to receive this "Cavalieri" or knight award. Because it was fifty years since the war, most recipients were retired like Consolato, entitling them to a small annuity. In 1972, the Italian Consul in Newark, NJ, presented Consolato with the Order of Vittorio Veneto and the Medaglia e Croce di Guerra al Valor Militare. After World War I, the later decoration was established to recognize valor for Italian military personnel who served in times of war.

Thirty-five-year-old Pietro also did his duty for America. On September 12, 1918, he reported to the Division 5 Local Draft Board in Paterson, New Jersey, and filled out his draft registration card. Though never called up, John Gandy, a draft board official, did not note any reason to disqualify Pietro from service.

The picture was likely taken in Austria-Hungary around World War I. Farthest left is Karoly Asztalos and sitting in uniform is Frantisek Eszterhay.

Welké Kapussany, Austro-Hungarian Empire
1910

The timing of Sandor's return was unfortunate for him and his family. Initially, life in Welké Kapussany was good. The economy was stable, and Sandor purchased a small farm for himself and his family to work. However, this was just four years before the start of World War I. Because of treaty obligations, the Austria-Hungarian Empire quickly allied with Germany at the start of the war in 1914. The Empire could not produce the necessary material and financial resources to cover the quickly growing demands of a rapidly expanding war machine. In addition, the four-year duration of the war demanded tremendous human, material, and financial sacrifices that were not anticipated when the monarchy committed to war.

The war took a toll on the Empire's youth and middle-aged citizenry. The Army had 7.8 million men in uniform at the height of the war. During its early part, Austro-Hungarians fought on three fronts that drew heavy casualties: an attack on Serbia, an Eastern front against the Russian Army, and in 1915, an Italian front. The Empire's military suffered 1.2 million deaths that had to be replaced with fresh recruits.

Because of the Empire's multinational nature, its citizens were not eager to volunteer for the Emperor's Army. Thus, the Empire had to resort to heavy conscription, which swooped up 78% of the military-aged men.

At age 51, Sandor was just outside the draft age when war broke out. However, Karoly was the prime age for conscription. The Austria-Hungarian government sought to draft Karoly into the Army but was unsuccessful because he was an American citizen. Karoly had the documentation to make his case. On December 8, 1913, he had the Hungarian church create a duplicate birth certificate documenting his birth and baptism in Pennsylvania sixteen years prior. These documents allowed him to live out the four years of war as a civilian in Welké Kapussany.

Not all members of the Asztalos family escaped conscription. In 1913, Sandor's eighteen-year-old daughter, Marie, wedded Frantisek Eszterhay from the same village and seven years her senior. Their only child Maria Borbala was born on February 4, 1914. Four months later, Archduke Franz Ferdinand and his wife were assassinated in Sarajevo, effectively starting World War I.

In retaliation for the assassination of the Empire's heir to the throne, Emperor Franz Joseph I ordered a general mobilization of the Austro-Hungarian Army for all servicemen aged twenty-one to forty-two on July 31, 1914. Frantisek was part of that call-up and went to war the same as other men did in countries across Europe. With much pomp and circumstance, Frantisek and fellow villagers paraded off to fight as their loved ones and friends lined the streets and wished them a safe and quick return. The following is what Frantisek experienced, mainly based on John R. Schindler's book: "Fall of the Double Eagle The Battle for Galicia and the Demise of Austria-Hungary."

The bulk of the Empire's Army was organized into sixteen corps, nearly all linked to territorial regions. These units were composed of local recruits, like Frantisek, who served as reservists during peacetime. Thus, Frantisek was likely assigned to the 39th Honvéd Infantry Division, part of the VI Army Corps. The Corps had approximately 60,000 troops from Northeast Hungary and was headquartered in Košice, a large city fifty miles from Welké Kapussany. The Corps commander was Commandant Svetozar Boroević von Bojna. Once mobilized, VI Corps became part of the Austro-Hungarian Imperial Forces 4th Army, commanded by Moritz von Auffenberg.

Throughout Europe, armies quickly mobilized upon declarations of war. Both sides, the Triple Entente and the Central Powers, believed they could strike a quick devastating blow to their rivals and win the war by Christmas. Austria-Hungary was no exception. Frantisek and his fellow soldiers were only permitted a few days after mustering in Košice to train on their weapons and tactics. Shortly after arriving, Austria-Hungary declared war on Russia on August 6. The 1st, 3rd, and 4th Armies were ordered to Galicia, a border province abutted against Russia and Russian Poland. They planned to attack the Russian Army along a 170-mile front before it could fully mobilize for an offensive.

Frantisek's commanding officer, General Boroević, was a disciplinarian who demanded fanatic loyalty to the Empire from the men of VI Corps. He led by example, marching with the troops, eating their same rations, and sleeping on straw in the field as they did. The General sent the following message to his senior officers on August 11:

> *"I am not impressed with what I have seen so far of the combat and service troops of this corps. There is a lack of serious discipline and order; the men are letting themselves go, and some of the officers too. There is a lack of focus, and concentration is not at the level that will be required in the imminent encounter with the enemy…Therefore it is a duty, and a requirement of wisdom too, without a moment's delay, to bring the officers and men to an understanding that the primary and most authoritative condition for success is iron discipline."*

On paper, Frantisek was part of a powerful force. The 4th Army consisted of nine infantry and two cavalry divisions for a total of 147 rifle battalions, seventy-four cavalry squadrons, and 438 cannons. However, Frantisek and his fellow soldiers saw problems while traveling 200 miles northeast toward the Russian Empire. First, units made up of different ethnicities from across the Empire spoke different languages, hindering communication. Second, they lugged outdated weapons and lacked adequate battle training. Third, their blue-grey uniforms looked impressive parading through hometowns, but they helped make them easy targets in battle. Lastly, unknown to Frantisek, his top generals clung to 18th-century military strategies that would prove deadly when facing a Russian Army that adopted modern artillery and machine-gun tactics.

Nevertheless, morale was high as Frantisek, and his fellow soldiers left Košice for a long train ride to Przemyśl in Galicia. Before packing into train cars, generals gave speeches about their Army's superiority over their Russian adversaries. They told Frantisek and the others that God was on their side. General Auffenberg told his men: *"Soldiers of the Fourth Army! Our cause is the most just and holy in the history of warfare. God is therefore with us...Our unshakeable will brings us forward to victory and glory!"* Predictions were made that they would all be home by Christmas. Because thousands of train cars packed with troops were heading in the same direction, travel was excruciatingly slow. Frantisek and the others entertained themselves by playing cards and singing army songs, accompanied by music played on violins and harmonicas carried by the soldiers.

Przemyśl was on the San River, about twenty-five miles from the Russian border. Around the city were two rings of fortresses that completely encircled the city. As troops arrived, they fanned out to take up offensive positions across the province. The 4th Army mustered its scattered troops and marched northeast toward the front. Frantisek paraded toward the Russian border carrying about fifty pounds of gear, including his heavy rifle, bayonet, ammunition, and shovel. On his back was a pack containing emergency provisions, including tinned meats, coffee extract, sugar, salt, rice, and biscuits, together with tin cooking and eating utensils. He also carried an extra pair of shoes and a blouse, underwear changes, a winter coat, other clothing, and part of a tent. The sixty-four-mile trek to the town of Tomaszów, under a hot summer sun, was challenging on Frantisek, who was in good shape, but it was incredibly exhausting on middle-aged reservists with him.

There was no rest for the 4th upon arrival. On August 20, Frantisek and the men of the 1st, 3rd, and 4th Armies were directed to advance out of Galicia into Russia and Poland. Three days later, the 1st made contact with the Imperial Russian Army and began what would be known as the

Battle of Galicia. The Galician Campaign consisted of four separate battles occurring between August 23 and September 11. The Austro-Hungarian forces were triumphant over the Russians during the first two battles, but with initial success came high casualties.

In the Battle of Kraśnik, which commenced on Sunday, August 23, the Austro-Hungarian 1st Army, accompanied by the 4th Army on its eastern flank, advanced into Russian Poland and drove back Russia's 4th Army. Frantisek and his exhausted fellow soldiers successfully advanced under a blazing sun northeast toward the town of Chełm.

Frantisek and his comrades would experience the full horror of war during the second five-day battle beginning on August 26, when the 4th Army drove northeast and defeated the Russian 5th Army in the Battle of Komarów.

As it marched northward from Tomaszów toward Komarów, Frantisek's 39th Honvéd Division battled the entire first day against the Russian XIX Corps. Frantisek saw nearly half his officers and hundreds of his comrades massacred in a single day. The morning began with skirmishes that intensified by the afternoon into hand-to-hand combat among hills and creeks. Finally, the fighting grew so intense that Frantisek's Division ran out of ammunition.

A sister regiment to Frantisek's, the 85th was raked with artillery and rifle fire when its men emerged from a dense forest near Pawłowka Hill. Nevertheless, the Regiment pushed forward with a frontal attack, two battalions abreast, bayonets fixed, with regimental colors flying. Despite deadly artillery and rifle fire that pummeled the line, the soldiers pressed on to capture the hill. From the high ground, the survivors surveyed the battlefield littered with more than 455 dead and 830 wounded comrades.

The following day, Frantisek and the other soldiers of VI Corps were again launched into lethal combat. They continued their advance toward Tomaszów under constant Russian resistance, especially while crossing the Huczwa River. Again, Frantisek's 39th Honvéd Division led the attack and suffered heavy losses. Despite the withering fire and swampy conditions, they advanced in an orderly manner and pushed back the Russian defenders. Finally, Frantisek and his exhausted fellow soldiers were ordered to bunk down for the night around midnight. The men crammed onto the limited dry ground along narrow roads that crossed wetlands or in scattered forests. However, the Russians had other ideas. At 2:00 a.m., they counterattacked. Frantisek and the others fought off waves of marauding enemy soldiers all night and into the next morning. Thousands of Austro-Hungarians lost their lives that night.

Despite the heavy losses, VI Corps attacked on the morning of August 28 and drove on the Russian forces. Because Frantisek's unit and others heroically advanced, they smashed through the Russian lines. VI Corps tactics and warfighting under General Boroević were credited as a decisive factor in the victory. The end of the battle left Frantisek and the other troops exhausted, jubilant that they won, yet horrified by the loss of so many comrades.

The Empire's success on the battlefield was short-lived, with the final two battles of the campaign resulting in a complete route of the Austro-Hungarian forces in Galicia. The Battle of Gnila Lipa saw a two-day massive Russian counterattack shatter the Austrian lines. After suffering significant casualties, whole units retreated in panic. The Austrian 3rd Army commander ordered a general retreat of his forces to the fortress city of Lemberg. Many retreating troops abandoned their weapons and cannons and formed long lines toward Lemberg.

While Austro-Hungarian forces collapsed around him, General Auffenberg pushed his 4th Army and threatened to encircle Russia's 5th Army. Leading the attack was the battle-tested VI Corps, driving the Russian V Corps back toward Komarów. The following two days saw intense fighting where Frantisek and his fellow VI Corps soldiers charged straight at the enemy, bayonets fixed, without regard for withering enemy fire or heavy casualties. August 30 brought General Auffenberg's Army within reach of a knockout blow to the Russians even as his ammunition ran low, and his casualties mounted. However, his position became tenuous as the 3rd Army and then the XII Corps collapsed on his flanks.

The Galicia battles were unlike the trench warfare on the Western Front. Instead, they were more traditional battles fought with massive infantry charges, where hundreds of thousands of troops collided with fixed bayonets and engaged in hand-to-hand combat. Among them were massive cavalry charges and cannon fire showering down on them. Airplanes flew overhead, sending back reports on enemy movements. The days were filled with attacks and counterattacks. The exhausted troops bedded down in open fields at night as hundreds of wounded soldiers cried out for help. Frantisek and his fellow troops truly experienced war in its most raw form.

Back in Welké Kapussany, Frantisek's wife Marie and the Asztalos family were desperate for news from the front. Villagers sensed a military disaster was occurring 200 miles to the northeast as thousands of notifications went out to families of loved ones killed in combat. The news came in from surrounding villages about the notifications. While the government placed heavy censorship on troop movements and suppressed information on the battle, the Asztalos family did get hold of sporadic newspaper reports that the troops had won a sweeping victory over the Russians and were pursuing them into western Poland. The stories boasted about the heroism of their troops and how they captured Russian soldiers. However, the reports admitted that casualties were heavy on both sides, making the villagers even more uneasy.

The doctors and nurses in Galicia were desperately treating massive numbers of wounded troops with horrific wounds. They also saw the first men suffering from severe shock, later called "shell shock." Also, unsanitary field conditions were beginning to breed cholera and typhus.

The Galician Campaign's final battle was the Battle of Rawa-Ruska from September 3 to 11, in which Austria-Hungary's powerful 4th Army, including VI Corps, was routed out of Galicia. General Auffenberg was ordered to turn south to protect the 3rd Army from the pursuing Russian 3rd and 8th Armies. The Austro-Hungarian 3rd Army was in disarray, having suffered heavy men and equipment losses during its hectic retreat. General Auffenberg was concerned about his troops, exhausted from long marches and constant fighting. However, he knew his current position was in danger of being encircled as his sister units collapsed around him. Complying with the order, General Auffenberg moved Frantisek and the 4th Army to the south and then to the east to assault the Russian 3rd Army.

Both sides exploded toward one another on September 3 at Rawa-Ruska, a key rail junction northwest of Lemberg. For four days, the two massive armies threw their exhausted men with dwindling supplies against one another. Frantisek was beyond tired and numb from the constant horror around him. The battlefields were littered with tens of thousands of killed and wounded men. Yet, neither Army could defeat the other.

As the battle raged on, the situation continued to deteriorate for the Austro-Hungarian forces. Finally, on September 11, as heavy rains covered the battlefield, the Austro-Hungarian high command realized it was in danger of losing its entire Northern Army. It ordered a general retreat of all forces back to the San River. The order ensued widespread panic and a 100-mile route of the Army out of Galicia. Germany was forced to dispatch troops from the Prussian front to cover the retreat and bolster the Empire's lines. This action saved the Empire from complete collapse.

Frantisek joined several hundred thousand exhausted, hungry, frightened, and war-weary soldiers in the chaotic retreat, slogging on muddy roads. Along the way, men died, deserted, and some just fell from exhaustion. The Russians captured tens of thousands of retreating troops. One of them was Frantisek Eszterhay.

The defeat in Galicia was a severe blow to the Army. It would never fully recover from the massive loss of between 420,000 and 450,000 casualties, including 100,000 dead and 220,000 wounded. It left behind large numbers of supplies, weapons, and train cars. It lost the fortress city of Lemberg, and the fortress of Przemyśl was cut off and under Russian siege. In addition to Frantisek, between 100,000 and 130,000 Austro-Hungarian soldiers were captured.

Carmelo and Carmela Diodato Blundo emigrated from Santa Croce
Camerina to Paterson, New Jersey, in 1916

Paterson, New Jersey
1916

Like Austria-Hungary, World War I shattered the Italian economy as it
could not keep up with the demand for industrial goods to supply its
large Army.   It lacked raw materials, a large domestic market, and an
established trading system forcing the country to borrow large sums of
money from Britain and the U.S. and print more money. The effect
devastated its citizens, including the Iozzia and Blundo families, when
inflation soared, and increasing quantities of money bought scarcer
goods.

Rent and wages failed to keep up with prices, which quadrupled during
the war.   Inflation decimated savings and caused middle-class
purchasing power to fall by about 25% between 1915 and 1918. Life
became dismal.

Even though Italy was on the victors' side, the war's end brought
continued misery to its population. Over 600,000 Italians were dead,
and 950,000 wounded.   The war cost more than the government had
spent in the previous fifty years, resulting in continued high inflation

and unemployment. In "victory," Italy received extraordinarily little at the Versailles Peace Accords. Italians believed that their government had been humiliated by their allies, was weak, and lacked pride in Italy. Like countries on the war's losing side, this resentment fueled a nationalist movement headed by Benito Mussolini.

Pietro came to the United in 1905 to escape his family, but now his house had become a way station for former neighbors and family members seeking to escape the devastation in Europe. With steady work at the energy utility company and then a rubber mill, he maintained his sizeable two-story house at 73 Beckwith Avenue. The house was in an Italian community close to mills and factories and had plenty of room for those needing to begin their lives in America.

In 1916, as the war raged in Europe, his house filled with a wave of Giuseppina's family. The steamship, Caserta, arrived in New York from Palermo, Italy, on July 2 with Giuseppina's elderly parents, Carmelo and Carmela Diodato Blundo, her 18-year-old sister Concetta, and 15-year-old brother Giuseppe. After resolving some issues with immigration officials, they departed Ellis Island and moved into the house's additional floor.

Born in 1855 in Santa Croce Camerina, Carmelo never attended school but learned to read and write in his native language. He ran a successful bakery and was considered "well-to-do." Carmelo, like his children, wore expensive jewelry and custom-made clothing--that is until the wartime economy robbed Carmelo of his business. In his late fifties, he worked as a stonemason while his teenage daughter worked in a shoemaker shop, and his son was an apprentice for a tinsmith.

Despite everyone in their family earning a wage, they stepped off the S.S. Caserta with little money in their pockets. But once in the U.S., they would contribute to the finances of their reunited family. Carmelo became a laborer in a piano shop until he could no longer work. On November 6, 1929, he passed away just eight days after the stock market collapse on "Black Tuesday." Eleven months after Carmelo passed, Carmela, who helped raise her young grandchildren, also passed. Concetta Americanized her name to Jennie, and Giuseppe would become Joseph Blondin. Giuseppe worked as a trackman on a rail line, and Concetta became a finisher in a silk mill. Both went on to have their own families, with Concetta marrying Consolato Foti, the Italian Navy war hero, on April 24, 1921, by Father Modesto Valenti at St. Anthony's Roman Catholic Church in Paterson.

Pietro and Giuseppina were married in 1909, and their house would become a haven for family members and former neighbors escaping wartime Italy.

Paterson, New Jersey
May 19, 1917

As their house filled with Sicilian relatives, Pietro continued working as a track laborer for the Public Service Electric and Gas. Giuseppina stayed home raising Carmen and Anthony while Thomas began classes at Public School No. 11. Thomas's eyes were weak, and he could not see distance, making Giuseppina extra watchful of her oldest son. Despite her caution, tragedy as part of a bizarre event struck the Iozzia household on Wednesday, May 23, 1917. The following describes the events as reported in the local newspapers.

During the four days between Saturday, May 19, and Tuesday, May 22, six local young boys went missing. On Saturday, Thomas Trainer, age 12, who lived at 2 Madison Terrace, and Kenneth Hardern, age 14, of 928 East 29th Street, disappeared after telling their parents they were heading to Garrett Mountain to play with their friends. Also missing that weekend were Walter Van Houten, age 14, of West Park, and Joseph Sueck, age 14, of Dundee.

It was not unusual for children to ascend Garrett Mountain. By mid-May, the weather warmed, and signs of Spring abound, especially in the woods along the mountain. A typical May weekend found hundreds of children enjoying "May walks" on the mountain, where they picked flowers and looked for curious plants and stones among the rock beds. However, panic set into the neighborhood when four children did not return home by Sunday night, and two more seven-year-olds, Thomas on Monday and William Demarest on Tuesday, went missing.

At noon Monday, Thomas left home for another day at school. The elementary school was located on Market Street, less than a mile from the house. He wore dark clothing and a black hat, with books under his arm. Teachers saw Thomas leave the schoolhouse with class ending at 3:00 p.m. When Thomas did not return home, Giuseppina, three months pregnant, frantically checked with the school staff and other parents, but nobody saw where Thomas went. Pietro rushed home from work and gathered family and neighbors to search for the boy.

After combing the neighborhood without turning up any trace of his son, Pietro reported him missing to the Police shortly before 10:00 p.m. The local patrolmen were instructed to look out for the boy. With lanterns in hand, Pietro and a half-dozen friends continued their search through the night.

The next morning, Tuesday, July 22, scores of panic-stricken neighbors visited the Iozzia home to console the family and offer assistance. Five missing children had sent terror through the entire neighborhood. Hundreds of people would spend the day searching for Thomas and the other lost boys.

That afternoon, Jefferson R. Potter, the Principal of Thomas' school, organized a posse of schoolchildren to search the mountain, which lasted several hours. Other search parties made up of Pietro's relatives and friends, including Detectives Pirolo and Eyres from the Paterson Police Department, also scoured the mountain. Later that day, neighbors told Pietro and Giuseppina about a sixth missing child the same age as Thomas.

William Demarest, who lived at 348 Straight Street, halfway between the Iozzia house and Public School No. 11, went missing that morning. He was a student at Public School No. 20 on East 37th Street. William's playmates and friends combed through all the yards and cellars in the vicinity of his home to no avail. That afternoon the boy's father reported him missing to Desk Sergeant Sautter at the Police Station. The Police immediately began a search for the boy. His parents believed William was kidnapped because he was too young to travel beyond his neighborhood. The search extended through the Sandy Hill section of Paterson. Neighbors openly feared that young William and Thomas were the victims of a "fiend" or met with "foul play."

The Police conducted a massive search for the "fiend" who took the young boy clad in blue overalls. That evening Detective Captain Tracey received a tip that William was being held by "Italians" in a stable behind a house on 327 Straight Street, a block from the boy's home. Detective Downey rushed to the scene but found no trace of the boy. Later that evening, the Police received another tip that the boy was held captive nearby in a cellar at 36 Essex Street. However, when Patrolmen Reid and Daly arrived on the scene, they also found this tip to prove fruitless.

The Demarest house was one block away from Bamford Mill, a silk dyeing factory located on Madison St. A few of the ladies who worked at the mill were discussing the missing boy when one remembered seeing a boy who fit his description playing in the mill yard earlier that afternoon. She took no notice of William because neighborhood boys and girls often played games in the yard. She told the mill superintendent, who instructed an engineer, Fred Polglaze, to carefully search the mill yard in case the boy met with an accident. Fred reported that he searched every nook and corner of the yard and found no trace of the boy.

Search parties were also looking for the other four missing boys. Police were mystified and assumed the children might have gotten lost on the mountain or had a mishap. Numerous groups searched the woods, ravines, notches, gullies, streams, and ponds among the mountains. Along the way, searchers found dozens of children picking flowers and playing. None reported any mishaps or seeing the missing children. Searchers found a few piles of rocks at the bottom of Garrett Rock, which might have fallen in an avalanche, but there was no evidence that the children were there. The police expanded the search area to the banks of the Passaic River and the region surrounding Passaic Falls. The Police continued to interview local children, and none of the missing boys' friends had heard from them since they went missing.

As night set in, Pietro and his fellow searchers returned to the mountain with lanterns and looked as far away as Albion Place, south of Garrett Mountain. Meanwhile, panic continued to grip the neighborhood, with parents fearing for their children. Two boys, Thomas Wille, age eight, and George Osborne, age ten, of 123 Jackson Street, were reported missing to Police by their older brothers. Desk Sergeant Perry had just entered the report into the Station logbook when young men came into the police station with the missing youngsters, whom they nabbed coming out of an ice cream store. Detectives Pirolo and Eyres broke away from the search party and hurried to nearby Lodi when Chief Bimson received a report of a lost boy found. He turned out to be from Passaic and was returned home.

When Fred Polglaze returned to the Bamford Mill at 7:00 a.m. the next morning, he reexamined the mill yard for young William. The only place he did not search was a reserve water tank, used as an auxiliary for the factory's sprinkler system, that was twenty feet long, twenty feet wide, and twelve feet deep. Atop the tank was a wooden roof covered with tin. When he examined the roof, he found two boards missing and decided to run the pumps that drain the tank. At 7:45, when ten feet of water drained out and only two feet left, he went atop the roof and peered in the tank. Shock overcame him when he saw the boy in a crouching position on the bottom of the tank with his knees drawn up, almost touching his chin. Awed by the gruesome discovery, Fred ran to the mill office and notified the superintendent. Upon receiving the mill's report, the Police dispatched Detectives William Elvin and Charles Eyres to the scene. They arrived to a large crowd, including William's grandfather, grandmother, father, brother, and sister. The detectives used long hooks to fish William's lifeless body out of the tank. At the sight of the body, his relatives and friends became frantic with grief as the police and neighbors tried to comfort them. Robert Armstrong, the Passaic County Physician, arrived and granted permission to remove the body after determining the death was accidental.

The community was digesting the horror of William's death when Thomas Trainer showed up at his home. He was the third child to return, joining Joseph Sueck and Kenneth Hardern, who previously returned. None of the boys explained their disappearance. Still, posses continued to search an ever-expanding area for Walter Van Houten and Thomas. They now scoured the Watchung Mountains, which are three long low ridges of volcanic origin, between four and five-hundred feet high, lying parallel to each other twenty-five miles south of Paterson and west of Newark. The Police also expanded their investigation as far as Newark. Detective Brooks drove fifteen miles south to work with Newark detectives in case the boys ran away to see the Ringling Brothers Circus, which came to town early that morning.

The Police remained hopeful that they would find the two boys alive. However, by midday, that hope was shattered. Close to sixty men and boys led by Detectives Pirolo and Eyres spread out along the mountain and the woods. Around noon a man was coming down the mountain on a trail called "Hunters' Path," which led to the edge of Devlin's Quarry (formerly called Pope Quarry) at the head of Van Winkle Ave. He spotted something unusual at the bottom of the old brownstone quarry. When he got closer, he saw it was the body of a boy. The body was draped over a large rock and partly covered with sand and rock. He called the Police, who identified the boy as Thomas. He was badly mangled and looked as if he lost his footing while climbing up or coming down the mountain and tumbled over the cliff side, plunging 30 feet below into the quarry and smashing his skull. The Police broke the news to Pietro and Giuseppina that they found their son's lifeless body less than two miles away on the mountain that overlooked their house.

They also told them that the other boy, Thomas' age, was also found dead in the water tank. The last boy, Walter Van Houten, was eventually found half-starved and dehydrated by Patrolman James Kearney.

The truth of what happened to Thomas has never been revealed, nor likely ever will. Children played various games on the mountain. Some games brought them to dangerous parts of the mountain where the rock bed and soil were loose and needed only the foot's touch to precipitate a slide. The choicest flowers often grew in perilous places, and boys relished the danger required to get the best blooms. Thus, nearly ninety-seven years later, Roseann told her family that he accidentally died while playing on the mountain. However, other family lore says the Mafia caused his death. People in the neighborhood were convinced that five missing children, including two deaths, were not a coincidence but the work of sinister forces. The Police were puzzled that they had not discovered the body previously as three or four search parties scoured that area of Garrett Mountain. Before finding the boy's body, Pietro expressed fear that Thomas had met with foul play. He told the police he could not explain his fears and did not know whether his boy had been kidnapped or hurled down from the mountain in play and killed. This statement led some family members to speculate that the Iozzia family ran afoul of the Mafia, which was rampant in Paterson, and in retaliation, they threw the young boy off Garrett Mountain. Whatever the truth, it pained the family for years until they finally could no longer utter his name or hang his picture on their wall.

Thomas's death devastated the family, and though they grieved, they also grew their family with the birth of their first daughter, Anna, six months later. Additionally, they continued to open their home to their Italian relatives. In 1919, Pietro's younger brother, Giuseppe, came to Paterson with his wife, Josephine. Other family members either temporarily resided there or visited him for advice and assistance as they assimilated into this new land.

Not only did the war and its economic devastation transform Pietro from an outcast to a beacon for his family, but it also created a new hub for the people of Santa Croce Camerina and the Iozzia-Blundo families in

New Jersey. World War I transformed them from the Old World to dual-world families.

Emigration is more than masses of people boarding ships and staking claims in new lands; it involves many subplots. One from this period is creating an Invisible Highway between Santa Croce Camerina and Paterson, New Jersey. The highway allowed a steady stream of villagers to escape the misery of early twentieth-century Europe, but as Italians built wealth in the U.S. and the European economy stabilized, the Invisible Highway evolved into a two-lane road.

Mike Marno was Giuseppina's second cousin. He worked in New Jersey until he saved enough to buy a farm in Santa Croce Camerina. He returned and, with his brother, built greenhouses to run a successful carnation business until he passed away. Another cousin, Pino Blundo, and his wife, Connie, also lived in New Jersey and returned once they could afford to start their business. There are hundreds of other similar stories.

Even today, signs exist of the invisible two-lane road in both Paterson and Santa Croce Camerina. In the village square of Santa Croce Camerina is a statue built by Paterson's Sicilian-Americans dedicated to villagers who lost their lives in World War II. The local church contains a cross, whose base bears an inscription that Pietro Iozzia and his family donated it. In New Jersey, the San Giuseppe Santa Croce Camerina Society remains active, and on St. Joseph's Day, March 19, they hold an annual feast and procession the same as when Pietro helped celebrate the inaugural festival in 1916. That feast is a weekend event where Italian natives and descendants bake pastries to fill a 400-square-foot table in their social hall and walk with a statue of St. Joseph, their patron saint, to Sunday mass just like it is done back in Italy.

Passport issued to Karoly Asztalos, November 26, 1920

Veľké Kapušany, Republic of Czechoslovakia (Formerly Welké Kapussany, Austro-Hungarian Empire)
1919

The war's end brought further upheaval to those who lived under the former Empire's rule. Post-war treaties dismembered the Austro-Hungarian Empire and formed new countries with little regard for native populations. Austria and Hungary were split into two new countries. Both lost large tracks of land to victorious neighboring states, including Poland, Romania, Yugoslavia, and Italy. The Republic of Czechoslovakia was created out of this carved-up land. Included was the Asztalos family homestead that was shifted seventeen miles over the border from its native Hungary to Czechoslovakia. Along with Germany, the shattered empire was forced to sign humiliating treaties, accept responsibility for the war, and pay reparations to the victors. The crippled economy could not provide for the welfare of its people, much less cover reparations.

The Asztalos family found itself thrust into a new country that was beleaguered by a poor economy, unemployment, inflation, and disillusionment over the war's senseless devastation and death. It also endured a government plagued by political instability. This upheaval was like that facing the Iozzia/Blundo families in Italy. Like them, a vibrant native community in the U.S. made it possible to begin new lives.

A favorite destination for many from Veľké Kapušany was Passaic, whose mills and factories sat a few miles downriver from those occupied by Italian immigrants in Paterson. Dutch settlers originally formed the settlement of Acquackanonk on this part of the Passaic River in 1679. Passaic was chartered as a city on April 2, 1873, as the area was fast becoming a textile and metalworking center. It contained various types of mills, but the dominating ones produced wool and silk textiles. Botany Mills, founded in 1889, supported a city of 20,000 inhabitants in 1921. Forstmann and Huffmann and New Jersey Worsted Company operated large textile mills in Passaic and its neighboring town of Garfield. Rubber mills also dominated the river's skyline with the Okonite mill, founded in 1888, and Manhattan Rubber Manufacturing founded four years later. Other industries included chemical manufacturing, leather tanning, paper production, and dye works. These mills grew precipitously from the turn of the century until the Great Depression.

Per the author, William W. Scott, the tie between Passaic and Hungary can be traced back to December 1879, sixteen years before Sandor began work in Youngstown, Ohio. Laborers were getting scarce, and George B. Waterhouse of Waterhouse Brothers conceived a plan to import untrained Slavic workers from Hungary. In December 1879, Mr. Waterhouse personally brought over seven men from Austria-Hungary, followed by two more six months later.

These Hungarians first worked in the Waterhouse Mill and then at the Rittenhouse Company, which manufactured wool. These pioneers taught other Slavs how to weave fabrics, which drew other immigrants to Passaic from Austria-Hungary. This action opened another lane in the Invisible Highway from Hungary to New Jersey.

Eventually, Hungarians created their neighborhood along the Passaic River known as "Lower Dundee." This industrial section on Passaic's east side bumped up against other Eastern European neighborhoods housing Poles, Russians, and Ukrainians. It was a very urban environment where blocks of boarding houses and shops surrounded the enormous mills. At its center was Saints Peter and Paul Austria-Hungarian Orthodox Cathedral.

Saints Peter and Paul Austria-Hungarian Orthodox Cathedral, at 134 years old, is now a Russian Orthodox Church.

One day in 1919, a gaunt, ragged, and exhausted traveler entered Veľké Kapušany. It was Frantisek Eszterhay, and the town he saw was quite different from the one he gloriously paraded out of five years prior. He returned to a place where the villagers tried to reconcile their lives with the political turmoil, economic hardship, and the loss of so many young men. Upon seeing him, Marie and her daughter Maria cried with relief after spending the war not knowing if he was alive or dead.

Frantisek told Sandor, Karoly, Alex, and the other villagers about his ordeal. After being captured in Galicia, he and the others from the 39th Honvéd Division were held in makeshift holding areas with soldiers from other units. Next, he spent several months traveling across Russia and her Ural Mountains, either marching or packed in filthy, unheated train cars and wagons. Finally arriving in Siberia in the dead of winter, he was placed in a Prisoner of War (POW) camp that would force him to live on the edge of survival for the war's duration.

Initially, there were no holding facilities for the tens of thousands of prisoners arriving each month, so Frantisek and his fellow Hungarians were crammed into warehouses and other large buildings. There was no running water or bedding and only makeshift sanitation facilities. Eventually, they received stoves for heating and wood to build bunks and spartan furniture. The environment outside the camps was so hostile that prisoners were left unguarded for much of the time. Escape was suicide. He and his fellow prisoners performed exhausting work in mines and on construction projects. There was never enough clothing to keep warm, and meals were meager or, many times, nonexistent.

He told how thousands of his comrades, who survived the unimaginable battle, died from the hunger and diseases that ravaged the camps. Others were worked to death or died from exposure. Frank spent most of his time cold, exhausted, and hungry, but the will to return to Marie and Maria kept him alive.

Frantisek went on that after the 1917 October Revolution, putting the Bolshevik government of Vladimir Lenin in power, things changed-- some better, some worse. After initial chaos from the new camp and local administration changing hands, the Bolsheviks declared Frantisek and the other POWs "free citizens" and reorganized the camps into cooperatives. In reality, this meant that the new government did not feel obligated to provide food and shelter to the POWs, and it was now up to Frantisek and the other "free citizens' to provide for themselves. Many former prisoners integrated into farming coops. Others found ways to leave Siberia and attempt to return home. All the newly free citizens were subject to endless hours of Marxist indoctrination. Like other Russians, Marxism was injected into every aspect of their lives. Frantisek knew that he did not want to live under a Marxist state, and upon the cessation of the war, he began his long journey home.

Karoly always felt like a visitor in his parent's homeland, and though he wanted to return to his native America during the war, he would have endangered himself by undertaking that trek. Not only was travel unsafe through war zones, but he also risked being held as an enemy alien traveling through countries at war with the U.S. or pressed into a U.S. ally's army. Besides the war's end, Karoly now had even more reasons to cross the Invisible Highway. He knew he had to take his sister, niece, and Frantisek to America to restart their lives together. Another reason was a woman who lived in America that he was arranged to marry and whom he loved.

The war forever changed how people traveled internationally. Before 1914, Western people were free to travel where they wanted and stay however long they pleased with minimal or no government permission. Neither permits nor visas were typically required to cross borders. World War I triggered a rash of security concerns that led to countries implementing border controls and the widespread use of passports and entrance visas. Added to the system were official photographs, health and vaccination certificates, letters of recommendation and invitation, and addresses of relatives and friends. When the long war ended, Karoly thought he could resume his life in America. Travel for Karoly was quite different from Sandor's emigration, which required only willpower and a ticket. Because of the new rules and an unstable world, Karoly had to plan extensively for his return trip to be successful.

With his planning and savings of money complete, Karoly would follow his dream by leaving Veľké Kapušany to re-Americanize himself and deliver his sister and her family. Thus, on November 26, 1920, he awoke and took out his razor to produce a close shave, only leaving an uncharacteristic thin mustache. He put on his only suit and tie with a stiff-collared white shirt. His hair was freshly cut and nicely groomed. He walked into the American Embassy in Prague, presented his birth and baptism certificates issued by the Hungarian Reform Church, and applied for a U.S. passport allowing him a return to Pennsylvania. He stated that his last legal domicile was in McKeesport, Pennsylvania, with his permanent residency at his brother-in-law Louis Kish's home, 150 South Sixth Street, Duquesne, Pennsylvania. After paying a $2.00 fee, Alan Winslow, the Second Secretary of Legation, completed the application, and Richard Crane, the Envoy Extraordinary and Minister Plenipotentiary (who, under the terms of the Congress of Vienna of

1815 was a mid-level diplomat below the Ambassador), dutifully issued him the passport he needed to resume his life in America.

Shortly after, the twenty-three-year-old, five-foot-seven, blue-eyed, brown-haired voyager gathered up Frantisek, Marie, and Maria and started his return home to the U.S. On November 27, they left Prague by train and traveled through Germany and France. On December 4, they boarded the RMS Aquitania in Cherbourg, France, and set sail for New York City.

One can only imagine his ride in steerage on the Aquitania. The ship was a Cunard Line ocean liner built in Clydebank, Scotland. A relatively new ship, she was launched on April 21, 1913, and sailed on her maiden voyage to New York on May 30, 1914. Aquitania was third in the Cunard Line's "grand trio" of express liners, with sister ships RMS Mauretania and RMS Lusitania. It was the last surviving four-funneled ocean liner. The press labeled her one of the most attractive ships of her time and nicknamed her "Ship Beautiful."

In 1920 the great steamships plied the Invisible Highway, not only transporting passengers but also cross-pollinating culture, society, business, and diplomacy between the new and old worlds. Their voyages attracted coverage in the news, business, society, and even sports sections of newspapers on both sides of the Atlantic. The voyage with Karoly and his family was no exception.

The Irish War of Independence was raging with the Irish Republican Army (IRA) engaged in a guerilla war against British forces. IRA members traveled incognito on the English ship to the U.S. to raise funds and obtain weapons for their cause. When Aquitania returned to Southampton, England, from New York, awaiting British police searched the ship. They arrested six passengers accused of belonging to the Irish nationalist group Sinn Fein and confiscated their stash of guns.

Once police cleared the ship of revolutionaries, they oversaw the loading of the largest shipment of gold ever carried on one steamship to the U.S. Under watchful eyes, workers loaded 384 crates, clamped with iron bands, containing $18,500,000 of gold bullion. The gold was destined for the U.S. Federal Reserve bank to pay England's share of a wartime Anglo-French loan. It would be stored in the Specie Room, with armed guards to thwart inquiring passengers.

The following day, Wednesday, December 1, the ship departed Southampton to Cherbourg, where Karoly, Frantisek, and his family joined the other 3,089 passengers to set sail for New York City. Newspaper reporters and the public eagerly awaited her arrival. In addition to gold, she carried Christmas mail and society elites coming to America for the holidays. Though they never met, Karoly shared the ship with royalty, including the Earl and Countess of Craven, Sir Ernest Hodder and Lady Williams, the Countess Jumilhac, and the Marquis of Carisbrooke, son of Her Royal Highness Princess Beatrice and a grandson of the late Queen Victoria. He was en route to visit Brigadier General Cornelius Vanderbilt.

Also in first class were pillars of business, including A. McClay Pentz of the shipping firm of Sanderson and Sons and Harold Vanderbilt, returning from a short stay in Paris to settle the estate of his late father, William K. Vanderbilt.

Diplomats and government officials also populated the ranks of first-class passengers. A. H. Saastamoinen, the Minister of Finland to the U.S., was returning after a six-month leave. He reported that conditions in Finland were normal, and the food outlook for the winter was good. Otto Praeger, the U.S. Second Assistant Postmaster General, returned from Madrid, Spain, after attending an international postal conference. *"There is intense interest in the airmail in Europe,"* he said. *"Practically every country has opened an airmail experimental line or plans to do so in the near future."*

The great ship's hull also bore a tale of diplomatic intrigue between the U.S. and the new Russian Bolshevik government. Washington D. Vanderlip, head of the Pacific Coast Bankers and Financiers' syndicate, provided a radio interview from the ship about his sixty-day sojourn across Soviet Russia. As Aquitania approached New York, he told the International News Service that *"the fire of communism is rapidly burning itself out"* and that Soviet leader Vladimir Lenin *"is bringing a change from left to right."* He believed that *"Russia considers America her only friend but will not beg on our doorstep much longer"* and that *"restoration of trade will do more than the League of Nations could do."* He said Russia was willing to concede 400,000 square miles of territory in return for a chance to purchase $3 billion of U.S. goods and added, *"I have blazed a trail."*

His journey through Soviet Russia was shrouded in mystery and controversy. His pro-Soviet statements and travels were extensively covered in the American press and drew sharp criticism from anti-communist groups. Reportedly, he obtained freedom for American prisoners, and Lenin held a military parade in his honor. He told Lenin and other Soviet leaders that he was there on behalf of Senator and presidential candidate Warren G. Harding. He offered U.S. recognition of the Soviet government in exchange for trade and land concessions. However, in late October, Secretary of State Bainbridge Colby denounced the mission, and Senator Harding denied all knowledge of Mr. Vanderlip, stating, *"I never heard of Mr. Vanderlip…He is not my agent, and I have no agent."* Washington never acted on Mr. Vanderlip's recommendations, and his offer from the Soviets lapsed with no further action.

Washington was also not enamored by the old Czarist regime. Major General Count A. Cherep Sipirdovich, a Russian General under the former army of the imperial regime, returned on Aquitania to America, where in 1908 he was well known among New York society. He now received a different welcome when he was detained on the ship by immigration officials who investigated his return to America. Mrs. Wendell Phillips of Boston, President of the Soviet Carry on Society, returned after representing the American Legion at several European conferences.

The great ship also brought European culture to the New World. Photographers flashed bulbs as a young lady departed the ship in a blond feather headpiece, the first to wear the European fashion piece in America. Moviegoers awaited the delivery of the 1918 Hungarian silent movie "Aphrodite" for its American debut in Baltimore. Afterward, the film would be copied and sent to theaters across the country.

However, the most popular passenger on the ship turned out to be a small gray kitten. Buried in a pile of 6,100 mail bags was a bonded mail sack packed in Manchester, England, eight days before being unloaded on a Hudson River pier. As longshoremen handled the bag, they detected a slight movement. Sensing something more than mail inside, they took it to the Grand Central Post Office, where it was opened, and out crawled a six-month-old kitten, weak and hungry. After several bowls of milk, the kitten purred, and reporters put its picture and story in newspapers across the country.

One must wonder how much Karoly and the Eszterhays knew of all the activity occurring on the upper decks and in the cargo holds of Aquitania. Accommodations-wise, the ride over was much better than the one Karoly's father took 25 years before. Because it was a modern ship, the food and berthing spaces were vast improvements over Sandor's cramped conditions in the hold of the Pennsylvania. However, sea conditions were not kind to the passengers on this sailing. North Atlantic storms battered the ship for much of the voyage. Even on arrival off the U.S. coast, a nor'easter forced it to delay docking for twenty-four hours.

On December 13, the ship, filled with war-ravaged immigrants seeking opportunity in a new land, pulled into port. The week Karoly and the Eszterhays arrived, Ellis Island officials inspected 18,000 immigrants. Arriving with Aquitania was the White Star liner Adriatic, filling the Quarantine station on Staten Island and Ellis Island's enormous processing rooms.

Frantisek, Marie, and Maria had to detour through the Ellis Island Immigration Center, which they cleared to start their new lives. The Eszterhays eventually settled in Newark, N.J., where Frantisek (American name Frank) got a job as a mason with a building construction company. Marie (Mary) became a nurse and worked at City Hospital. Mary died in 1934, and Frank later married Elizabeth Stefanko. He passed away on September 20, 1959

Karoly and 28 other steerage passengers were classified as C1 (Citizens of the United States) on the ship's manifest. These passengers attained citizenship through marriage, lineage, or other means and bypassed Ellis Island's immigration process. Karoly could read, write, and speak English. He also knew what to expect in the U.S., all of which made the trip less harrowing than his fellow first-time travelers in the steerage compartments of Aquitania. Karoly was declared disease-free by the health authorities and walked down the gangplank onto the street. He stood on the pier, waiting for the Eszterhay family to return from Ellis Island. With his suitcase in hand and $17.00 in his pocket, he was ready to begin his second life in America and meet the woman he planned to marry.

From left to right: Unknown man, Frantisek and Mary Eszterhay, Charles, Bertha and Karoly Asztalos, Steven Horvath and Elizabeth Kovacs Horvath

Chapter 3
The Roaring Twenties

Bertha Kovacs embroidery in Hungarian. The translation is "In a small boat on a Danube River swing through, in my heart the love has an awakening, Kovacs, Bertha, June 1, 1920."

Garfield, New Jersey
December 13, 1920

Post-World War I, the U.S. economy was the opposite of Europe's. After a short postwar depression, the country entered the decade of the "Roaring Twenties," which saw political stability and prosperity that further illuminated America as a safe harbor for war-weary immigrants.

The country retooled its wartime industrial strength for domestic production. Factories that created tanks and guns now built automobiles, radios, tools, appliances, and other mass-produced consumer products. These industries provided steady paychecks and products that made life more convenient and created a consumer culture of buying and selling products. As a result, large department stores and small shops sprang up, bringing these new products into workers' neighborhoods.

With a road to citizenship and stable employment, many European transplants chose to participate in their new country's prosperity. Money saved working in the mills allowed immigrants to create small businesses and own homes. Because of child labor laws and a booming economy with increased wages, children entered public schools where they learned English and civic values, which enabled them to integrate faster into American society. They also opened their homes to their friends and family in Europe, encouraging them to leave the war-ravaged continent.

On December 13, 1920, Karoly walked off the S.S. Aquitania in New York City, and while he took in the sights of the New World, his mind was on a woman he met in the old one. His parents arranged for him to share his life with a beautiful eighteen-year-old named Bertha Kovacs, who lived in Garfield, N.J. In June, they met in Hungary and got to know one another sailing on the Danube River. Six months ago, they gave their hearts to one another, as their parents had planned. Thus, Karoly deviated from the path he laid out for Allan Winslow at the U.S. Embassy in Prague. Instead of transiting to the Pittsburgh area, he crossed the Hudson River and went to Passaic, where Bertha's family provided him a room and a job at the Manhattan Rubber mill. The mill began operation in 1894 and employed 3,000 people when Karoly set foot on the factory floor.

Karoly went to work with a fellow Hungarian who was a pressman at the mill. Fifty-year-old Janos Kovacs was born in Borsod, Hungary, in 1870, immigrated to the U.S. in 1892, and became "John." In 1897, he married Lizzie Juhaze, who arrived the prior year from Abony, which is about eighty miles south of Borsod. They had four daughters who, in 1920, were Lizzie, 21 and married; Margaret, 15; Sussie, 12; and Karoly's future wife, Bertha. Sussie attended school, and Bertha and Margaret helped support the family by working in a nearby wool mill.

Bertha was born on June 12, 1902, in Woodbridge, NJ. The family moved to Garfield when she was a child so her father could work as a presser at a factory in Passaic. She attended public school until sixth grade, then worked as a handler in a wool mill. Always smiling, Bertha and her sister Sussie believed they had a psychic connection to the afterlife. They would tell fortunes and conduct seances. Maybe it was Bertha's sixth sense that attracted Karoly to her.

In this era, it was common for arranged marriages, such as Janos and Lizzie and Sandor and Maria. Janos came to the U.S. to create a new life, and once established, he was expected to receive the bride his family chose for him. This was also the case with Karoly. Janos and Sandor knew each other from when Sandor spent time in Passaic. Thus, Karoly and Bertha's marriage was arranged, and while not all arranged marriages pair up the right people, they created one that would last until death did them part.

Maybe the match was right because nobody was better at matching up eligible young men and women than Lizzie. She ensured that her three beautiful daughters were married and starting their own families before each turned 21. Karoly was a handsome man and a good provider. Lizzie had plans for Karoly.

On April 2, 1922, just one year and five months after arriving in New York, 24-year-old Karoly walked into the Hungarian Reformed Church on 220 4th Street in Passaic to marry Bertha Kovacs. He wore a black tuxedo juxtaposed with a white pocket square, tuxedo shirt, silk bow tie, and a boutonniere on his left lapel. On his feet were button-down black shoes and his hands wore white gloves. Bertha's three sisters made up the bridal party, including 17-year-old Margaret, the maid of honor. Her paired groomsman was her soon-to-be husband, Frank Lazer, born in Hungary in 1900 and arrived in the U.S. ten years later. Behind them marched Karoly's beautiful 19-year-old bride, Bertha, with a beaded and lace headpiece, a mid-calf length white dress, white high heel shoes, and a long-flowing lace train. She carried a bouquet of 24 white roses with fern leaves and ribbons that were curled and flowed to the floor. Standing next to Karoly were his groomsmen dressed in their best nonmatching suits with white shirts, stiff collars, ties, and boutonnieres. They were his fellow mill workers and future relatives. Paired with Lizzie was her husband Stephan Horvath, born the same year as Karoly but in Hungary. Bertha's parents looked on as the Reverend Lazlo Jegre declared the couple husband and wife.

For immigrants, life during this time revolved around their ethnic community, built around the mills filled with workers from their native country. Within a small radius contained family, friends, social gathering places, sporting fields, and shops. Immigrants had limited means and reasons to venture outside of their neighborhoods. While Karoly and Pietro worked in rubber mills on the same river, 7.7 miles from each other, they never met until the late 1940s, when their children Roseann and Charles would date.

Young Bertha Kovacs. Charles and Bertha Asztalos married on April 2, 1922

Paterson, New Jersey
1920's

While Pietro and Giuseppina took in their Old World family members, 73 Beckwith Avenue's small rooms were also filled with immediate family members. In addition to Carmen, Anthony, and Anna, Roseann, their last child was born in 1926. Originally named Rose after her paternal grandmother, who never left Sicily, she later changed it to Roseann because she did not like being called "Rosie."

Pietro and Giuseppina worked hard to ensure that their children and their Sicilian family members could enjoy life in the U.S. After the war,

Pietro found steady employment as a laborer in a local rubber mill. Several years later, he would be promoted to a "molder" position. A molder made rubber objects using a "casting mold." Once the rubber is poured into it, it shapes the rubber into formed objects such as an automobile tire. Giuseppina also helped with finances and took a job as an operator in a shirt factory. She kept the job until Roseann was born mid-decade. Their oldest son, Carmen, also added to the family's income by working as a caddie on a golf course once he finished high school.

The results of Pietro and Giuseppina's hard work and dedication to the family paid off. All their children attended public grammar school. Roseann advanced the furthest to graduate high school and attend one year of college. Unlike their parents, who only spoke Italian at home, they learned to read and write English at an early age.

Pietro and Giuseppina in front of 790 East 18th Street during the 1950s and the house in 2018. The wrap-around porches were removed, and the neighborhood is primarily Hispanic and with only a small Italian enclave.

Around the same time Roseann was born, Giuseppina and Pietro paid $13,000 in cash for a three-story house at 790 East 18th Street. In March 1896, William J. McFalan paid Edward A. Kavanaugh $2,825 to build the house. It was less than a mile from their current house, but it was in a nice middle-class area away from the mills. The house was also close to Market Street, the heart of the Italian enclave in Paterson. The neighborhood was the perfect spot to raise a family. Saint Joseph Catholic Church and a multitude of stores run by fellow Italian immigrants were within walking distance from the house. On corners were newspaper stands selling *Il Messagero,* the Italian language paper published for the community. Nearby schools included Public School No. 15, six blocks away, and Eastside High School, three blocks closer.

The larger house allowed Pietro and Giuseppina to further supplement their income by taking in renters. In 1930, Enzio Gulino, a local barber, his wife Sadie, daughter, and son paid Pietro $38.00 a month to live on the first floor.

During the 1920s, Giuseppina and Pietro focused their money on giving their large family a life with necessities and few frills. There was food on the table and clothes to wear, but luxuries were rare. When Roseann was born, she had a crib and blanket, but her parents could not afford to host a party to celebrate the birth. She was baptized at Saint Anthony's Catholic Church with Consolato and Concetta as her godparents, but to their sadness, they did not have the money to open their house to celebrate Roseann's entrance into the church. They lived comfortably but only one level above poverty--until the Great Depression.

Charles and Karoly in his 1926 Ford Model T

The town of Garfield sat across the Passaic River from the city of Passaic. At the turn of the century, it had pockets of mills and other industries along the river. While it was primarily wilderness and farmland, some saw the town as a future suburban haven for Passaic's mill workers. In the late nineteenth century, Gilbert Ditmus Bogart launched the village of "East Passaic," which boasted affordable homes with yards within walking distance of the mills. He backed that claim by building a bridge from Garfield to the mills in Passaic. The bridge is still there today, and a section of Garfield retains the name of Bogart Heights.

Eventually, a series of bridges were erected across the river, and trollies traveled between Garfield and the mills. These bridges and trollies allowed immigrant workers to find homes away from congested urban Passaic as other sections of Garfield developed. The town did not originate in one area and expand out as many towns do; instead, it was formed by seven separate self-contained communities separated by farmland. Each community had a distinct ethnicity, shopping, and community services. For example, the section called Plauderville, founded by German immigrants in the 1890s, contained a factory, post office, fire company, and even a railroad station.

Like Janos, many Hungarians settled in Garfield's Belmont section, just across the river from Lower Dundee and not far from Plauderville. Belmont is derived from two French words: "beu," which means "beautiful or lovely," and "mont," which means "a hill" due to a large hill that sits in the middle of that area. By the turn of the century, the community had a public school and fire department. Its hub was Orchard Street, which had been growing since its first houses were constructed in the 1870s.

After marrying Lizzie in 1897, Janos saved his money and took out a mortgage on a two-story house at 115 Orchard Street. Like Pietro's on Beckwith Ave, his house became an entry point for his native compatriots traveling the Invisible Highway. It was kept full of immediate and extended family members and other newly-arrived Hungarian boarders. In 1910, Janos housed his wife, four daughters, and three boarders who were factory workers and a florist.

After their marriage, Karoly and Bertha moved into Janos' house while Karoly continued to work at the rubber plant. On January 23, 1923, nine months after their marriage, Bertha gave birth to Charles, named after the English version of his father's name. Charles was to be the only child of Karoly and Bertha. Like other mill workers, Karoly enjoyed a decent wage from the booming economy. Although raised with modest means, Charles enjoyed some luxuries all little boys should have: a nice baby carriage, a toy fire engine, and a baseball and glove. Though his clothes were hand-me-downs from his cousins, he always had a warm jacket and proper footwear. Bertha also sported nice clothes that she and her sisters made, including a "Sunday's Best" outfit with a brimmed bonnet and gloves. Karoly drew the line on luxuries. He refused to buy a radio because he told Bertha they could walk over to Sussie and Kurt Wehrmann's house when they wanted to hear the news or music. Eventually, he saved up $520.00, and one day in 1926 came home with one of the most famous cars ever produced in the U.S.: a brand-new Ford Model T.

Henry Ford conceived an idea to transform how Americans traveled by building an inexpensive car and marketing it to the masses. Before Henry Ford's Model T, cars were luxury items owned by a few wealthy individuals. On October 1, 1908, Ford Motor Company's first Model T rolled off the assembly line. More than 15 million were made when production ceased in 1927.

Ford kept the price low by building a single model with interchangeable parts via a moving assembly line. This process sped up production and allowed the employment of unskilled workers. Karoly, like other Americans, sought the independence and freedom that came with owning a car. He purchased his Model T as it was coming to the end of production. In 1926, Ford was retooling its cars to meet Americans' growing demand for more style, speed, and luxury than the Model T could offer. A year after Karoly bought his car, the last Model T rolled off the assembly line.

The economy of the 1920s was good for Janos and his extended family, but Janos also had the drive necessary to take advantage of his steady salary. He was a stubborn man with a temper when things did not go his way. One day he got so mad at his mule that he bit the mule's ear off. Janos turned his stubborn determination toward real estate by purchasing two more houses on Orchard Street worth $5,000.00 each. By the decade's end, Karoly and his family rented 115 Orchard Street for $22.00 per month. Bertha's sister Lizzie, her husband Stephen, and two children owned the house next door. A few doors down, 99 Orchard Street was owned by Janos and Lizzie, who rented the top floor to daughter Sussie, her husband Kurt, and Kurt Junior for $22.00 per month. Surrounding them all were houses full of extended Hungarian families. Orchard Street was a vibrant community where fellow Hungarians intermarried and helped each other prosper. While the Belmont section's Hungarian population was minimal in 2018, a dwindling number of Janos' decedents still resided on Orchard Street.

99 and 115 Orchard Street in 2018 (the numbering says 117, but the old 115 is now linked to the 117-house next door).

The American founders wrote in the Declaration of Independence, "*all Men are created equal, that they are endowed by their Creator with certain unalienable Rights, that among these are life, Liberty and the Pursuit of Happiness.*"

At the same time, Pietro, Janos, and Karoly were pursuing happiness as envisioned by the Founders James Truslow Adams coined the phrase "the American dream." He wrote:

> *"...that dream of a land in which life should be better and richer and fuller for everyone, with opportunity for each according to ability or achievement. It is a difficult dream for the European upper classes to interpret adequately, and too many of us ourselves have grown weary and mistrustful of it. It is not a dream of motor cars and high wages merely, but a dream of social order in which each man and each woman shall be able to attain to the fullest stature of which they are innately capable, and be recognized by others for what they are, regardless of the fortuitous circumstances of birth or position."*

The American Dream took shape for Karoly in the later part of the Roaring Twenties. Shortly after buying his Model T, he translated the skills he learned at the rubber plant to repair and make shoes and set up his own small business. He asked John Kungel, who--with his wife Julia and two children--owned a house at 22 Dewey Street, to rent the house's small storefront for a shoe repair shop. John and Julia were born in Hungary but spoke German and emigrated in 1907. John was a laborer in a wool factory and willing to help a fellow Hungarian and supplement the family's income with rent. So Karoly purchased the machinery needed for his new craft and quit his job at the mill. In 17 years, Karoly went from a subsistence farmhand in war-ravaged Europe to a car-owning family man and small business owner. It is the classic American Dream story.

Chapter 4
The Great Depression in the Hoover Years

Northern New Jersey
October 29, 1929

It was an ordinary Tuesday with Karoly and Pietro going about their day repairing shoes and casting rubber molds, not knowing that their world had fundamentally changed twenty miles across the Hudson River in Manhattan. The optimism and feeling that prosperity was boundless propelled Karoly and Pietro to pursue the American Dream in their own ways. Unfortunately, those same feelings pushed other Americans to unwittingly join in a financial bubble by recklessly borrowing to get their piece of the endlessly expanding stock market.

On that day, the bubble burst, and the Roaring Twenties came to an immediate halt with a cataclysmic crash of the stock market. It is forever known as "Black Tuesday" and the dividing line between the Roaring Twenties and the Great Depression.

During the 1920s, real estate values were on a seemingly endless rise, but by mid-decade, when Janos and Pietro purchased their houses, real estate values were beginning to slow. This began to put pressure on the exploding stock market. The market's unceasing incline tempted Americans to speculate with borrowed money. Some brokers would lend investors more than two-thirds of the stock value purchased. This resulted in the sum of stock loans exceeding the total sum of all currency circulating in the U.S. The market was propped up by borrowed money from loans, which, if called, could not be paid.

Even though there were signs of a bursting bubble, investors continued to pour more money into the market, hoping more could be made. Stocks steadily declined for most of September and October. Five days before the crash, the big bankers attempted to stop the decline by purchasing large amounts of various "blue chip" stocks. This scheme worked to halt the decline temporarily. However, on "Black Monday," general faith in the market started to collapse, and an exodus began with the market losing 13% of its value. The following day, Black Tuesday, the exodus turned into a stampede when the Dow Jones Industrial

Average lost another 12%, nearly one-half its value in less than two months. The Rockefellers and other prominent families tried to bolster market confidence by purchasing large quantities of stock to no avail, with the stock market effectively crashing as public confidence dissipated.

Back across the Hudson at about 7:00 p.m., Karoly finished his work and walked the half-mile home where he ate a simple dinner with Bertha and Charles. Pietro also finished a full day of work and took the bus home. On the way, they may have heard newsboys selling the evening newspapers calling out the headline "Wall Street Panics as Stocks Crash." Surrounded by Giuseppina and his four children Pietro also ate dinner. Afterward, he played cards with his brother-in-law Consolato (the Italian Navy war hero), who finished his coal delivery route. After cards, Consolato drove the 1.8 miles home, and Pietro went to bed. Without money invested in the stock market, the ramifications of Black Tuesday would be lost on them, that their lives would be radically altered for the worse.

Garfield, New Jersey
1930's

It is impossible for those of us who did not experience the Great Depression to grasp its horrific toll. As challenging as 1973, 2008, or other post-World War II recessions were, they pale compared to the catastrophe of the 1930s. Americans, including immigrants, stored their wealth in their homes, businesses, and the stock market. The Great Depression annihilated billions of dollars in wealth through the collapse of the real estate and stock markets. With the disappearance of wealth came the collapse of consumerism that fueled the Roaring 20s, and businesses shuttered in droves. Eventually, stock losses and loan defaults caused banks to close, so even money tucked "safely" away in savings accounts disappeared. The entire economy and much of society would lay in tatters for nearly a decade.

Post-crash, the stock market floundered for the next few years until it fell so low that it was a stock market in name only. After Black Tuesday, the market continued to fall to a low on November 13 at

198.60. It then rallied nearly a hundred points by April 1930, only to slide again until July 8, 1932, when the Dow hit rock bottom at 41.22. By then, the market had completely collapsed and lost 89% of its value since Black Tuesday.

The real estate market also began its collapse in 1929, and by 1932, it had lost over two-thirds of its value. The house that Karoly would buy on Dewey Street plunged from $6,800 in 1930 to $1,500 in 1940. Janos' three Orchard Street properties, each valued between $4,000 and $5,000 in 1930, lost approximately half their value by 1940. Houses in Paterson suffered even more significant devaluations. Pietro's house on East 18th Street fell from $13,000 in value in 1930 to $2,234 in 1940, when the country and the real estate market finally climbed out of the depths of the Depression. Considering that Pietro's income was $1,040 in 1940, this is an devastating loss of wealth.

For Karoly, it took all the survival skills he learned in life to provide for his family.   John Kungel was having difficulty keeping his Dewey Street house even though his tenant Karoly was making enough money in his shoemaker shop to pay rent. John was typical of homeowners in the early 1930s. In 1932, 273,000 families were evicted from their homes, and by 1934, nearly one-half of all residential loans were delinquent. At the height of the Depression, Karoly bought the house, and he, Bertha, and Charles moved in with the Kungel family. During the back end of the Depression, the Kungel family moved out to a new place.

Karoly loved to grow things. His green thumb came from his youth working on the farm in Hungary. In his yard were fruit trees, apples, pears, and a large vegetable garden.   This skill helped the Asztalos family persevere through this tough time when many suffered from malnutrition and starvation. When business was so slow, he could not afford food for the table, so his home-grown vegetables and fruits sustained his family. Another trait that helped the Asztalos family survive was Karoly's work ethic. When work appeared, he completed jobs of high quality with a quick turnaround. It was not uncommon for Karoly to work twelve-hour days, six days a week and half days on Sunday, only taking time off in the morning to attend services across the river at the Hungarian Reformed Church in Passaic.

During those Depression years, young Charles attended grammar school at Garfield's Public School No. 8, four blocks and across a park from his house. Located at 147 Cedar Street, it opened in 1926, housing students from kindergarten to eighth grade. Though new when Charles attended, classes were full as immigrant family students were transferred in from the older crowded schools. Charles enjoyed school, but his education eventually fell victim to the Depression.

On June 17, 1937, he completed the eighth grade and graduated from Public School No. 8. His friends wished him a nice summer and looked forward to four more years of high school with him at Abraham Lincoln Public School, which was primarily a grade school but served as the town's high school. Charles completed one year of high school, where he focused on mechanics, but the Depression would not allow him to continue.

Instead of sitting in a classroom, Charles found he needed to help support the family. So, he took an apprenticeship at Tydol Gas Station, where he worked as an attendant and assisted the mechanics with car repairs. Shortly after, Charles obtained a job as a garage attendant at Joe's Service Station on Harrison Avenue and provided his paycheck to his parents to help keep the roof over their heads and food on the table. He held that job until October 1939, when at age 16, he joined the ranks of the unemployed. Charles would not receive a high school diploma until August 4, 2005, when at 82 years old, Heartland of Zephyrhills in Zephyrhills, Florida, provided him and other World War II veterans with an honorary diploma in recognition of their service.

Paterson, New Jersey
1930's

The economy's collapse was like nothing the country had ever experienced before. Between 1929 and 1933, unemployment spiraled upward to 25%, and a quarter of the nation's families did not have any employed wage earner. Workers who were lucky enough to have a job suffered drastic pay cuts and reductions in working hours. In 1932, 90% of all companies reported pay cuts for workers, and three-quarters of all workers were only working part-time.

Pietro was not exempt from the economic misery gripping the country. In 1930, he lost his job at the rubber mill and could not find steady work for several years. So, he worked odd jobs when available and sometimes walked to a nearby country club to caddy on a golf course for tips. Fortunately, he did well because the golfers liked him--they called him "Pops." He also occasionally worked at night guarding produce stands from vandals, where his pay consisted of taking home unsellable food and sometimes a little cash.

Pietro was the same person who ventured to the U.S. to establish a new life for himself and then for his family members when he was a young man. Now this proud man was carrying golf clubs for tips and guarding produce stands for blemished food; however, he did what had to be done to keep a roof over his family's heads.

Finding enough money to survive was not limited to the breadwinner. Carmen and Anthony, Pietro's sons, came of age during this time and sought--but could not find--any steady work to help with the family's income. Carmen left Paterson's Public School No. 15 after completing the sixth grade and eventually became a silk worker in a mill. Unfortunately, he lost that job in 1930 when his father was laid off.

At age 18, Carmen and his younger brother Anthony were forced to work odd jobs like going with Pietro to the golf course and caddying for tips. Giuseppina, who was a dressmaker in Sicily, found occasional work sewing garments. When things got very bad, she sold the fine jewelry she brought over from Sicily. When that was gone, and it looked like her family was going to join the ranks of the homeless, she sold her and Pietro's gold wedding rings. Pietro and Giuseppina lived without wedding rings until 1959, when their children bought them new bands to celebrate their fiftieth wedding anniversary.

During those dark days with no steady work, keeping the house consumed all the family's energy. Industrial towns such as Paterson were hit especially hard as the demand for manufacturing plummeted and thousands of workers were laid off. Paterson's families became homeless by the thousands as they were evicted from their dwellings. They were forced to live in shantytowns called "Hoovervilles," named after the tainted U.S. President. These shantytowns in and around

Paterson had no running water, electricity, sanitary facilities, or sewers. Local governments could not help these people, and they spiraled into misery and hopelessness. While life was difficult, sheer willpower kept the Iozzia family from succumbing to the Great Depression's catastrophic effects.

To maximize the rent they could collect, the family moved into their three-story house's unfinished top floor. The first and second floors were centrally heated and easier to rent, but Pietro was handy with tools and spent his time out of work fixing up the attic, so it was comfortable for his family.

Pietro made life on the third floor as hospitable for his family as possible. He built an indoor bathroom with a bathtub while many of his neighborhood's houses still utilized outhouses. Heat consisted of a stove in the kitchen that burned wood or coal. There was a comfortable living room with a blue velour couch and two maroon club chairs with crochet scarves. However, this room was seldom used, especially during winter when it was closed off by sliding doors to conserve heat.

The apartment had three bedrooms. One was for Giuseppina and Pietro. Anthony and Carmen slept in a second room until they left to work in government programs, and Anna and Roseann slept in the middle bedroom. It was a small room with one window that looked out at a neighbor's house that was so close they could touch the wall. Because the alley was so narrow, little light made it into the room, but it was close to the kitchen, where the wood-burning stove kept it warm. Playtime was outside. The children and their friends played dress-up, marbles or told stories on the large front and back porches.

Pietro did all the repairs and painting to ensure the house stayed in good condition. His neighbors appreciated his skills, and he supplemented his income by doing repairs and handiwork on nearby homes. However, Pietro was nearly fifty years old, and the work could be difficult. One day he came home bloody and swollen after falling off a ladder while painting a neighbor's house. While he was battered and bruised, he was fortunate not to have any permanent injuries.

Giuseppina and Pietro paid $13,000 in cash for the house in the 1920s and were, therefore, free from a mortgage. Sadly, during the depth of the economic collapse, they were forced to do the unthinkable: mortgage the property. After much anguish and no alternative for money, they asked the bank for over $3,500 in much-needed cash to pay for necessities. However, that meant they faced a monthly bill with no certain income.

Being a landlord was a struggle unto itself since renters also fell out of work. Even though they could barely maintain their house, Pietro was sympathetic to many of his tenants who asked for additional time to pay their rent. One family who owed eight months' rent moved out in the middle of the night, leaving the apartment empty and the rent unpaid.

During these dark days, families starved, and men, desperate to feed them, transformed into beggars on Paterson's streets. Others took the dramatic step of abandoning their loved ones to become "hobos," riding the rails across the country searching for work. Soup kitchens, organized by churches and local organizations, sprang up across Paterson, but they became overwhelmed by the sheer numbers of destitute families.

Next to keeping a roof over the family's heads, getting food on the table was the big challenge. Pietro's produce stand guard job paid little money but allowed him to bring home bruised fruits and vegetables that Giuseppina could turn into meals. Like Karoly, Pietro tapped into the farming skills he learned as a boy in Europe as he and Giuseppina grew vegetables in a garden. He made wine out of bruised grapes from the fruit stands and soft drinks from roots, including great-tasting root beer soda made from the sassafras plant's root.

Young Roseann was a cheerful child who loved to learn, and Giuseppina did all she could to shield her from the upheaval of the day. While Roseann had few outfits, Giuseppina ensured she had nice clothes to wear to school. Roseann's favorite outfit was a grey knee-length pleated wool skirt, a pink long-sleeve sweater, bobby socks, and black and white saddle shoes. She walked six blocks up the hill to Public School No. 15. She loved her teachers and thirsted for learning.

Giuseppina stretched every nickel brought in to feed the family. With no car or money for the bus, they walked everywhere. There was not enough food to have a pet, so young Roseann had to settle for playing with a stray cat she named Mickey, who lived behind their yard. Giuseppina made all food from scratch, so their money was only spent on the basic staples. The one treat she maintained was her Saturday night baking, where she baked marble cupcakes and an entire cake that she rationed over the upcoming week.

Washington, District of Columbia
1929

Herbert Hoover was starting his presidency when the stock market crashed in 1929. Like most economists of the day, he believed the economy was experiencing a temporary dip. When the economic "dip" continued to freefall in 1931, the President amplified efforts to shore it up with minimal federal intervention. He refused to use the Federal government to control prices or directly intervene in the economy. Instead, he believed a balanced budget and conservative fiscal policies would eventually allow American volunteerism and local initiatives to heal the economy.

The President conducted meetings with business leaders at the White House, urging them not to lay off or cut wages to workers and assisting them with loans from a newly created Reconstruction Finance Corporation. He also encouraged local aid for public works projects to employ workers and relief programs for needy individuals supported by individual states and the private sector.

In April 1932, the Director of New Jersey's State Emergency Relief Administration painted a grim picture of the state. He reported that the state's unemployment grew to an alarming level, with approximately 600,000 destitute people. He also reported that private charities and municipalities could not keep up with the demand for basic food and shelter for New Jersians out of work and that $20 million in immediate relief was needed.

The shorthand term for these local programs for the poor was "relief." In Paterson, one program provided needy families with a monthly supply of staple foods such as flour, beans, and rice. Giuseppina saw the broken families, proud men forced to beg on the streets, and the hopeless souls living in Hoovervilles.   She was too proud to accept these handouts, saying instead to distribute the food to others who need it more than they do. Because as bad as it was for them, Giuseppina had her family, her house, and hope to make it through the hard times.

Chapter 5
The Great Depression and the New Deal

Charles on a Civilian Conservation Corps tractor, 1940

Garfield, New Jersey
1932

The Presidential election was a philosophical fight over how to best fix the economy. It pitted President Hoover against Democrat Franklin Delano Roosevelt, who promised the nation a "New Deal" that would put the federal government's full strength toward providing relief to suffering Americans. Roosevelt solidly defeated President Hoover, receiving 57.3% of the vote.

Saturday, March 4, 1933, was Inauguration Day, and the country was socially and economically hopeless. Industrial production was sliding toward half its 1929 level, jobs continued to hemorrhage, driving up rampant unemployment, and most banks had disappeared with their customers' life savings. Karoly, Bertha, Lizzie, Margaret, and Sussie, along with their husbands Stephan Horvath, Frank Lazer, and Kurt Wehrmann, huddled around Sussie and Kurt's radio to hear the incoming president's inaugural address, where he promised them immediate action. He told them to keep hope: "*This great nation will endure as it has endured, will revive and prosper*," he went on. "*The only thing we have to fear is fear itself.*" The weather in Garfield was grey, overcast, and thirty-eight degrees. Thus, inside and playing with his toy firetruck, ten-year-old Charles did not hear the president's speech, though he later became a direct benefactor of the new President's plan laid out that day.

In his first 100 days in office, President Roosevelt and Congress initiated aggressive programs to attack the economy's failings. He instituted a banking holiday and, with Congress, created legislation to restore the banking system, provide relief for farmers, and give direct aid to unemployed workers. He also created several public works job programs, including the Civilian Conservation Corps (CCC).

Seventeen days after his inauguration, President Roosevelt addressed Congress with his "Three Essentials for Unemployment Relief" speech. He said:

> "*I propose to create a Civilian Conservation Corps to be used in simple work not interfering with normal employment and confining itself to forestry, the prevention of soil erosion, flood control, and similar projects. I call your attention to the fact that this type of work is of definite, practical value, not only through the prevention of great present financial loss but also as a means of creating future national wealth.*"

Congress agreed and established the CCC as a civilian army that employed young men between eighteen and twenty-five, mainly recruited from local welfare boards and often from families where the father was unemployed. They enrolled for six months, which could be extended by six-month stints for up to two years. They built bridges, dams, roads, and highways and planted more than three billion trees. Workers were paid $30 a month, where they could keep $5 and send the remaining $25 home to support their families. Enrollees received room, board, and medical care and, in return, worked eight hours a day, five days a week. The camps had organized recreational and educational activities during off-hours.

The President focused various federal government resources on getting unemployed young men into the CCC camps as quickly as possible. His goal set in March 1933 was to have 250,000 men in camps by the end of July. Running at speed unseen in a peacetime government, all federal government branches and agencies worked together. The Army, tasked to spearhead the job, quickly built camps, and the first enrollee was sworn in on April 7, only 34 days after the president's March 4 inauguration.

Paterson, New Jersey
1933

The CCC and other programs of the New Deal were a godsend to the Iozzia family. In 1933, Carmen and Anthony were twenty and eighteen, respectively. They and their father spent the last three years with no steady work except for intermittent odd jobs. The Iozzia family barely survived day-to-day, the same as 25% of American families without a breadwinner. This unsustainable situation could become tolerable if one of their sons could land the family's first real job since the Depression hit. If accepted into the CCC, the $25 per month would be a blessing for the family.

In mid-April, the County Relief Administration was notified that Paterson, and its surrounding areas would receive 196 slots for young men to participate in the "national reforestation army." This is what the CCC was called in its early days. They called for applications from local men between eighteen and twenty-five who were U.S. citizens, had dependents, and were known to local officials to need relief aid.

Carmen and Tony were determined to keep the Iozzia family intact. Since the announcement activating the CCC, a long steady stream of desperate young men, including the Iozzia brothers, stood in line outside the Emergency Relief Administration office at School No. 1 on Fair Street in Paterson. While both brothers met the criteria for service, only one person per family could serve in the CCC at any given time. One brother could join now, and the second could enroll once his brother's service concluded. Anthony and Carmen argued about who would go first to no resolution. Finally, they agreed to flip a coin, and Anthony won the toss.   On May 2, Anthony completed his application for "Emergency Conservation Work."   His last odd job was assisting a driver delivering newspapers.   However, he lost that job seven months prior.   Anthony was told that if accepted, he had to enlist for six months, pass a medical examination, and accept and immediately proceed to his duty assignment.   He had no say in where he would be assigned.

The Administration Board spent the next three weeks reviewing applications, then Theodore F. Sloan, the Municipal Relief Director for Paterson, informed five hundred applicants to report to the National Guard Armory on Wednesday, May 17 through Friday, May 19, where 196 applicants would be selected for service.

Anthony was directed to report on Wednesday, the first day of application reviews.   He passed a cursory medical exam and successfully answered the Board's questions on the need for family assistance.   After being awarded a slot, Anthony joined a group of men who filled three buses.   First Lieutenant C. W. Scovel Jr., an Army Reserve Field Artillery Officer, escorted them to Camp Dix, an Army post in central New Jersey, for two weeks of physical conditioning.

There was a festive mood in the Armory as the group waited for the buses to fill.   After three years of Depression, the men were looking forward to the camp.   Two recruits from Passaic with a guitar and mandolin played and sang "hillbilly" songs.   Family members and sweethearts were on hand to wave goodbye.   There were lots of smiles, hugs, and tears.

Upon arrival, Anthony joined other men his age from towns across Northern New Jersey to form the nucleus of CCC Company 296.   Major C.F. Davis, U.S. Army Medical Corps, gave him a medical examination and Typhoid and Smallpox vaccinations.   Next, he was shuttled to the barber shop and military clothing, where he was issued a mirror, toothbrush, razor, work clothes, an overcoat, two pairs of shoes, and a duffle bag.   He remained at Camp Dix for seventeen days completing an orientation to the CCC and performing military-style conditioning exercises.

On Saturday, June 3, Anthony and the other Company 296 members boarded a train to take them cross-country to their assigned workplace in Idaho. They arrived in Boise, Idaho four days later and were transported by truck about seventy miles northeast to Centerville in the Boise National Forest.

With large tracks of forest land, Idaho was the site of extensive CCC operations. At the same time, Anthony was in processing at Camp Dix, a large contingent of U.S. Army officers arrived in Boise to establish up to 164 conservation forestry camps in that state. Their target was to recruit 25,000 workers from the Atlantic seaboard, mainly from the New York City area. By 1935 Idaho would have 79 camps with 15,000 men. The Boise area contained seventeen companies, eleven of which were filled with workers from the East Coast.

Centerville had a brief, but rich history tied to gold. In 1860, gold was discovered in Pierce, Idaho, then other sites across the state, launching the Idaho gold rush. The news of the gold strikes traveled across the country, drawing prospectors from both coasts. On August 2, 1862, prospectors searching the Boise National Forest found their prize panning the waters of Grimes Creek. The prospectors named the creek after their leader, George Grimes, who was killed, allegedly by Indians, not long after his gold discovery. Soon the creek bed was teeming with prospectors, and the mining town of Centerville was formed.

Within eight years, prospectors had mined the most easily accessible gold and moved on to other areas in Idaho, Montana, and Nevada. The town's population, which was 3,000 in 1863, plunged just as fast as it grew. When Anthony arrived, two dredges were still mining gold and quartz on Grimes Creek near Centerville.

Company 296 dismounted their trucks in a field along Grimes Creek, an old mining camp where prospectors mined and dredged for gold. Here they would establish CCC Camp S-230 by pitching a headquarters, mess tents, and squad tents. The locals assisting with the camp told the "city boys from back east" that enough gold was found on this site to pay the U.S. debt from the Civil War.

As told by Elizabeth M. Smith in her book, "History of the Boise National Forest 1905-1976," the Boise National Forest, one of the nation's largest national forests, was plagued with uncontrolled forest fires, especially in 1931.

"The 1931 fire season was very severe, and the Quartzburg fire of that year was the worst conflagration in the forest's history. Well over 40,000 acres were destroyed by this fire before a force of 1,000 men finally brought the flames under control. Weather factors that summer created tinderbox conditions on the forest and throughout the state. This lightning-caused blaze swept through the slashings of cutover land so rapidly that men were at times hard pressed to keep out of its path... Starting west of Quartzburg on August 19, 1931, the fire gained a head start because available firefighters were still on the Macks Creek fire, which burned 22,000 acres east and north of Shafer Butte the same year.

"The flames destroyed part of Granite City, most of Quartzburg, and the Gold Hill mine. Placerville was saved only through the determined efforts of the townspeople. Some buildings at the Missouri mine on Big Muddy Creek, the Charlotte Gulch sawmill, the Golden Age mill on Grimes Creek, and many flumes were destroyed. Placerville and Quartzburg were evacuated; the residents loaded belongings on wagons and moved out, camping in the hills away from the fire, and a baby girl born in the camp was named Smoky. At the same time as the Quartzburg fire, there were twenty other fires burning south of the South Fork of the Payette River, and another lightning storm started a fire near Centerville that burned 1,500 acres and then combined with the major Quartzburg fire.

"On August 23, the forest was closed, and Idaho's Governor C. Ben Ross issued a proclamation banning camping and smoking on Protective Association lands...Many of the fires in the northern part of Boise Basin burned together, and a total of over 60,000 acres of national-forest land burned in August of 1931...

"One of the results of the disastrous season of 1931 was that fire planning was subsequently done on a project-fire basis. In addition, the CCC labor that became available in 1933 was used to a great extent to improve buildings and trails needed for better fire control. Roads were built in 1933 and 1934 by the CCC to Scott Mountain, Deadwood, Bear Valley Mountain,

Whitehawk, and Gold Fork lookouts. Fire protection also benefited indirectly from the campground improvement and construction done by the CCC's during the mid-1930s, since the campgrounds helped to limit man-caused fires."

Company 296 was an integral part of the fire plan. Anthony and his teammates used picks, axes, saws, and shovels to create fire trails. First, dynamiting crews cleared the right-of-way for roads by blasting rocks, tree stumps, and snags through virgin timber. Then the company members cleared obstacles and leveled the roads using hand tools. These roads were fire trails for easy access to possible forest fires. In all, the Company built thirty-six miles of these roads in approximately 4 ½ months. Additionally, the crews were called off-road building to fight four forest fires. One was close to their camp, and the others were within forty miles.

On October 8, Anthony's six-month tour was coming to an end, and he opted to return home, giving his older brother Carmen a chance to enlist. He boarded a train in Boise and crossed the country arriving at Camp Dix three days later. There he received his final physical, collected his last pay, and was rated as an "excellent" worker for this entire tour. On Friday, October 13, he was given a ride back to Paterson.

For each of Anthony's six months of service, the Iozzia family received $25, while Anthony kept $5. The money allowed the Iozzia family to keep its house and have food on its table. The tour out west made a lasting impression on Anthony. Growing up in inner-city Paterson, he was amazed at the number of stars in the Idaho night sky. The stories of getting rich by finding gold also stayed with him. The Boise Basin produced at least 2.3 million ounces of gold, with a value usually given between $60 million and $100 million. Many men struck it rich working its creeks and mines. Years later, Anthony returned to the area to strike it rich in the gold fields. However, like many before, he found more hazards and hardship than riches and returned home.

Today, very little mining activity remains in the Boise National Forest. Many of the gold rush towns have vanished, including Centerville. Its Post Office closed in 1952, and its buildings have been reclaimed by the forest.

Though small in stature, at only five feet one and 103 pounds, Carmen looked forward to his turn to support the family. On September 29, after receiving a letter announcing Anthony's plans to return, Carmen applied for enrollment. He explained to James Montgomery how he and his father had been laid off from their jobs for three years, that his brother would be coming home, and that it was his turn to work. He stated that he would be willing to work on conservation projects under the U.S. Army's direction. Mr. Montgomery told him to report back when his brother returned in three weeks for transportation to Camp Dix for further processing.

On October 23, Carmen and a group of inner-city youth from Paterson boarded a bus and rode seventy-nine miles to Camp Dix. Like Anthony and the other CCC recruits from that state, Carmen first reported to the post for some rudimentary basic training, including physicals, inoculations, and conditioning, before being sent to his assigned work camp. Upon arrival, Army Captain Tom Bankart explained the rules and obtained Carmen's agreement with them. Navy Lieutenant H. K. Sessions gave him a clean bill of health and two vaccinations. After two weeks of training and physical conditioning, he boarded a bus to serve at Camp SP-10 in Marion, Virginia, his home for the next fifteen months.

Carmen arrived at the camp on November 7, 1933, and was assigned to Company 1249 as a laborer. There was much work ahead for Carmen and the other 199 men in his company. First, they had to turn their skills and talents on the camp itself, making it ready to accommodate the workers' needs. SP-10 opened three weeks before Carmen arrived. He and his co-workers turned the rudimentary buildings into a working camp where the men could live, eat, sleep, enjoy recreational activities, and plan their workdays.

The Virginia countryside was suffering from three centuries of neglect. Forests were unprotected from fire, overcut and were being reseeded by inferior species. Shoddy farming practices led to massive soil erosion and fields stripped of topsoil. While flush with natural beauty, Virginia did not have any state parks for its citizens to enjoy its natural wonders. One of the top goals for the CCC in Virginia was developing a state park system. The CCC provided labor and materials to create six state parks for a grand opening slated for 1936. The primary mission of Company 1249 was to prepare Hungry Mother State Park in Smyth County, west of Marion, for the grand opening.

It was up to Carmen and the other enrollees to develop tracts of land into a functioning park by creating trails, recreational areas and building public facilities and structures. Projects included picnic shelters, campgrounds, cabins, lodges, bathhouses, swimming pools, superintendent lodging, restaurants, boathouses, stables, barns, and maintenance structures. Some of the landscape features they constructed were dams, spillways, bridle trails, stairs, bridges, campgrounds, paths, beaches, and a man-made lake.

Because the Army ran the camp, life during the week was regimented through military discipline, management, and organization. They followed a strict schedule from reveille at 6:15 in the morning to mealtimes and work projects each day. However, evenings were free for recreation, including playing sports, reading *Happy Days* (the weekly newspaper of the CCC), or taking education classes until lights out at 10:00 p.m. On weekends, Carmen and his fellow enrollees visited nearby Marion to patronize the stores, movie theaters, billiard rooms, dance halls, churches, and restaurants. Some of Carmen's fellow workers met their future wives while in town. While suspicious of strangers, the townspeople looked forward to the approximately $5,000 a month camp workers spent boosting their anemic local economy.

The work of Carmen and the hundreds of other CCC workers who followed him at Camp SP-10 culminated in a ceremony on June 13, 1936, when Governor George C. Peery presided over the official opening ceremony for the first of six parks making up the Virginia State Parks System. The ceremony was held at Hungry Mother State Park, the park that Carmen worked on. The celebration was attended by thousands of Virginians and included concerts, a water pageant, and a bathing beauty contest.

On December 22, 1934, Carmen took a discharge physical that found him healthy and 16 pounds heavier than when he joined. He was honorably discharged from the CCC in Marion and put on a train to make it home in time to spend Christmas with his family in Paterson.

While he was happy to be heading home for the holidays, he felt an ominous feeling overcome him, realizing he was also heading back into the world of the unemployed.

Carmen spent the next fifteen months with no work except for occasional odd jobs. Then, on May 12, 1936, he returned to the Relief office on Fair Street and reapplied to the CCC. Mr. J. O. Gorman approved his application, and Carmen was back in the CCC for a five-month stint.

Since his last enrollment, the CCC had grown very active in New Jersey, with camps established throughout the state to help with tree planting and reforestation. The CCC established or improved many of the parks used today in the Garden State. So, it was no surprise that Carmen remained in state for his next assignment. He was transported thirty-one miles on Route 23 through Morris County to CCC Camp P-66 in Newfoundland, New Jersey.

Carmen was amazed that a short bus ride could transport him into a world unlike where he lived. He boarded a bus from the center of congested Paterson, where the air and water were dirty, trees were sparse, and most of the view was concrete and asphalt. When he stepped off the bus, he was in a rugged land known as the Farny Highlands. It contained continuous forests of tall red, white, and black oaks. Interspersed through the area were large boulder fields made by receding glaciers from an earlier time. Splitrock Reservoir, swamps, and numerous headwater streams flowed through the area toward the Passaic, Delaware, and Hudson River basins, which gave the region a waterscape and mountainous landscape. Hawks, owls, and songbirds were in abundance. He saw remnants of businesses that came and went, with old logging roads and iron mining and smelting industry relics dotting the area.

In Newfoundland, Carmen and his coworkers from Company 120 helped rebuild private forest land, which supplied drinking water to one-third of New Jersey residents. Work projects included seeding, vista clearing, tree planting, insect control, and fighting forest fires when needed.

Less than four months into his assignment at Camp P-66, Carmen was transferred to Company 3221 at Camp MC-55 in Leipsic, Delaware, to work on mosquito control projects. This task was extremely difficult for the workers and generated controversy for the CCC.

Kathleen Duxbury's book titled "The Boys of Bergen" describes that program. In the early twentieth century, the medical community determined that mosquitoes transmitted diseases such as malaria and yellow fever. Some in the healthcare field claimed the solution was to drain the saltwater marshes where mosquitos breed. Delaware picked up on the argument, partly because the tiny state did not have any state forests to avail itself of the benefits of the CCC program. In 1933, the Delaware Mosquito Extermination Association convinced policymakers to add mosquito control to the CCC missions. Delaware won approval for two mosquito control camps.

Carmen was assigned to Camp MC-55 for only a little over three weeks, where his time there was filled with backbreaking and dangerous work. Each morning, he strapped a cylinder filled with either oil or larvicide onto his back with a flexible hose and spray nozzle extended from it. Wading in hip-deep salt marshes, Carmen sprayed the thick fluids atop the stagnant water to smother mosquito larvae. All the while, he and his coworkers were assaulted by flies and insects while watching for water snakes and other predatory animals. When he was not spraying, Carmen helped dig ditches and construct tide gates to drain the swamp waters. Barges brought lunch consisting of soup, coffee, and sandwiches to the workers, who ate their noon meal among the putrid swamp waters.

On September 30, 1936, Carmen completed his enlistment and was discharged from Camp MC-55. The records state that work did not impair his health, and he was considered satisfactory by his superiors. He hopped a ride to nearby Clayton, Delaware, where he caught a bus that ultimately took him to Paterson. When he arrived home, Carmen was relieved to hear that his dad, Pietro, had finally found steady employment at a silk-dying plant.

During its five years of existence, the CCC's mosquito control projects met strong opposition from hunters, anglers, and wildlife advocates because it was wreaking havoc on the other creatures that survived in and around the swamps. Finally, in 1938, two years after Carmen completed his work, the CCC leadership decided to discontinue all mosquito control projects and closed those camps.

Garfield, New Jersey
1940

Six months after losing his job at Joe's Service Station, Charles walked into the Garfield Welfare Office on Outwater Lane and enrolled in the CCC. It was April 9, 1940. Charles and a group of inner-city youth from Garfield completed applications and were assigned to a camp near the New Jersey/New York line, where workers were developing a state park. He boarded a bus and rode nine miles to the CCC induction center in Teaneck, NJ., where he received a physical examination and vaccinations against typhoid and smallpox. Dr. Thomas D. Campbell certified him as qualified to join, and Charles agreed to enlist for six months.

He climbed on another bus, which departed from the induction center and rode fifty-four miles northwest into the countryside near the New York border. When it entered Branchville, NJ., the bus traveled down Grau Road and arrived at CCC Camp S-71. Charles and the other enrollees reported to the camp headquarters in an 1813 carriage house and a cabin built in 1860, the original home sites when the land belonged to the Skellinger family. They were assigned to Company 1266 and shown their barracks to live in for the next six months.

Tragedy struck during Charles's first week at the Camp. Karoly and Bertha asked their family members if they wanted to visit Charles during his first-weekend break. Bertha's sister Lizzie and her ten-year-old daughter Dorothy volunteered. Lizzie's son-in-law Teddy Kalemba offered to drive. On Sunday morning, April 14, they all piled into Teddy's new Dodge sedan, a wedding gift from Lizzie to him and his wife Betty two months prior. Teddy and Karoly rode upfront while Bertha and Dorothy sat in the back. Lizzie took the rumble seat, which was an exterior seat that folded into the automobile's trunk area. They had driven approximately forty of the fifty-mile trip when outside of Sparta, young Dorothy accidentally opened the door and fell out of the car. As she fell, Lizzie lunged forward out of the rumble seat and tried to catch her daughter. Both tumbled onto the road, with Lizzie impacting the pavement head-first. Teddy was not driving fast, so he immediately stopped the car. While Dorothy only had minor bruises, Lizzie fractured the base of her skull. State troopers rushed her eight miles to Newton Memorial Hospital, where doctors did their best to save her. Sadly, she succumbed to her injury the next morning. Lizzie was only forty years old. Instead of a happy family visit, Charles returned to Garfield and attended his aunt's funeral that following Friday.

Kathleen Duxbury provides a vivid picture of life in the CCC camps in New Jersey. With the Army's responsibility to administer the camps and induct, organize, equip, and transport the enrollees, the camps, including those that housed Anthony, Carmen, and Charles-- looked and were run as quasi-military compounds. Most of Charles's camp consisted of nondescript wooden buildings that housed a mess hall, officers' quarters, warehouses, an infirmary, latrines, facilities to provide water, light, heat, and army-style barracks.

During his first days at the camp, Charles received classes in forestry and job training in road maintenance. In July, he also attended classes in carpentry.

Five days a week, Charles followed a routine that his future brothers-in-law, Anthony and Carmen, went through in 1933 and 1936. He was awakened by a bugler playing reveille at 6:15 a.m. and ate breakfast at 6:45, followed by a barracks cleaning. At 7:45, a work call sounded, and by 8:00, Charles and his fellow workers loaded onto trucks for a five-mile ride northwest to where they worked "pick and shovel" duty to help develop an area near Kittatinny Lake that later became Stokes State Forest. CCC enrollees at Branchville constructed cabins, privies, roads, bridges, and impoundments for holding water to fight forest fires. Their artesian handiworks are still visible today, especially the fine stonework on the bridges crossing the Flatbrook River and its tributaries. Charles's time at the camp was his first taste of life outside a city. He learned to work with the land and drive a tractor.

Workers returned to the camp in time to shower and eat their evening meal in the mess hall at 5:00 p.m. After the evening meal, enrollees assembled on the parade ground for news and updates from Rolland G. Scott, their Company Commander.

Evenings were free to read in the library, box in a makeshift ring, play table tennis, or enjoy other activities in the recreation center. High school classes were offered for those wanting to continue their education. Charles loved baseball, so his recreation was playing on the camp's baseball team. At 10:00 p.m., it was lights out and setting the fire watch while the camp fell silent for eight hours.

Carmen adapted well to the quasi-military life, but it was not for Charles. He performed "satisfactory" and did not excel in the Corps like some of his fellow workers; he was even subject to disciplinary action on one occasion. Charles was homesick and did not return to camp on time after spending the weekend of September 7 and 8 at home. He was docked one day's pay for missing roll call on Monday morning. While he did not enjoy this rigid life, his superiors found him cheerful and honest. His camp commander commented that he had a positive attitude and developed as a man. Though Charles could re-up for another six months, he chose to go home once he completed his enlistment.

On Monday, September 30, Charles was honorably discharged by Rolland Scott. With $29 in his pocket, he boarded a bus that took him to Passaic, where he wrongly thought his military-like life was forever past.

Currently, the former camp S-71 is the site of the New Jersey School of Conservation run by Montclair University. Even today, it is in a desolate part of the state that requires an effort to find. One must turn off the main road and follow a long narrow country road across a CCC-built bridge that straddles a babbling stream, then over and down another hill before arriving at the former camp. It looks like it did when the bus rolled up to it with Charles in 1940. Amidst a meadow next to a lake, the original buildings are still used by the University. The cedar red dining facility, barracks, and other CCC workers' buildings are strewn across the meadow and situated along the lake's banks. Across the road are concrete structures that appear to have been smokers. The original Skellinger family house has been restored and is still in use.

The carriage house, which served as a blacksmith shop, is reduced to a partial frame and foundation with the blacksmith's tools still visible. There is a statue of a CCC worker with the inscription "CCC Enrollee, 1933-1942, Dedicated to Stokes State Forrest (S-71), Companies 218 and 1266, Donated by Henry Billitz and N.A.C.C.C.A. Chapter 8, 1996." The Americans of CCC heritage landmark statue was dedicated to all the former CCC camp workers on November 4, 1996.

The CCC helped prepare Carmen, Charles, and others in their generation for the challenges they would soon face with the U.S. entry into World War II. With the onset of war, the Director of the CCC, Robert Fechner, said that because of the camp training and discipline, discharged CCC workers were "*85% prepared for military life*" and could be "*turned into fighting men at almost an instant's notice.*" It turned out that 75% of the CCC workers, like Carmen and Charles, went on to serve in the Armed Forces during World War II. Carmen and Charles started their CCC service at Camp Dix and later returned to it wearing American G.I uniforms.

Left: Likely camp dining facility. Right: The original cabin was used as an administration building.

Left: Stream near the entrance to Camp S-71. Right: Statute of a CCC worker at Camp S-71.

Left: Charles Asztalos (back row, third from the left) on the Civilian Conservation Corps baseball team in 1940. Note barracks in the background. Right: Those same barracks in 2018.

Paterson, New Jersey
1935

By the mid-1930s, the nation's economic hemorrhaging had finally begun to slow. However, President Roosevelt sought even more aggressive action to spur the economy. He launched his "Second New Deal" of additional federal programs to provide workers jobs and economic stability. New programs included the Social Security Act, the Rural Electrification Administration, the National Labor Relations Act, and the Fair Labor Standards Act.

Like America, the Iozzia family also slowly clawed its way out of the lowest depths of the Depression. Pietro obtained a silk dyer position, dying material for clothing sheets at the National Dyeing and Print Company. However, before being offered a permanent job, he had to work for two weeks without pay. On December 10, 1936, Pietro received his Social Security card, assuring him retirement income. This resulted from President Roosevelt signing the Social Security Act of 1935, which guaranteed pensions to millions of Americans, including Pietro. He joined a newly formed union, the Paterson Dyers Local 1733, and eventually retired as a dyer in 1957.

Life also improved for Carmen. After returning from the CCC, he worked intermittently as an auto mechanic. By 1938 the work became steady while employed by a Paterson shop owned by Tom Brown. Carmen repaired motors, chassis, and transmissions on trucks and automobiles. He also relined, repaired, and adjusted breaks and performed general overhaul work. Other tasks included repairing the ignition system and other electrical units, oiling, lubricating vehicles, and making replacement parts. By 1940 he was earning twenty dollars a week, which was good money.

While the mid-1930s began a long slow climb out of the depths of the Depression for Americans and the Iozzia family, poverty and desperation still abounded. In 1936, New Jersey created a relief program allowing a family of three to receive $55 per month, which was the bare minimum to sustain them. Hundreds of thousands of needy families applied and immediately bankrupted the program. The New Jersey Emergency Relief Administration shut it down shortly after it opened its doors.

Another program created by the "Second New Deal" was the Works Progress Administration (WPA) which provided unemployed people jobs. It was an infrastructure improvement program that built post offices, bridges, schools, highways, and parks. It also funded work in art theaters and literary projects. Between 1935 and 1943, the WPA provided work to 8.5 million people on more than 250,000 projects.

WPA workers built multiple schools, stadiums, and other projects across New Jersey, including the Lincoln Tunnel, the Jersey City

Armory, and Hinchliffe Stadium in Paterson. That stadium hosted professional baseball games in its prime, including games played by the Negro Leagues, professional football games, and high school athletic competitions from baseball to football to track and field, auto racing, and music concerts.

Since his six-month stint in the CCC, Anthony spent much of the last three years without steady work. He secured a chauffeur position for two years, but that job evaporated in 1937. After two months of futile job hunting, he applied for a position with the WPA. On March 23, 1937, Anthony was certified eligible to work as a laborer.

On September 20, he received his first assignment: to meet a bus at the Hill and Oliver Station at 7:00 a.m. on September 22. The bus drove him and fellow WPA workers fifteen miles to the future site of the Butler Kakeout Reservoir outside Kinnelon, NJ. Anthony joined one hundred workers from Morris, Union, and Passaic Counties who worked on a nine-month project to repair problems with Butler's water supply and the surrounding municipalities that were growing acute in the mid-1930s. This project built the 900,000,000-gallon Butler Kakeout Reservoir to provide water for the area residents' needs.

On November 19, Anthony and the other WPA workers completed the new reservoir, which began storing water for the local population. At a pay rate of forty-five cents an hour, Anthony brought home $116.55 for his two months' work. The money was much-needed income for his parents struggling to pay the mortgage and buy necessities. He did not have any work for the holiday season but received his next assignment to begin on December 31.

At 8:00 a.m. on December 31, Anthony reported for work at the corner of East 5th Avenue and East 6th Street. This was an industrial part of town near the Passaic River. Anthony was eager to return to work. A new year brought him a five-cent per hour raise, thus now earning fifty cents an hour. Except for two weeks in April, Anthony worked for the entire year of 1938 as a common laborer on various projects across Paterson.

One project was restoring a landmark in the mountains overlooking Paterson. Everyone who lives in the city knows of Lambert Castle, which overlooks the city from 500 feet above sea level on a perch atop Garrett Mountain. It is a castle-like structure with a tower high on a cliff. In 1892, Catholina Lambert, who owned silk mills in Paterson, built this house modeled after the castles of Yorkshire, England. Four years later, he added a seventy-foot observation tower on the cliff's crest to look down on his mills.

In 1923, Catholina died, and his son sold the castle to the City of Paterson, which turned it into a county park in 1928. A museum was added in 1934. However, years of disrepair had caught up with the structure. In the late 1930s, the WPA designated it as a project, and workers, including Anthony, were hired. Anthony was part of a team that fixed up the observation tower, cleared overgrown areas, and built up the grounds. They improved the tower by fitting it with a new concrete roof, steps and guard rails, stucco-covered metal-lath walls, and a concrete shelter. They also built a picnic area around it. Drainage was provided for the whole area, and Anthony and his WPA coworkers carried out a general beautification program.

Lambert Castle on Garrett Mountain in 2018. Charles and Roseann's granddaughter, Courtney, is standing at the base of the Castle.

Working on Garrett Mountain brought young Anthony happy and painful memories. During the darkest years of the Depression, the only relief for the Iozzia family was escaping to Garrett Mountain for weekend picnics. His Uncle Consolato somehow maintained his coal delivery business through those painful years. On weekends, Anthony and his family, Aunt Concetta, Uncle Consolato, and cousins, would pack blankets and a picnic lunch. They would then pile into the back of the coal delivery truck to spend the entire day enjoying nature on the mountain, which provided a respite from the daily worry of survival. Painfully, the family would reflect that this was where Anthony's brother, Thomas, was killed in 1917. The mountain held so much emotion, and now it provided Anthony with a steady paycheck.

While they picnicked, one wonders if they whispered about Thomas and the Mafia lords in their neighborhoods. Did they shake their head as they compared how the Iozzia family witnessed the best of the Mafia when it helped Consolato keep his coal delivery route or found odd jobs for Pietro, Carmen, and Anthony during the dark days of the Depression? Then they saw its worst with the death of Thomas

Family lore about Mafia ties was prevalent as Iozzia's gathered around the Sunday dinner table and whispered stories of how Pietro and his sons caddied for members of the "Cosa Nostra" or that the Mafia helped prop up Consolato's coal business during hard times. Later in life, Carmen did not socialize much with his brother and sisters. Innuendo abounded that his low profile and eventual move out west were related to underworld activities. It is possible that the family interacted with the mob. The prohibition of alcohol from 1920 to 1933 grew the Mafia as it became the source of liquor for the population that still wished to drink. This allowed the mob to expand its influence in the 1920s and 1930s, making it an omnificent force in the Italian neighborhoods in Paterson and Northern New Jersey. They controlled many of the jobs, services, and entertainment. Regular interaction in the Italian neighborhood required operating in Mafia territory. However, much of the Mafia's history is unwritten and disappeared with the participants' death, so we will never really know how many, if any, ties existed between the Iozzia family and the mob.

Pietro's steady work and his sons' employment allowed the family to begin enjoying some treats. Meat returned to their diet with Giuseppina making stuffed chicken baked with potatoes and vegetables on weekends. Young Roseann's childhood began looking up. Her brother Carmen saved enough money to buy an old Ford with a rumble seat and a handle under the front grill used to crank-start the engine. After work, he would pile Roseann and her friends in the rumble seat and take them for rides. On weekends, those rides included a stop for ice cream if he had the money.

Her brothers worked hard to make up for the childhood that she lost during those early Depression years. Carmen shared his income with his little sister, buying her roller skates, a tennis racquet, and a typewriter. When Roseann was in the eighth grade, all her friends had bicycles except her. So, Carmen bought her a blue bicycle on timed payments. Anthony was a practical jokester, always bringing humor into the house. One day he set back all the clocks in the house and almost made her late for a school dance.

Roseann's best friend was her cousin Josephine, her Aunt Concetta, and Uncle Consolato's daughter. Born three years apart on the same day, July 5, they were inseparable and spent many weekends together. During the dark days of the Depression, they would occasionally visit the Jersey Shore, where both learned to swim. They started as babies floating in rubber tubes, eventually gaining the confidence to swim from their tubes and realizing they shared a love of the water. As the coal delivery business improved, trips to the Jersey shore became more frequent. Consolato would wash his coal truck--a flatbed with sides--until it shined. He put benches in it and drove Roseann, Josephine, and their friends to the beach, where they would share stories, laugh, and joke the entire way.

On January 9, 1939, Anthony's job was terminated due to a lack of area projects. He was formally removed from the WPA on July 6. His biweekly salary of $30 would be missed by the Iozzia family and eventually put pressure on his young sister, Roseann, to help with family finances.

Garfield, New Jersey
Late 1930's

There were also fun times for the youthful Charles several miles away in Garfield. With its mix of diverse neighborhoods made up of immigrants from common lands working in the same mills, the town possessed character and many fantastic small businesses. When Bertha could afford to buy something special for Charles, it was a baked treat from Kohout's Bakery. Kohout's was established in 1924 by Charles and Josephine Kohout, who emigrated from Czechoslovakia during

World War I. Today, their decedents still operate the bakery, much as Charles and Josephine did. Bertha would have also taken Charles down the hill from their house to Meltzer's general store for an egg cream soda at the lunch counter. Founded by Samuel and Jennie Meltzer, who emigrated from Russia in 1913, it continued to be operated by the Meltzer family as a sporting goods store until it closed in 2015 after 101 years of operation. On special occasions, he was treated to a chocolate drink that Natale Olivier, a fellow Garfield resident, began producing in 1928. He called the new drink, "Yoo-hoo."

Down the hill in the other direction was a lake called "Pump House" because of an old water pumping station that sat next to it. The lake was a favorite place for Charles and his friends to ice skate in the winter. Also by his house was Belmont Hill Park, which had amazing slopes to sled ride. The town also had a very active youth program. Within walking distance for Charles were the public library and a YMCA, both established in 1923, the year he was born. Charles saved enough money to pay the YMCA a nominal membership fee and took advantage of all the YMCA's sporting activities, including tennis, baseball, and basketball.

Life was starting to improve for the Asztalos and Iozzia families, but it would take several more years until the start of World War II before the nightmare of the Great Depression finally ended.

Paterson, New Jersey
1930's

Because Americans longed for humor during the dark days of the 1930s and '40s, comedy teams became popular. Humor from Stan Laurel and Oliver Hardy, George Burns and Gracie Allen, The Three Stooges, and Bud Abbott and Lou Costello transported Americans to a world of laughter that was far from the rigors of war and the Depression.

One of the most famous comedy teams was Abbott and Costello, with Lou Costello coming from the same neighborhood as the Iozzia family. On March 6, 1906, Louis Francis Cristillo was born on Madison Street, directly behind the Iozzia family house.   His father, Sebastiano

Cristillo, emigrated along the Invisible Highway to Paterson from Calabria, Italy. Lou attended the same public school and played on the same playgrounds as the Iozzia boys. Though small in stature, Lou was a skilled basketball player and was watched by all the neighborhood kids, including the younger Carmen and Anthony. Lou dropped out of Central High School and eventually went to Hollywood in 1927. After a year with little success, he returned to Paterson, Americanized his last name to Costello, and became a burlesque comedian. The following year he met Bud Abbott, and they formed one of the most popular comedy duos of the twentieth century.

Carmen and Lou developed a friendship during those Depression years. Lou gave him odd jobs and hired him to caddy his clubs on the golf course. Despite his meteoric rise to fame and eventual move to Hollywood, Lou never forgot his roots and remained a familiar face around the old neighborhood. He returned to visit children in local hospitals, perform at fundraisers for children's athletic clubs, and generously contributed to charities for underprivileged children and toward building a new Catholic church on Beech Street. He also made it a point to visit the Iozzia family. The Iozzias hosted him for a meal at their house whenever Lou was in town. They especially enjoyed it when he brought his partner Bud along. The two were generally close friends and would entertain the Iozzia family with stories and jokes well into the evening. His philanthropy and positive spirit uplifted the country, his old neighborhood, and the Iozzia family.

Northern New Jersey
1930's

The immigrants' creed to take care of one another and help extended family and fellow countrymen succeed in life, regardless of living in less-than-ideal circumstances, helped the Kovacs and Iozzia families survive the devastation of the Great Depression. On Orchard Street, the families of Stephan and Lizzie, Frank and Margaret, Kurt and Sussie, and Karoly and Bertha all looked after one another.

Frank held onto his job as a weaver in a wool mill, and Kurt maintained his bus driver job through the Depression despite suffering pay cuts and reduced hours. However, stress from the economic downturn and the turmoil and repression in his native Germany took a toll on Kurt. After a decade of marriage and fatherhood, in June 1940, Kurt left Sussie and Kurt Junior to live in an apartment in Passaic. Five months later, he took the oath of citizenship and walked away from his German roots.

The Kovacs bonded together to support their extended family. They took care of Sussie and Kurt Junior. They provided for their big sister when Lizzie's husband Stephan lost his job as a molder at the rubber mill in the early '30s, then for Stephan when Lizzie tragically died. As immigrants, they knew the importance of depending on each other and always helping those less fortunate. Karoly and Frank ensured that Lizzie, Stephan, Sussie, and Kurt Junior had a roof over their heads and food on their table.

The same was true for the elderly Janos and Lizzie, who saved and gave all to develop this close-knit Kovacs community. Janos passed away during the Depression, leaving his widow, who moved in with Frank and Margaret. They ensured the remaining years of her life were good, and surrounded by family members she helped grow. On December 14, 1943, Lizzie passed away in the house she and Janos built and passed on to their children.

That same immigrant spirit was the bedrock of the Iozzia family's survival. Pietro was there on the docks greeting Concettina when the S.S. Caserta pulled into New York Harbor in 1916. He opened his house for her and her family and supported them until they settled into their new life. Without Pietro, she may have never left tattered and war-torn Sicily. So, when Pietro lost his job and struggled to care for his family while Consolato maintained his business, Concettina shared it all. She brought over portions of their meager meals, and Consolato took the children on weekends so that Pietro and Giuseppina did not have to worry about feeding them. Consolato would also host get-togethers with the extended family on weekends to share food and foster the family spirit and cooperation. He would gather Pietro and Giuseppina, Joseph, and Margaret Blondin (Giuseppina's brother and sister-in-law), Giuseppe and Josephine Iozzia (Pietro's brother and sister-in-law), and their children. The women cooked the delicious food provided by Consolato, the men played cards, and the cousins played in the yard. On the first Sunday of May, he hosted a large family reunion at his home, where he shared his food and ensured the children had lots of playtime.

The lessons learned from the First World War and immigrating to the U.S. that families and neighbors must support each other when one hits hard times or starts up the economic ladder of life were vital to the Kovacs and Iozzia families. These lessons helped them survive this horrific economic period. They also helped shape young Charles and Roseann.

Chapter 6
The Second World War During Neutrality

Northern New Jersey
1930's

During the 1930s, Europe and its problems seemed far away from the minds of Americans, who focused on their survival. However, news from immigrants still traveling westward on the Invisible Highway told of ominous happenings.

Through his efforts with the San Giuseppe Santa Croce Camerina Society in Paterson, Pietro heard firsthand accounts from new immigrants about Benito Mussolini's tactics and his Fascist administration. In March of 1919, Mussolini formed the Fascist Party out of several smaller right-wing groups under the banner of restoring Italy to its great Roman past.

During the 1920s, Mussolini gradually replaced all democratic institutions with pro-fascist organizations and made himself dictator, taking the title "Il Duce" or "The Leader." His reign was marked by strict policies accompanied by terror and repression of dissidents. All forms of influence on the public, including the media, education system, youth programs, public works projects, and especially the police, were devoted to reinforcing his control, eliminating his enemies, and promoting the regime's interests.

Even though Santa Croce Camerina sat in a far corner of Sicily, about as far from Rome as a town can get, it was still subject to the regime's total repression. Like other towns across Italy, it had a Podestà, a commissar whose job was to ensure that local politicians and officials towed the Fascist Party line. He possessed extensive powers as Rome's eyes, ears, and hands in that small town. The Podestà ordered the arrest and imprisonment of any individual--including journalists and teachers--who criticized fascism. The Regime further expanded its tentacles into Sicily's small villages so that by the mid-1930's most police officers, judges, military officers, and even Catholic priests were loyal Fascists helping the Podestàs.

Sicily's Fascists, like the regime in Rome, viewed the U.S. and the thousands of Sicilians touched by the Invisible Highway with suspicion. America had condemned Italy's brutal invasion of Ethiopia in 1935, and relations became more bellicose as the Mussolini regime grew closer to Nazi Germany, culminating in the signing of the May 1939 "Pact of Steel." Mail to and from Santa Croce Camerina that revealed too much about life in Sicily under Fascism was a criminal offense. Podestàs monitored citizens, looking if they entertained "foreign" ideas or studied English, which was banned from public schools. People who made it to the U.S. told Pietro and his fellow Society members about dark times descending over their old village.

The news from Hungary that filtered into the Belmont section of Garfield also grew bleak as World War II approached. Hungary was politically and socially stable during most of the 1920s and '30s. However, as World War II drew closer, its government aligned with the German Third Reich. In the late 1930s, Hungary's fascist Arrow Cross Party was on the rise, and the government implemented Jewish policies modeled after its Nazi neighbor. On November 20, 1940, Hungary joined the Tripartite Pact, which allied the country with Germany, Italy, and Japan, bringing its people into the escalating war.

Paterson, New Jersey
September 1, 1939

In June 1939, Roseann graduated from Public School No. 15 and was excited to continue her education. She loved school and learning. She especially excelled in geography and history. Though Pietro had steady employment in the silk dying plant, and Anthony was finishing his assignment with the Works Progress Administration, money was still scarce for the Iozzia family. Nevertheless, Giuseppina was determined to make whatever sacrifices necessary to allow Roseann to continue her education.

On Friday, September 1, 1939, Roseann looked forward to her final taste of summer with a Labor Day Weekend get-together at Uncle Consolato and Aunt Concettina's house. Once Tuesday came, it would be time to experience the thrill of her first day of high school.

All summer, she had been dreaming about walking into Eastside High School. Opened in 1928, it was a large school with extensive sports and extracurricular programs. Its teams were called "the Ghosts" because it was said that the school was built on an old cemetery. Roseann was anticipating all the new subjects she could learn and sports teams she could join. However, world events that so often clouded her young life would do so again.

The headlines on Friday, September 1, were ominous: "German Army Attacks Poland; Cities Bombed, Ports Blockaded; Danzig is Accepted into Reich." Roseann read the New York Times story by Otto Tolischus aloud as her family listened to her words:

> *"Berlin, Friday, Sept. 1--Charging that Germany had been attacked, Chancellor Hitler at 5:11 o'clock this morning issued a proclamation to the army declaring that from now on force will be met with force and calling on the armed forces 'to fulfill their duty to the end.'*
>
> *"The text of the proclamation reads:*
>
> *"To the defense forces:*
>
> *"The Polish nation refused my efforts for a peaceful regulation of neighborly relations; instead, it has appealed to weapons.*
>
> *"Germans in Poland are persecuted with a bloody terror and are driven from their homes. The series of border violations, which are unbearable to a great power, prove that the Poles no longer are willing to respect the German frontier. In order to put an end to this frantic activity, no other means is left to me now than to meet force with force.*
>
> *"German defense forces will carry on the battle for the honor of the living rights of the reawakened German people with firm determination. I expect every German soldier, in view of the great tradition of eternal German soldiery, to do his duty until the end. Remember always in all situations you are the representatives of National Socialist Greater Germany!*

"Long live our people and our Reich!

"Berlin, Sept. 1, 1939.

"Adolf Hitler."

Roseann was interrupted by the sound of air raid sirens going off. In response to the attack, anti-air raid defenses mobilized throughout the country, and cities tested civil defense warnings.

Despite the disturbing news coming from Europe, the Foti family held its traditional weekend get-together. While the children played, they noticed the adults were subdued, reading extra editions of the newspaper as they hit the streets, and stopping conversations to listen to the radio. As the weekend progressed, the news worsened.

Sunday saw a significant expansion of the war. The headline proclaimed, "England Declares War On Germany," with a news report on the radio stating, "*today France considered herself at war with Germany in as much as she has said she would follow whatever steps Britain took.*"

Great Britain gave Germany an ultimatum to withdraw its troops from Poland by Sunday, 11:00 a.m. London time (5:00 a.m. in Paterson) or face war. Thirty minutes after the expiration of the deadline, England declared war on Germany.

The news reported that President Roosevelt would address the nation that evening in a radio broadcast. The group of concerned adults and children, gathered around Consolato's radio, hushed as the President took to the airwaves:

> *"Tonight, my single duty is to speak to the whole of America,"* said the President. *"Until 4:30 this morning I had hoped against hope that some miracle would prevent a devastating war in Europe and bring to an end to the invasion of Poland by Germany.*
>
> *"For four long years, a succession of actual wars and constant crises have shaken the entire world and have threatened in each*

case to bring on the gigantic conflict which is today unhappily a fact...

"It is easy for you and me to shrug our shoulders and say that conflicts taking place thousands of miles from the continental United States, and, indeed, the whole American hemisphere, do not seriously affect the Americas—and that all the United States has to do is to ignore them and go about our own business. Passionately though we may desire detachment, we are forced to realize that every word that comes through the air, every ship that sails the sea, every battle that is fought does affect the American future.

"Let no man or woman thoughtlessly or falsely talk of America sending its armies to European fields. At this moment, there is being prepared a proclamation of American neutrality...We seek to keep war from our firesides by keeping war from coming to the Americas. For that, we have historic precedent that goes back to the days of the administration of President George Washington. It is serious enough and tragic enough to every American family in every State in the Union to live in a world that is torn by wars on other continents. Today they affect every American home. It is our national duty to use every effort to keep them out of the Americas...

"I hope the United States will keep out of this war. I believe that it will. And I give you assurances that every effort of your Government will be directed toward that end. As long as it remains within my power to prevent, there will be no blackout of peace in the United States."

On Tuesday, September 5, as the German Army was defeating the beleaguered Polish Army and the U.S. officially declared its neutrality, Roseann walked through Eastside High School's doors, ready to become a part of its world.

Paterson's Eastside High School in 2018

Paterson, New Jersey
1940

The shadow of the growing world war hung over Roseann's time at Eastside High School. On the one hand, she tried to maintain a typical high schooler's life. She loved the coursework required to complete her Commercial Diploma, geared to prepare her for a traditional female caste job in business. Over the next four years, she would take typing, stenography, bookkeeping, and advertising. Because she enjoyed writing, her favorite class was English. Her love of school brought her acceptance into the exclusive "Leaders Club," established to foster future community leaders. She also completed commercial drawing courses, which would serve her when it was time to "do her part" in the war effort.

She also did the things outside of class that typical high schoolers do. Though Roseann was petite and not a superstar athlete, she tried out for all the after-school sports programs, including baseball, basketball, and tennis. She eventually became the sports score manager and enjoyed keeping score at the athletic events.

Her outgoing personality allowed her to develop close friends. Roseann, Violet Polser, and Mae Turner were inseparable. They were known as "The Three Musketeers" and could be found at the movies or hanging out in the ice cream shop.

However, the war was never far off. The radio in the Iozzia house brought the distant war into their living room each evening. Broadcast pioneers working for CBS--such as Edward R. Murrow in England-- painted a vivid picture of the Battle of Britain and the "blitz" on London; William Shirer and Howard K. Smith, perched in Berlin, hauntingly described, in graphic detail, the rise of the National Socialist Party into power and the atrocities against its citizens; Eric Sevareid stayed in Paris to give a first-hand account of the fall of France, then reported on the war from other parts of Europe, Asia, Africa, and Central and South America; and Larry LeSueur covered the London Blitz on CBS's London After Dark, then covered the German assault on the Soviet Union.

Violence and intolerance also festered up from neighboring immigrant communities, whose populations suffered years of economic hardship. Out of the German neighborhoods in Paterson and other parts of the state emerged groups that espoused Nazi hate and rhetoric. The most notorious organization was the Amnerika-Deutscher Volksbund, or German-American Bund, which was intensely loyal to Adolf Hitler, and was the de facto American arm of the Nazi Party.

Because New Jersey and New York had large immigrant populations, the bulk of the Bund's membership and activity were in those states. Northern New Jersey cities saw parades and protests, where brown shirt-clad Bund members carried Nazi flags and hurled hateful speech at the crowds. Accompanying these rallies were fistfights and violence between pro-and anti-Nazi gangs. It is no coincidence that in February 1939, the Bund held its largest rally at Madison Square Garden in New York City. Attending were many German immigrants from Paterson and other North Jersey cities to produce a crowd of 22,000. The bigoted speech and violence by brown shirt American Stormtroopers and pro-Nazi spectators revolted most Americans, including many in Paterson's Italian enclave who suffered under previous autocratic European governments.

Law enforcement eventually cracked down on the Bund, especially after the Reich invaded Poland. Contained in the Selective Service Act of September 1940 was a provision to exclude Bund members from working in any defense industry plant. The new law caused the dismissal of many Bund members and their sympathizers from the growing number of plants, including the Wright Aeronautical Corporation of Paterson. Though she did not know it, these vacancies would directly impact young Roseann's life.

Private Carmen Iozzio

Paterson, New Jersey
November 30, 1940

The Selective Service Act of September 1940 had another impact on the Iozzia family. It opened the way for Carmen to enlist in an army on the front end of a transformation, which would see it grow by 47.5 times in six years. Before Germany invaded Poland in September 1939, the 174,000-man U.S. Army ranked nineteenth globally, behind Portugal and slightly ahead of Bulgaria. In addition to few soldiers, the Great Depression and American isolationist tendencies forced troops to endure inadequate training with obsolete World War I-era equipment.

The diminutive Army lacked a foreign presence, with its mission limited by Congress to defend U.S. territory. Except for a small contingent in China, the Army's area of operation was restricted to the continental

U.S. and its territories, including Hawaii, the Philippines, and the Panama Canal Zone. In the forty-eight states, soldiers were stationed in half-strength and ill-equipped divisions scattered across the country's numerous posts.

With the German invasion of Poland and the subsequent fall of France and the lowland countries in 1940, President Roosevelt convinced an isolationist Congress and the public to strengthen the American military. Congress passed legislation, and the War Department developed plans to raise and equip a 1.5 million-man force. This was accomplished by Congress authorizing the National Guard's induction into federal service and activation of the Reserves. Congress also created the nation's first peacetime draft of untrained civilian manpower.

The draft commenced in October 1940 by requiring all men between the ages of twenty-one and thirty-six to register for a potential twelve-month enlistment, limited to the Army's existing service area of the Western Hemisphere and U.S. territories or possessions. About twenty million men across the country registered for the draft.

In New Jersey, 541,000 men registered, including Carmen and Anthony, who, on October 6, walked into the draft board and filled out the D.S.S. Form 1, Registration Cards. The next task was for the 202 local draft boards in municipalities throughout the state to produce between 12,000 and 13,000 recruits for the initial Army draft of 400,000 new soldiers.

In Paterson, six local draft boards met in schools across the city to assign each registrant a number, then a national lottery was held to rank registrants across the country. Paterson School No. 13 on 15th Avenue, located six blocks from the Iozzia residence, housed Local Board No. 15. This Board had jurisdiction over men who lived in Paterson's Fifth and Eleventh Wards, including Carmen and Anthony. Its 31 board members, chaired by Garret Platract, were given a quota to produce ten recruits.

On lottery day, Tuesday, October 29, papers with the numbers 1 through 7,836 printed on them were placed into capsules. Each capsule contained one number. The capsules were poured into a giant fishbowl and stirred with a wooden spoon fashioned from part of a beam from Philadelphia's Independence Hall. Then, a blindfolded Secretary of

War, Henry Stimson, drew capsules from the bowl one by one to establish the draft order. President Roosevelt announced the numbers.

Local men with numbers who came up early received an "order to report for induction" letter from their draft board. The letter informed them to report to a draft board in Paterson to determine their enlistment eligibility and receive a medical examination. In early and mid-November, men poured into the Boards throughout Paterson and the rest of the country to fill out questionnaires, be evaluated by Board Members for eligibility to serve, receive a medical examination by civilian physicians and have lab work, including a Wassermann test for syphilis.

Like other boards, Local Board's No. 15 goal was to fill as many quotas as possible with volunteers before inducting draftees. Though Carmen had a draft number that did not target him for induction, he chose to volunteer. So, in mid-November, Carmen walked into School No. 13 to be interviewed by draft board members on his background and receive his initial physical. He was classified as 1-A, fit for immediate induction.

Nationwide, the first draftees entered military service on November 18. The following day, Carmen and nine other volunteers were notified by Draft Board No. 15 to report for induction into the Army at 8:00 am on Friday, November 29. His nine fellow inductees were:

- Frank Francis Camps of 291 Market Street;
- John Lewis Grove of 774 Madison Avenue;
- Lawrence Hershkowitz of 502 12th Avenue;
- Isaac Jacobowitz of 505 12th Avenue;
- Elmer Vincent De Augustinis of 975 East 24th Street;
- Thomas Firth Braithwaite of 267 18th Avenue;
- Thomas Angelo Vitagliano of 129 Park Avenue;
- Clifford William Skubas of 360 East 13th Street; and
- Charles Nelson Anderson of 1037 East 22nd Street.

During the week of November 25, 118 men who answered the call reported to draft boards across Passaic County to ship out to Fort Dix for basic training and a one-year enlistment in the Army. Monday night Carmen and the other Paterson inductees participated in a large send-off party at the Elks Club on Ellison Street. At 8:00 a.m. on Friday,

November 29, Carmen and the other nine volunteers mustered at School No. 13. There was a brief ceremony where Draft Board No. 15 members and local dignitaries thanked the men for their service. William G. Wollen, a Board member, gave the men a brief address, their orders were read, and Clifford William Skubas was chosen as the group's leader. Family members cried while Red Cross and Salvation Army volunteers passed out coffee, sandwiches, and tins of cigarettes.

A chartered Public Service bus began the journey of picking up all the inductees, starting with twelve from Board No. 16 at Paterson School No. 9. The men marched out of the school to their awaiting coach to find all the school students lining the street waving American flags and cheering them on. Then at 8:25, Carmen and the men from Draft Board No. 15 boarded the bus. It then picked up sixteen more from Clifton Boards 4 and 5. Many family members from Paterson, including Anthony and Roseann, followed the bus to Clifton for the brief but well-attended ceremonies at each stop. Once all thirty-eight inductees were aboard, the bus drove forty-three miles to the Army induction center in Somerville.

There Carmen received an in-depth physical examination from First Lieutenant Saul Solomon, an Army doctor. Carmen was: five-feet-two-and-one-half inches, taller than the five-feet minimum; eight pounds heavier than the minimum 105 pounds; had 20/20 vision; and was missing only two teeth, which was well above the requirement to have at least half his teeth. Dr. Solomon also noted Carmen had brown hair, blue eyes, a ruddy complexion, and a tonsillectomy in 1926. His physical results were normal, including his lab work and chest x-ray, and the doctor certified him as *mentally and physically qualified for the active military service of the United States.* Since he was never convicted of a crime and could read and write, he was *accepted for active military service and inducted into the Army of the United States.*

A soldier took fingerprints of the five fingers on Carmen's right hand. Then Carmen stood in front of First Lieutenant Fred Krug, raised his right hand, and swore an oath that ushered in five years of military service. He joined other volunteers, draftees, National Guardsmen, and reservists who more than doubled the Army's size during the last six months of 1940 and, by mid-1941, grew it to 1.5 million soldiers.

Like he did seven years prior when he joined the CCC, Carmen, with his luggage in hand, boarded a bus to begin his initial training at Camp Dix, renamed Fort Dix. Just months before Carmen arrived, the Army started transforming the post to house and train thousands of draftees from all over the East Coast. It more than doubled its size as 35,000 acres of surrounding farms and pinelands were converted into areas for maneuvers and artillery ranges. Structures were going up across the base. More than 160 new buildings, including barracks, hospitals, and PXs, were under construction when Carmen arrived. However, the base lacked enough wooden barracks to house the mass influx of draftees.

With drill instructors barking orders, Carmen was commanded to berth in one of the hundreds of tents pitched on Fort Dix's green. It was winter, unseasonably cold, wet, and muddy, and he and his fellow soldiers were shivering in the slushy mud surrounding their tent. Though they had a stove, it had no coal in it. The only warmth came when his tentmates "found" coal in the Officer's Kitchen.

His initial time at Fort Dix could only be described as "languishing in no-mans-land." He spent four days at the "recruit reception center." Then it was two weeks of quarantine to ensure he and his fellow inductees did not have any illnesses that could spread into the general Army population.

The supply system was plagued with the same shortages as base housing. Carmen and the other recruits wallowed in their tents for days before they were issued uniforms or gear. When their gear did arrive, it was leftover World War I equipment, including Springfield rifles, "Sam Browne" leather belts, and doughboy-style tin hats.

The Army of 1940 was nowhere near trained nor equipped as the one that would storm Hitler's "Fortress Europe" four years later. Carmen participated in maneuvers that included cannons on caissons drawn by horses. Shortages of guns, artillery pieces, ammunition, and vehicles forced some troops to use broomsticks for guns and rain spouts for cannons.

A peacetime draft was new to the country and highly controversial for a populace that wanted no part in another European war. The Army had to transition the men and the country into accepting a large peacetime force fed by draftees. Thus, on Sunday, Carmen's second day at Fort Dix, the post put him and the 2,737 other recruits on display for the public. Catholic, Protestant, and Jewish services were held in the recreation building for newly arrived soldiers. The Army then opened the Fort to 10,000 visitors, including the new men's family members. After spending time with their friends and family, the new troops jammed back into the recreation center for an evening vaudeville show featuring ten variety acts from Broadway and an orchestra. Two days later, Major General Clifford Powell, the commanding general, announced that he was suspending training from December 21 to January 2 and furloughing 13,500 soldiers to enjoy the holidays with their families and friends. When Carmen's quarantine period ended, he was paid fourteen dollars, taken to the bus station, and then to East 18th Street for a few days' leave.

On January 3, with the holidays in the rear-view mirror, Carmen was assigned to Company B of the 1229 Recruit Training Battalion. Their first task was to break down the tent city and move into newly built barracks, a job Carmen was happy to undertake. After completing a month of basic training, Carmen, with the 185 men in his unit, was transferred fifty-nine miles across New Jersey and up the Sandy Hook peninsula to a Coastal Artillery unit at Fort Hancock.

With over 12,000 miles of coastline, seacoast defense had always been an integral part of the country's defense. Starting in 1901, the Army organized the fortifications protecting our shoreline and harbors into the Coast Artillery Corps. World War I saw a surge in coastal fortifications, but like the entire military, much of the Corps demobilized post-war and what remained fell into disrepair from funding cuts. After Germany invaded Poland, the Roosevelt Administration began to refortify coastal positions to defend against sea and air attacks.

With about 4,000 soldiers of the 7th, 52nd, and 245th Coastal Artillery units, Fort Hancock sat on the tip of a peninsula that juts out into the Atlantic Ocean, about 10 miles south of the entrance to New York Harbor. Its strategic importance permitted the Fort to play a critical role in harbor defense and navigation since 1764, when its first structure, a lighthouse, was built. Over time, fortifications were added, and the installation was named Fort Hancock in 1899, with the completion of thirty-four buildings. In 1941, the Fort was a significant part of the nation's plan to keep New York Harbor safe from invasion or incursion by unfriendly submarines or warships.

When Carmen and his fellow soldiers arrived on a cold winter day, there were no barracks for them. Instead, they winced as they marched toward tents. Each "winterized" tent held approximately twenty-five soldiers. Latrine and shower facilities were also located outside. Tent City was cold, snowy and subject to bitter winds blowing off the ocean. Carmen and his fellow tentmates slept on cots alongside potbelly stoves, which were incapable of heating the large tents. Sometimes it was so cold that Carmen put an extra mattress on top of himself to stay warm! The cold was especially bitter with the blizzards of February 28 and March 7, which dropped fourteen, then seven inches of snow, wreaking havoc on the post.

Carmen was one of the first draftees to arrive at the Fort, whose staff were federalized National Guard soldiers assigned to instruct them. Pre-Pearl Harbor career soldiers looked down on draftees and did not embrace them coming into "their Army." They were hard on the new soldiers and strictly enforced military discipline. Under their guidance, Carmen would continue to hone his basic training skills. He continued to drill and practice the competencies every soldier must initially master.

The soldiers also received coastal defense training, including operating heavy artillery and mine laying. With training came cleaning, chipping paint, and polishing the weapons. While the work was hard and tedious, he spent time overlooking the beautiful Atlantic Ocean. On a clear day, when cleaning the right gun turret, he could see Coney Island. He learned that soldiers must enjoy beauty whenever and wherever they can find it.

He also stared down upon the familiar beach below him. Sandy Hook beach was where his parents took him as a child, and he swam as a teenager (when he and his friends could scrape together enough gas money). He spent many days having fun on that beach. Now he was in uniform, helping to lay mines and fire artillery at targets out to sea. This contrast indeed showed how much the world was changing.

Fear of an invasion of New York City, and other American east coast cities, drove an increased training tempo for the coastal defenders. Carmen and his fellow soldiers spent long days participating in invasion exercises and firing their weapons. On March 13 and 24, Carmen's unit and thousands of other troops from Forts Hancock and Tilden repelled naval "attacks" on Sandy Hook. It was the first comprehensive tactical inspection of the Sandy Hook harbor defenses since the expansion of the country's military forces. Men of the 7th, 52^{nd,} and 245th Coastal Artillery units were summoned to battle positions when the sea "attack" was launched by harbor patrol boats representing invading warships. More than 5,000 soldiers from Fort Hancock protected the six-mile shoreline of Sandy Hook. Others at Fort Tilden prevented "landing parties" from reaching Long Island. A similar exercise was repeated eleven days later.

April 1 found Carmen and 4,000 fellow soldiers manning their posts in the freezing rain during a practice nighttime alert. All the Fort's soldiers, vehicles, and other mechanized equipment went to battle positions for the 8:00 p.m. to midnight exercise.

On April 17, a coastal defense exercise took place to repel mock submarine and bomber assaults on New York, Boston, and Philadelphia. The exercise included a concentration of enemy submarine and air attacks against Fort Hancock and other New York City defenses. The lack of Atlantic seaboard warships, due to their repositioning to the Pacific Ocean, put additional pressure on coastal defenses to keep the shoreline safe against hostile dreadnaughts. Between these drills, the Fort conducted firing exercises for its heavy, 155 mm, anti-aircraft, and subcaliber guns for twenty-eight of thirty-six days between March 26 and April 30. It was a busy time for Carmen and the other coastal defenders.

Carmen also settled into a soldier's lifestyle. He learned to ration his off-duty entertainment until the first of the month when it was pay call. Then he and the other soldiers lined up in the base gymnasium at 8:30 a.m. to receive their monthly pay. He was compensated thirty dollars for his service, of which twenty-one dollars went directly to Pietro and Giuseppina. Two dollars was for insurance, and seven dollars had to last thirty days. However, the paymaster further whittled that down by requiring Carmen to settle any debts for laundry, haircuts, movie tickets, or anything else Carmen owed Uncle Sam.

Occasional off-base liberty had Carmen join his fellow soldiers piling in covered trucks that took them to the Elks Club in nearby Long Branch for dances and mingling with the local ladies. Other times local girls would visit the troops for social events at the service club on base. A rare overnight pass into nearby New York City or even Paterson was highly coveted.

"The more life changes, the more it remains the same," thought Carmen when four months after arriving at Fort Hancock, he got his next set of orders to Fort Eustis, Virginia. Like his 1933 CCC service, he began his military enlistment at Fort Dix and was now on a train that would take him back to Virginia's wilderness.

Originally established as a camp by the Army in World War I, Fort Eustis was mothballed during the Great Depression, and its land was transferred to the Federal Relief Agency and the Bureau of Prisons.

The Army reestablished the post as the Coast Artillery Replacement Training Center in August 1940. Its first trainees to learn seacoast and antiaircraft artillery arrived from Fort McPherson, Georgia, six weeks before Carmen, on March 29, 1941, when the Fort was re-designated one of two training centers for anti-aircraft artillery. The other was Camp Callan in La Jolla, California.

The concept of a "replacement center" was new to the Army. The Fort's primary purpose was to train soldiers and serve as a reservoir for other units. Recruits went through eight weeks of intense training, which molded them into basic soldiers that could, if called upon, serve in a coast artillery battery or the field. An additional four weeks of training made them minor specialists in qualifications such as plotters, observers, gun pointers, machine gunners, or searchlight personnel.

Initially, the plan was to train the draftees at the Fort for one year and allow them to return to civilian life, where they would serve as a pool of trained civilians, subject to recall in an emergency. Should war occur, these troops would supply men to form new regiments, raise existing ones to prescribed strength, and replace losses due to battle casualties.

Private Iozzio's train pulled into the Lee Hall Virginia Railroad Station. Then a truck drove him the remaining two miles onto the Fort. Carmen entered a sprawling base of 8,300 acres of forests, wetlands, and open plains, much of which was designated as training areas and ranges. Miles of unpaved roads afforded access to the Fort's remote sections providing soldiers with realistic terrain for training. It also had a 31-mile loop of railroad tracks for rail training. The Fort was rehabilitated with temporary wooden buildings, replacing the original structures. *"At least," he thought, "I am not in another tent!"* Like his CCC camp in Marion, Virginia, life was primitive, surrounded by vast wilderness with only necessities provided by the Army. The Army chose the perfect place to train with little distraction for Carmen and his fellow troops.

The base was also growing around him. He joined approximately 2,800 soldiers preparing to train 12,000 recruits at a time. Fourteen training battalions had been stood up, and plans were in place to establish a fifteenth. That battalion would be Carmen's home for the following year. The base was undergoing a significant construction program to accommodate all these personnel. Over 570 buildings, including twelve large warehouses, barracks, and mess halls, were constructed for the service unit and fifteen training battalions. Also under construction were fifteen large recreation buildings, two theaters, school buildings, an 850-bed hospital, laundry, bakery, cold storage plant, five guardhouses, and six post exchanges.

Soldiers run on food for their stomachs and mail for their minds! By April, the massive buildup of troops overwhelmed the postal service in Newport News, which experienced a 120% increase in business over April 1940. Each day twice as much mail and four to five times as many packages were sent to Fort Eustis as distributed in all of Newport News. Delays occurred as the overwhelmed post office delivered an average of 10,000 to 12,000 pieces of mail a day to the Fort. Sometimes that number, especially around the holidays, was as high as 25,000.

Further delaying the mail were letters generally addressed to "(Soldiers Name) Fort Eustis VA." To get these letters into the hands of eager soldiers, postal clerks had to match names to everchanging unit rosters. The mail delay drove homesick soldiers to stand in long lines outside the telephone pay stations each evening and deposit seventy cents for a three-minute conversation with loved ones back home. The Army's solution was to increase its postal force with newly arrived troops, including Carmen.

General Order #14 from Headquarters, Ft Eustis, dated May 15, 1941, established the 15th Coastal Artillery Training Battalion and made its initial assignments, including Carmen. He was attached to the Headquarters and Headquarters Detachment as a postal clerk. He spent his first year at the Fort clearing the backlog and moving mail to the Fort's occupants. It was a time-consuming job but rewarding because he got to bring cheer to his fellow soldiers. Soldiers appreciated more timely mail calls and the person handing them their letters from home! He fell into a routine and fit into his new unit. While his barracks was primitive, he was not in a tent, and workers were building amenities, including service clubs and a nearby signal office to call home. An occasional stomach pain and sinus infection brought him to sick call, where medicine was issued to relieve his symptoms.

Exactly three months later, on August 15, the fifteen battalions finished training their first groups, and 11,500 new soldiers departed to take up permanent assignments at Army posts in the eastern U.S. and its territories. These soldiers were trained in infantry drill, marching, bivouacking, rifle marksmanship, pistol operation, antiaircraft defense, chemical attack procedures, tent stitching, first aid, interior guard, military courtesy, customs of the service, elementary map, and aerial photograph reading, and basic signaling. They also received indoctrination in the Articles of War (rules of combat). In addition, most took advanced training, allowing them to occupy clerical, supply, mess, artillery, and communications billets in their new units.

With the class preparing to graduate in early August, Carmen was issued leave to visit his family in Paterson. Young Roseann was thrilled to see her older brother and the family intently listening to Carmen tell stories about Army life. On several nights, he and his friends from the neighborhood took the train into New York City to enjoy the nightlife.

As Carmen was enjoying his leave, events were occurring in Washington that would significantly alter his life. Earlier that summer, President Roosevelt asked Congress to extend the enlistment for draftees from twelve to as long as thirty months, plus any additional time deemed necessary for national security. On August 12, as Carmen said goodbye to his family and prepared to head back to his post, the House of Representatives approved the extension by one vote. The bill then sailed through the Senate, and the President signed the Service Extension Act of 1941 into law on August 18. His signature ensured that Carmen, whose enlistment would have ended a week before the Pearl Harbor attack, would now serve in the Army for the next five years. While Carmen eventually accepted his fate, other draftees threatened to desert when their original twelve-month service expired. In protest, they painted "O H I O" (Over the hill in October) on their barracks' walls.

Being in a Headquarters Company of a Coastal Artillery unit, Carmen had a front-row seat to the war clouds building between September and December 1941. Each day more troops poured into the Fort as efforts to fortify the country's coastal defenses moved at a frenzied pace. Additionally, the news in the Atlantic, beyond the range of coastal defensive weapons, was not good. On September 4, the destroyer USS Greer (DD-145) was attacked but undamaged while tracking a German U-boat 175 miles southwest of Iceland. Eight days later, the Coast Guard cutter Northland (PG-49) seized the Norwegian trawler Buskoe, which was headed to Greenland to establish and service German radio and weather stations.

October brought more ominous news. On the 17th, the destroyer USS Kearny (DD-432) was torpedoed and damaged southwest of Iceland. Two days later, a German U-boat torpedoed and sank the U.S. merchant ship, Lehigh, off West Africa. The month's end found the oiler USS Salinas (AO-19) torpedoed and damaged 700 miles east of Newfoundland. Worse, on the last day of the month, the destroyer USS Ruben James (DD-245) was sunk by German torpedoes off western Iceland. The Ruben James was the first U.S. Navy vessel lost to enemy action in World War II.

After October, the situation grew tenser. On November 6th, the cruiser USS Omaha (CL-4) and the destroyer USS Somers (DD-381) captured the German blockade runner Odenwald, disguised as a U.S. ship, and on December 3rd, the Sagadahoc, a U.S. merchant vessel, was torpedoed and sunk in the South Atlantic.

While not yet a national holiday, the President issued a proclamation declaring Thursday, November 20, 1941, as Thanksgiving. At Fort Eustis, Carmen and his fellow soldiers attended services and ate a traditional Thanksgiving meal. At the service, the Chaplain read the President's proclamation, which said:

> *"I, Franklin D. Roosevelt, President of the United States of America, do hereby designate and set aside Thursday, the twentieth day of November 1941, as a day to be observed in giving thanks to the Heavenly Source of our earthly blessings.*

> *"Our beloved country is free and strong. Our moral and physical defenses against the forces of threatened aggression are mounting daily in magnitude and effectiveness…*

> *"In the interest of our own future, we are sending succor at increasing pace to those peoples abroad who are bravely defending their homes and their precious liberties against annihilation.*

> *"We have not lost our faith in the spiritual dignity of man, our proud belief in the right of all people to live out their lives in freedom, and with equal treatment. The love of democracy still burns brightly in our hearts.*

> *"Let us ask the Divine Blessing on our decision and determination to protect our way of life against the forces of evil and slavery which seek in these days to encompass us…."*

In the mess hall, Carmen and his fellow GIs discussed how the President's proclamation omitted the earlier calls for peace and keeping the U.S. out of the war. The consensus among the soldiers was that war is at hand. While the President delivered his message, 6,913 miles west of Fort Eustis, a Japanese fleet consisting of six aircraft carriers with 414 airplanes, two battleships, three cruisers, nine destroyers, eight tankers, twenty-three submarines, and four midget submarines was preparing to get underway. Its destination was Pearl Harbor, which would ensure that PFC Iozzio's Army service would last a long time.

Chapter 7
The Second World War and Fortress America

Garfield, New Jersey
December 7, 1941

On December 6, 1941, if you asked seventeen-year-old Charles where he would be in seven months, the last answer would have been "*in Fort Eustis, Virginia, learning how to be a soldier.*" After Charles returned from his CCC stint on September 30, 1940, he secured a wool comber job in a local mill, making a decent $26.00 per week. The economy was returning to normal, and jobs were opening for young men and women seeking to help their families recover from years of economic hardship.

Just like the news shouted by paperboys on Black Tuesday twelve years prior or President Roosevelt's September 3, 1939, address to the nation on the outbreak of war in Europe, the radio broadcast Charles heard on the afternoon of December 7, 1941, was life-changing. On that Sunday, the weather was clear and cold, with the temperature hovering around freezing. Gusty winds made it feel even colder, so Charles and his friends skipped playing outside, and instead, at 2:00 p.m. Charles--like many others in northern New Jersey and New York--turned the radio to WOR for the kickoff of a football game between the New York Giants and the Brooklyn Dodgers. As the plays were being called, about a half-hour into the game, there was a bulletin: "*The White House announces Japanese attack on Pearl Harbor.*" Just like Pietro and Karoly did not grasp the full meaning of the stock market crash when they first heard the news, Charles was puzzled and asked his friends, "*Where is Pearl Harbor?*"

About an hour after the first bulletin, Charles heard a report that the Japanese torpedoed an army transport carrying lumber 1,300 miles west of San Francisco. "*That is a lot closer to home than an island in the middle of the Pacific Ocean,*" he thought. There were other false reports of naval battles and Japanese paratroopers landing in Honolulu. The image coming through the radio painted a stunning picture of the tragedy unfolding in Hawaii and the entire area, from the U.S. west coast to the east coast of Asia erupting in war.

As the afternoon wore on, Karoly came in from the shoemaker shop and joined Bertha, Charles, and his friends around the radio. The Dodgers would beat the Giants twenty-one to seven, but not before an announcement directing all servicemen to report to their units. Neighbors stopped by to listen. There were hugs, gasps, and hands over mouths as news reports shed more information on the attack and broadcast false reports that Manila, Burma, and Guam were bombed. While many of these frightening reports were inaccurate, they painted an ominous picture of the Japanese expansion that would occur over the next few weeks and months.

Charles could not pull himself away from the radio as programming was periodically interrupted with bulletins about other countries declaring war on Japan and interviews with senators and congressmen calling for a declaration of war. At around 8:00 p.m., New York City Mayor Fiorello LaGuardia ordered all Japanese subjects confined to their homes. Two hours later, an announcement was made that President Roosevelt would address a joint session of Congress the following day. Despite world events, tomorrow was a workday, so Charles went to bed.

The next morning, Charles, Frank Lazer, and the other workers on the wool mill floor shared the news as bulletins came across the radio. Reported casualty estimates went from 104 killed the day before to 1500. American warships were now reported sunk. Passengers shared the latest bulletins with Kurt Wehrmann as they boarded his bus. At 12:15 p.m., life paused as Americans huddled around radios to hear President Roosevelt before the microphones in a packed House of Representatives chamber.

With all eyes and ears focused on the radio, Americans heard microphones crackle, then the President said, *"Mr. Vice President, Mr. Speaker, Members of the Senate, and of the House of Representatives. Yesterday, December 7, 1941, a date which will live in infamy, the United States of America was suddenly and deliberately attacked by naval and air forces of the Empire of Japan."*

As the mill workers listened in disbelief, the President described to his stunned nation the scope of aggression in the Pacific and the extent of the Pearl Harbor attack. He also informed the nation that Japan used peace talks to help conceal the attack. The President went on, *"the Japanese government has deliberately sought to deceive the United States by false statements and expressions of hope for continued peace."*

He concluded his remarks:

> *"With confidence in our armed forces, with the unbounding determination of our people, we will gain the inevitable triumph -- so help us God. I ask that the Congress declare that since the unprovoked and dastardly attack by Japan on Sunday, December 7, 1941, a state of war has existed between the United States and the Japanese empire."*

Once the President concluded his remarks, Charles and the other young mill workers lifted their gaze from the radio and stared at each other. Without saying a word, they all knew what had to be done next: they had to head to the recruiting office in downtown Passaic.

Paterson, New Jersey
December 7, 1941

A few miles away, the entire Iozzia family also found a radio to huddle around. Fourteen-year-old Roseann already loved listening to the radio. All her life, she would enjoy hearing music or news filling her house as background noise. She also knew the power of the words that came out of its speakers.

One Sunday evening three years prior, Roseann listened to the Orson Welles radio broadcast of "War of the Worlds." This radio dramatization of a Martian invasion of Earth caused panic around the country, including in Paterson. Roseann heard the beginning of the show announcing that it was a dramatization. Despite her cautions, she watched people panicking in the street and within her own family. Roseann learned that Orson Welles Mercury Theater characters' acting coming through the radio was more potent than a young girl's caution to family members that the show was not real. The radio, she thought, is a powerful instrument.

While Roseann listened to President Roosevelt's words, her mind was on her older brother Carmen who was one year into his Army enlistment.

Fort Eustis, Virginia
December 7, 1941

Carmen watched the Pearl Harbor raid flip a switch on the base. The training program, established during peacetime to create a territorial army, now morphed into producing an offensive force whose goal would be to dislodge the Axis powers from conquered territories and destroy their homelands.

The directive from Washington was to produce as many soldiers as quickly as possible. The Headquarters cut the training program from twelve to eight weeks. It also modified the training to emphasize extended order drill, bayonet training, and chemical weapon defense. To further mold this offensive force, it erected more bayonet courses and gas chambers.

Not long after the bombing, the Fort and localities in the Hampton Roads area conducted the first extensive blackout exercise. Scheduled for three hours, the blackout lasted only a few minutes when spotters determined that the area was fully compliant with darkness policies. Blackouts then became part of life on the Fort.

Thursday, December 25, 1941, was only eighteen days after Pearl Harbor. Americans were still dazed and shocked from the devastating casualties suffered in the surprise attack. With the Pacific fleet in ruins, Wake Island fallen, Singapore besieged, and the Philippines invaded, Americans were quickly transitioning from peacetime to war footing. Christmas 1941 saw a blending of wartime preparation with the trimmings of peacetime that would soon be phased out.

Many families were apprehensive while relishing the ability to spend the holiday together, knowing that the men would soon be sent off to fight and maybe die. Women also knew they would soon leave home to assume military support jobs in the armed services, service support groups like the USO and Red Cross, or war plants. Rationing of goods had not yet started. So, holiday shoppers still found street lamps glittering and storefronts filled with luxury gifts that would soon vanish as the wartime economy prepared to swallow up most resources for the military.

Yet signs of war were all around. Along the nation's coastlines, anti-aircraft guns, of which many were obsolete, were hurriedly erected on roofs of buildings and alongside docks. Sentries often dressed in World War I uniforms carrying 1918-vintage rifles were posted at railway stations and armaments factories. Brigadier General John C. MacDonnell, the nation's air-raid warning commander, directed his volunteer civilian observers to man their posts on Christmas. *"Experience in war,"* he declared, *"has taught that advantage is taken of relaxation in vigilance to strike when and where the blow is least expected."*

Carmen's Christmas was also altered by the attack eighteen days prior. He planned to hop a train to Paterson and enjoy Giuseppina's Christmas feast with his family. He was approved for a week pass and could taste his mother's pasta, meatballs, and sausage from the butcher down the street. December 7 would keep his dreams just a dream. All furloughs, including Carmen's, were withdrawn or denied. The training pace significantly accelerated, requiring recruits and the staff to pack in more activity hours each day. This training pressure curtailed time off for the Christmas holidays. Drills were only suspended on Christmas and New Year's Day. Otherwise, the troops trained right up to and after the two holidays.

On Christmas Eve, many off-duty soldiers at Fort Eustis gathered around radios to hear the President and British Prime Minister, Winston Churchill, address the nation. At 5:00 p.m., the Marine Band on the South Lawn of the White House began a medley of holiday songs, beginning with "Joy to the World" and concluding with "Hail to the Chief." President Roosevelt then addressed the nation and the world. He said:

> *"It is in the spirit of peace and good will, and with particular thoughtfulness of those, our sons and brothers, who serve in our armed forces on land and sea, near and far — those who serve*

and endure for us — that we light our Christmas candles now across this continent from one coast to the other on this Christmas evening."

Following the President was Prime Minister Churchill, who stated it was *"a strange Christmas eve,"* because:

"Here, in the midst of war, raging and soaring over all the lands and seas, creeping nearer to our hearts and our homes, here, amid the tumult, we have tonight the peace of the spirit in each cottage home and in each generous heart. There, we may cast aside for this night at least the cares and dangers which beset us and make for our children an evening of happiness in a world of storm. Here, then, for one night only, each home throughout the English-speaking world should be a brightly lighted island of happiness and peace."

Nevertheless, he told Americans to:

"Let the children have their night of fun and laughter. Let the gifts of Father Christmas delight their play. Let us grown-ups share to the full in their unstinted pleasures before we turn again to the stern task and the formidable years that lie before us, resolved that by our sacrifice and daring, these same children shall not be robbed of their inheritance or denied their right to live in a free and decent world. And so, in God's mercy, a happy Christmas to you all."

Just as the Radio City Music Hall's Rockettes sought to high-step away the nation's war melancholy, the Army had plans to temporarily lift the Fort Eustis soldiers' morale. Traditional Christmas dinners with all the trimmings were served in the mess halls. USO volunteers and local ladies decorated the base service clubs with holiday decorations, then danced and entertained the troops. Santa even arrived in a jeep wearing his traditional red outfit and a helmet. Though the Army and the local population tried to normalize the troops' holiday, signs of war were everywhere. Troops and family members were told not to make long-distance calls on Christmas day unless necessary. The lines were cleared for national defense matters. On New Year's Day, troops listened to the annual Rose Bowl game with Duke University playing Oregon State.

But invasion hysteria caused officials to move the game out of California to Durham, North Carolina.

The tempo of training and the number of soldiers flowing through the Fort grew exponentially during the first six months of 1942. Live fire on the ranges and into the James River became constant. At night soldiers trained large searchlights on the sky, followed by antiaircraft fire.

Four to eight-week schools were established for automotive mechanics, bakers, buglers, clerical workers, cooks and mess sergeants, meteorology workers, observers, radio and telephone operators, and general mechanics. Hundreds of soldiers were selected from the enlisted ranks for Officer Candidate School and sent to Coast Artillery, Infantry, Quartermaster, Armed Forces, Ordinance, Medical Administration, or Chemical Warfare Officer Candidate Schools. Trains continuously transported raw recruits in and took out soldiers who built the units that would one day storm the beaches of Europe, Africa, and multiple Pacific atolls.

The air raid on Pearl Harbor also made the Army reform its obsolete plan to defend U.S. harbors against marauding battleships with large-caliber guns. Planes and aircraft carriers were a new threat, and the plan shifted from fixed heavy batteries to antiaircraft artillery training. Plans were underway to rewrite how artillerymen trained. Before December 7, the Fort trained troops to man large-fixed guns and await the enemy to come within range. America needed an offensive, not a defensive force, and antiaircraft artillery met that task. It could either be emplaced for defensive action or made mobile with infantry and armor units. This policy would significantly impact Carmen's Army career and have an even more significant impact on a future soldier named Charles.

On March 9, the Coast Artillery Replacement Training Center was redesignated as an Antiaircraft Replacement Training Center. The training battalions, including the 15th, were redesignated as antiaircraft artillery training battalions, and antiaircraft artillery orientation replaced heavy artillery training. With the reorganization and Carmen's knowledge of automobiles, it is not surprising that he was transferred to a new assignment as one of the detachment's three heavy truck drivers.

Thus, his new job was to drive heavy and light trucks within the Headquarters Detachment of the newly designated 15th Antiaircraft Artillery Training Battalion, 1310th Service Unit.

Though they had an intense work schedule, Carmen and the troops did find time for recreation. Three afternoons a week, over 5,000 soldiers participated in softball games. Two leagues formed in mid-May, the National and American Leagues, consisting of thirteen teams.

Not all of Carmen's driving was hard duty. On May 1, or May Day, Carmen was one of the drivers transporting 620 enlisted troops to the College of William and Mary gymnasium, where they danced with the college girls. Then, of course, Carmen had to wait at the school to safely return the dancing troops to the Fort. He also occasionally drove in "tactical training convoys" to the restored Colonial Williamsburg. Each day a battery of troops visited the historical town for tours and American heritage lectures. It was part of a citizen education program for the soldiers to understand better why they were going to war and what they were fighting to preserve. Carmen enjoyed strolling the town and eating the home-cooked food brought by the local workers.

The Fort also worked to increase the public's support for the war effort. Monday, April 6, was Army Day, commemorating the nation's entry into World War I. To celebrate, the Fort opened its gates to throngs of civilians who watched soldiers demonstrate their skills, such as how they lived in the field and fired small arms. Civilians roamed through barracks, mess halls, and recreation facilities. After driving VIPs around most of the morning and early afternoon, Carmen rushed back to the barracks to prepare to march in formation. Brigadier General Forrest F. Willford reviewed him and the other soldiers. Two months later, on June 14, Flag Day, the Fort put on a salute to the flags of the U.S. and its twenty-seven allied nations as Carmen and the other troops stood in mass formation, listening to music provided by both white and colored bands and a sixteen-voice chorus. Both were long days but made Carmen and the other soldiers on the Fort proud to be in the Army.

Passaic, New Jersey
July 3, 1942

The day after Pearl Harbor, recruiting stations across the country were jammed with Americans wanting to enlist. The small but growing military did not have the equipment, bases, or infrastructure to equip and train the massive military necessary to defeat the Axis powers. Thus, recruits were absorbed as new bases and equipment became available.

Charles's day to enlist finally arrived. On June 30, Charles returned to the draft board and filled out his draft registration card. Later that week, on Friday, July 3, 1942, he sat across the desk from Staff Sergeant Frank Arnold at the Passaic army recruiting station. At nineteen-and-a-half years old, Charles offered to enlist for the duration of the war, plus six months. He had no disqualifying qualities in his background. At the end of his interview, the staff sergeant dismissed Charles with instructions to report to the army recruiting station in Newark, NJ, the following Monday. Charles got to go home and enjoy the Fourth of July weekend. It would be four years until he would enjoy another one as a civilian.

Monday was a long day of "hurry up and wait," a fitting welcome to military life for Charles. He was fingerprinted, x-rayed, and had his vision, hearing, and urine tested. Once all test results returned normal, Dr. R. N. Carrier gave him a complete physical and signed him off as qualified for the U.S. Army. The following day, Charles completed the remainder of the paperwork and reported to a steadily filling room. After about 100 new enlistees gathered up, the door opened, and in walked First Lieutenant John Corser with a noncommissioned officer who hollered, *"Raise your right hand and repeat after the officer."*

Lieutenant Corser spoke, and all the enlistees repeated:

> *"I (Charles Asztalos) do solemnly swear that I will bear true faith and allegiance to the United States of America, and that I will serve them honestly and faithfully against all their enemies whomsoever, and I will obey the orders of the President of the United States and the orders of the officers appointed over me, according to the rules and articles for the government of the*

Army. And I do further swear that all statements made by me as now given are correct."

With that, Lieutenant Corser said, *"Congratulations, men,"* and the new soldiers shook each other's hands.

As a new army private, Charles's pay was about a dollar per day or $31.00 a month. This was a substantial pay cut from his $113.00 monthly salary as a wool coomber at the mill. He was assigned to join Carmen in the Coast Artillery Corps. The importance of defending the coastline and territorial waters was even made apparent during Charles's short time at the recruiting station. From July 3 to 7, while Charles was processed into the Army:

- The Alexander Macomb, an American Liberty ship loaded with supplies for England, was sunk off Cape Cod by the German submarine U-215. That submarine, while on a mission to lay mines off Boston Harbor, was then depth charged and sunk by a British warship;
- In two separate actions, the Japanese destroyers Nenohi and Arare were torpedoed and sunk off the Alaskan islands of Attu and Kiska (respectively) by American submarines; and
- A German submarine, U-701, was depth charged and sunk off Cape Hatteras, North Carolina, by an Army Air Corps coastal reconnaissance aircraft.

All these actions occurred off the U.S. coast while Charles stood in line to be processed into the Army. The country needed to rebuild its coastal defenses; it needed men to man it, and like his future brother-in-law Carmen, Charles was designated to help fill that need.

Soldiers have a saying that all plans are subject to change based on the "needs of the Army." Charles soon discovered the meaning of that saying. He was ordered to Fort Eustis, VA, to begin a journey that would not take him to a U.S. coastal battery but instead across the invisible highway to wage war on European soil.

Charles was about to join Carmen in the greatest military buildup ever experienced by their country. When Charles entered the recruiting office to take his oath, the Army had grown to three million soldiers, with all but a few hundred thousand having served more than two years. By war's end, that number of soldiers would climb to over eight million.

It took two years of training on American soil before Charles faced the enemy. Lieutenant Colonel George Dyer articulated the reason for the lengthy period in his historical compilation "XII CORPS Spearhead of Patton's Third Army." He says:

> *"97 percent of the army had to be produced by hastily warming over a bunch of confirmed civilians. The Army had to make civilians into soldiers. It then had to form these soldiers into fighting units. Lastly, it had to teach these units to work together to produce a cohesive and effective army."*

A training plan that implemented Lieutenant Colonel Dyer's description was put forth in "Training Directive Number 40" issued by Headquarters, Second Army, on November 1, 1942, as described in the transcript, "History of the Second Army." The plan was intended to ready units for combat against the enemy by creating four periods of mobilization training. The first thirteen-week period provided the individual with the skills necessary to be a soldier. This was followed by eleven weeks of unit training to develop each unit into "*an aggressive fighting team.*" The third period of eleven weeks taught "*combined training*," where units of all arms and types operated together as a "*hard-hitting, aggressive team.*" The fourth and final training period lasted until the unit embarked overseas, and it emphasized exercises and other training to hone skills learned in the previous periods.

After receiving training in the Articles of War and conduct for soldiers in Newark, Charles was put on a train and arrived at Fort Eustis near Williamsburg, Virginia, on July 15. He began his first period of training, where he learned to be a soldier--it was his "boot camp."

Charles's train pulled into the Lee Hall Virginia Railroad Station, where a Sergeant, Corporal, and a handful of Private First Classes greeted him and the other trainees. They lined the new soldiers up and marched them two miles to camp. During the march, the Sergeant, who carried a walking stick, waved it around and barked, "*you, soldier, you, soldier, get in line, watch your step.*" Charles and the other recruits yelled back: "*Yes sir, yes sir,*" and kept marching as best they could.

Charles was assigned to Battery A, 4th Antiaircraft Training Battalion, where he began his eight weeks of basic training and learned basic artillery skills. He was taught to dress and act like a soldier. He learned how to fold his clothes, eat his food, and receive lots of vaccinations. He also learned to march, for there was lots of marching. His training included multiple twenty-mile forced marches and running obstacle courses in the oppressive summer heat and steamy swamps along the Charles River. He and his fellow soldiers got to experience a new 500-yard obstacle course that included swinging on ropes over fourteen obstacles and conquering high walls, ladders, rope swings, wire entanglements, trenches, ditches, and pipe tunnels. The Army built up his endurance by starting with two-mile marches each day, and by the end of basic training, he completed a twenty-four miler with his full field pack and rifle.

Charles also learned how to fire weapons. For the first time in his life, he would fire small arms and learn the basic skills necessary to fight in a war. Charles also spent long hours learning to operate fixed, railway, and tractor-drawn artillery pieces at ranges on the Fort and in the town of Grande View. He fired rounds into the James River and anti-aircraft target practice at free-flying balloons.

Though training consisted of long days with little time off, there was occasional recreation to help Charles and the other soldiers unwind. A month after arriving, Charles and another 10,000 enlisted troops were treated to the "Fort Eustis Cavalcade of Stars." Starting at 8:00 p.m. on August 25 and under a bright full moon, the troops watched a continuous performance of comedians, tap dancers, magicians, vocalists, instrumentalists, and girl choruses. After more than two hours of performances, an antiaircraft searchlight lit an American flag, and the National Anthem played as the curtain fell on the final act.

Charles spent his free time on Sunday afternoons standing in a long line outside the small post signal office in the rain or hot sun, waiting to make a long-distance call home. By September, waiting in line got easier as the Fort began publishing a weekly newspaper. On Friday, September 4th, the first eight-page edition of "Sky Watch" was distributed to the troops. Now while standing in the multitude of lines, Charles could peruse the paper's pictures, news, sports, and cartoons.

Life was getting better just as he prepared to ship out to his next duty assignment in mid-September. On the 12th, he watched the Eastern Army grid team (the Fort's local football team) defeat the New York Giants professionals sixteen to nothing. However, his biggest thrill was playing on the 4th AA Training Group's softball team. Like his days at the CCC, he loved playing ball. To his disappointment, the 4th did not make the playoffs for the Detachment Softball Championship. However, he was treated to exciting playoff games where the Military Police defeated the 33rd General Hospital in two straight contests for the right to meet the 2nd AA Training Group team for the post title. The 2nd then won the crown by taking two out of three games from the Military Police. The 2nd's pitcher, Private Bob Konold, pitched three shutouts in the semifinals and finals. Charles thought: *Watching good baseball is the next best thing to playing!*

The 4th Antiaircraft Training Battalion was located near Carmen's 15th Training Battalion. One wonders if Charles stood in a line behind Carmen or sat next to him at a USO show. Both loved baseball. Did they sit next to each other and cheer their teams on against the other? They may have even exchanged words, and then their faces faded into their clouded memories filled with the blurry faces of thousands of GIs they would meet during the war.

Fort Sheridan Illinois
July 1942

A few weeks after Charles arrived at Fort Eustis, Carmen was transferred to the newly created 405th Coastal Artillery Battalion at Fort Sheridan, Illinois, for an advanced motor transportation course for enlisted personnel. The Army watched the mechanized German army decimate opponents whose soldiers rode horses and bicycles into combat. It knew that the U.S. Army had to fight the Germans on par, which meant an array of vehicles to move troops and weapons quickly. Those vehicles needed soldiers to service and fix them. They needed mechanics, welders, and sheet metal repair personnel. However, the Great Depression limited civilian automobiles and trucks. Thus, a large pool of mechanics did not exist in the civilian population. The Army opened a series of motor transportation schools to address the shortage, including one at Fort Sheridan.

The Fort, on Lake Michigan's shore, was about an hour north of Chicago and just south of the massive Navy Training Center at Great Lakes. It opened in 1887. In addition to the motor transportation school, the post had one of the country's four Recruit Reception Centers, processing large numbers of recruits. It also housed the headquarters for prisoner-of-war camps in Illinois, Michigan, and Wisconsin. When Carmen arrived, these camps were preparing to receive Axis prisoners from the upcoming North African Campaign.

For the next six months, Carmen and Edward Novalcik, his friend who grew up near him in Boonton, NJ, would take courses to repair and keep vehicles operating. These courses covered all aspects of motor transportation, including tire, battery, engine, track repairs, and vehicle servicing, both in quarters and in tactical situations. On December 1, Technician Fifth Grade Iozzio and Private First Class Novalcik were among twenty-five students to graduate from Ordnance Automotive School. They were awarded a certificate of completion by Colonel E. H. Besse, the Commandant of the School.

When not learning about mechanics, Carmen was occasionally permitted to take the bus into Chicago for entertainment. He enjoyed his time at the USO Club in the "Windy City," but he was ready to leave by November. First, the weather was turning cold, being on Lake Michigan's shore, and second, he had a date back in Paterson he could not miss.

Tank Destroyer Training Center
Camp Hood, Texas
September 1942

On September 18, 1942, Camp Hood, Texas, officially opened as an Army post, and Charles completed his training in Virginia. He was rated excellent in character and satisfactory on his soldier skills, much the same rating he received during his regimented time in the CCC. The new soldier boarded a train for the newly opened camp, where he would be molded into a Tank Destroyerman.

Charles was one of the first to train in a newly devised type of warfare at the just constructed post. He was a pioneer, and with that came excitement, mental and physical challenges, frustration, and rustic living.

If Charles felt his CCC camp in New Jersey was in the wilderness, he had to marvel at the vastness of Camp Hood's desolate landscape. Twenty times larger than Fort Eustis, it was 160,000 acres of various terrains, including sandy plains, rocky hills, steep bluffs, wooded valleys, and rolling hills. The terrain was very rough, with snakes as the major occupants. The nearest towns with amenities were Belton and Waco, located approximately forty miles away.

In addition to a desolate location, the living conditions were primitive. The site for Camp Hood was chosen in January 1942, only nine months before Charles arrived. Construction of the main base could not start until some 300 farming and ranching families were given short notice to surrender their land five months before his arrival. The soldiers before Charles lived in extremely primitive conditions. As the main post was under construction, training and work battalions lived in field tents under theater of operations conditions. They drew equipment and food from rail and truck heads and drank purified creek water. It was not until a few weeks before Charles arrived that troops began to occupy hastily constructed and spartan barracks and buildings.

Charles was assigned to Company B of the Student Regiment for his initial two months of training. He then graduated to advance training with Company D of the 127th Training Battalion. Along with a Headquarters Company and the 126th and 128th Training Battalions, the Company made up the Tank Destroyer Replacement Training Center's first class. Company D consisted of personnel who would become motor mechanics, supply men, and clerks.

Charles and the other soldiers received their introduction to the new training center. They piled into a furniture-less room where an officer stood before them and described this new type of warfare aimed to destroy German and Japanese tanks. He said:

> *"World War II, as you know, is a mechanized war. The early stages of the conflict were characterized by the overwhelming superiority of the Nazi Panzer Divisions which penetrated like a devastating meteor into the lowlands of Poland and France. The speed with which the Nazi legions conquered those powerful nations convinced the Army that it was necessary to form a specialized striking force specifically designed to meet this challenge. Thus, was the Tank Destroyer born, child of American ingenuity and American adaptability.*

> *"That in response to this new method of warfare, General Marshall activated the Tank Destroyer Force on 21 November 1941. It was charged with the mission to SEEK, STRIKE and DESTROY enemy tanks. Five weeks after the start of the U.S. involvement in World War II, it was announced that this Tank Destroyer Tactical and Firing Center would be established. The first major unit, the 893d Tank Destroyer Battalion, arrived here from Fort Meade, Maryland on 2 April 1942.*

> *"You are in a sense going to school. The Army realizes the value of complete and adequate training facilities. Here in the RTC, you will go to class and learn about your weapons and how to use them and the tactics of employing them. You will learn everything that is necessary for you to become familiar with the Army, and the ways of the Army. When you have completed your cycle of training in the Center, you will no longer be a trainee but a well-rounded soldier ready for duty...*

> *"From the very first, on battle conditioning and infiltration courses, you will learn combat discipline, self-preservation, offensive measures, how to conquer fear, and to have confidence in the techniques you have learned on Hood's far-flung acres. You will learn to destroy enemy tanks with modern*

weapons, and even with only your hands and the wreckage of battlefields."

Soldiers who reported after Charles would read this history in the "Welcome to the Tank Destroyer Replacement Training Center" booklet issued to them on arrival. For the next two months--in classrooms and on the field--Charles learned every known method of tank destruction, from the massed fire of mobile self-propelled heavy weapons to guerilla-style ambushing of tanks.

He became intimately familiar with the M-3 half-track mounted with a 75mm gun and a top speed of about 43 miles per hour. It was the first self-propelled tank destroyer. He learned that the M-3 had to combat the enemy tanks' firepower with greater firepower and a high-velocity flat trajectory. The Destroyers also used greater mobility and independence of operations to overcome the enemy tanks' mobility. The Destroyers' tactic was to fire four or five rounds from one position, dash to an alternate position, and reopen fire before the enemy's guns began to register.

Though a critical mission, Charles and the new students suffered from a lack of training facilities and battle conditioning short on realism because they were quickly improvised. Given the limited time, budgets, and resources, the Center attempted but did not always make training realistic. A mock-up of a Japanese tank welcomed Charles and the other soldiers to help them envision what they would be up against in future duty assignments. However, the school lacked American and enemy vehicles, guns, and equipment for training.

In addition to the mental challenge of learning newly developed and untested weapons systems, Charles and his fellow soldiers were pushed to their physical breaking points. They faced five grueling days on the Tank Hunting Course, where obstacles and infiltration courses challenged them. They crawled through weeds, across ravines and trenches, and under barbed wire while live machine gun rounds streaked overhead. They practiced tank destroying skills in a mock Nazi village. The course contained ranges where they learned to fire 45mm pistols and Tommy Guns fast and accurately from the hip in darkness and daylight. They also practiced assaulting tanks with Molotov cocktails and "sticky grenades" as the tanks traversed a field of debris and other various terrains.

December put Charles's skills as a soldier to the test. In the middle of the month, he participated in a 26-mile forced march with full gear and then a major anti-tank exercise against a co-located tank battalion. Adding to training demands was the ad-hoc nature of being one of the first classes of a new warfare. Lessons were being learned, and the training was being developed and refined as it was taught. Also, a lack of equipment required constant improvising. Lectures took place in garage sheds and dayrooms void of tables or chairs. Supplies, including weapons, ammunition, and even blackboards were at a premium, and some texts arrived late, if at all. A week after Charles left the camp, the entire Replacement Training Center was placed in quarantine due to a measles outbreak.

Meals were an essential part of the soldier's day, and Charles was served three meals a day. They were generally of good quality but often poorly cooked, monotonous at best, and unfamiliar to him and the other new soldiers. Soldiers were taught to eat Army style, as dictated by the following rules, which hung in the chow hall:

> "1. Never take more food on your plate than you need to eat.
> 2. Eat all the food you take on your plate.
> 3. Do not think just because you are one among millions that the food you waste doesn't count. If the millions waste a little it adds up to a lot.
> 4. You are not saving food merely because you have been asked to. Food is a weapon; you are helping to win the war when you do not waste it."

While life was consumed by long days of training, the Army did provide entertainment on weekends or an occasional evening for soldiers off duty. On December 10, the soldiers stationed in the vast desolate camp were provided regular news about the base, surrounding communities, and the world when the camp published its first biweekly newspaper called the "Hood Panther." In addition to the newspaper, the camp had a library, chapel with services for all denominations, and theater with movies most nights. December movies included *Flying Fortress* and *Road to Morocco.*

Several USO shows visited the camp during Charles's training, including a December 16 pre-Christmas presentation with the Ray Herbeck's Orchestra and All Girl Revue. On those rare occasions when he was granted off-base liberty, Charles visited a USO Club in a neighboring town. However, unlike Garfield's social gathering places, they were racially segregated by law, with one club for white and another for black soldiers.

Charles loved sports, and there were many sports teams and events, including baseball, basketball, bowling, and lacrosse. Boxing matches were very popular.

His time at the school extended over the 1942 holiday season, and his training prevented him and his fellow trainees from taking leave, but the Army still tried to make the holidays festive. On Thanksgiving, November 26, the mess hall served a special meal consisting of an oyster cocktail, roasted turkey with sage dressing and cranberry sauce, snowflake potatoes, candied sweet potatoes, creamed corn, and Waldorf Salad. For dessert, there were pumpkin and mincemeat pies and fruitcakes. Post-desert cigarettes and cigars were also distributed. This was a much-improved menu compared to the usual dishes of spam and chip beef on toast.

Over the holidays, Charles attended Auto Mechanics School learning how to operate and fix the Tank Destroyers' various vehicles. Training halted on Christmas Eve and Christmas Day so soldiers could enjoy the holiday. Services for various denominations were held. The major camp buildings, including the Post Headquarters, PX, mess hall, and motor pool, were decorated with holly wreaths and tinsel. The Camp Commander encouraged his soldiers to enjoy the "*holiday spirit while Christmas tree lights twinkle*" because they bring "*encouragement to an*

Army fighting for peace." He also told them, "*in the company messes, Uncle Sam will give one of the biggest Christmas meals in history. The menu calls for turkey and all the trimmings.*"

In mid-February 1943, Charles was coming to the end of his training and listened to a briefing by Colonel Thomas J. Heavey, the Second Tank Destroyer Brigade's Executive Officer who had just returned from a 30,000-mile tour as an observer in England and North Africa. He told the soon-to-be Tank Destroyerman, "*Tank Destroyers in Africa have proved their usefulness and are the talk of the new campaign there.*" Colonel Heavey opined that he did not think "*the Allies are going to have all easy time in Africa. It is very evident that the German forces in Tunisia are well-trained and well-equipped and that they have a very high morale. They are battle-seasoned.*" Colonel Heavey found "*high praise from officers everywhere in North Africa for the self-propelled 75-millimeter tank destroyer, the familiar half track. One tank destroyer was credited with knocking out five German Mark IV tanks with seven rounds.*"

On March 8, 1943, Charles completed training with the 127th Training Battalion. With his graduation, Charles sewed the patch of a Tank Destroyerman onto his uniform. The round yellow, black, and red patch depicts the tank destroying Black Panther, crushing an enemy tank between its powerful jaws. He was now a trained Tank Destroyerman. However, Charles would learn for the second time in his short Army career that the Army is entitled to change its mind and often does.

Paterson, New Jersey
Fall, 1942

Roseann was a junior at Eastside when the bombs fell on Pearl Harbor. After that, the men in her neighborhood began to disappear. During the remainder of her time at Eastside, the U.S. military added 7.3 million men to its existing 1.8 million, including Carmen. Older brothers of friends were drafted or volunteered. Passaic County, which includes Paterson, would later suffer 759 troops killed in the war and thousands of young men wounded. Roseann would learn how to attend funerals for people she intended to grow up with only a year or two earlier.

When Roseann entered her senior year, her elderly parents still struggled financially. Giuseppina was 58 years old and suffered from arthritis. Pietro was 59 and working a physically demanding job dying silk in the mill for subsistence wages. They were trying to meet daily finances while continuing to pay off the mortgage they were forced to take out during the height of the Depression.

The household lightened with Carmen in the Army and Anthony and Anna getting married. In December 1936, Anna married Thomas Baeli, and they rented an apartment at 87 Lodi Street in Hackensack. Thomas worked as a Color Mixer, earning $1,450 per year, while Anna was a Sewing Machine Operator. Four years later, Anthony married Carmella Tonzillo, a neighborhood Italian girl, and they moved around the corner from his parents into an apartment on 78 Cedar Street.

Without her siblings, it fell on Roseann to support her parents. On Saturdays, while her friends went to the movies and did fun things, Roseann cleaned the house, including washing floors and cleaning the kitchen, bathrooms, and bedrooms.

Pietro and Giuseppina fell behind on their mortgage payments. Giuseppina asked Roseann to help support the family financially. Though she had 97 points of the 100 required to earn her sports "Letter E," Roseann dropped off her sports teams and took an after-school job filing at a credit bureau. Except for a small allowance, her entire salary went to her parents so they could pay the mortgage.

Though they struggled, they all found joy in early December 1942. Technician 5th Grade Iozzio completed his training at Fort Sheridan and was transferred to the 501st Coastal Artillery Battalion at Camp Edwards, Massachusetts. The Army gave him leave between the move, allowing Carmen to make his way to Paterson for a family reunion and get married! Carmen had been corresponding with Lillian Brown, a beautiful Paterson girl. Lillian came from a large family with eight brothers and sisters that lived on River Street, about two miles from the Italian section. Her grandparents immigrated to the U.S. from Northern Ireland and Belgium, and her parents met and settled in Paterson. John, her dad, worked as a carpenter at a machine company and her mother, Mary, stayed home. Sadly, John passed away several years before the wedding, leaving Mary to care for Lillian and six of her siblings, who ranged in age from twelve to twenty-eight.

On December 6, American troops were locked in brutal fighting against the Nazis across North Africa and the Imperial Japanese Army on Guadalcanal. The first steps toward wresting territory from the Axis powers were occurring. Despite all the world's problems, it was a happy day for the Iozzia and Brown families with the marriage of thirty-year-old Carmen and eighteen-year-old Lillian.

The two families and all the guests arrived at Our Lady of Lourdes Church in Paterson. Carmen wore his crisp Army dress uniform with two stripes and a "T" on his arm, designating his Technician 5th Grade rank. Lillian wore a beautiful white silk dress with a lace veil and a long flowing train. In her hand was a bouquet of two dozen white roses and on her face was the biggest smile. The rest of the wedding party wore tuxedos with white boutonnieres, and the women wore white silk and lace gowns. Carmen's best man was Lillian's twenty-seven-year-old brother Thomas, and the maid of honor was sixteen-year-old Roseann. Father O'Connell performed the ceremony.

It was a rare moment in a troubled time, both globally and for the two families, to dress up, have fun and enjoy one of life's pleasures, the bonding of two people who found love.

With his furlough completed, Carmen boarded a train to Boston and then hitched a ride to Camp Edwards on Cape Cod, where he was assigned to the Headquarters Company of the 501st Coastal Artillery Battalion. He was shortly promoted to Technician 4th Grade. Carmen's health did not do well in the damp Massachusetts coastal climate. Between March and August, he made fifteen trips to sick call for congestion and stomach ailments. Carmen preferred the south's warmer climate, and fortunately or unfortunately for him, his time would be short in the Bay State.

Carmen Iozzio and Lillian Brown's wedding in Paterson, December 6, 1942

Camp Hood, Texas
March 5, 1943

Instead of transferring to a Tank Destroyer unit, Charles received orders to the 267th Field Artillery Battalion, which was activated four days prior. It was stationed at Camp Shelby outside Hattiesburg, Mississippi, in the southeastern part of the state. Charles was ordered to depart Camp Hood on March 8 and arrive at Camp Shelby two days later. Train travel was slow because railroads were clogged with troop trains and freight cars moving massive quantities of equipment toward the ports. On March 10, the steam locomotive pulling his train that belonged to the Bonhomie & Hattiesburg Southern pulled into the Hattiesburg Train Depot. The welcoming station was impeccably clean and housed in a classic brick train station building constructed in 1910. Under a large canopy was the passenger platform with "donut girls" and Red Cross volunteers serving coffee and snacks to weary travelers. Across the railyard, Charles could see downtown Hattiesburg with its shops, warehouses, and businesses built up around the railyard.

He and the other Army train passengers were driven twelve miles south down Highway 49 to Lee Street, through the Camp's south gate, to its reception center, where he got a meal and a ride to the 267th barracks.

Camp Shelby was first activated on July 18, 1917, to train doughboys to fight in World War I. It was one of sixteen "National Army" camps established by the War Department to prepare mobilized National Guard soldiers for European battlefields. Less than two years after it opened, the war ended, and the Camp was deactivated. It subsequently became a training post for the Mississippi National Guard. In November 1940, when the U.S. began its military buildup, the Camp was again federalized to support the Army.

When Charles arrived on March 10, 1943, Camp Shelby was a massive post of 360,000 acres, with another 400,000 acres leased for maneuvers that stretched into Louisiana. This gave the Army over a thousand square miles of training areas and ranges needed to school the newly formed artillery and infantry units stationed on the post. Charles arrived at the back end of another base construction boom. A total of 17,000 civilian workers and Army engineer units constructed more than 1,800 new buildings and laid 250 miles of roads to accommodate over 100,000 troops and support personnel. The camp that Charles entered was larger than any city in Mississippi.

The growing intensity of the war effort expanded the diversity of Charles's Army life. Camp Shelby held infantry divisions and tank destroyer, engineer, artillery, and field hospital units, all training independently and in joint operations. Its cantonment area contained white and "colored" housing, reflecting an army that still fought segregated on the battlefield. On the northern end was a large hospital complex providing care to soldiers wounded on the North African battlefield. After he arrived, a POW stockade housing German soldiers from that same battlefield was established on its west side. Charles also met Japanese-American soldiers who served with the 442nd Regimental Combat Team. The 442nd eventually served in Europe and became the most highly decorated unit based on its size and length of service. Arriving at the camp simultaneously with Charles were women in uniform who later became the Women's Army Corps or WACs. The

Camp provided Charles with a microcosm of the war he was preparing to enter.

Charles was told that after his initial introduction to artillery, he would be granted fifteen days of leave, allowing him to visit his family and friends in Garfield. Charles had not been home since July 6, 1942, when the bus took him to Newark for his induction.

He was attached to Battery "C" of the 267th and received two weeks of orientation to the base and his new assignment. Then on March 25, 1943, Charles was given his signed fifteen-days leave papers. He caught a bus where he sat in the front "whites only" section to the Hattiesburg train depot. Charles walked past black and white segregated restrooms and waiting areas toward his train going north. It had been over eight long months, and he was going home!

Charles home on leave with Karoly in front of their house in Garfield

Garfield, New Jersey
March 27, 1943

After two days of travel, Charles returned to a very different Garfield and family--his town and parents had also "gone to war." In the early part of World War II, the survival of the Republic was not guaranteed. The Great Depression made people question the viability of capitalism, and in the aftermath of World War I, the U.S. watched one democracy after another fall to either communist or fascist totalitarianism. As Charles was shipping out in 1942, the Japanese expanded their empire across the Pacific and Asia, threatening Australia and India with invasion. The Nazi regime had conquered all continental Europe and was on the outskirts of Moscow. England was isolated and feared an impending invasion that would strike the Union Jack forever. As German Panzers made their way across the Sahara Desert toward the Middle East and the Japanese Army probed India's eastern border, planners in Washington feared a Japanese/German sphere of control that would circle the globe.

America's "two oceans defense" to protect the Western Hemisphere from Europe and Asia's tyranny did not seem so reassuring. Pro-fascist regimes in the southern part of our hemisphere were sympathetic to the Third Reich. Since the Pearl Harbor attack and while Charles was training, German U-boats were sinking cargo ships within view of the American Atlantic and Gulf of Mexico coastlines and landing spies on U.S. shores. The Pacific coast felt an even more significant threat. The Japanese Army overran the American territories of the Philippines, Guam, and Wake Island and, in June 1942, occupied the islands of Attu and Kiska--part of Alaska. Japanese submarines occasionally but ineffectively shelled coastal areas in California and Oregon. With our Pacific fleet sitting at the bottom of Pearl Harbor, Americans feared that an imminent invasion of the West Coast could not be thwarted. This fear even worked its way into the Hungarian neighborhood of Garfield.

In addition to assembling a military large enough to fight a two-front war, the Roosevelt Administration created the Office of Civilian Defense in May 1941 to mobilize the civilian population to respond to aerial or naval attacks on the country. Also created was the Coast Guard Auxiliary to patrol the coastal waters and the Civil Air Patrol to monitor the skies. Coast Watchers manned towers along the American shoreline. The Civil Defense organization grew into a massive institution of ten million volunteers organized down to the block level in communities. Civilians were trained in first aid, firefighting, and decontamination from chemical attacks. The person responsible for Charles's old neighborhood was Air Raid Warden Karoly Asztalos.

So, when Charles went home, he did not just walk into his house and father's shoemaker shop. He walked into the command post for Dewey Street's defense plan. Karoly's Air Raid Warden job was to ensure that

Dewey Street was prepared for an air raid and coordinate rescue and recovery efforts after one occurred. Once he was approved for the job by the Garfield Defense Council Chairman, Everett Hughes, and Chief Air Raid Warden Byron Christie, he was issued a uniform consisting of a white armband with the Office of Civil Defense symbol, a red and white striped triangle inside a blue circle. On his head was a steel helmet of WWI vintage painted white and bore the same Civil Defense symbol as his armband. He also carried a gas mask, gas-protective clothing, heavy work gloves, and a warden's whistle.

Charles and Bertha sitting on the steps of 22 Dewey Street in 1943 and the house in 2018

Karoly received extensive training, including:

- A ten-hour first aid practical course conducted by the American Red Cross;
- Lectures and drills by Garfield Fire Department personnel who were specially trained at Civilian Defense Schools on methods to combat incendiary bombs;
- Lectures conducted by Reserve Officers on how to protect yourself and your neighbors in a chemical gas attack; and
- How to fill out, forward, and record reports delivered by the Chief Warden.

Karoly was issued and expected to memorize the "Air Raid Warden's Handbook." Excerpts from Karoly's handbook include:

"Your Duties as Air Raid Warden.

"You have been chosen as Air Raid Warden of your Sector (of 500 individuals) because you are known to be reliable and responsible and because you have the needed qualities to lead, direct, and help the people entrusted to your care.

"In your Sector are the homes of some hundreds of your friends and neighbors. It will be your responsibility to see that everything possible is done to protect and safeguard those homes and citizens from the new hazards created by an attack from the air or by enemies from within our gates. As an Air Raid Warden, you have specific duties to perform. You must study them, review them, practice them over and over so that you may carry them out in an air raid without failure or error. You must know your Sector as intimately as others know their own homes. You must know your people well. To them, you are the embodiment of all Civilian Defense. In every way, you must seek to gain their confidence so that in any time of stress you may more easily calm and reassure them and avert panic. As you become better acquainted with the individuals in your Sector, you will learn whom to call upon for informal help at such times.

"You are not a policeman nor a fireman nor a doctor, although your duties are related to theirs. As an Air Raid Warden, you have a unique position in American community life. It is a position of leadership and trust that demands an effort not less than your best."

Another section of the Handbook brings to light the responsibility Karoly could have had to assume:

"The Air Raid Warden in War.

"In time of war or other emergency, think of yourself first as a leader chosen from your neighborhood to do the right thing, with your neighbors and for them. The keynote of your conduct must be courage and presence of mind. When a warning is

given, go at once to your post, wear your arm band and secure your equipment. Reassure all those you meet and try to persuade them to go about their ordinary tasks until the sirens sound."

As part of Karoly's duties to prepare his neighbors for air attacks, he supervised blackout drills that commenced with an air-raid alarm signal. Karoly patrolled up and down Dewey Street after the siren blasted, looking for any escaping light from its houses. He also ensured that people caught out on the street or in cars stopped and found shelter in the nearest building.

Like Charles, Karoly was part of the defense of his country.

Charles also found a Garfield that was not just ready for war but a town that was an engine to launch him and the other U.S. troops across the Invisible Highway to Europe and Japan. Six months after France fell to the Nazis and a year and a half before Charles's enlistment, President Roosevelt gave a speech to the nation where he said that to preserve universal freedom, *"we must have more ships, more guns, more planes, more of everything. We must be the great arsenal of democracy."* These words especially rang true when Charles arrived back home. At that time, most of the world's industrialized areas were either under the Axis powers' domination or aerial assault by their air forces. To win the war, it would fall on the U.S. to produce the ships, planes, weapons, food, uniforms, etc., that allied military forces needed to win. President Roosevelt refocused the country's industrial power into a war production machine.

As part of that plan, Garfield's industries mobilized to support the war effort. According to Howard Lanza in his book, "Images of America Garfield," the Heyden Chemical Plant received a contract in 1943 to manufacture penicillin for wounded soldiers. Hartmann Embroidery Works in the Plauderville section converted operations to become the country's largest manufacturer of military insignia. On Randolph Avenue, the massive Forstmann Woolen Mill produced woolen uniforms and blankets for the troops. Perhaps Charles's uniform was made just down the street from his house.

The immigrant community did not forget fellow countrymen left behind in the nightmare of World War II Europe. In 1943, the predominantly

Polish St. Stanislaus Kostka Catholic Church's parishioners collected $1,000.00 and purchased an ambulance that they donated to the Polish Army. That church would one day be the parish for the Charles and Roseann Asztalos family.

Garfield's St. Stanislaus Kostka Catholic Church in 2018, looking the same as it did in 1943.

A "Six-Man Tent" was standard quarters at Camp Shelby, and the 267th FAB former barracks area is open fields and a tank wash area in 2017

Camp Shelby, MS
April 9, 1943

After a long train ride, Charles arrived back at Camp Shelby and reported in with the 267th. The unit was billeted in the far southeastern section of the cantonment area between 38th and 42nd Streets and 9th and 15th Avenues. Artillery units billeted in the most recently developed--yet unfinished--section of the Camp.

Charles returned to his five buddies, who shared a "six-man tent" with him. As standard quarters for enlisted personnel at the camp, the sixteen-by-sixteen-foot structure was made of wooden floors and walls with a canvas roof. Chicken wire-type screening encircled the area between the canvas roof and wooden half-walls. A wood or coal-burning stove was in the center of the tent. They were cramped and provided minimal protection from the heat, bugs, violent summer thunderstorms, or the winter chill. Eventually, the Battalion replaced the six-man tents with fifteen-man "hutments," which were all-wooden temporary structures containing two stoves for heat. They provided slightly better protection from the elements than the old structures.

When the 267th arrived at the artillery section, they found that toilet facilities were not yet built, so they had to use open-air latrines. Each week, someone from Charles's gun crew would be assigned the wretched latrine duty. It was not the kind of latrine duty one gets when there are regular flushing toilets that only involve cleaning. This duty required soldiers to pump the sewage out of the pits and dispose of the waste. "Pumping detail" was the worst duty and generally doled out as punishment or what Charles's Sergeant liked to call *motivational training.*

The 267th Field Artillery Battalion was activated as part of the Third Army to fire truck-drawn 155mm howitzers. The Battalion was non-divisional; it was an independent battalion assigned in combat to whatever Third Army unit needed additional fire support. It could be assigned to a field artillery group or directly to the headquarters of an Army Corps. The purpose of independent artillery battalions was to augment organic artillery units in heavy combat areas.

The 267th officers were activated reservists and recent graduates of the Field Artillery Officer Candidate School at Fort Sill, Oklahoma. The enlisted members were almost entirely personnel called to active duty with the Georgia National Guard and transferred from the 179th Field Artillery Group, also located at Camp Shelby. The Field Artillery Replacement Training Centers at Fort Bragg and Fort Sill furnished most filler-enlisted men, many of whom were draftees. A few, like Charles, were pulled from the Tank Destroyer school to help fill the Battalion's ranks.

The enlisted medical detachment consisted of personnel from the 78th Infantry Division at Camp Butler, North Carolina. Lieutenant Colonel Walter Hinsch assumed command of the Battalion, which was attached to the 403rd Field Artillery Group while it trained at Camp Shelby.

Colonel Hinsch was a true soldier. He served as a Private in World War I and received an officer commission in the Army Reserves after the armistice. Between March and December 1922, he commanded the 185th Field Artillery Brigade, a reserve brigade headquartered in Chicago. Colonel Hinsch was the first commanding officer of the newly created Brigade and oversaw its summer training at Fort Sheridan. He also commanded the reserve 3rd Field Artillery Battalion for five years.

Before coming to Camp Shelby to take charge of the 267th, he commanded the 26th Battalion at the Fort Sill Replacement Center. That was the primary training center for field artillery. He also attended the field officers' course in the winter of 1942. He was an experienced soldier, a combat veteran, an avid golfer (when he found time to play), and an able leader for the 267th.

The Battalion's weapons were twelve 155mm M1 howitzers that fired a 95-pound projectile a maximum distance of about nine miles. These medium artillery pieces were brand new, as the model had just gone into production in 1942. Firing the gun was a complex process. The 155's ammunition was not a single projectile with a cartridge case--instead, it had four components loaded separately into the breech. First, gunners prepared the projectile by fitting its nose with a standard fuse to explode on impact or a proximity fuse that could be set to explode a few feet above the ground for antipersonnel firing missions. The gunners then loaded the projectile, a separate bag of propellant charge, a fuse, and a primer for firing. The number of individual powder bags in the propelling charge determined the projectile's distance. After each round was fired, the 155mm tubes' powder chambers had to be swabbed and inspected because excess powder residue in the barrel could cause a catastrophic explosion when the next projectile was fired.

Smoke shells were used to mark target areas. Forward Ground Observers and Airborne Observers in a light aircraft assigned to the Battalion guided the guns onto their targets. This process was called "registration" by the gunners.

Firing the guns also required intense logistical coordination. Delivering ammunition in wartime was a daunting task, even for the brave. Drivers transported the projectiles on pallets containing eight projectiles each and weighing over 800 pounds. A standard Army truck could carry between 50 and 60 projectiles per trip from the ammo dump to the batteries. Drivers also had to transport crates of fuses and bags of high-explosive gunpowder. These are not items you want in the back of your truck while traversing a battlefield. When the ammo arrived, it took several artillerymen to unload and store the 95-pound projectiles.

The 267th had the standard structure of a medium artillery battalion. The "TO"--or Table of Organization for the Battalion--was approximately 550 enlisted men and thirty officers. It had three firing batteries (A, B, and C) with four guns and around 120 men assigned to each. It also had a headquarters battery with the Commanding Officer, Colonel Hinsch, his Executive Officer, Major William Collins, and staff, including the fire direction, communications, and administrative personnel, and a service battery with supply personnel, drivers, and mechanics. The 267th had a Georgia flavor that was detectable in its soldiers' southern drawls, mannerisms, and love of comfort food. It also had a handful of Midwesterners and northerners, including a Hungarian from New Jersey who tried to fit into this foreign culture and make his mark on the Battalion.

The three firing batteries were broken down into gun sections, which crewed a howitzer and led by a sergeant who served as the Section Chief. Under him were nineteen personnel, including a gunner corporal, assistant gunners, cannoneers, a driver, and an assistant driver. Though each soldier had a specific job, they were all cross-trained to step into other jobs if necessary.

The 267th prepared for deployment to war by following the four-phase training plan laid out in the Unit Training Programs for Field Artillery and a similar Second Army plan described earlier. During the Battalion's first two months, the programs ensured its troops had the skills necessary for a soldier. On April 27, the unit completed its Physical Fitness Test with a score of 93%. Despite being hampered by a lack of equipment and primitive living conditions, it completed Phase One on May 1.

On Friday, May 14, the Battalion celebrated its creation with an "activation dance" held at Service Club 5 on base. In addition to a speech from Colonel Hinsch, the men were treated to a song entitled "267th F.A. March," composed by Private Howard Marsh of Headquarters Battery. Before joining the Army, Private Marsh attended Mansfield College for music and was a music teacher for ten years in Pocono, PA. Song sheets with the words were passed out to the soldiers and guests. They then sang along with the band as the song was played for the first time. In August, Private Marsh participated in the 403rd Field Artillery Group Sing-Off, performing a monologue on his experiences as a soldier. The performance was well-received by the crowd gathered around an open-air stage.

Since Charles started his training later than most of the unit, he continued his individual training into May when he completed Cannoneer School and the Infiltration Course. According to the U.S. Army Military Occupational Specialty (MOS) code definition, a cannoneer is:

> *"Responsible for the actual safe firing of the Howitzer; loads the projectile and receives the powder charge; ensures the correct fuse and the correct amount of propellant charge in each fire mission; responsible for keeping Howitzer combat loaded with rounds at all times; also, responsible for keeping the breech and bore of the Howitzer clean after firing; understands all fire commands."*

In other words, they do all the heavy work necessary to fire the weapon.

On July 5, Charles was promoted one rank to Private First Class. While he strove to do the best job possible, he did not expect a promotion beyond this rank. Like most artillery units, all the 267th noncommissioned officer billets were filled with career army personnel who had priority for advancement.

The next few months were occupied with unit training, emphasizing proficiency in firing their howitzers quickly and accurately. Soldiers learned how to do their jobs in coordination with one another, so the Battalion acted as a cohesive unit. They conducted field exercises to establish the gun emplacements, assemble the guns, and determine and fire at targets. In August, the batteries were evaluated on how well they fired in two tests, and the 267th completed them with scores in the 80s.

Once they learned their weapons, the Battalion conducted maneuvers with the 69th Division, which was activated two months after the 267th. On Sundays, the troops would head out into Camp Shelby's wilderness areas and conduct themselves under tactical wartime conditions from 6:00 p.m. that evening until 6:00 p.m. on Thursday. Charles and his fellow artillerymen were prohibited from smoking cigarettes and lighting matches or fires in the dark. Food rations and latrine facilities were field conditions. They learned to support an infantry division as it assaulted simulated enemy strongholds. At 6:00 p.m. on Thursday, battlefield conditions ceased, and there were three days for the leadership to debrief on the week's actions and plan for the next field operation, which would begin the following Sunday. The rest of the Battalion conducted maintenance on the equipment.

The troops occasionally mixed fun with their training. When the 403rd Field Artillery Group commemorated its new obstacle course on Friday, July 23, with an obstacle course race among its battalions, Charles's Battery C won hands down. Battery C took the prize with an average time of 119 seconds. The four-man team and their times were: Sergeant Walker, 113 seconds, PFC Perez, 114 seconds, PFC Small, 113 seconds, and PFC Brierly 139 seconds. Second place went to Battery B of the 268th Field Artillery Battalion, whose average time was two-and-one-half seconds slower. Battery C's "prize" for winning was to put on a clown act for the second race held on August 13. Their performance was a hit with the audience!

Softball, wrestling, and boxing were popular on Camp Shelby. The Artillery Group also organized events for these sports. One of Charles's sergeants, Everett Walker, made his way into the boxing finals losing to Theodore Pysh from the 265th Field Artillery Battalion, and 267th Private Mercuri won a semifinal lightweight wrestling bout over Private Meza from the 265th. The entire Battalion was there to cheer them on.

Occasionally, Charles got free time to visit one of the Camp's Service Clubs, PX, or even utilize an "Honor Pass" to go into Hattiesburg for the day. Honor passes were cards provided to soldiers with a "clear record" that allowed them to travel past the camp's guard shack. Downtown Hattiesburg was full of shops, soda fountains, a movie theater, and other places soldiers could entertain themselves. The people were extremely friendly to the troops and made their short-lived liberty enjoyable.

Like other towns close to bases, Hattiesburg had USO clubs where Charles and his fellow soldiers could eat, relax, and enjoy some recreational activities, which included talking with women his age who staffed the clubs. However, this was the Deep South, and like the area around Camp Hood, these clubs were segregated, with black servicemen restricted to only the East Sixth Street USO. As Charles walked past the courthouse, he read on a statue dedicated in 1910 to the town's Confederate soldiers, *"When their country called they held back nothing. They cheerfully gave their property and their lives."* The city's leaders were the sons and grandsons of those Confederate Army soldiers. They were proud of their relatives who fought in gray and sought to keep their southern way of life, which meant segregation and degradation of black Americans, including black soldiers.

Over the week of September 12, the Battalion was subject to three tests that evaluated how well it performed. It was evaluated on its ability to move, set up, communicate, keep supplies flowing, and fire timely and accurately. It passed the Battalion I, II, and III tests with scores of 68%, 85%, and 81%, respectively. Upon completing Battalion Test III on September 17, the 267th cleared unit training and moved on to the next phase of combined training, where units of all arms and types learned to work in coordination.

Paterson, New Jersey
June 24, 1943

Graduation day finally arrived, and Roseann earned her Commercial diploma from Eastside High School. It was right in the heart of America's military buildup. Men were being pulled out of the labor force into the military while the demand for weapons, ships, planes, and supplies grew exponentially. To fill the demand for workers to maintain this "arsenal for democracy," the government and businesses embarked on a campaign to recruit women into the workplace.

Patriotic posters plastered areas where people congregated, reminding them of such things as "Loose Lips Sink Ships" or "Buy War Bonds." They were especially concentrated in heavy industrial areas such as Paterson. A month before she graduated, Roseann picked up the May 29 Saturday Evening Post and looked at the cover, which featured a picture of "Rosie the Riveter." Rosie was a young, strong, and pretty woman wearing work clothes and goggles. On her lap was a rivet gun and a sandwich in her hand. The American flag was behind her, and patriotic pins were displayed on her overalls. The cover was then replicated in a new poster that appeared around industrial Paterson. Rosie was one part of a major effort to move women from home into the industrial workplace--an effort that would eventually recruit six million women into the workforce.

In 1942, President Roosevelt created the War Manpower Commission (which should have been called the War Womanpower Commission) to oversee labor issues in the war effort's military, industrial, and other civilian sectors. As the demand grew, it implemented programs to recruit housewives and then single women into the war effort. One program gave female high school graduates a crash course in wartime industrial sector skills.

Upon graduation, a teacher talked Roseann and other female graduates into taking government-funded courses through the New Jersey College for Women (now Rutgers University) to be held over the summer at the Eastside. Girls who completed the program received one year of college credit. The courses included algebra, trigonometry, and calculus. Roseann found these courses extremely difficult and spent long hours studying each night. At the end of the summer, she passed her courses and was the first in her class to receive a job offer. Roseann was about to join all the "Rosie the Riveters" who fulfilled President Roosevelt's "arsenal for democracy."

Santa Croce Camerina, Sicily, Republic of Italy
July 9, 1943

Across the invisible highway, an army of 180,000 troops from General Omar Bradley's II Corps and the 7th Army under General George S. Patton amassed in North Africa for an invasion of Sicily that would result in Santa Croce Camerina becoming one of the first European towns liberated from the Nazi grip. On Friday, July 9, the invasion commenced with an airborne assault on the Island. Past sunset, paratroopers of the 505th Parachute Regimental Combat Team, part of the 82nd Airborne Division, jumped into Sicily to the east of Santa Croce Camerina. The 2nd Battalion of the 505th, commanded by Major Mark Alexander, reorganized its scattered troops and headed to the coastal village of Marina Di Ragusa. It quickly captured the Italian battery and took the village four-and-one-half miles southeast of Santa Croce Camerina.

During those early morning hours, the coastal area south of Santa Croce Camerina was subject to continuous naval gunfire and bombing from the U.S. Army Air Forces. Sunrise revealed soldiers of the 157th Infantry Regiment of the 45th Infantry Division on the beach several miles west of the 505th. The American soldiers began their amphibious assault at 3:00 a.m., and after making their way through rough waves and surf, poured out of their landing crafts onto the beach, intending to move inland to capture Santa Croce Camerina. By 9:00 a.m., the beachhead was established, and the first American amphibious assault on a European beachhead in World War II was a success. The 157th then set out toward the town.

The 157th and the 505th faced light resistance from Italian XVIII Coastal Brigade units as they moved towards San Croce from the southeast and southwest. Morale among the Italian Army and its civilian population was at a low. Military forces and war-weary civilians were ready to abandon Mussolini. The soldiers standing between the Allied invaders and Santa Croce Camerina had lost confidence in themselves and their commanders, who believed the war was already lost.

By 1:00 p.m., the 1st Battalion of the 157th took the high ground to the west of Santa Croce Camerina and prepared to assault the town. The 505th took up a position just east of town, and unbeknownst to each unit, they simultaneously stormed the town from two sides. The Italian garrison resisted the 157th's approach from the west. However, the garrison commander surrendered with the assault from the 505th. By 3:45 p.m., all of Santa Croce Camerina was under Allied control.

One of the many Axis machine gun bunkers located around Santa Croce Camerina in 1980.

The American military was accelerating its offensives against the Axis fortresses in Europe and the Pacific. U.S. and British forces had driven the German/Italian force from Africa and Sicily, and an invasion of Italy proper had begun. In the Pacific, American forces won a hard-fought campaign to secure the central Solomon Islands. These offensives, and ones in the planning stage, required massive amounts of manpower, and one way to obtain trained troops was by draining the defensive coastal units.

Back on Cape Cod, while attached to the Headquarters Company of the 501st, Carmen was briefly transferred to Battery C, 512th Antiaircraft Artillery Gun Battalion, with further orders to transfer to ECP #2, Camp Edwards in October. There he was processed for overseas deployment. He was issued additional clothing and immunizations. In July, the replacement processing center opened on Camp Edwards to funnel men into the growing number of units preparing to ship overseas. Though the Army did not tell him, he was about to participate in one of the greatest logistical and supply operations ever conducted. He was to serve in India in support of the British East Indies and Nationalist Chinese Army front against the Japanese. This operation was known as the China Burma India Campaign (CBI).

Japan's quest for an empire or "Greater East Asia Co-Prosperity Sphere" began in 1931 with its invasion of China's Manchuria Province and systematically spread further into that country. By 1937, Japan controlled most of China's major cities and cut its supply line from the rest of the world. In desperation, China's Nationalist leader, Generalissimo Chiang Kai-shek, built a 600-mile road to Burma that allowed his forces and the Chinese people living under his control to receive strategic imports of war and relief supplies. Supplies arrived by ship at the Burmese port of Rangoon, then loaded onto trains that traveled through Mandalay into the mountains to the railhead at Lashio. There the goods were put on trucks and driven along the Burma Road to Kunming, China.

However, the Japanese continued to drive west, seeking to completely deprive the Chinese Nationalist Forces and the civilians under its control of any relief or war supplies. In 1941, the Japanese Army lunged into Indochina, routing the British defenders from Burma in just seventy-five days. The collapse of Burma and Rangoon's seizure closed the Burma Road and again cut China off from the rest of the world. Without a sufficient supply route, Chinese forces began to wither. The Japanese Empire now set its sights on bringing India into its co-prosperity sphere.

The title of a March 16, 1942 article in LIFE Magazine summed up Japanese ambitions in that part of the world: "The Conquerors Throw Dice for Richest, Oldest Prize of All." The article describes the reasons why Japan sought to conquer India and speculates on its chances of success.

LIFE notes that even though the population suffers from intense poverty inflamed by British colonial policies, India is as large as the European part of the Soviet Union and viewed as a significant prize to many conquering armies. LIFE went on:

> *"But the true treasure of India is not in its glittering array of temples and mosques and palaces. It is not even India's second-rate mineral deposits or third-rate industrial plant. What the onrushing Japs want from India is a treasure surpassing all these. They are ravenous for India's labor supply of 300,000,000 people, 20% of the working hands in all the world. And this vast labor reservoir is overwhelmingly docile, intelligent, skilled, used to obedience and small pay. The ruler for whom it works and from whom it buys has always heretofore been the most powerful ruler in the world."*

Another reason the Japanese coveted India was to provide it with a ground link to the expanding Nazi empire. In 1941, Adolf Hitler and Benito Mussolini's forces were expanding eastward in North Africa, and its agents were openly operating in the Middle East. In June 1941, Hitler's army thrust into the Soviet Union and marched east and south. The ultimate goal was to link up Japanese and German forces in a friendly India and create an Axis belt extending across European and Asian continents.

While India was considered the crown jewel of the British Empire, there was uncertainty in London and the U.S. about whether the Indian people would actively participate in the war against Japan. The Indian people, whose civilization goes back 5,000 years, spent much of that time as subjects of outside conquerors. They yearned for freedom from the British, who suppressed all attempts to release them from their empire. Leaders of the Indian people were not eager to fight for an empire that crushed their freedom. However, they recognized that Japanese occupation would not differ from British Imperialism.

In February 1942, Chiang Kai-shek visited India to coax its leaders into joining the war against Japan. He met with the popular Hindu leader Mahatma Gandhi and Jawaharlal Nehru, the Congress Party's leader. Gandhi opposed coming to any agreement that supported an empire he believed was on the brink of collapse. LIFE Magazine provided an account of the talks in its April 1942 edition. LIFE wrote:

> *"The proposition brought to India a month later by Sir Stafford Cripps was that India would become a Dominion after the war, united or disunited as its separate parts decided for themselves. After much talk, Gandhi and Jawaharlal Nehru, the Congress Party, the Moslem League and the Untouchables all rejected this proposal, all for totally different reasons. Britain thereupon withdrew its offer. The comment of Nehru was typically that of an Indian leader: "Sir Stafford took the attitude, peculiar to the British, that they are always in the right, and the other is always wrong and damnably wrong." He therefore decided that Indians will not be among the men who make the peace, but that India will wait to petition the winner. Nehru and Cripps aged visibly during the talks under a full moon within smell of rose gardens. Gandhi remained calm. And Chiang Kai-shek went home without change of expression."*

Chiang returned to China without an agreement from his neighbor, an agreement he needed for his regime to survive.

The Japanese Army butted against the Indian border, which further inflamed religious and nationalist loyalties among Indians. Much to the

Japanese government's delight, Indians intensified protests against the British. LIFE Magazine further reported in April 1942:

"The native Indian peoples were of many religions but the majorities were either Hindu or Moslem. They were not very compatible and their differences were always present as we made our way through the teeming streets of humanity. There were opposing factions everywhere. At the same time that World War II engulfed Calcutta with the threat of the Japanese army moving into the Province of Bengal, there was much internal agitation by both the Hindu and Moslem groups to unseat the British government. The Indian fight for freedom and an independent country was going on at the same time as this influx of soldiers and troops of all kinds were trying to defend its borders from the Japanese invaders. It was a strange situation. In the midst of all of this, Mahatma Ghandi, popular leader of the Hindu and also the majority of the Indian people, was waging a war of passive resistance to the British government. He was seeking independence from British rule. He would be arrested for his resistance and placed in jail. He would then go on a hunger strike and as he became weaker, his followers would become more violent, until the British would be forced to release him. He owned nothing except his clothing and spectacles but was the most revered man in all India."

Eventually, on August 8, 1942, Nehru, at the Bombay meeting of the Congress Party convention, advocated a combined policy of passive resistance against the British while pledging support to the Chinese people to maintain their freedom against Japan. This gave passive agreement to the effort to support the Chinese and eventually turn back the Japanese advance.

In the aftermath of the Pearl Harbor attack, the U.S. developed plans to contain the Axis expansion and buy time to strengthen its war production and military. President Roosevelt was concerned that Japan occupied all Southeast Asia, isolating Chiang Kai-shek's forces, while British colonial policies were causing India's instability. U.S. war planners deemed India a priority to stabilize and funnel supplies and equipment to the Chinese Army. So long as the Chinese Army remained a viable fighting force, it would tie up fifteen to twenty-two Japanese combat divisions and support troops, nearly one million men. Until it could build its industrial and military might, the U.S. could not afford to have an additional million Japanese troops free to attack Australia, the Hawaiian Islands, or even its own West Coast. Also, early war planners looked at China as a potential base of operations to attack Japan.

In January 1942, President Roosevelt activated the CBI theater by sending Lieutenant General Joseph Stillwell to China with a staff of thirty-five officers and five enlisted men. General Stillwell's nickname was "Vinegar Joe" for a good reason. He was a driven officer who pushed his men to whatever level necessary to complete the mission. The General and his staff determined that the only way to sustain the Chinese Army was to transport supplies from India over the Himalayan Mountains, "the Hump," to Kunming, China. He planned to use cargo airplanes until he could build a road from India to China. Simultaneously, he needed to thwart the Japanese advance into India.

The first American troop units to arrive in the CBI theater were Army Air Force personnel who landed in Karachi, India, on March 12 with 28 trucks, some bombs, and small arms ammunition. Afterward, troops and supplies began to pour into Karachi, with the first Services of Supply troop units, the 393rd Quartermaster Battalion and the 159th Station Hospital, arriving on May 16.

American pilots soon began flying a steady stream of cargo planes over the Hump from India to Kunming, China. However, these planes, which endured high altitude, unstable air over the mountains, terrible weather, and Japanese fighter planes, could only deliver a fraction of the supplies needed by the Chinese. General Stillwell's forces embarked on a two-fold plan to transport supplies and equipment more easily from India: Begin to build the 500-mile "Ledo Road" that started in Ledo, India to meet the Burma Road, and push the Japanese back so the Burma Road can reopen. Both were highly ambitious goals.

The 95,500 CBI force that Carmen would join in late 1943 did not consist of infantry or armored units. Instead, it was formed by troops from the Army Corp of Engineers and Army Air Force personnel building airfields in China and India; quartermasters and supply personnel unloading, moving, and delivering supplies; pilots and aircrew flying the Hump, and engineering troops laboring on the Ledo-Burma Road and a parallel oil pipeline. No U.S. combat units were deployed to the CBI theater except for 3,000 volunteer soldiers known as "Merrill's Marauders."

Carmen was ordered to participate in a complicated corner of the World War. When Frantisek went to war 29 years prior, he was painted a clear picture of the war in terms of good v. evil. But good v. evil was blurred in India. Americans fought to protect Indians and preserve their system of government, which they spurned. Carmen could rationalize fighting against Japan, but fighting for British hegemony over a people who yearned for freedom would cause mixed feelings. Additionally, culture and politics were incredibly foreign, and the people were extraordinarily impoverished and deeply divided by religion and sects. To Carmen, it would not feel like God was on his side in India.

As the train took Carmen from Boston to Hampton, Virginia, the convoy that would take him across the Atlantic Ocean started to assemble. On October 2, thirty-two merchant vessels and warships led by the USS Dorian and escorted by the Auk-class minesweepers USS Tide, Threat, and Nuthatch departed New York Harbor for a one-day journey to Virginia. The convoy was officially labeled UGS-20 (NY Section).

The train ride to Virginia was familiar to Carmen. He rode it several times during his tenure with the CCC and when stationed at Fort Eustis. His mind wandered while watching the familiar countryside. He did not know where he would sail to, but he knew it was through the U-boat-infested Atlantic Ocean. Being with Coastal Artillery, he heard about many ships torpedoed or sunk by mines in the Atlantic. He had even witnessed the destruction from U-boats off the New Jersey shore.

The American war machine was in high gear and determined to move troops and equipment overseas. Equally determined to stop the flow were the German and Japanese navies. Thus, 1943 saw the highest number of U-boats at sea and the war's biggest convoy battles. Fortunately for Carmen and the other troops and sailors on the forming convoy, antisubmarine efforts were finally stemming the U-boats' effectiveness in the Atlantic. In May 1943, U.S. and Allied forces inflicted the highest loss to befall the U-boat fleet, with forty-one boats sunk. Overall losses for 1943 were 244 U-boats sunk with 10,065 men killed and only 1,837 survivors. Between October 5 and 23, when this convoy crossed the ocean, the German Navy lost eighteen U-boats.

The train took Carmen to Hampton, VA, where he was driven to the pier and lined up in front of a waiting troopship. It was Monday, October 4, and the busy harbor was full of ships loading men and equipment. An Army band played heart-pumping patriotic tunes while fireworks shot off and bystanders waved flags for the assembled troops. Carmen and the other men boarding dozens of Liberty ships experienced mixed emotions, including fear, apprehension, and excitement. Staff Sergeant Robert Tessmer gives insight into what Carmen experienced once he boarded his ship in his story: "Life Aboard a Troop Transport" about a similar crossing.

> *"We were herded like cattle, struggling under the weight of 100 pound duffel bags, packs with bed rolls, rifles and steel helmets into a gaping hole in the side of the towering ship...*

> *"Once we had climbed the gangway and gotten aboard, each of us simply followed the man in front of us through a maze of hatches and companionways until we reached our assigned area. This consisted of a forest of steel pipes supporting canvas strips stretched tightly with ropes. Each "hammock" was approximately two feet wide by six feet long, and was strung about two feet from the "hammock" above. These hammocks were tiered three high and the man on the uppermost one stared into a tangle of pipes immediately above his face. The men below had to contend with the indentation made by the bodies of the men above them, and each had to adjust his position to provide adequate clearance.*

> *"Aisles between the hammocks were extremely narrow and packed with duffel bags and gear, so we were constantly climbing over something."*

Once he found his hammock, Carmen settled into his quarters for the voyage. The troopships were newly constructed Liberty ships. Built to be expendable, they were uncomfortable with minimal amenities for the troops. Though crowded and cramped, they were new ships and not an "old rust bucket" he would ride later in his voyage.

Carmen's ship was filled with replacement soldiers, equipment, and rumors. Lots of rumors about their ultimate destination. Since the destination was classified as "secret," it was known by only a few on ship. To the rest, where they were headed was something to occupy their minds over long days at sea.

Pier Number Two of the Naval Operating Base Norfolk was also busy as the warships of Destroyer Division 21, who would form much of Task Force 65, also prepared for the crossing. The Task Force was given the mission to protect the seventy-two merchant ships during the Atlantic crossing to the Straits of Gibraltar at the Mediterranean Sea entrance. Thereupon, the Task Force would accompany ten ships to Casablanca, Morocco. A force of British ships would escort the remainder of the convoy through the Mediterranean Sea as it dispatched ships to Oran Algeria, Gibraltar, and Malta, ultimately terminating in Port Said, Egypt. At 2:00 p.m., the warship captains met on board the convoy flagship, the USS Livermore, followed at 4:30 with a convoy conference of all the Convoy UGS-20 ship captains. A major topic of the meetings was protecting the ships from U-boats. The threat weighed on all the captains' minds.

The previous convoy, UGS-19, was completing its voyage with its escort carrier, USS Card. As the UGS-20 captains were meeting, the Card, working on intelligence obtained from cracking the German "Ultra" secret code, detached from the convoy to reconnoiter a remote area north of the Azores, away from shipping lanes. The intelligence proved accurate when one of the Card's spotter planes found three U-boats refueling from a submarine tanker. Three waves of planes attacked the tethered submarines, sinking two of them. Depth charges from Avenger and Wildcat aircraft sunk U-460 causing sixty-two deaths and two survivors. U-422 met its demise by a Fido homing torpedo from an Avenger and two Wildcat aircraft. All forty-nine crew were lost. One submarine managed to escape, and unknown to the Allies at the time, the tanker submarine was lost during its escape dive. Word of the attack flowed back to the captains and reinforced that they were about to sail in harm's way.

Task Force 65 got underway at 9:00 p.m. to meet the merchant vessels and commence a screen for the convoy. That night the vast merchant fleet also made its way through the channel and into the Atlantic. At 8:00 a.m., the first merchant ships emerged from the channel. By 11:00, Convoy UGS-20 formed several rows of merchant ships flanked by destroyers on all sides. They set an easterly course at 9.5 knots per hour using evasive tactics that made it difficult for German submarines to obtain a fix on them.

While the first day ended uneventfully, Carmen was awakened early in the morning of October 7 by the ship jerking right and left, then the sound of explosions in the distance. With the convoy heading on a southeasterly course, the U.S. Coast Guard Cutters (USCGCs) Duane and Campbell conducted sonar sweeps, searching for U-boat sounds. The Duane picked up an underwater sound contact at 3:47 a.m. Fifteen minutes later, it detected another contact and attacked with depth charges. The convoy commenced emergency zigzagging with a forty-five-degree turn to starboard and then port to move the fleet away from the suspected U-boat. A half-hour later, the Campbell detected another sonar hit and steamed to the contact. Its sonarmen reported it was a positive submarine contact, and the ship went to General Quarters. At 5:02, the Campbell dropped a full pattern of depth charges then searched the area for any sign of wreckage. Daylight brought no evidence of debris. However, a review of the sonar readings showed a probable sub and near hit.

Below deck, Carmen settled into the monotonous routine of a soldier on a troopship. The Army required him to always carry his lifejacket, even when he went to the head to relieve himself, mess deck to eat, or his hammock to sleep. Being caught without it brought punishment, usually extra duty that involved scrubbing and cleaning unpleasant things.

Reveille at 6:00 a.m. took him out of his hammock to await his turn to use the head. Out of the faucets and showerheads flowed unheated seawater, so the troops were issued special salt water soap bars that were rock hard and produced no lather. When the salt dried on Carmen's skin, he felt dirtier than before. Like many of his fellow GIs, washing was such an unpleasant experience that it fell by the wayside as the voyage progressed, further contributing to the poor air quality below deck.

Once finished with his morning hygiene, his next task was to stand in line for the first of two daily meals. The line would take hours and snake around the ship's passageways. When Carmen made it to the serving area, the messmen ladled canned, tasteless food into his mess kit. Standard breakfast menu items were powdered eggs and chipped beef in gravy on toast (the troops called it S.O.S or Shit on a Shingle). Canned meats, vegetables, and powdered milk made up the evening meal. Consuming the bland food was also an experience. He stood while eating at a chest-high stainless-steel table that ran the width of the ship. It had a rolled edge on all sides to keep the mess kits from sliding onto the deck. He had to gulp down his food and make space for the masses of soldiers behind him, seeking to do the same. At the end of the table, Carmen readied his mess kit for the next meal by washing it in huge garbage cans with soapy water and then clear water for rinsing. In heavy seas, the ship rolled and pitched as he consumed his meal, mixing bland food with a queasy stomach. Sometimes seasickness made him forgo the meal. Other times he forced the food down then shortly vomited it back up in the head or over the side of the ship.

Carmen found life below decks claustrophobic. The berthing decks contained hot, stuffy, and cramped compartments filled with men reading, writing letters and diaries, playing cards or dice games, and preparing their gear for the next surprise inspection. Prime "real estate" was near the ventilator shafts that pumped in some fresh air. When seas were calm, Carmen and the other troops were permitted topside, where he walked over soldiers stretched out until he found an open spot to enjoy fresh air and sunshine. He also passed the time watching warships conduct weapons firing and antiair and antisubmarine drills. Topside was the only respite for Carmen to escape the noise, crowded conditions, and permeating smell of seasick troops who could not handle the bobbing motion from heavy North Atlantic seas.

The monotony was regularly punctuated by abandon ship, man overboard, and other drills. Other tasks included standing random guard duty beside some hatch or passageway for an unknown reason or fire watches to ensure no one ignited a deadly fire, which would be a catastrophe under such crowded conditions. Lastly, the USO provided shows that were difficult to watch because of the crowded conditions, but they were a sought-after activity.

On October 8, the convoy sailed on an easterly course as the Atlantic Ocean's war was in full fury. Allied aircraft sank three German submarines, the U-419, U-610, and U-643. Convoy SC-143 was traveling north of UGS-20 from the U.S. to Britain. U-378 fired a torpedo into one of its escort warships, the Polish destroyer Orkan, sending it to the bottom in less than five minutes. Out of its crew of 229, 186 perished, including her Commanding Officer.

When UGS-20 cleared the range of U.S.-based aircraft, it was joined by Task Group 21.15, consisting of the USS Greene, Goldsborough, Belnap, and the Core, a newly built escort carrier. On her deck were twelve Grumman F4F Wildcat fighters and nine Grumman TBF Avenger torpedo bombers. This was Core's third combat patrol. Carmen spent the afternoon on deck, watching the ship and her planes conduct exercises. At 12:17, the fighters catapulted off her deck to conduct mock strafing runs on the destroyers, paralleling the convoy. Shortly after 1:00 p.m., they fired on a target towed by a destroyer. About an hour after they commenced firing, the planes began to land back on Core. At 2:10, F4F #8 was approaching to land when it suddenly crashed into the ocean about fifty yards astern of Core. Carmen and the rest of the troops on deck watched in awe as the carrier changed course and the destroyers Greene and Goldsborough raced to rescue the pilot. The crew of Goldsborough plucked W.C. Webb from the ocean and, after giving him a medical checkup, pulled alongside the Core to transfer the downed pilot. By dinner time, Webb was back on his ship, and Carmen headed below deck to begin the long process to fill his mess kit. The past two days made the war real to him.

The following five days were relatively calm for the convoy. Each day, destroyers picked up at least one sonar hit that caused them to scramble and take offensive action. All proved to be false contacts.

On October 9, Task Group 21.15 with Core, Greene, Goldsborough, and Belknap broke away from the convoy to join the Escort Carrier USS Card Task Group to search for enemy submarines near the Azores Islands. Four days later, an Avenger from the Card found U-378, which had earlier sunk the Polish destroyer Orkan, but her torpedo missed, and the submarine escaped.

October 12 saw a Merchant Marine messman on one of the Liberty ships experience a medical emergency requiring transfer to the Campbell by stretcher rigged from a line between the two ships.

Thursday, October 14, a panic fell over the troops as the destroyers picked up another sonar contact, and the fleet commenced emergency zigzags. At 8:30 p.m., the Campbell's sonar picked up a contact that the Howard also heard. The Howard, Ericsson, and Campbell steamed toward the contact while the convoy turned away from the danger. The target was identified as a probable submarine, and over the next half-hour, the Campbell and Howard launched two patterns of depth charges followed by hedgehog attacks. All this time, the convoy was executing evasive maneuvers. By 9:06 p.m., a search of the area found no submarine debris and one scared whale.

Four days later, the convoy got the first sign that it was on the voyage's back end. Around 4:00 p.m., lookouts spotted a U.S. Army B-24 Liberator airplane. It was part of the Antisubmarine 2037 Wing out of Port Lyautey, Morocco, and provided cover for the convoy. The following afternoon, a patrol off the Core spotted U-378, the boat that sunk Orkan and eluded the Card's pilots. The leader of Core's squadron VC-13, Lieutenant Commander Charles W. Brewer, who was flying a Wildcat, strafed the sub, causing ammunition in the conning tower to explode. Two depth charges obliterated the submarine and killed all forty-eight crewmembers.

On Wednesday morning, October 20, Carmen knew the convoy was close to its destination when, on deck, he saw several American planes from Morocco circling the convoy. Later that day, three British warships, HMS Brilliant, Antelope, and Velox, appeared on the horizon. Then two U.S. ships, the USS PC-481 and USS PC-482, rendezvoused with the convoy to escort nine merchant ships to Casablanca. At 4:20

p.m., those ships and the Duane, Campbell, and Kearny departed for Casablanca. The remaining ships, including Carmen's, proceeded through the Straits of Gibraltar into the Mediterranean Sea. Carmen sat on deck watching the North African coastline, which looked foreign to him. Brown and desolate, it had occasional structures that looked like nothing built in the states. Dolphins played in the wake of the ships, and the waters of the Mediterranean Sea were calm compared to the crashing waves of the last fifteen days. Scuttlebutt was again rampant that the ship was heading to no less than five different ports. At this point, Carmen and the other troops learned that the destination of their ship was Oran, Algeria.

The British organized the convoy in four columns and moved it through the Mediterranean Sea toward Port Said, Egypt. On a cloudy and wet October 22, twenty-three merchant ships from the convoy split off and pulled into Oran's crowded harbor. Only three could dock. The remainder were left anchored outside the harbor or diverted to Arzew, Algeria, about thirty miles up the coast. Carmen's ship was one of the delayed vessels, and it would be another two days before he could exit the cramped ship and feel land under his feet.

Battery A of the 267th at Camp Shelby MS. Charles was in Battery C.

As the 267th prepared to participate in its first combined arms wargame, eighty-five of Charles's fellow artillerymen were transferred to the 65th Infantry Division to become infantrymen. That Division was activated at the Camp two months prior. It needed troops, and co-located units were asked to shed all nonessential personnel to the new Division. Those troops would train for the next year and a half and enter combat in Germany two months before hostilities ceased.

At 6:30 the following morning, a slimmed-down 267th began a two-month training mission when it convoyed from Camp Shelby to participate in the Louisiana Army maneuvers. It traveled 165 miles through the Mississippi countryside, crossing the entire state until it arrived at the U.S. Army Recreation Area, three miles east of Natchez, Mississippi. At 3:00 p.m., the convoy rolled past the guard shack and entered a large area of ballfields and other sports and recreation areas. After setting up gun emplacements, the artillerymen traveled to the camp section with tents and Quonset Huts, where the 267th was served hot meals and bedded down for the night.

At 7:30 the next morning, the Battalion set out on a 133-mile convoy to Zimmerman, Louisiana. It crossed the Mississippi River using the Natchez–Vidalia Bridge, built by the Works Progress Administration in 1940. The Battalion spent the next month participating in the Fourth Period 1943 Third Army maneuvers, part of the larger annual Louisiana Army maneuvers. This exercise brought hundreds of thousands of troops from all facets of the Army to train in unison.

As the Army grew in number and mission, it needed large training areas to practice realistic wargames. To meet that need, the Army purchased 3,400 square miles in central Louisiana between the Sabine and Red Rivers, which was rural and sparsely populated. Large-scale maneuvers were conducted annually from 1941 to 1944, where hundreds of thousands of men comprising all battlefield roles were divided into opposing armies for simulated battles.

The Generals sought to make the battlefield realistic and challenging. General George Marshall said, "*I want the mistakes made in Louisiana, not made in Europe.*" The colorful General Patton said, "*If you could take these tanks through Louisiana, you could take them through Hell.*" Thus, the troops lived in battlefield conditions like those they would face in the European Theater, and tactics mimicked those they would face from the Wehrmacht.

Since the war games were held over a large area, it was typical for troops' formations to transverse through private property. Locals found troops bivouacked in their yards and gardens, but the native Louisianans were good hosts and happy to have Charles and the other soldiers there. Since the troops survived on field rations, they were glad to accept fresh milk from the men or fresh baked bread and tea cakes from the ladies. Other locals did laundry and pressed uniforms.

On November 1, 1943, the Battalion completed its wargaming. It was bivouacked six miles north of Leesville, on the grounds of Fort Polk, when it assembled into a convoy and departed for Camp Van Dorn, Louisiana. It left at 7:15 a.m. and traveled through Natchez, then south toward a remote area in southwest Mississippi just above the Louisiana line. In thirteen hours, it covered 209 miles past worn-out farmland, piney woods, and swamps.

Oran, French Algeria
October 24, 1943

As Carmen's ship lay anchored outside Oran's harbor, he looked around the bustling Algerian port and hillside city. The city was liberated from the Reich eleven months earlier when the allies launched "Operation Torch," the Anglo–American invasion of French North Africa. Officially Algeria was a colony of Vichy France and was halfheartedly defended by troops with mixed loyalties. Along with Casablanca and Algiers, the city became the Americans' first beachhead against the Axis, allowing the Allies to eventually expel the Germans and Italians from North Africa and launch the first European landings on Sicily and Italy proper.

The city of Oran runs from the harbor up a hillside, with its downtown area approximately 450 feet above the Mediterranean Sea. From there is a commanding view of the well-protected and deep-water harbor below. Together with the harbors at Mers-e-Kabir, five miles west, and Arzeu, thirty miles east, this area served as a staging area for ships and troops heading to fight the Axis forces in Europe, the Middle East, and the CBI.

With all his gear in hand, Carmen stood on deck and prepared to walk on land for the first time in twenty days. The sky was grey, and the air damp. On the horizon were scattered rainstorms. He would soon learn that while Algeria has a hot desert climate in the summer, it is cold and rainy during the winter. About the middle of October, the sky turns grey with low clouds and rainstorms. The temperature begins to fall, making November quite unpleasant with cloudy, cold, and wet weather.

As Carmen and his fellow soldiers filed off the ships, he moved past natives calling out *"chewing gum Joe"* or *"hey Joe cigarette"* toward open trucks for his ride toward "camp." Algeria did not have housing or infrastructure to support the thousands of troops pouring into the country to move further north or east into battle. Thus, living conditions were highly primitive for Carmen and his fellow soldiers. They were trucked to a transient troop holding area outside Oran, an old olive grove consisting of a large muddy field with a few Quonset huts. They erected Army-issued tents with eight to ten bunk beds made of chicken wire, dug slit trenches for latrines, and set up a field kitchen. Like his days at Forts Dix and Hancock, these conditions would be his home for the next month.

Life in Oran was physically and mentally taxing on Carmen. The climate was miserable. The temperature was usually 100 degrees at noon and then plunged to around freezing at night. The tents provided little protection from the cold, so troops did all they could to stay warm, including supplementing their Army-issued blankets by reversing their buttoned overcoats to mimic sleeping bags. After a few days, some farmers sold them straw to fill old mattress covers and insulate the ground underneath them. In addition to the cold, fleas and lice crept into the tents. Everywhere was thick mud that stuck to their boots and clothing. The only way to clean themselves was with cold rainwater collected in their helmets.

German reconnaissance planes regularly flew overhead, requiring the troops to live in blackout conditions and forgo fires that could provide some comfort at night. The food was no better than that served aboard ship. Carman had a choice of either canned field rations or dates, oranges, and onion sandwiches. The latter was fresh but foreign to him and his fellow soldiers. Diarrhea and even dysentery usually followed these meals. The cold and mud were especially impactful when Carmen had to slog his way to use the slit trench latrines at night, usually through cold rain and mud, with no lights permitted.

Generally restricted to camp, Carmen had lots of idle time to dwell on the uncertainty of where he was going or why and how long he must wait. Boredom and hunger pushed Carmen and his tentmates to volunteer for Kitchen Police duty to have the first crack at better food. To make time pass faster, they played softball in the muddy fields and were occasionally permitted to take short sightseeing tours of the surrounding towns. They also organized talent shows for themselves in the nearby Quonset huts or listened to "Axis Sally" broadcast a mixture of American music with Nazi propaganda. The night before he would board his next convoy across the Mediterranean Sea, Axis Sally announced the locations of convoys and that they would face German bombers. Carmen thought, whatever his future, he was ready to leave here and face it.

Camp Van Dorn, Mississippi
November 1943

Camp Van Dorn could be a poster for "the middle of nowhere." It was a vast tar paper shack-type base in a nearly inaccessible part of Mississippi halfway between McComb, MS, in the northeast and Baton Rouge, LA, in the southwest. Crude dirt roads were the only access to the Camp. Camp Van Dorn was hastily constructed and activated on September 20, 1942, just three months after a hammer hit its first nail. It generally hosted 41,000 military personnel at any one time. Just to its north was the town of Centreville, a small, impoverished rail station with a population of 1,800. The Camp was a major boon to the depressed local economy.

Van Dorn was a "Theatre of Operations Camp" with primitive living conditions and lots of open space for field training. The buildings' spartan and temporary architecture reflected that the Camp was constructed for troops to live and practice in the field. Most buildings were made of wood and tarpaper atop cinderblock foundations with wood-burning stoves for heat. In the barren mess hall, troops ate food ladled into their mess kits. Though the Camp had service clubs, a theater, PX, and a library, the tarpaper buildings gave it a bleak and incomplete look.

Centreville had little to offer the troops. What little off-duty time they had was spent on base in the Beer Garden, PX, or one of the service clubs playing ping pong or shooting pool. The clubs were staffed by young ladies who traveled from Natchez, McComb, and Baton Rouge to make the troops' lives a bit better, and some would also say to find a husband! Occasionally, girls from McComb or Baton Rouge were bussed in by the USO for dances. Another distraction from the long hours of training were stray dogs that units adopted as mascots.

For seventeen days, the 267th participated in combined training with the 364th Infantry Regiment, an all-black unit shrouded in controversy and a shadowy relationship with the nearby town. The unit responded violently to intense racism inflicted on it by white soldiers and local civilians. Much of the unit's story is documented and supported; however, controversy exists about whether 1,200 soldiers of the 364th were massacred at the hands of white soldiers and local townspeople.

A 2001 article titled, "The Mystery of the 364th," by Geoffrey F.X. O'Connell for Gambit Weekly says:

> *"The 364th was an all-black regiment of soldiers that had been stationed in Jim Crow-era Centreville, Mississippi. At that time, the Army had begun intensifying its efforts to recruit blacks but was still racially segregated. The few black regiments designated for combat were typically under-trained, under-supplied and sent to stations where they were isolated and subject to insult and attack from hostile, white civilians.*
>
> *"Before arriving in Centreville, members of the 364th Regiment had already been involved in three race riots. In fact, the Army*

created the 364th to reorganize the 367th, a regiment of black soldiers that had been demoralized by the January 1942 "Lee Street Riot" in Alexandria, Louisiana in which dozens were injured and, according to some reports, as many as 10 were killed. After the newly created 364th had been relocated to Phoenix, Arizona, racially motivated fighting erupted twice, killing at least three people. Ironically, it was in response to the Phoenix riots that the government shuttled the 364th to Centreville...

"...In May 1943, when the beleaguered 364th arrived in Centreville, Mississippi, the treatment it received was no exception. The men of the 364th, some of whom had already survived three previous race riots, came to Centreville announcing they were going to "clean up" the base and surrounding towns, and challenged Jim Crow laws at every turn.

"White civilians, who were heavily armed, braced for a violent clash. The Army high command in Washington warned base and regimental commanders that they were to end racial violence or lose their jobs. But on May 30, within days of the 364th's arrival, the local sheriff killed one of its men, Pvt. William Walker, who had been scuffling with white MPs near the entrance to the base. Members of Walker's company broke into base storerooms, stole rifles and headed for Centreville, swearing revenge.

"What followed the 364th's rally and cry is subject to conflicting reports. Allegations range from minor skirmishes and disciplinary action to wholesale slaughter {of 1,200 black soldiers} ...

"...{An} Army Inspector General report concludes: 'In light of the recent riotous conduct of the 364th Infantry, vigorous and prompt corrective action was necessary in order to place this regiment in such a disciplinary state that it would not again resort to mutinous conduct and to protect the lives of the citizens of Centreville and other innocent persons'...

"...{B}lack vets...remember that punishment. In effect, they were subject to house arrest in a cordoned-off area within the

base. White vets...patrolled the perimeter in jeeps and half-tracks mounted with .50-caliber machine guns. {Letters and interviews} make reference to sporadic gunfire exchanges across the cordon line...

"...There was chaos to be sure. The 364th's Morning Reports, a kind of company-by-company daily attendance sheet, note dozens of soldiers as AWOL following the Walker shooting and its aftermath. Files in the National Archives trace some who made their way north, seeking from their local induction boards asylum from what they called a life-threatening situation...

"...In September 1943, Col. Lathe Row of the Army Inspector General's Office studied the situation and concluded, 'The presence of the 364th Infantry constitutes a threat to the normal peaceful conditions at Camp Van Dorn ... [and] should be transferred at an early date ... for overseas duty.'

"According to most 364th regimental documents, those troops not transferred to other units left Camp Van Dorn by train Dec. 26, 1943. After waiting a month or so at Ft. Lawton, near Seattle, Wash., they embarked on three ships for the Aleutian Islands off the coast of Alaska...It was then that their personnel roster began to show signs of hemorrhage. Records show that between 800 and 1,000 of the 3,000 men left the 364th before the war's end. In other words, from June 1943 until Japan's surrender, about one soldier's name per day disappeared from the 364th's roster.

"Pressured by Mississippi Congressman Bennie Thompson and the NAACP -- who feared a massacre had occurred at Centreville -- the Army committed thousands of hours and hundreds of thousands of dollars to explain the massive losses. A report was finally issued on Dec. 23, 1999. 'There is no documentary evidence whatsoever that any unusual or inexplicable loss of personnel occurred,' the report contends.

"But inconsistencies in the Army's report have diminished its credibility, leaving unanswered the same haunting questions that journalists have been investigating for years."

The questions about whether a thousand-plus black soldiers were gunned down by white soldiers in a racially motivated shootout and buried in a mass grave somewhere on the sprawling base or "stacked like cordwood" and shipped north on boxcars remain unanswered today. The 1999 Pentagon probe disputing the story left many questions unanswered. Additionally, a 2001 History Channel documentary, "The Mystery of the 364th," gave credibility to the allegations of a massacre and a sixty-year cover-up of 1,200 black soldiers.

Today in Centreville is the Camp Van Dorn Museum, a small building with three staff and a handful of volunteers dedicated to preserving the Camp's memory. A pamphlet freely shared with visitors titled "The Rumor about Camp Van Dorn Truth or Myth?" reiterates arguments debunking a massacre.

On Monday, November 15, the men of the 267th awoke unaware that the Battalion would suffer its only death in the war. The Battalion was coming off a day of rest after two weeks of intense field training. The artillerymen spent Sunday at the base chapel, then onto the PX, library, or recreation center. After standing in line to send a telegram or make a phone call home, the day was topped off by having a drink at the service club with ladies from the surrounding communities or the Woman Army Corps unit stationed at the camp.

Feeling a bit refreshed, the Battalion mustered early Monday morning to drive to the range for artillery practice using live ammunition. Lieutenant Colonel Hinsch, First Lieutenant Leonard J. Wisnniewski, Second Lieutenants James W. Pollard, and Clair K. Sparks, with Private Clyde R. Minshall, directed the exercise from a forward observation post where they could see how accurately the projectiles were falling on targets. During the afternoon, a round from an 81mm mortar fell short of its intended distance and landed on the observation post. The round killed Colonel Hinsch and wounded Second Lieutenants Sparks and Pollard and Private Minshall. Lt. Sparks was the most severely injured.

The following day, with three wounded men recovering in the station hospital, the artillerymen gathered at the hospital chapel for a memorial service to their fallen leader. First Lieutenant Wisnniewski, standing arm's length from Colonel Hinsch when the round exploded and was unharmed, accompanied Colonel Hinsch's body back home to Chicago. A month later, Major William B. Collins would assume command and lead the 267th throughout the war.

A day after the memorial service, a somber 267th mustered in darkness and cold air at 7:00 a.m. and boarded their vehicles for a 148-mile convoy back to Camp Shelby. Just past noon, as the trucks rolled past the Camp Shelby guard shack, Charles and the rest of the artillerymen were happy to be out of Camp Van Dorn and back in their regular chow hall for lunch. They ate with little talk and reflected on the cursed feeling they lived under at Van Dorn. It was a wretched place, and the safety of Camp Shelby warmed their cold bodies.

Back at Shelby, the Battalion also discerned that their training was ending, and soon it would be time to put their knowledge to work fighting Nazis. For the rest of November and December, the Battalion wrapped up loose ends on its Phase Three training plan. On November 19, Charles completed an Ammunition Handling Course. The leaders of the 267th debriefed on the two months' training maneuvers and conducted post-maneuver training, where they drilled the artillerymen in areas where they saw deficiencies and incorporated new operational techniques.

Another sign indicating the artillerymen were entering a new training phase that would end with them in combat was the generous leave policy announced for the upcoming Thanksgiving holiday. All personnel except those on duty were granted two weeks of leave. On November 23, Charles again took a train from the Hattiesburg train depot going north to New Jersey. Two days later, he made it in time to join Bertha and Charles for a Thanksgiving feast. His entry through the door the morning of Thursday, November 25, truly put thanksgiving into the holiday.

The former Wright Aeronautical Corporation Defense Plant, Paterson, 2018

Paterson, New Jersey
December 1943

As Charles was enjoying his fourteen-day leave, the war continued to transform the Iozzia family and the city of Paterson. A sprawling six-and-a-half-acre aircraft engine plant was located on Beckwith Avenue, not far from Pietro and Giuseppina's first house and less than a mile from their current East 18th Street home. The Wright Aeronautical Corporation first opened its aircraft engine plant in Paterson in 1916, and by the 1920's it became a leading spot for cutting-edge technology to develop airplane engines. Wright engines produced at the plant were used in aircraft flown by pioneer aviators such as Charles Lindbergh, Richard Byrd, and Amelia Earhart. Wright Aeronautical continually expanded its operations through the 1920s and '30s. On the eve of World War II, the plant was the largest airplane engine factory in the U.S. and--some claim--in the world. It employed over 2,400 workers and produced the Whirlwind and the more powerful Cyclone engines for military and civilian use.

With the advent of war, Wright Aeronautical further expanded its Paterson plant to respond to the enormously increasing demand for military aircraft engines. It built a massive industrial structure comprising 2.3 million square feet of floor space housing additional manufacturing and warehousing areas as well as a new testing facility.

Wright Aeronautical had to hire additional workers to meet the military's growing demand for more powerful engines to fly larger planes. Like other industries, it turned to women workers. During the war years, aviation saw the greatest increase in female workers than any other industry. More than 310,000 women worked in the U.S. aircraft industry in 1943. This represented 65% of the industry's total workforce compared to just 1% in the pre-war years.

One of those 310,000 women was Roseann. After successfully completing her mathematics studies at the New Jersey College for Women, she was hired as a Junior Pattern Design Worker in the Pattern Design Department. There she designed parts, including various specialty screws that went into military aircraft engines. Her work relied heavily on the calculus, trigonometry, and algebra she had learned the previous summer. Parts designed by Roseann were installed in the B-17 Flying Fortress, the B-25 Mitchell medium bomber, and the B-29 Superfortress, which includes the Enola Gay that dropped the atomic bomb on Hiroshima in August 1945.

Roseann also became an active member of the Engineers and Salaried Employees Association of Wright Aeronautical Corporation, the union representing the company's 8,000 white-collar workers. She served on the entertainment committee and helped plan and conduct social events to keep morale high.

During the war, Roseann and the other women workers helped double aircraft industrial production and delivered a staggering 300,000 aircraft to the military. The Wright Aeronautical plant built 139,000 aircraft engines, more than any other plant in the country. Its engines powered every major bomber used by the Army Air Force in the war.

The war also fundamentally changed Pietro and Giuseppina. In 1943, Pietro took the most significant step to Americanize the Iozzia family since he boarded a ship bound for America in 1905. On December 15, 1943, at age sixty, Pietro put on his rarely-worn suit and headed to the Passaic County Courthouse to give up his Italian citizenship and become a naturalized American citizen. At 9:45 a.m., he and 103 other prospective citizens appeared in front of Judge Alexander MacLeod. After an eighty-five-minute hearing, the judge approved Pietro to take the oath of citizenship. Shortly after, Pietro raised his right hand and repeated the oath of allegiance administered by Catherine Meyer, the Deputy County Clerk. At five feet, four inches, and 145 pounds, the new American citizen looked very distinguished in his grey suit and black silk tie. Shortly after his second country officially became his home, the beaming new citizen went to the County Board of Elections office and registered to vote in the next election with Clerk Margaret M. Mott.

The decision to change his citizenship did not come easy. He was a proud Italian, active in the San Giuseppe Santa Croce Camerina Society and other informal cultural groups. Italian was the language spoken at home and the newspaper he read. However, it was difficult to watch the repression of his friends and relatives back in Sicily from the Mussolini regime. Being an Italian-American, it was even more difficult to watch Benito Mussolini stand on his balcony with the German and Japanese ambassadors to berate and declare war on the U.S. four days after the Pearl Harbor attack. In World War I, Italian-Americans flocked to Italy to serve in that ally's armed forces. Now, American GIs would never again come home to New Jersey at the hands of Italian troops in North Africa and on the Italian peninsula. These troops served in the same army as his son, Carmen, and his daughter Roseann supported as a war plant worker.

Five months before Pietro took the oath, the British and U.S. forces that landed on Sicily were welcomed by most Sicilians--including the villagers of Santa Croce Camerina--as liberators. Afterward, refugees and returning troops brought back stories of the mistreatment suffered by fellow Sicilians. How could an Italian government mistreat its people so badly?

With the Allied invasion came two governments in Italy: one in the Allied-occupied territory and friendly to the Allies and the other reconstituted by the Nazis and led by Mussolini. The Italian Army was also divided, with some troops fighting on the side of the Nazis, others alongside the allies, while others just went home. There was no sense of what being an Italian stood for. Pietro compared that to his newly-adopted country's government which provided Carmen and Anthony with much-needed jobs through the CCC and the WPA. He was at peace with his decision.

On March 6, 1945, a little over a year later, Giuseppina took the same oath. Giuseppina and 102 other prospective citizens appeared before Judge MacLeod in Naturalization Court. When the process was complete, she and sixty-eight others were approved for citizenship. Like she did for Pietro, Catherine Meyer administered the oath of allegiance, and to cheers from friends and family members, Giuseppina became an American. The following week the entire Iozzia family celebrated with a reception at the YMCA.

Pietro and Giuseppina's naturalization documents

Oran, French Algeria
November 25, 1943

In North Africa, Carmen's monthlong pause in his journey toward his ultimate duty station was ending. Carlton Jackson's book, "Allied Secret, The Sinking of HMT Rohna," describes Carmen's next voyage through the Mediterranean Sea. On Thanksgiving Day, Carmen awoke to face another cold and wet day. His unit was ordered to pack their gear and prepare to board another troopship. He and his unit assembled their gear and were trucked to the outskirts of Oran. Then with full packs and all their equipment in hand, they marched two miles in a blinding rainstorm to the harbor. The troops were divided among six troopships: His Majesty's Transports (HMTs), Egra, Karoa, Rajula, Ranchi (an armed merchant cruiser), and Rohna, and the S.S. Banfora.

Wet and cold, with full packs, gas masks, rifles, bazookas, and other gear, Carmen and the others made their way down narrow stairwells and passageways deep into the ship. As he made his way, his nose was overwhelmed by the rancid smell of engine oil that permeated the ship. He was also disturbed to see rats and mice scurry from the army of intruders.

In their civilian capacity, each of these ships comfortably carried approximately 100 passengers. Today, over 2,000 troops poured onto each ship, occupying every available space. A few lucky men claimed a bunk. Most would sleep in hammocks, on mess deck tables, or on the deck using their duffel bags as pillows. However, those troops who spread their blankets on the deck quickly found that they had to share their space with the rats that scurried about the ship after the lights went out. Troops were packed into the ships to the point that crewmembers were concerned about overloading. Also of concern were the German reconnaissance planes flying over the harbor, watching the entire operation.

By early morning the loading of troops was complete, and the Captain ordered a boat drill. After the drill, Carmen and his shipmates got their first taste of British transport food. Instead of a traditional American breakfast of powdered eggs and coffee, each was served a large greasy sausage, about one-quarter meat and three-quarters soybean, a plate of slippery fried onions, a slice of bread, and weak coffee that resembled light tea.

At 12:30 p.m., the six troopships, loaded with soldiers who only had guesses where they were going, headed into the Mediterranean Sea and took a northeasterly course. The Rajula developed engine trouble and returned to port. Three hours after leaving the dock, the Banfora, Egra, Karoa, Ranchi, and Rohna joined Convoy KMF.26, transiting from Great Britain to Egypt.

KMF convoys transited from the United Kingdom to the Mediterranean Sea and consisted of Fast ships. Hence the acronym KMF. Initially, they were invasion convoys, but as the Mediterranean became somewhat secure, KMF convoys added troopships, ferrying soldiers to the Indian Ocean. Navy escorts guided the five troopships to their designated positions in the convoy of ten escorts and eighteen troopships. Rumors on their destination swirled about the vessel. Some thought they would join the Italian offensive. Others predicted Greece, while others believed they would head into Suez Canal to India or China. After finishing their Thanksgiving meal of watery canned chicken, dehydrated potatoes, fruit cocktail, and slimy camel butter spread on doughy rolls infested with weevils, the cramped soldiers found wherever space available to make the most of a quiet night at sea. Some read books while others wrote letters they hoped to mail someday soon. Others joined in large, raucous craps or poker games found in most troop compartments. Darkness brought a thick layer of fog that blanketed the convoy and settled the troops in for the night.

Unbeknownst to Carmen and the other troops, the Germans began shadowing the convoy the next morning, November 26. One of the escorts, the ORP Ślązak, an A56-class torpedo boat serving with the Free Polish Navy, reported an aircraft at 8:46 a.m., and the British Hunt-class destroyer HMS Atherstone, escorting a merchant vessel that fell twenty miles astern of the convoy, reported another aircraft shadowing them at 9:24.

Carmen needed to get some air. The ship was rocking from rising wind and waves. Added to the oil-soaked air below decks was the smell of vomit and diarrhea from seasick soldiers, whose stomachs rebelled against the foreign food. The deck was crowded, but the fresh air on his face felt good. He could see the Algerian coast in the distance and heard singing coming from a nearby transport. A chaplain was holding choir practice on the deck of the nearby HMT Reina del Pacifico. He could also see British and American warships escorting the transports.

With six columns, four ships each, the convoy traveled approximately 400 miles. By 4:30 p.m., it was about 15 miles off the coast near Bougie, now Béjaïa, Algeria. The ships had limited air escort of four land-based Free French Air Force Spitfires. Suddenly, Carmen heard gunfire from other ships in the distance, which did not cause concern since gunners periodically practiced firing their guns. Next, he heard the klaxon's horn sound of the air raid siren and saw the crew and soldiers running about the ship. All troops were ordered below decks to their compartments. The convoy came under assault by thirty German planes, including fourteen Luftwaffe Heinkel He 177A heavy bombers escorted by Junkers Ju 88 aircraft. The planes took off from a base in Bordeaux, France, with the mission to bomb the convoy.

One of Carmen's shipmates could peer out a porthole and called out the battle as it unfolded. He reported a formation of thirty to fifty German planes in the distance. The British gunners were firing in their direction, with the tracer bullets falling short of the formation. A group of planes peeled off and attacked a British corvette. He then reported seeing smoke billowing above the corvette from every one of its guns firing at the planes. Then he shrieked that the planes dispersed and attacked the ships in the front and the middle of the convoy. They were dropping bombs on the convoy, but all fell harmlessly between the ships.

The battle intensified. Carmen felt the ship jerk as the convoy sped up and zigzagged to evade the attackers. He heard his ship's gunners firing machine guns, Oerlikon autocannons, and even rounds from her 12-pounder gun. Within about half an hour, between six and nine German torpedo bombers and eighteen Royal Air Force Spitfires, Beaufighters, and P-39s from bases in Algeria and Tunisia joined in the air war. Flack covered the sky, creating a wall of lead that effectively kept the Luftwaffe attackers at bay. Carmen could hear the sound, amid the artillery noise, of two German planes losing control and spiraling into the Mediterranean Sea.

The mood in the compartment was surreal, almost like that of a sporting event. Men cheered as allied gunners hit their mark or British fighters chased the Luftwaffe aggressors. However, a somber mood fell over the troops when they felt the concussion from near-miss 500-pound bombs and heard the impact of German rounds striking the vessel's upper deck. One bomb exploded so close to the ship that paint chips fell from the overhead on Carmen and the others.

Unable to penetrate the heavy antiaircraft barrage and strike its prey, the Luftwaffe retreated over the horizon. Carmen and his shipmates breathed a collective sigh of relief when the soldier at the porthole reported that the German planes were departing.

But the break in the attack was short-lived as a third and final wave bore down on the convoy. Heinkel He 177As, armed with Henschel Hs 293 radio-guided rocket-boosted glide bombs, headed for the troopships. The bomb was a German secret weapon, a winged missile aimed at its target by remote control. It was a forerunner of the V1 and V2 rockets and the first radio-controlled guided missile. Though they fired nearly thirty at the convoy throughout the attack, almost all missed their mark due to the heavy antiaircraft flak.

The convoy was effectively defending itself against the aerial onslaught. However, its luck was about to run out. The Rohna remained in formation with the convoy, and her 195 crewmembers worked furiously to protect their passengers, which included 1,988 American soldiers and seven Red Cross volunteers. About forty-five minutes into the battle, Luftwaffe pilot Major Hans Dochtermann set his sights on the Banfora, next to Rohna, and released a glide bomb. Gunners hit the bomb and sheer off one of its wings. This caused the bomb to veer out to sea, but not before striking the Banfora's radio antenna and scattering large pieces of debris on her deck.

Major Dochtermann then banked his plane and returned for another pass. He flew his plane over the HMS Atherstone, turned thirty degrees toward the troopships, and fired his missile forward and down toward the Rohna. The missile's nose turned red from the heat, and black smoke spewed out of its tail. George Zuther, the bombardier, guided the missile toward the Rohna. At 370 miles per hour, the 650-pound warhead impacted the ship on her port side, at the aft section of her engine room, and on a troop deck quartering the 853rd Aviation Engineer Battalion. It instantly killed about 300 men.

Carmen heard a plane fly directly over his ship, and his shipmate at the porthole yelled: "*What the devil is that?*" What they actually heard was the missile. Next, the passengers heard and then felt a tremendous explosion. Carmen's shipmate at the window reported that an explosion had ripped through a nearby ship, sending up a cloud of smoke nearly three times the height of the ship's mast and encircling the entire aft one-third of the ship. He could see a seventy-five-foot or so hole in her side. Once the smoke cleared, he updated his report that he could see straight through the ship's hull.

The bomb provided a mortal blow to Rohna. Though it hit fifteen feet above the waterline, the explosion blew out the hull on the starboard side below the waterline. The explosion caused the engine room to flood, knocked out all electrical power, including her pumps, and caused the ship to burn out of control. Hans Dochtermann and George Zuther were the first to successfully use a German guided missile in combat.

There was nothing unusual about the Rohna. The 8,602-ton passenger and cargo liner was owned by the British India Steam Navigation Company and constructed in Tyneside, England, in 1926. She was named after a village in Sonipat, Punjab, India. In 1940, the British government requisitioned her as a troopship and since sailed her in harm's way delivering soldiers. She was constructed with a standard freighter design, and her five boilers provided a standard cruising speed of 12.5 knots.

Her crew muttered when she was directed to take up position twelve in the convoy, putting her second in the port column. This position was called "Coffin Corner" because it was vulnerable to air attacks. The sailors worried about riding in the "Corner" during a "Suicide Alley" run from Algeria to Tunisia. Sailors' superstitions are usually rooted in truth.

Deep in the bowels of another typical troopship, Carmen sat with his eyes closed as he memorized the emergency escape route, he was taught the day before. He replayed his Sergeant's instructions, when he first boarded the ship, how to wear and deploy his life belt: *"The belt is to be worn around your waist and is inflated by squeezing the belt's levers that pierce two CO2 cartridges. If the cartridges do not work, then inflate the belt by blowing into the two tubes. Wear it at all times, especially when you are sleeping."* His concentration was broken by crying and prayers from his fellow shipmates, asking God that they not suffer the same fate.

Over 1,500 frantic passengers, many badly wounded, poured out from any hatch that could open onto Rohna's deck. They joined the crew in a desperate dash to the lifeboats, as trained during their lifeboat drills. To their horror, they found six of the twenty-two lifeboats destroyed, and none of the portside boats could be lowered into the water because of warped plates in the hull from the bomb blast. Troops jumped into the churning and oil-soaked sea. They overloaded the few surviving lifeboats, only to have them swamp or capsize.

As the convoy with Carmen sped away on its easterly course, the Rohna was dead in the water, ablaze and listing twelve degrees to starboard. Men were still pouring into the Gulf of Boguie. Responding to German planes strafing the floating survivors, the Atherstone provided anti-aircraft cover and created a smokescreen. This allowed the Auk-class minesweeper USS Pioneer, British corvette Holcombe and cargo ship Clan Campbell to pick up survivors. By 5:50 p.m., about thirty-five minutes after the bomb strike, most of the men had abandoned the ship, which burned furiously.

Fifteen to twenty-foot waves prevented the Atherstone and Pioneer from launching their small boats, so the Pioneer scrambled from one group of survivors to another. The Clan Campbell had a high freeboard requiring her to lower a cargo net for survivors to climb aboard. The climb was about thirty feet from the sea to the deck, which was exhaustive for many of the exhausted survivors. Many stricken soldiers died within arm's reach of the ship's hull.

About an hour after the Rohna was struck, survivors and crew on the rescue ships heard the distinct sounds of her collapsing bulkheads. Smoke billowed from her number three hold, and the bow rose toward the sky as the ship slid under by her stern. Then she was gone.

When darkness fell, the Atherstone discontinued anti-aircraft duty and joined in rescuing survivors. The rescue tug HMS Mindful dispatched from Bougie, also joined the operation. The ships continued their rescue efforts until 2:15 a.m. on November 27, when they ceased finding survivors. In total, 819 survivors, some terribly burned, were taken to Philippeville (now Skikda Algeria). The Pioneer rescued 606, while the Clan Campbell rescued about eighty-three and the Atherstone about seventy.

Of the 2,193 souls on board Rohna, 1,138 men, including 1,015 U.S. personnel, lost their lives. Thirty-five GIs later died from their wounds. Five of Rohna's officers and 117 of her 195 crew were killed, plus one of her twelve attached Navy gunners and one hospital orderly. The attack is the greatest loss of U.S. troops at sea due to enemy action in a single incident and claimed the lives of almost one-third of the 3,604 American personnel killed at sea in the European Theater.

As the sky calmed and Carmen continued to sail east, he was fortunate to be below decks and miss the carnage playing out behind him. He was also fortunate that he did not board the Rohna. The convoy would encounter German planes two more times. Two nights after the Rohna sinking, at approximately 2:00 a.m., just off North Africa's coast about 100 miles northwest of Bizerte, Tunisia, the Luftwaffe returned to finish the job. They could be seen on the horizon, dropping flares in search of the convoy. However, they were too far away to find their prey. On the evening of November 29, the convoy was directly south of Sicily when at 5:00 p.m., a formation of approximately twenty German planes dive-bombed the convoy. The Egra was the first ship to open fire. The attack was brief, with the enemy driven off without damaging the convoy. Carmen watched one German plane crash in flames.

On Tuesday, November 30, the convoy finally docked in Alexandria, Egypt. While tied to the pier, Carmen witnessed his ship's former escort, the HMS Birmingham, limp into the harbor with extensive battle damage. With the forward third of the ship flooded, she was bow down, drawing thirty-three feet forward and sixteen feet aft. The Birmingham was detached from the convoy for another mission. At 12:22 p.m. on November 28, while sailing from Malta, she was torpedoed by a U-boat off Cyrenaica, Libya. The torpedo hit forward, flooding several compartments. Casualties included twenty-nine men killed and twenty-eight wounded.

Also hobbling into the harbor was the Ranchi. During the November 26 attack, a bomb struck her forecastle, penetrated the troops' heads, then exited through the ship's hull before exploding. One man died, and three were wounded.

Because the Allies did not want the Nazis to know how successful their new missile was, they did not report the Rohna sinking to the American public. As documented in the "Admiralty War Diaries of World War II, Levant Command September to November 1943," the official record of the time omits any mention of the Rohna sinking, stating:

"November 29th

"Attack on Convoy K.M.F. 26

"O.R.P. SLAZAK (S.O.) escort reported one shadower at 0846 and H.M.S. ATHERSTONE escorting 1 M.V. overtaking 20 miles astern, reported one shadower at 0924. A dusk attack was foreseen and the fighter escort increased to 12. When it materialized at 1710, the fighters broke up a force of 15 J.U. 88s and claimed 2 shot down, 1 probable, and 1 damaged. The S.S. RANCHI suffered superficial damage from a near miss and had a man killed and 3 wounded, no other damage to the convoy. O.R.P. KRAKOWIAK and H.H.M.S. THEMISTOCLES joined H.M.S. ATHERSTONE before sunset, but no attack developed...

"PART II

"APPRECIATION OF EVENTS FOR NOVEMBER 1943

"General

"5. Early warning was received of impending air attack on convoy K.M.F. 26 on the 29th when part of the convoy and 1 joiner astern were shadowed from 0900. Enough fighters were up at dusk to break up the attack when it materialized at 1710 with the result that only 1 ship in the convoy suffered superficial damage and 2 out of the attacking force of 15 J.U.88s were shot down. No attack was made on the merchant ship astern which like the convoy had been joined by 2 Hunts before dark."

The attack was classified as "secret," with survivors and rescue personnel sworn to secrecy. The Allies also suppressed all news, with family members of those killed telegrammed that their serviceman was "missing in action" or "killed in action" in the North African Area. It was not until 1993 that the story about the sinking went public with a report from reporter Charles Osgood and the first reunion of the KMF.26 Convoy survivors was held in Gatlinburg, Tennessee. Carmen was eighty years old. Since then, several books have been written, and the History Channel produced a documentary on the controversy surrounding the incident and its coverup.

The day after entering Alexandria Harbor, the three undamaged troopships that left Oran together, the Egra, Karoa, and Banfora, independently sailed to Port Said, Egypt. They then convoyed through the Suez Canal, into the Red Sea, then along the Gulf of Aden to the Port of Aden. The three ships were part of the first convoy to transit the Suez Canal since early 1941 when the Germans captured the island of Crete. Carmen and his shipmates eventually recovered from the initial shock from the attack and found the voyage to Aden pleasant. However, there was palpable tension on the ships' bridges as officers read dispatches from the British Mediterranean Fleet Levant Command about the waters ahead of them.

> *"November 29th, 1943*
>
> *"The S.S. ATHINA LIVANOS was torpedoed in position 12-20N, 44-00E (the Gulf of Aden) at 1630 and a submarine's periscope was seen. 25 survivors were picked up.*
>
> *"This reopened the question of how the S.S. SAMBO was sunk on the 10th (ten miles S. of Perim Island in the Red Sea off the coast of Yemen) ...Three of her crew and nine gunners were lost. 35 survivors rescued by Norwegian MV Helgøy...A submarine had been ruled out, but that decision was now reconsidered."*

On October 19, 1943, while Carmen traveled across the Atlantic toward Africa, His Imperial Japanese Majesty's Ship (HIJMS) Submarine I-27, captained by Commander Fukumura, departed Penang Malaysia on a westerly course. Commencing her ninth war patrol: the I-27's mission was to raid enemy communications and shipping in the Gulf of Aden and the Arabian Sea. By the end of the month, she was reconnoitering Allied shipping traffic along the coast of Yemen. Over the next forty-five days, she torpedoed five ships, sinking four. The casualties included:

- November 10, I-27 spotted the 7,219-ton British SAM-class Liberty ship Sambo in his periscope. Sambo was on her maiden voyage from Iquique, Peru, to Suez with nitrate and general cargo. Commander Fukumura launched a torpedo, which sank the lone merchant ship and killed three sailors and nine gunners.

- November 18, I-27 torpedoed the 7,176-ton British SAM-class Liberty ship Sambridge southeast of Aden. She was on her maiden voyage from Madras to Aden with 365 tons of general cargo and 1,000 tons of sand ballast.
- Eleven days later, she torpedoed the 4,824-ton Greek steamer Athina Livanos, killing nine sailors and two passengers.
- December 2, I-27 torpedoed the 4,732-ton Greek steamer Nitsa south of Aden. She was en route from Calcutta, India, to Aden. Eleven sailors were lost.
- The following day, she torpedoed and damaged the 7,126-ton British freighter Fort Camosun off Somalia's coast. The ship transmitted an SSS signal. A code only used when being torpedoed by a submarine.

The Banfora and Karoa sailed into Aden Harbor on Thursday, December 9, followed by the Egra that Saturday. Arriving with the Egra was the Clan Campbell, one of the vessels that rescued Rohna's survivors. Carmen and the other soldiers were able to spend some of the weekend enjoying dry land at the British outpost before having to sail again on Monday.

As the crew restocked the ship with coal and supplies for its next convoy, Carmen and the other soldiers departed down the gangplank, walked past with guards at the harbor entrance, and strolled into the town. They visited a shopping area where merchants targeted Americans for sales. The next day Carmen and his friends visited northwest of the city. There was a high wire fence separating Aden from Yemen. All he could see there were dry, sandy flatlands. Nearby there was a library with interesting pictures of that territory. All hands had to return to the ship upon darkness or about 6.30 p.m.

On Monday, December 13, Convoy AB.24A departed the harbor for a six-day voyage to Bombay, India. It consisted of five veterans of Convoy KMF.26, the Banfora, Egra, Karoa, Derbyshire, and Reina Del Pacifico. Protecting the small convoy was the HMS Aimwell, an armed Favourite-class tugboat.

At the captains' meeting before sailing, there was anxiety over the Japanese submarine hunting in the waters off Aden. Watches and gun crews were to be on full alert upon departing the harbor. Unknown to the convoy captains, I-27 received orders to return to its base in Malaysia and was well east of AB.24A on a southeasterly heading similar to the convoy. The convoy crossed the Arabian Sea without incident.

As the ship made its way into the bustling port of Bombay, Carmen and his fellow soldiers covered every square inch of the deck to view their new home. Carmen's senses were immediately overwhelmed by the country's heat, sights, and smells, which wrapped him like a putrid fog, a fog he knew would encircle him for many years. As foreign as the land in front of him looked, Carmen was anxious to go ashore. He also witnessed lingering damage to the harbor from massive explosions that occurred eight months prior.

On April 14, a Liberty ship with a deadly load of TNT and gray ammonal caught fire while unloading its cargo. As firefighters and crew fought the flames, the ship morphed into a massive fireball, whose explosion was heard up to fifty miles away. Shortly after, a second, more powerful explosion occurred, lifting the 5,000-ton ship sixty feet in the air and decimating the port and whole blocks of the town. The toll was horrendous, with 1,500 killed and 3000 wounded. Twenty-seven ships were sunk or burned.

He thumbed through a booklet issued to him entitled "A Pocket Guide to India." He stopped on a page with a map and read:

> *"ONE glance at the world map below will show you why the United Nations must hold India and why that need is great enough that American forces have been sent to share in the undertaking. This sub-continent, jutting into the Indian Ocean, lies across some of the most vital sea lanes of the United Nations. It is the greatest territorial barrier to the joining of the major forces of our Axis enemies. India is just about equi-distant between Rome, Berlin, and Tokyo.*
>
> *"It is 2,000 miles from Aden, the important base covering the southern end of the Red Sea and protecting the Allies supply lines looping around South Africa to serve our forces in Egypt, the Middle East and Russia. Singapore, the gate on the Malacca Strait which is the main highway to the waters of eastern Asia,*

is a like distance away. Thus India might become the main base of our advance against Japan's positions in Burma, Malaya, and Thailand, or the springboard by which the Japanese can drive westward against the positions which enable the forces of the United Nations to control the Middle East and the Indian Ocean.

"The forces of the United Nations hold India's numerous excellent ports. Likewise, the United Nations hold the great naval base at Trincomalee in Ceylon, and the strong British base at Aden which covers the entrance to the Red sea. These holdings give our side strategic command of a body of water - the Indian Ocean - which serves three continents. Were Axis forces to gain control of the bases, we would no longer have command of the seas. India is the principal base which must be strengthened to assure the continuation of this command. Our forces and those of the British Empire are cooperating toward this end."

Despite his sensory overload from the sights, smells, and sounds, Carmen had enough of that loose queasy feeling in his stomach from weeks at sea, spartan living conditions, and bland food. Carmen longed for solid land under him and a permanent barracks so he could stop living out of a duffle bag in a cramped compartment. He was also ready to do the job his country sent him to do.

His stay in Bombay was short-lived. However, it was long enough to reinforce the sense that he was about to begin an unimaginable experience. Once he disembarked the ship, he was further overcome by the sights, smells, and sounds around him. The crush of humanity, incredible poverty and grime, the squalor and appalling smells of everyday living conditions far exceeded any misery he witnessed at the height of the Depression in Paterson.

 He would only have dry land under his feet long enough to transfer over to a local vessel that would transport him 550 miles up British India's northwest coast to the port of Karachi, where he would come ashore four days before Christmas 1943. There, his seventy-nine-day voyage from America would end, and his two-year stint in India would begin.

Camp Shelby, Mississippi
December 12, 1943

After a fourteen-day respite from his drab and regimented Army life, Charles returned to his post. It was a sad goodbye when he left Garfield, but it was back to training upon return. However, between drills, Charles listened to leave stories from the other battalion members. Captain Jack Fugate from Charles's Battery married Marilyn Hrdlicka in Houston, Texas, at 11:00 a.m. on Thanksgiving. His dad was the best man. Then all the wedding guests shared a Thanksgiving dinner at the home of the bride's parents. Captain Huron, Major Heenan, and Lieutenants Ainslie and Berkowitz were visited by their wives and enjoyed Hattiesburg and the surrounding Mississippi countryside with their families.

Four days after Charles and the rest of his Battalion returned from leave, they completed their final Third Phase test with a 93% score on the Air-Ground Test. Three days later, a ceremony was held for Major Collins to formally assume command of the Battalion. Lt. Col. Hinsch was on everyone's mind that day.

The Battalion entered the fourth and final training period, which lasted until the unit embarked overseas. This was a waiting period where the unit moved in the queue for transport to the European Theater of Operation. Until departure, it emphasized exercises and other training to hone skills learned in the previous periods. Rumors were rampant that the Third Army would be moving out to England. That is when the Army--being the Army--changed the plan for the 267th.

It received orders to depart Camp Shelby on Christmas Eve for Fort Bragg, North Carolina, and retrain on massive 240mm howitzers, an entirely new gun! For Charles, this was Army Standard Operating Procedure. He joined the Army Coastal Defense Force and, after his training, was sent to Tank Destroyer School. Once he graduated, he was sent to a 155mm artillery unit. After nine months of learning that weapon, he was assigned to a new one--all on the eve of being shipped out to fight the enemy.

On December 24, the 267th assembled in front of its barracks, and with a band playing "Dixie" and "There's No Place Like Home," it marched across the base toward the train station. Packs, rifles, gas masks, and heavy overcoats weighed them down as they moved past the other soldiers who wished them well. Exhausted from the long march, they boarded a special train that took them out of the Camp. The Battalion traveled all-day Christmas and arrived at Fort Bragg the following day to be relieved of its assignment to the Third Army, XIX Corps, 403rd Field Artillery Group, and assigned to the Second Army, XII Corps, 402nd Field Artillery Group. The Battalion's training plan, which was in the last phase, was reset back to the start.

The 240mm M1 Modified Tractor Drawn Howitzer was the largest and most powerful mobile artillery piece in the Army's arsenal. It fired a 360-pound shell up to 14.3 miles and was nicknamed the "Black Dragon." The Army began to develop the gun in 1941. Its first action occurred when the 697th Field Artillery Battalion deployed in response to an urgent request by General Marshall for heavy artillery in the Italian Theater. Battlefield reports noted that the guns launched deadly and relatively accurate firepower against German fortifications and tank concentrations. With these positive results, the Army eventually purchased 315 of the massive guns. Of the 238 separate field artillery battalions operating in the European Theater of Operation, only the 267th and fourteen others were assigned 240mm howitzers.

The 240mm's history goes back to the early 1920s. After World War I, the U.S. slowly developed an earlier version, the 240mm M1918 howitzer. It was not until 1934 that a workable gun and carriage were produced. In June 1940, the 79th Field Artillery Battalion was formed as the first 240mm M1918 howitzer battalion. A total of 48 M1918M1A1s were produced. However, they were obsolete by early 1941, and the Army began to replace them with the M1 design. The 267th was initially given M1918s for training purposes, which were substituted with M1s when they became available.

The weapon came with benefits and drawbacks. The gun's benefit was providing super heavy field artillery capable of destroying heavily reinforced targets, like those along the Siegfried Line that Army planners knew would be the Wehrmacht's defiant stand between its homeland and advancing Allied armies. The downfall of the weapon was mobility and manpower challenges. The World War II battlefield required artillery to continually move with advancing infantry and armored forces. The 240mm was a heavy gun--over 29 tons--requiring extensive manpower and equipment to move and emplace it. The 12.5-ton gun barrel and 20-ton carriage were disassembled from each other and towed separately by 38-ton M33 tractors that traveled up to 21 miles per hour. The gun's weight limited the areas it could travel, especially in the European campaign's muddy conditions. Once in a new position, getting the gun into firing position could take a couple of hours, as the crew dug a recoil pit, hoisted the barrel by crane onto the gun carriage, and reassembled the weapon. A minimum of fourteen personnel were needed to load and fire it. Most of them were needed to move and load the 360-pound projectiles and seventy-eight-pound bags of gunpowder, plus swab out the long barrel after each fire.

The 267th was issued six guns, and its three firing batteries (A, B, and C) received two guns each. It retained its Headquarters and Service batteries. Charles was assigned to the Second Gun Section of Battery C. With him were the following personnel:

1. Sergeant William F. Potter, Atlanta, GA;
2. Sergeant Everett L. Walker, Sacramento, CA;
3. Sergeant Henry A. Jones, Hemlock, NC;
4. Sergeant Herbert C. Myers, Wise, VA;
5. Corporal Elmer L. Toth, Cleveland, OH;
6. Monroe Bailey, Monroe, WV;
7. Austin Bishop, Cincinnati, OH;
8. Frank A. Percival, Ravena, NY;
9. John C. Johnston, Corning, NY;
10. Rogelio Herrera, Mission, TX;
11. Richmond Howse, Atlanta, GA;
12. George I. Basher, Cavalier, ND;
13. James F. Jahnke, Marshfield, WI;
14. John D. Mussey, Salisbury, NH; and
15. Oliver W. Privett, Sawyer, KY.

New Year's Day 1944 transformed many of the artillerymen's rumors and expectations into reality with two significant orders.

First, the 267th was officially converted from 155mm to 240mm howitzers and directed to train its personnel on the new weapons and vehicles until mid-February. During this time, designated enlisted personnel were sent to Tractor School at Fort Sill, Oklahoma, and Tank Drivers School at Fort Knox, Kentucky. The schools were six weeks of intensive training. Charles completed a Night Infiltration Course on January 5 and, ten days later, a Carbine Course as a Marksman with a score of 152.

Secondly, the Third Army was alerted to prepare for deployment to England as a stepping stone to invade the European mainland. The opening of a second front on "Fortress Europe" was a hotly debated topic among the Allies since the U.S. entered the war. Joseph Stalin, the Premier of the Union of Soviet Socialists Republics, led his country in a costly war against the Germans. To take some pressure off his army, he called on the U.S. and Britain to invade the European Continent in 1942. The U.S. felt its army was not ready to conduct a massive invasion and direct assault against Germany. The disastrous August 1942 British raid on the German-occupied port of Dieppe, where nearly 60% of the raiders were killed, wounded, or captured by Axis coastal defenders, and the rookie performance of U.S. forces against Germany's North Africa Corps demonstrated that Allied forces needed time before they could take Germany head-on. The U.S. administration believed that 1944 was a more realistic date. 1944 had just arrived.

Between February 13 and April 22, the Battalion trained for long hours learning their new guns. The 267th had already developed the cohesiveness that a unit needs in combat; this training applied that cohesiveness to firing the new gun rapidly and accurately. Punctuating that mission was the standard training a unit set to deploy must complete. In March, Charles and the other artillerymen were also schooled on Hygiene and Sexual Conduct, Malaria Control, and the Articles of War.

By the end of March, the 267th felt sufficiently trained to challenge the new weapons proficiency tests. On March 31, it completed Battalion Test II with a score of 80%. Five days later, it breezed through a modified Battalion Test III with an excellent rating. At the same time, it passed its tests, the Battalion received its movement orders for overseas shipment. The artillerymen worked with station artillery personnel to make final repairs or replacements of their guns and equipment. They then packed their guns and field equipment for separate shipment from the men. They also waterproofed and conducted maintenance on their personal gear that would accompany them.

On April 22, the Battalion boarded trains to the area of bases collectively called the "New York Port of Embarkation," where they spent the next four months moving between posts while awaiting their slot to cross the Atlantic. These bases for transient troops, located in the Greater New York area, consisted of Fort Slocum, Camp Kilmer, and Camp Shanks, which were primarily established as staging areas to parcel out troops and material to convoys heading to Europe. Nearby, Fort Dix also served as a processing and final training center.

At Fort Bragg, Charles and his unit waited at the depot for several hours before boarding a Pullman train to New York City. It rode through Virginia, stopping in Washington, D.C., then through Maryland, Pennsylvania, his home state of New Jersey, and into Pennsylvania Station in New York City. It was Sunday night when they arrived. Even though Charles was just twelve miles from home, he could not visit his family or enjoy New York City's nightlife because he had a mission to accomplish. The Battalion changed to a New York, New Haven, and Hartford Railroad (NYNH&H RR) train to New Rochelle, NY. They then boarded a ferry to Fort Slocum.

Fort Slocum was an Army post occupying Davids' Island in the East River off New Rochelle. The name was significant to the Battalion because it was named after Henry Warner Slocum, a Civil War Union General who commanded the XII Corps, the parent unit of the 267th. Fort Slocum was pleasant duty for Charles and his unit. The staff was well-organized and hospitable to the troops, conducting a field artillery school with last-minute training for the 267th. Quality liberty time was plentiful. One-quarter of the enlisted men and officers were allowed into New York City on a pass when not training. Some troops, like Charles, who lived locally, got passes to go home. Charles enjoyed being back in the north after nearly two years. He was around people who talked like him, ate the same food he liked, and were culturally similar. Charles also enjoyed going home on short visits and taking his fellow artillerymen into New York City, especially those who had never been there.

The 1940s was the era of big bands, and New York City was the place to experience them. Large bands that could be compared to mini orchestras traveled the country playing for young adults. New York City was home to the most popular bands led by Tommy Dorsey, Jimmy Dorsey, Glenn Miller, and Benny Goodman, to name a few. Charles, Roseann, and others in their generation judged each other by how well they danced. Dance halls or hotel ballrooms, filled with big band music, were the places men and women would meet and fall in love.

Outside the ballrooms, New York was a city filled with energy. Young men in uniform enjoyed life with the mindset that their visit to the city could be the last fun they would experience in their short lives. Women knew this too and were willing participants in fostering pleasant thoughts for servicemen to recollect as they headed into battle. New Yorkers--a group of people known as indifferent--treated servicemen with warmth and respect. USO clubs in the City gave them a safe and secure area to unwind when they experienced too much city life. A night of liberty in the Big Apple was the antidote to the tedium of Army training and no-frills living. Morale for both Charles and the Battalion significantly improved after several visits to the City.

During this time, the Battalion's Advanced Detachment was in England, coordinating with XII Corps staff for the arrival of the main body. They arranged quarters, training areas, and supplies for the rest of the unit. They also had to locate the Battalion's artillery pieces, vehicles, and field equipment shipped separately and interspersed with equipment designated for other units. At the beginning of May, they operated out of Llanover, Monmouthshire. The following month they relocated to Peover, England, and then finally to Bude, Cornwall in July to meet the main body.

After almost two weeks awaiting transit overseas, the Army changed plans again. It determined that the 267th would not partake in the D-Day or initial invasion of Europe. The unit's weapons were too heavy to transport to the French coastline in the initial D-Day landings.

Instead, the 267th, along with other 240mm units, would be moved into the European Theater of Operation at a later phase. Limited troopship transportation meant the 267th had to step back for other units going over for the initial invasion.

On May 5, the Battalion boarded a ferry then a train to Fort Dix, the same fort where Charles's military service started. There the Battalion spent nearly two months continuing to perfect its operation of 240mms. It also used this time to conduct final preparations for deployment. Charles and the artillerymen received inoculations, spectacle prescriptions, and allotments or insurance changes. Any missing training was completed, such as weapons qualifications on the rifle range. All field equipment was turned in for salvage, and new gear was issued.

Charles was given eight days leave in Garfield and returned to Fort Dix on May 25. Based on news reports from Europe, Charles and his parents felt that the assault against Hitler's "Fortress Europe" would soon commence, and that Charles would be part of it. They all harbored the thought that this could be the last time they would see each other for a long time, if not forever.

Training at Fort Dix lasted until June 26, when word came again that it was time to ship out.

Karachi, British India
December 20, 1943

Carmen's ship pulled into Karachi's port, an artificial harbor filled with a hundred tall cranes. Beside the harbor was the city of Karachi, sitting on a mud flat. Carmen was struck by the number of guns deployed in a port so far from the front. The Imperial Japanese Army Air Service had set its sights on American shipping entering the CBI Theater. Its planes conducted a major bombing raid on India's port of Calcutta earlier in the month. During the December 4 morning raid, Japanese planes concentrated their bombs on its Kidderpore docks, causing considerable damage. Many civilians working the docks were killed, and three merchant vessels, one navy ship, and fifteen barges were damaged. The raid also extended to the town, resulting in about 350 dead and many more wounded civilians. One military personnel was killed, and thirteen were wounded. The British defenders were no match for the attackers as Japanese pilots shot down nine British Hurricanes in the ensuing dogfights. The Japanese lost one plane, with another damaged. One plane was forced to land when it ran out of fuel. While Calcutta was 1,300 miles closer to the front, the raid prompted extensive security around the Karachi port.

Though tensions in the port were running high, Carmen was surprised that it was not as busy as the other ports he had transited. Four months after the Pearl Harbor attack, the U.S. chose Karachi as the initial port to funnel supplies through India to Chinese forces fighting the Japanese. But the pitfalls of choosing a port so far from the front lines became quickly apparent. While the port was modern and could unload large quantities of military tonnage, supplies backed up in overflowing warehouses due to India's poor transportation infrastructure. Loaded down troop and cargo trains would make the nearly two thousand-mile trek across the hot Central Plains of India to its eastern border with China and Burma. Because India did not have a standardized railroad track size, the track changed gauge size several times, and all freight had to be unloaded, stacked, guarded against pilferage, and then reloaded onto different size railcars. It took a soldier, on his way up to work or fight in Burma or China, three or four weeks to make the trip.

By the time Carmen arrived, most of the American cargo was heading to Calcutta. With this shift, the soldiers who unloaded ships were transferred from Karachi to Calcutta. Only a small Army staff supervising native labor now handled port activities at Karachi.

Despite reduced port activities, Karachi still hosted a significant military presence. "Base Section No. 1 Karachi" was activated on May 27, 1942, covering an area of 360,000 square miles. It had a major airfield, initially developed by the British and greatly expanded by the U.S. Army Air Corps in 1942, to handle aircraft flying supplies and personnel from the U.S. via Brazil and Africa to forward bases in the CBI. Also on base were aircraft assembly plants that put together crated combat aircraft for deployment further east against the Japanese. The airfield and a Bombing Practice Range trained Nationalist Chinese and U.S.

units and personnel prior to entering combat. The base also contained extensive medical facilities to treat personnel stationed in India and those evacuated from China and Burma.

Once he departed the ship, Carmen was trucked about sixteen miles east to Replacement Depot #1 in North Malir and assigned to its Headquarters Company. Malir held the largest concentration of American servicemen in the area, with a cantonment that could accommodate 20,000 troops. It contained thirty-eight mess halls, 300 barracks, and other support facilities. The function of the Replacement Depot was to receive fresh troops and supplies, then ship them on trains across India to Assam on the eastern border. From Assam, supplies were either distributed locally or carried by airplanes over "the Hump" to the Kunming China area, then transported to Chungking and finally to Chinese forces on the front lines by rail, truck, boat, or carried by people or animals. By December 1943, many of the depot's functions and personnel were shifted east to Replacement Depot #2 near Calcutta. Malir's hospital, refrigeration facilities, rail transportation office, and other logistic services remained busy despite the shift.

The sprawling base sat on a bare, dusty, and often windy plain. Lacking shade, the summers were unbearably hot, water was rationed, and sand was blown into everything. Barracks and other buildings were situated amongst large thorny acacia bushes that extended over the horizon and into the desert. Carmen looked around and thought how it reminded him of Oran, not a happy thought. But he put all that out of his mind. Christmas was right around the corner, and not having a decent meal since he left the U.S. three months earlier, all he could focus on was a posted menu of turkey, real potatoes, gravy, cranberries, pies, and cigars. Christmas could not come soon enough!

From left to right: Eskew Steffens, Roseann, and two friends.

Paterson, New Jersey
April 1944

While still a young lady, Roseann's parents tried to impose the old-world tradition of an arranged marriage on Roseann. Despite Pietro and Giuseppina having escaped Sicily so they could marry each other based on love, they still felt it their duty to arrange their daughters' future husband. One day Giuseppina and Pietro sat with Roseann and told her about a Major in the Italian Army, also from Santa Croce Camerina. As Giuseppina showed Roseann his picture and correspondence, she informed her that this man would be her husband. In one of those transitional moments where the Iozzia family moved from an Italian to an American family, Roseann defied generations of tradition and responded that she would select her husband based on American, not Sicilian values. Despite this new American freedom, she did not have time to date boys In high school. She only went on one date during the entire four years, and not until just before her graduation. It was a movie date with a fellow student she rated "*so-so.*"

After her graduation, she and her "Musketeer" friends felt it was "their duty" to attend dances frequented by soldiers and sailors. During the war, the big band circuit included Paterson, where its dancehalls came to life most weekends. Troops home on leave were at these dances to unwind, and the "Three Musketeers" were there to ensure their "boys" had dance and flirt partners.

One Saturday evening in April 1944, as the war raged on, a sailor stood out to Roseann from all the other GIs in the dancehall. The sailor was tall and had beautiful eyes that mesmerized her. He saw Roseann looking at him and asked her to dance. They danced for hours, and she was amazed at how he glided on the dance floor. After the dance, they talked until early into the morning. As he was shortly shipping out to the West Coast, he asked if he could take her to a movie later that day, and she said yes. Time was not a luxury for young people during wartime.

The sailor's name was Eskew Steffens. He was the 22-year-old son of Blanche and William Steffens. Blanche was born and raised in Kanawha County, West Virginia, and was a widow after her first husband of four months died while working in a coal mine. William was from Brooklyn, NY, and a veteran of World War I. After the war, he worked in a West Virginia coal mine, where he met and quickly married Blanche. Blanche and William left the mountains of Appalachia for Paterson shortly after Eskew was born. With a thick West Virginia accent, she and her family settled in Paterson's Italian district not far from Pietro and Giuseppina's house. Eskew had one brother, William Jr., and three sisters, Margaret, Blanche, and June.

William was a painter and lost his job at a silk dying plant during the early days of the Depression, like Pietro. He spent much of the Depression unemployed. This forced Eskew to cut his education short, leaving high school after one year to help the family earn enough money to survive. Eskew and his younger brother worked sixty hours a week as farmhands on a local farm. Before being drafted into the Navy, Eskew was hired as a guard at the Picatinny Arsenal, a military munitions production site in Morris County.

The arsenal was founded in 1880 as the Picatinny Powder Depot. The Navy assumed a portion of the 6,400 acres installation and established Lake Denmark Naval Ammunition Depot, a major gunpowder manufacturer until after World War I. Meanwhile, the arsenal shifted production to heavy munitions and research and development activities.

Eskew worked at the arsenal during the height of its wartime activity with 18,000 employees.

On January 20, 1944, Eskew joined the Navy for the duration of the war plus six months. He completed his boot camp in Great Lakes, Illinois, and was home on nine days of leave before shipping out to the Pacific.

That evening, Eskew and Roseann went to a movie and then for coffee. The next day, Roseann met Eskew at the Paterson Station, less than a mile from her house. In 1944, train stations across the world were emotional places. Men in uniform--or their last set of civilian clothes-- were on train platforms hugging their girlfriends, mothers, and friends. Children were crying, and fathers could be seen wiping back tears. It was the spot where friends, lovers, and family members would share what could be their last hug or utter their last words to each other. As the trains pulled out, everyone feared it was the last glimpse they would have of one another. Roseann found it hard to say goodbye as Eskew boarded a train to take a cross-country voyage that would end on the USS Intrepid (CV-11).

Roseann and the "Musketeers"

Camp Kilmer, New Jersey
June 26, 1944

The 267th completed a short train ride and arrived at its new post to again wait in line for transportation to war. Opened in mid-1942, Camp Kilmer was built as a transportation hub that would ultimately process over twenty divisions to participate in the European Theater. The 1,600-

acre camp was located between Edison and Piscataway, about forty miles south of Charles's hometown of Garfield. The post was named after the poet Joyce Kilmer, who enlisted in the U.S. Army during World War I and was killed in action in the Aisne-Marne Offensive. The camp had 1,120 buildings, including rows of wooden barracks, seven chapels, five theaters, nine post exchanges, a gym, three libraries, four telephone centers, a post office, a 1,000-bed hospital, twenty-eight miles of roadway, and about eleven railheads that fed into the main line. These facilities accommodated the 1.3 million servicemen who were temporarily staged there before being deployed to Europe,

For the last three weeks, Charles and the artillerymen followed the D-Day landings and expanding Allied beachhead in France. War correspondents reported Wehrmacht defense tactics at places the 267th studied in its training scenarios.

It started on June 6 when Charles and his gun section huddled around a radio to listen to NBC News reports of German radio bulletins coming in that the Allied invasion of Europe had begun. Later that morning, the British government confirmed that the invasion had commenced. That message was shortly followed by a communication from General Eisenhower, the Supreme Commander of the Allies in Europe, to his troops. His message was short and optimistic but sober. His voice came over the radio:

"Soldiers, Sailors, and Airmen of the Allied Expeditionary Force:

"You are about to embark upon the Great Crusade, toward which we have striven these many months. The eyes of the world are upon you. The hopes and prayers of liberty-loving people everywhere march with you. In company with our brave Allies and brothers-in-arms on other Fronts you will bring about the destruction of the German war machine, the elimination of Nazi tyranny over oppressed peoples of Europe, and security for ourselves in a free world. Your task will not be an easy one. Your enemy is well trained, well equipped, and battle-hardened. He will fight savagely.

"But this is the year 1944. Much has happened since the Nazi triumphs of 1940-41. The United Nations have inflicted upon the Germans great defeats, in open battle, man-to-man. Our air offensive has seriously reduced their strength in the air and their capacity to wage war on the ground. Our Home Fronts have given us an overwhelming superiority in weapons and munitions of war and placed at our disposal great reserves of trained fighting men. The tide has turned. The free men of the world are marching together to victory.

"I have full confidence in your courage, devotion to duty, and skill in battle. We will accept nothing less than full victory. Good Luck! And let us all beseech the blessing of Almighty God upon this great and noble undertaking."

Since that day, the men of the 267th traded rumors and news stories about the Allies' progress. The invasion and subsequent war reports made the war more real as they continually checked their gear and refreshed their training. A constant stream of rumors about when and where they were shipping out kept the men guessing as they welcomed new units arriving at Camp Kilmer and waved goodbye to others departing for their ships.

The Army found ways to occupy the soldiers' time with a long list of monotonous tasks. Charles and his fellow artillerymen spent their days scrubbing the barracks, viewing training movies, lectures, boat drills, exercises, and, of course, policing up the campgrounds. Interspersed were standing in endless lines for chow, medical instructions, phone calls, and additional immunizations.

In mid-July, the officers gathered the troops of the 267th to announce that they were shipping out of New York City to the European Theater of Operation on July 23. They were given their final packing lists and weight limits on the gear they were permitted to take with them. Anything outside those weight limits or packing lists had to be shipped home or left behind.

As Charles packed his gear for the journey, the war in Europe intensified. The difficult and bloody Battle of the Hedgerows in Northern France finally ended with U.S. forces capturing the French town of St. Lo.   On the ride to New York, he also heard that Adolf Hitler survived an assassination attempt by a member of his inner circle while going over war plans with his military leaders. They were heading into chaos.

Drydock Number 4, Hunter's Point Shipyard, San Francisco, California
May 1, 1944

The train ride to San Francisco took five long, tedious days. To meet the wartime demand, train companies purged their boneyards of every engine and passenger car that could roll on tracks. A cross-country train ride had servicemen go from one leg in a plush Pullman car to the next in a Civil War-era rattletrap.   In addition to being uncomfortable, traveling servicemen usually occupied every space. They filled every seat, stood in the aisles, and even stretched out in overhead baggage racks.

Civilians tried to help make the ride easier for Eskew and his fellow troops. "Donut Girls" passed out coffee and donuts at train stops. Eskew received homemade pies, cakes, and cookies from the ladies of Council Bluff, Iowa, as his train pulled through that town. Despite all the goodwill, it was still a relief to exit the train in San Francisco after five days of uncomfortable sleeping, no bathing, and being doused with soot from coal-fired steam engines.

According to the Ship's Deck Log, May 1, 1944, was a typical day for the USS Intrepid as it sat in San Francisco's Hunter's Point Shipyard Drydock Number 4. She had been there undergoing repairs since March 22. At 9:40 a.m., Chief Pay Clerk O. A. Carver and Ensign A. N. Diaz inspected 110 gallons of ice cream delivered by the Golden State Company. Later that day, the ship received 511 pounds of asparagus from the Half Moon Fruit and Produce Company, 600 pounds of beets from Giovannoni Brothers, and 507 pounds of avocados and 507 pounds of squash from the American Fruit Company. At 11:35 a.m., Seamen First Class H.C. Hilton and Wilson Cox were transferred to the Treasure Island Naval Hospital for treatment.

Ensign H.C. Small assumed the duty as Officer of the Deck at noon for a four-hour watch. During his shift, 290 sailors reported on board for duty with their bags, hammocks, records, and transfer papers. One of those sailors was Navy Seaman Second Class Eskew Steffens, three-and-a-half months after joining the Navy. As he arrived at the end of the pier, he was in awe, standing in the shadow of the massive ship. He then made his way up the long gangplank. A new ship, the Intrepid was commissioned on August 16, 1943. She was 872 feet long, 147 feet wide, and displaced 27,100 tons. Inside her hull were eight boilers that propelled her through the sea at thirty-three knots. Eskew joined three thousand men to make up the ship's crew, which grew to over 3,300 when ninety to one-hundred planes came on board with their flight crews. She was under the command of Captain William Dodge Sample.

At the end of the gangplank, Eskew stopped, faced aft, and snapped a smart salute at the American flag, then one to Ensign Small. He said, *"Request permission to come aboard."* After reviewing his identification card, the Ensign responded, *"permission granted."* Below his feet, he felt a surge of power from one of the mightiest ships in the greatest Navy in the world.

A shipmate from his new department escorted him to his quarters. It was a small room where every space was filled with sleeping compartments, "racks," and lockers stacked three high from the deck to the overhead. He stowed his gear in a locker and put bedding on his new rack. He next visited the bathroom or "head." It was equipped with showers, sinks, and urinals. Since freshwater was a commodity, salt water flowed in them. The commode was a separate compartment with a twenty-foot-long V-shaped metal trough with seats formed by two planks that Eskew adjusted to fit the width of his bottom. A continuous stream of seawater flowed from one end to the other, flushing refuse out to sea. With his business done, he was ready to explore his new ship.

The ship was like a small city with a maze of passageways and ladder wells, many led to dead ends. Inside the hull of Intrepid were barbers, bakers, butchers, chaplains, shoemakers, plumbers, carpenters, and any other occupation found in a typical American town. It also had a library, mess hall, sickbay (hospital), and a "gedunk" stand (ice cream and candy store) that helped support Eskew's smoking habit by selling cigarettes for five cents a pack. In 1944, nearly all the crew smoked cigarettes. As he roamed a passageway, Eskew heard a bugle blow over the ship's intercom system, called the 1MC or One Main Circuit. Sailors emerged from all compartments and headed in one direction. When he asked one where he was going, the response was "chow time." He followed the sailor to a long line that snaked to a big pile of metal trays. He picked one up and went through a line where sailors piled meat, potatoes, vegetables, bread, and dessert on it. The food was good, Eskew thought, and the bakers made some great bread and dessert.

Eskew quickly learned that the 1MC dictated life on the ship. From reveille waking him up until taps sent him to bed at night, it directed him through every part of his day, including when to work, eat, go on liberty, and how to protect himself and the ship in combat. He also learned that in exchange for his work on Intrepid, she provided back many amenities. Free haircuts were dispensed by four sailors in the barbershop. Dirty laundry was collected in the morning and returned clean in the evening, though it was not folded. Shoemakers repaired shoes, dentists and corpsmen fixed health problems, and chaplains conducted daily services.

An Essex-class carrier, the Intrepid was constructed at Newport News Shipbuilding & Dry Dock Company and commissioned in August. Once battle-ready, she was sent to the Pacific Theater, and by January 1944, she took part in the invasion of Kwajalein in the Marshall Islands. She then immediately participated in raids on the Japanese stronghold island of Truk, located in the middle of Micronesia. On the night of February 17, Intrepid took a torpedo hit from a Japanese G4M aircraft on its starboard quarter fifteen feet below the waterline, flooding several compartments and jamming her rudder hard to port. The damage forced the carrier back to San Francisco for repairs in the shipyard.

With repairs nearly completed toward the end of May, Captain Joseph Francis Bolger assumed command of the ship. On June 3, she passed her sea trials and was certified as fully repaired and ready to return to the fleet. The following day, she tied up at Alameda Naval Air Station and on-loaded spare aircraft, motorized equipment, and miscellaneous cargo for transport to the Pacific theater.

The Intrepid was ready to sail but did not see combat until September. Thus, Eskew got time to adjust to shipboard life while the carrier conducted non-combat operations. On June 9, with Eskew on board, and loaded with troops, trucks, planes, and other critical cargo, Intrepid sailed 2,345 miles to Pearl Harbor, arriving on June 14. Eskew was happy to see Hawaii because the ship had more passengers than beds, so he had to "hot rack," meaning that he had to share his rack with an Army passenger. When Eskew would return to his berthing from watch, his Army bunkmate would vacate the rack, and Eskew would climb between hot clammy sheets--thus the name "hot rack." He looked forward to offloading the human cargo at Pearl Harbor so he could return to full-time ownership of his rack.

As the ship pulled into Pearl Harbor toward Ford Island, she passed the attack's remaining shoreline debris. Tugs eased the ship into a berth that was occupied by one of the doomed battleships on that December day three years prior. The USS Arizona submerged hulk lay visible with the burned and twisted bridge tower and gun turrets protruding above the water. It turned Eskew's stomach to see this watery grave for a mighty battleship and over 1,100 of her crew. The solemnness of the moment intensified at sundown when a lone bugler sounded taps, and the ship's colors were slowly lowered on a dockside mast.

Intrepid offloaded its passengers and cargo. It then reloaded with relief planes and pilots to commence the remainder of its cargo run on June 23 to the Eniwetok Atoll in the Marshall Islands. Escorting Intrepid were the destroyers USS Smalley (DD-565) and USS Leutze (DD-481). After three days in Eniwetok, the Intrepid loaded hundreds of soldiers, sailors, and Marines and headed back to Pearl Harbor on the Fourth of July. Some of the new passengers were wounded in the battle for Saipan and needed hospitalization in the rear, while others were transferred to new duty stations.

After arriving at Pearl Harbor on July 11, Eskew spent the next month learning about sailors' traditions and the benefits of liberty ashore. The Intrepid's crew was given generous liberty to enjoy Honolulu or Waikiki Beach, knowing they would soon spend extensive time in combat.

July 27 was a big day for Eskew and the Intrepid crew. He pressed his dress white "crackerjacks" uniform and made sure it was up to military standards with no spots or fray strands called "Irish pennants." After a successful inspection by his Chief Petty Officer, he was assigned to join fellow crewmates to "line the rails." This tradition is used on special occasions or special port calls where the crew, in dress uniform, stands in formation on deck around the ship's perimeter. The occasion for this ceremony was a visit by President Roosevelt to the base. Another memorable day was August 1, when Eskew stood in formation on the flight deck for promotion to Seaman First Class. He also discovered the importance of cake to sailors. Cakes are used to celebrate important events in the Navy. On August 16, Eskew enjoyed a piece of a massive 300-pound cake made in the ship's bakeshop to celebrate the first anniversary of Intrepid's commissioning. It also signified the end of a brief breather in Hawaii.

Eskew learned that "old salts" liked to play jokes on new sailors. So, he and the other junior sailors were sent to the engineering department to requisition nonexistent "left-handed smoke shifters" and "skyhooks" and stood duty as a lookout for the mythical "mail buoy" in the middle of the Pacific Ocean.

Each day Eskew had off-duty time, he would keep his promise to Roseann to write her a letter. He also looked forward to mail call because she also kept that same promise. They shared their experiences via pen and paper, which drew them more intimate with each other. Each Sunday, Roseann visited with Eskew's mother, Blanche, and his sisters. They grew fond of each other, and she grew especially close to Eskew's older sister, Margaret. Eskew received letters from his family, sharing the wonderful times that they were having with Roseann. Then one day, he penned a letter asking her to marry him. A few weeks later came her response, "yes," and they were engaged.

Once the crew finished eating cake, the Intrepid, with the planes of Air Group Eighteen, the carriers Independence and Enterprise, and four destroyers, sailed 4,000 miles in six days to Eniwetok. There it conducted training exercises, including gunnery practice.

Camp Kilmer, New Jersey
July 22, 1944

On Saturday evening, as darkness set in, the men of the 267th shouldered their gear and departed Camp Kilmer for the docks. Troops were transported at night, but if they had to during the day, they did so with curtains covering all the windows. This was to prevent German spies from identifying troop movements. They boarded the ferry, S.S. NY 22, for a ride down the Raritan River, along the coast of Staten Island, into New York Harbor, and up the Hudson River to a pier at the west end of 48th Street. As the ferry closed on the pier, Charles and his fellow soldiers saw a great ship under the dock's floodlights. The hulking gray vessel was the S.S. Queen Mary or S.S. 490, which was her wartime designation. She was also known as the "Gray Ghost" for her wartime paint job and the speed she sailed.

The men applauded when they saw the massive ship because they knew the trip to England would take only a week. A smaller ship, such as the Liberty ship that Carmen sailed on, traveled in a slow-moving convoy, escorted by warships, and took at least two weeks. German submarines could not target the large ocean liners like the Queen Mary because they were too fast for the slower subs.

The Queen Mary was built for Cunard Lines at the John Brown & Co. shipyard in Clydebank, Scotland, between 1930 and 1936. She was 1,019.5 feet in length with a 118-foot beam. Her sixteen geared turbines and quadruple propellers moved her at a breakneck cruising speed of 28.5 knots. In addition to speed, the ship's prewar luxury and advanced technology made her popular with British Royalty, Hollywood celebrities, and dignitaries. They enjoyed the fine living the ship offered as she plied the Middle and the Far East seas.

In 1940, when all of Europe, North Africa, and Asia plunged into war, the Queen Mary's role as a passenger ocean liner seemed over. However, her record-breaking speed and size caught the eye of war planners, and she was retrofitted to serve as a troopship.

Charles disembarked the ferry and stared down Pier 88, and even though it was nightfall, there was a world of activity. A band played, "Praise the Lord and Pass the Ammunition" as Red Cross donut girls distributed hot coffee and snacks. With his arms full of the gear that would sustain him in battle, including his huge duffel bag, a field bag, cartridge belt, bayonet, canteen, gas mask, and M-1 rifle, Charles struggled up the long, steep, and narrow gangplank into the belly of the massive ship.

Hilary St. George Saunders described life on the Queen Mary in an article published in the July 9, 1945, edition of Life Magazine. He described the experience for Charles and thousands of other GIs who rode the Queen Mary to war:

> *"At the dark entrance stands a white helmeted M.P. 'Keep goin' soldier!' he will say, and those three words will ring in your ears like the refrain of a litany throughout the trip, varied on occasion by the sharp command, 'Put out that cigarette!' In your hand is a blue card and, once inside, you will find yourself in a long alleyway with a staircase on the far end. It smells hot and stuffy, but you bump your way down it til you reach the stairway and then climb up or down. Here and there you will catch a glimpse of a steward in a white coat or a British seaman in dark blue trousers and a polo-necked pullover...."*

Charles and his fellow artillerymen navigated through the maze of passageways and ladder wells until they arrived at their staterooms. In peacetime, the small cabin would have slept four. For this voyage, the furniture was removed and replaced with "standees," which were stretcher-like aluminum and canvas beds stacked in tiers from two to six high. They fold up against the bulkhead or each other when not used, allowing this small space to berth eighteen soldiers. Charles studied his standee to determine how he would sleep because there were less than two feet of open space from the bottom of his rack to the bottom of the rack above him. Then he planned the acrobatic maneuvering it would take to climb in and out of his rack. Charles stowed his gear and found the nearest head, only to find more soldiers quartered in the bathroom. In fact, any space which could be used to house troops, including the grand saloons and dining rooms, was full of occupied standees. Charles was told to find his rack and remain in his quarters for the night. That was fine with him as it had been a long day, and it felt good to have a rack to finally settle into a night's sleep.

He awoke the next morning after a sound sleep to his sergeant setting shifts to use the nearby head, which could only accommodate a few soldiers at a time. As he was going toward the head, his sergeant reminded him to wear his lifebelt that contained his life jacket and survival gear if he went into the water. Military Police (MP's) wandered the passageways looking for soldiers who made the mistake of leaving their cabins without their belts. Charles found that freshwater was a precious commodity on board the Queen. Warm salt water and soap that did not lather were abundant, so after a saltwater shave, he returned to his cabin to hear a horn give a long blast, then he felt a shudder of the deck below his feet. He looked at his watch; it was 7:00 a.m., and he was heading out on the Invisible Highway toward Europe.

The Queen Mary sailed down New York Harbor with all passing vessels blowing their whistles to honor the ship and her passengers. She then sailed through the submarine nets and toward open seas. The air and ship escort followed until she was offshore; then, she set her engines to full speed ahead and left them in her wake as her speed made it safer for her to sail unescorted through enemy submarine infested waters.

The Queen Mary began her 38th round-trip wartime cruise designated WW #38E. She sailed under the command of Captain Bisset from New York City to Gourock, Scotland, traveling 3,315 miles at an average speed of 28.02 knots. The crossing took four days, twenty-two hours, and eighteen minutes. On board were 1,130 crew and 12,009 troops, including Second Lieutenant John Doud Eisenhower, the son of General Dwight D. Eisenhower.

Charles looked at the card issued to him. Each soldier was given a red, white, or blue card that listed his sleeping quarters, the areas of the ship he was authorized to enter, and the location and time to eat his two meals a day. The ship could only serve its 12,000 soldiers breakfast and dinner. To serve three meals was physically impossible. He brought his mess kit to the dining room just as his sergeant instructed. After standing in a long line, the mess crew served him a choice of boiled or baked eggs, sloppy meats--usually sausage--and bitter coffee that made him realize why the British drink tea. The food was not appetizing, but it quelled his hunger. With a full mess kit in hand, he had to wait until someone rose from a table. Noncommissioned Officers ensured that

Charles ate quickly and turned his seat over to other waiting soldiers. Once he rose, he washed his mess kit in warm salt water at a washing station near the exit and stowed it until the next meal. Such would be his routine for each meal while at sea.

After breakfast, all passengers and crew participated in a series of drills that included General Quarters, abandon ship, man overboard, and lifeboat and life raft handling. These drills were repeated at different times each day, including after dark.

Though on different oceans, Charles and Eskew had something in common: hot racking. Because the Queen Mary had room for 8,000 standees and 12,000 passengers, the lower rank soldiers, like Charles, shared their rack. So, for twelve hours each day, he had to find a place to occupy himself while another soldier utilized his standee. Charles roamed his designated area of the great liner, trying to imagine what it was like to sail on it before the war. Wartime configuration made it difficult because standees occupied every space except for the passageways, two lounges, and two dining rooms retained for feeding soldiers and providing some area for recreation. The great swimming pools were also converted into dining rooms.

The squash courts were turned into ship's stores and stocked with English biscuits and ginger beer. Charles thought he would pick up some snacks to hold him over between his breakfasts and dinners, but when he got to the store, he realized that most of the 6,000 soldiers who were awake had the same idea. Torn between the thought of, "*Why wait in line with hundreds of soldiers in front of me?*" or, "*Do it because I have nothing else to do,*" Charles stood in the line for hours only to be told the store ran out of its allotment of items to be sold that day.

During his four days at sea, there was little Charles had to do outside of eating meals, sleeping, and participating in drills. Movies were shown in troop quarters. USO and talent shows occurred at various times, and nonstop card and dice games were found in most compartments. The public-address system was very active, with prayers from the Chaplains, updates from superior officers, and the day's news read at noon. Nevertheless, interspersed between all these activities were long periods of boredom.

Outside, the ship steamed east, but not in a straight line. Every so often, the helmsman jolted the ship toward the starboard or port side. The crew explained to their "landlubber" passengers that the course was changed every few minutes to zigzag so that an enemy submarine could not lie in wait ahead of them. Occasionally, a false alarm would send gun crews manning their stations. Like her earlier voyages, the Queen Mary did not encounter any enemy vessels. Of course, the Army was not immune from that naval tradition called "scuttlebutt," where rumors of U-boat sightings traveled throughout the ship.

After four days of calm seas, a rarity for the North Atlantic, the great ship reached the straits between Ireland and Great Britain, where an oil film, placed on the water, marked a safe course for the ship to transit a minefield. She reached the River Clyde and eased her way upriver. Soldiers poured out onto the decks to get their first glimpses of Scotland. They could see rolling green hills, colorful foliage, and cottages dotting the landscape. Once inside the harbor, the Queen Mary was surrounded by vessels of all types. Other passenger liners in wartime configuration lined the harbor, along with hospital ships, submarines, aircraft carriers, cruisers, and destroyers. The ship made her way into a berth and tied up. Charles was happy to disembark and put his feet back on solid land even though he had just entered the war's European Theater.

Chapter 8
The Second World War and the American Offensive

Greenock Scotland, United Kingdom
July 30, 1944

As Charles walked down the Queen Mary's gangplank, he and his fellow GIs were greeted with the sound of bagpipes from Scots dressed in military regalia. Families waved to the Americans streaming off the ship onto foreign-looking British railway cars. The train differed from any Charles had ridden in the U.S. Each car was divided into several compartments, each with two facing seats. Unlike American trains, the corridor was on the side of the car instead of the middle.

As Charles settled in a seat, he was mixed with emotion, looking out at his first-ever foreign country, and mentally digesting his secrecy indoctrination lecture, "Dangers of the Theater of War." The foreignness of the land set in as the train rolled to their assigned training area 500 miles away, nearly across the entire British Isle. He marveled at the neatly kept countryside containing miles of stone fences and little stone cottages with thatched roofs that he only saw in movies. Instead of coffee and donuts, tea and scones served at each stop reinforced that he was not in America.

The next morning, Sunday, July 30, 1944, the train rolled into Bude, Cornwall, located in England's most southwestern region. Members of the Battalion's advanced party greeted them at the station platform; they had been in-country for three months.

They shared a story with Charles and the others about how General Patton assumed command of the Third Army and addressed his men in England two days prior. The men said:

> *"With his troops assembled, the General exited his long black car, shining resplendently in the bright sun. He was impeccably dressed in high boots, a shiny helmet, and pearl-handled revolvers hanging from his hips. He inspected the honor guard, eyeballing them up and down, then staring intently into their faces, and then mounted a platform to address the troops that he*

would soon take into combat. As he marched to the microphone, the men snapped to their feet and stood silently. General Patton surveyed them grimly then said, "Be seated." This was not a request but a command. The General's voice rose high and clear:

"Men, this stuff we hear about America wanting to stay out of the war, not wanting to fight, is a lot of bull... Americans love to fight—traditionally. All real Americans love the sting and clash of battle. When you were kids you all admired the champion marble player, the fastest runner, the big league ball players, the toughest boxers. Americans play to win—all the time. I wouldn't give a hoot in hell for a man who lost and laughed. That's why Americans have never lost, nor ever will lose a war, for the very thought of losing is hateful to an American...."

Charles knew there was no tougher general than George Patton. Knowing he would be under his command was reassuring yet troubling at the same time.

Bude is Cornwall's most northern town and was usually a quaint English seaside village. Its long sandy beach, pounded by the fury of the open Atlantic Ocean, catered to Britons from various classes "on holiday." Bude was a popular seaside resort for the aristocracy during Victorian times. In 1898, a railroad was built to connect it to Britain's cities. It then caught on with the middle class, who were discovering the attraction of "sea bathing." In the decade before the war, the town built the Bude Sea Pool to provide a safe swimming environment for its vacationers. This semi-natural pool, measuring 298 feet long by 147 feet wide, was created under the curve of the cliffs on the shoreline. It gave holiday-goers the experience of being in the sea, close to the Atlantic Ocean's ferocity but sheltered from its pounding waves.

During the months just before and after D-Day, the entire British island was honeycombed with temporary bases filled with Allied troops and supplies--Bude was no exception. As the train rolled into the station, it passed dozens of temporary camps housing troops in endless rows of bell tents. Charles also saw vast quantities of tanks, vehicles, artillery, supplies, and other military equipment stored in the woods and camouflaged by the treetops against spying German planes. What stood out were the tons of ammunition stored anywhere it could be stacked and hidden from aerial view.

Above his head was the constant drone of aircraft engines. Eight operational air forces operated out of the area, and an anti-aircraft training camp was continually firing.

Charles was happy when he was marched past the rows of tents to a beautiful stone three-story house with a porch on each level and surrounded by a decorative rock fence. When he came alongside it, Sergeant Potter barked out for him to bivouac there. The villa was a stone's throw from the unit's portable kitchen and within walking distance to the beach.

The day after the unit arrived in Bude, Major Collins assembled the troops to update them on the war and their part in it. He first shared that enough of the Third Army had arrived in France to make it operational effective noon that day. He informed the men that General Patton would immediately commence combat operations. He added that the 267th had also received a message alerting it for movement into France to commence combat operations. War was becoming more of a reality for Charles.

It would take two weeks before the rest of the world caught up to Charles's information about General Patton. Not until August 15 did the Allied Supreme Headquarters officially announce for worldwide dissemination that the Third Army was operational on the Continent under the command of Lieutenant General George S. Patton, Jr. The revelation that George Patton was on his way struck fear in the German generals.

With that news, the 267th would spend the entire month of August in Bude, preparing for its crossing of the English Channel and entry into the war. Since its troops shipped out of New York with only their personal equipment, the Battalion had to be re-equipped with its guns, vehicles, and equipment and then fit into the continuous stream of men and supplies moving from Britain to France. Because the 267th was attached to XII Corps, these tasks fell to the XII Corps Headquarters' staff 200 miles away in Camp Bewdley outside Kidderminster. Previously established "Buildup Priority Tables" dictated how and when units moved into France. With tons of supplies and thousands of troops scattered across the entire island, planners lost track of units and/or their materials. Timelines slipped. Units unprepared to deploy were held back, and others were sent quicker than initially planned. With their need for specialized equipment and ammunition, artillery units were some of the Headquarters' personnel's biggest challenges.

A primary task of the 267th Advance Party was coordinating with Headquarters to locate and route all the Battalion's artillery, trucks, and other equipment to Bude before the Main Body arrived. It was no easy feat because, at the same time, sixty-one other Third Army units scattered across the United Kingdom were also trying to repatriate their equipment. Adding to the frantic pace to locate and arrange shipment was scuttlebutt about how earlier in the month, three artillery battalions awaiting their weapons in the United Kingdom were reassigned to POW escort and infantry duty. The Advanced Party was determined not to allow this fate to fall upon the 267th.

Track equipment used to tow the 155mm, five-inch howitzer, eight-inch gun, and 240mm howitzers were unloaded at Liverpool, Manchester, and Glasgow, often as much as 300 miles from the parent unit's station. These vehicles could not move long distances on hard surface roads because they would cause excessive wear of their tracks and undercarriage. The Third Army Transportation Corps moved some smaller equipment by train; however, most of these vehicles and guns were too high and wide for rail movement. Two ordnance evacuation battalions equipped with tank transporters moved the equipment to units, including the 267th, via one of the Ordnance Depots scattered across England. The Advanced Party staff successfully had all the gear waiting in Bude when the Main Body arrived.

After Major Collins' update, the artillerymen marched to a field containing their vehicles, guns, and equipment, along with the smiling faces of the Advance Party members who received a pat on the back for not making the 267th a tempting target for reassignment. The artillerymen's downside to finding their weapons came when they were issued solvents and rags to scrub away the thick sticky grease called

"Cosmoline" that protected the artillery equipment during transit. Charles called it *"a real sticky mess."*

Artillery ranges were established in Wales and southern England, including the Bude, Cornwall, area. The troops of the 267th spent the next few weeks in training, firing their guns, and preparing them for use against the enemy. Particular emphasis was placed on coordinating fire on targets by multiple battalions with different caliber cannons. They fired their cannons from cliffs at targets six to twelve miles out in the Atlantic Ocean. This was the only time Charles got to see his shells land as they splashed and exploded in the sea. At the same time, mechanics equipped the motors of trucks and other vehicles with air-breathing "snorkels" to travel in three to four feet of water if necessary while disembarking from the ships.

Despite long workdays and a 10:30 p.m. curfew, Charles and his fellow GIs also found time to enjoy the beautiful landscape and friendly inhabitants. When not working, liberal liberty was granted, giving troops time to enjoy the seaside or countryside. Locals were grateful for troops protecting their homeland and opened their houses for dinner and companionship. GIs learned the nuances of driving on the left side of the road to move gear or head to their favorite local pub. Charles loved the ocean and spent most of his time at the Bude Sea Pool, where he swam and mingled with the locals. He also loved baseball and the "double British summer time," where the sun did not set until after midnight, allowing them to play softball into the wee hours of the morning.

Disappointment fell on Charles and the GIs when the order came to ship out to Weymouth for transport to France. But after a month, the 267th was certified as battle-ready and slated to go to war.

Left: House where Charles was quartered and Right: liberty time at the Bude Pool in Bude Cornwell, August 1944

On August 28, the 267th, with all its gear loaded, set out on a sixteen-day trek that would land it on the front lines in combat against the German Wehrmacht. The first leg was a four-day convoy to Weymouth for transit across the English Channel. Just shy of three months from D-Day, England's roads remained congested with troops and supplies moving to English seaports. The approximately 119-mile transit over congested highways was slow-going. Though the weather was fair and roads passable, the 267th moved only thirty-two miles on day one, bivouacking one mile west of Okehampton. The convoy covered another thirty-eight miles the next day, putting in at Honiton, Devonshire, for the second night. Forty-three miles were covered on day three, taking it to a concentration area outside Piddlehinton. On August 31, the 267th traveled 6 miles to the port of Weymouth. The weather was cold and rainy.

Weymouth has a rich seagoing history that dates to the earliest settlers on the British Isles. It also played a crucial role in the war up to this point. Charles's convoy rolled into a town heavily bombed by the Luftwaffe during the "Blitz" of 1940 and 1941, then periodically after. The last bombing raid occurred on May 28, 1944, nine days before the D-Day Operation. Over nineteen bombs fell on the town, damaging the hospital, severely damaging 100 houses, and causing slight damage to another 300. Four people were killed, including three members of the Civil Defense Rescue Service.

Being 84 miles from Cherbourg, France, Weymouth's harbor served as a major jumping-off point for military operations. In 1940, many of its inhabitants took to their small boats to evacuate the British Expeditionary Force from Dunkirk. Throughout the war, the harbor received numerous refugees escaping Nazi-occupied Europe. Three months earlier, legions of British and American soldiers left England's shores from Weymouth to participate in the D-Day landings in Normandy.

Charles looked out over the harbor. It was full of every amphibious craft the Navy had in its inventory. Rows of LCTs (Landing Crafts, Tank), LCs (Landing Crafts), LSTs (Landing Ships, Tank), and other various types of troop and material transport vessels filled the harbor. Charles was taken aback by how rusted and worn the crafts looked. The vessels and their crews ran continuous operations to France since D-Day, and the wear was clearly visible.

On D-Day, the amphibious Navy in England ferried 130,000 troops and vast quantities of tanks, vehicles, artillery, supplies, and equipment to Normandy's beaches. Since the invasion, the fleet transported 11,000 tons of supplies and a steady stream of troops each day across the rough and unpredictable waters of the English Channel. Once all the cargo was offloaded, they would return with wounded Allied troops and Axis Prisoners of War.

On the way toward the harbor, Charles and his fellow soldiers stopped at an American Red Cross tent adjacent to Greenhill Gardens, where smiling American and British volunteers served them coffee and donuts. A sign on the tent read: *From the folks back home through the American Red Cross.* As they marched toward the pier, Charles noticed an insignia on the ramp of an LST that read '357' and pictured a stork carrying a baby with the words *"We Deliver." "Funny sailors,"* he thought.

The harbor was full of activity, with hundreds of amphibious craft being loaded with supplies, traversing the harbor, being serviced, or making other preparations for their next runs. Overhead were hundreds of barrage balloons, which were small blimp-shaped balloons tethered with metal cables that defended against attacking enemy aircraft. The metal cables made the attacking fighter craft's approach more difficult or even destroyed it upon collision. British and American soldiers stood guard all along the harbor, and members of Britain's Coastal Defense manned antiaircraft guns.

Major Collins marched the Battalion to the piers with waiting amphibious crafts moored to them. The Major and his Headquarters Company boarded the LST B1365, which is much larger than the LCTs. The LST displaced 1,780 tons and had huge doors in its bow that opened to drop a ramp in shallow water at a beach so tanks and other vehicles could drive off under their own power. The smaller LCT only displaced 284 tons. Charles and the other Second Gun Section members were directed to board LCT 594.

In 1940, U.S. war planners were greatly concerned that the country had no amphibious vessels as they watched Britain evacuate its troops from Dunkirk. The British--who also lacked large ocean-going amphibious craft--left vast quantities of tanks, vehicles, and supplies behind because they did not have an expeditious way to extract them from the beach. While the evacuation from Dunkirk saved 330,000 men from capture, the British Army was left virtually devoid of tanks, artillery, and mobile equipment. These concerns led the Navy to develop the LCT Mark 5 in early 1942, a 117-foot craft that could accommodate five thirty-ton tanks or 150 tons of cargo. LCT 594 was a Mark 6-- a later version of the Mark 5.

A flat bottom vessel, she was 119 feet in length with a 32-foot beam. She displaced 284 tons and could carry 150 tons of men or supplies. With a crew of twelve, her three diesel engines generated 225 horsepower that lumbered her through the water at a very slow speed of seven knots. She had two 20mm antiaircraft guns and four 50 caliber machine guns for protection.

LCT 594 was built by the Pidgeon-Thomas Iron Company in Memphis, TN, and her keel was laid on September 24, 1943. Thirty-two days later, she was launched and, on October 30, delivered to the Navy. On D-Day, she was part of the first wave on Utah Beach. Under a withering fusillade, she delivered Company A of the 70th Tank Battalion onto the Green Beach sector of the landing.

K. L. Dixon, the Officer in Charge of the vessel, directed his sailors to assist the green soldiers onto their craft. D. I. Eidemiller, the Assistant Officer in Charge, directed the loading operations. Once all the troops were loaded, the artillery and movers secured, and the barrage balloons tethered, LCT 594 moved out of the harbor to rendezvous with the other vessels. As the fleet set out, a storm blew into the Channel. Charles's LCT and the larger LSTs continued onto France while most of the LCTs behind him turned back to Weymouth to wait out the storm. The LCT had a flat bottom and an open well that held the troops and their equipment; both were not ideal for a vicious storm. The troops took shelter wherever it could be found and fought seasickness.

Charles Asztalos and artillerymen on an LCT in Weymouth Harbor and crossing the Channel, September 1, 1944

In the darkness of night, LCT 594 completed its ninety-mile voyage when it anchored in the safety of the artificial harbor created by the Allies at Utah Beach. Because the Navy had a policy that it did not offload vessels after 10:00 p.m., the troops of the 267th hunkered down for some sleep wherever they could find a comfortable spot, which included atop camouflage nets, piles of gear, and inside or around their vehicles.

When the sun rose, LCT 594 weighed anchor to deliver its cargo onto Utah Beach. The beach was a buzz of activity with loading and unloading vessels and was covered with all types of vehicles and staged supplies. U.S. and British Navy Beachmasters somehow choreographed all this activity. The Beachmasters directed the LCT onto a narrow strip of unoccupied beach. Despite heavy surf from the swirling offshore storm, the sailors ran the LCT aground at the right spot. Once secured to the beach, the front ramp went down, and Battery C personnel and gear went ashore.

As they set foot on the beach, Charles and his fellow soldiers looked at their boots, touching the same sand and water that ran blood-red from the 4,400 D-Day allied casualties less than three months prior. They could all feel that they were standing on hallow ground.

Charles and the Second Gun Section marveled at Utah Beach's destruction from the intense battle. In the surf were hulks of ships sunk by aerial bombardment. The beach's perimeter was ringed with demolished German pillboxes and gun emplacements. Large craters caused by intense naval bombardment were everywhere. They also saw their first hostile German. Utah Beach was still subject to an occasional ME-109 Luftwaffe fighter that dodged the barrage balloons in quest of an Allied vehicle to strafe.

MPs directed the Second Gun Section and other members of the 267th onto waiting trucks for a nine-mile convoy over narrow, dust-choked roads to Assembly Area B at the U.S. Third Army Assembly Area near Sainte-Mère-Église. Charles remembered how he and the other artillerymen had seen this as the scene of fighting in newsreels at home. Upon arrival at Assembly Area B, the troops were greeted by a huge billboard, like the ones that advertised products along the roads back in the U.S. On the billboard, printed in large letters was the following:

"This is Third Army Area

Fine for not wearing helmet $25.00
Fine for not carrying gas mask $25.00
Fine for not saluting officer $40.00

-By Command of Gen. George S. Patton, Jr."

As the 267th transited from Weymouth to Utah Beach, two significant events occurred that directly impacted the Battalion. First, the Third Army suffered the first of what would become a chronic problem: gasoline shortages. As its supply points were dry and unit loads were disappearing fast, the Twelfth U.S. Army Group notified it on August 30 that no gasoline would be available in appreciable amounts until September 3. This shortage gripped the entire Third Army by restricting vehicular movement in most areas and completely immobilizing all field artillery units. Secondly, an Army directive dated September 2, 1944, ordered XV Corps to an assembly area in preparation to seize a line of the Moselle River and then advance northeast to seize Karlsruhe, Germany, and secure a bridgehead across the Rhine River. The XV Corps consisted of the 79th Infantry Division, 83rd Infantry Division, 2nd French Armored Division, and supporting troops.

At Assembly Area B, the rear echelon members of XII Corps mapped out the Battalion's next moves once all its troops arrived. Major Collins was directed to take the 267th to Sens, France. Once there, it would receive orders attaching it to the 410th Field Artillery Group. The Battalion would join the 177th, 182nd, 183rd, and 404th Field Artillery Groups and the 176th, 191st, 253rd, 255th, 512th, 558th, 696th, 738th, 752nd, 775th, and 974th Field Artillery Battalions that were supporting that Corps assault on the Wehrmacht in northern France. Those units all had either 105 or 155 howitzers. The 267th would be the first unit to provide XII Corps with the powerful 240mm guns. XII Corps was currently liberating Joinville as it raced across France, or as General Patton liked to say, conducting "reverse blitzkrieg." In front of it lie the towns of Toul, Pont-à-Mousson, and Nancy.

On Monday, September 4, the remainder of the 267th and another 240mm howitzer battalion arrived on Utah Beach. Also, the Third Army finally received much-needed gasoline allowing it to resume its advance to the east toward the heavily fortified cities of Metz and Nancy in Alsace-Lorraine, and the 267th to convoy toward combat. Sergeant Potter notified the Gun Section that they were moving out the next morning.

With fair weather and the convoy loaded, the 267th began its next leg of the journey toward the frontlines. Charles was struck by the damage he saw in this recently liberated area. Hundreds of destroyed vehicles lined the roads, and dead cattle and horses littered adjoining fields. The smell of death was overpowering. Though this area was considered "the rear," it was still dangerous. Everywhere along the road were signs warning that mines were cleared to the shoulder of the road. Ordinance was everywhere. At one stop, Charles saw live German grenades in a ditch. Another sight that made Charles and his fellow artillerymen pause was the stream of convoys headed in the opposite direction. They were filled with gaunt, filthy, and glazed-eyed troops, coming off the frontlines for some rest and relaxation. They asked each other, *"Will that be us in a few weeks?"*

After driving 101 miles, the convoy stopped to bivouac for the night near Saint-Mars-d'Égrenne. To their pleasant surprise, local farmers, grateful for their liberators, approached the bivouacked soldiers with fresh milk, eggs, and bread. They even slipped in some Calvados, a locally-produced apple brandy. After a solid week of eating military B- and C-rations, the fresh food was much appreciated.

The 267th Field Artillery Battalion convoy stops for chow somewhere in France.

PFC Iozzio in India

Karachi, British India
August 15, 1944

Tuesday was another hot, humid day, punctuated by afternoon thunderstorms rolling off the Indian Ocean. Damage was everywhere from the cyclone that pummeled the area a little over two weeks prior, leaving 10,000 Indians homeless. PFC Carmen Iozzio wiped the sweat off his brow as he lugged his duffle bag and all other worldly possessions into the office of his new assignment. Two days ago, he received orders attaching him to the 185th Quartermaster Company (Depot Supply) to work as an automotive mechanic.

The 185th was created on February 20, 1942, at Camp Shelby, Mississippi, from soldiers drawn from Company D of the 118th Quartermaster Regiment. The Company completed three months of training as a Depot Supply unit, including a course in practical training in the Quartermaster Warehouse.

Exactly three months after its creation, the 185th left Camp Shelby, arriving at the Overseas Discharge and Replacement Depot, Charleston Port of Embarkation in Charleston, SC. On May 22, the Company boarded the SS Mariposa for a 53-day voyage to Karachi, with port calls in Freetown, Sierra Leone, and Cape Town, South Africa. Upon arrival in British India, the Company was assigned to duty in the Headquarters and Quartermaster Sections of General Depot #1. The Company set up shop and took responsibility for offloading supplies from U.S. ships and arranging their transportation across India to Burma and China.

Carmen's initial assignment to the base's Headquarters Company provided him with off-duty time to experience Karachi. Neither his CCC assignments in the forests and swamps nor his time in Oran could prepare him for India. In a booklet provided to him called "Guide to Karachi – A Service to a New-Comer!" the Army called Karachi the "*Paris of India*" and the "*Gateway of India*." For Carmen, it was a land that challenged all his senses. Most sections of town assaulted his nostrils with every imaginable odor, most being unpleasant. India lacked sanitation and hygiene. Upper-class Indians burned their dead and threw the ashes into the holy river. Deceased members of lower-class families, too poor to buy wood for a funeral bonfire, were just tossed into the river. This left a rancid stench hovering over the river and streams where others washed their clothes and bathed. Putrid smoke from cooking fires also hung in the air. Cows are sacred in Hindu areas and roamed the streets at will. Their manure was everywhere. Women picked up the fresh droppings with their bare hands, formed them into patties, then placed them in a container on their heads to bring home. The manure patties were then patted onto the sides of their bamboo huts, dried, and used as fuel for cooking and heat, a flammable but foul-smelling fuel.

His other senses were also overwhelmed from a continuous stream of lepers, beggars, and children yelling out American expressions such as "*OK*" and "*What's cookin'?*" all seeking some of Carmen's monthly pay. Add in magicians and con artists looking to lure him over with bizarre performances. Everywhere he heard bells. Karachi city was permeated with the warning jangling of bells on the camels that darted down streets pulling carts with their splayfeet that plopped on the ground. Finally, there was the constant sound from the crush of people bartering in the markets and communicating with one another. Like Oran, Karachi was primarily occupied by Muslims. Thus, everything ground to a halt five times a day while prayer rugs were rolled out, and the devout would face Mecca to pray.

Despite the foreign culture, Carmen found the locals friendly, courteous and enthralled by his American humor. He was treated with great hospitality when invited into their private homes as families joyfully shared their modest possessions. His interactions with the locals were written up in the following article printed in Paterson's newspaper, the Morning Call on March 24, 1945.

"In Far Off India Paterson Dyer, Finds Natives Interesting; They are Being Educated in Americanese

"Strange bits of Americana transplant themselves to far-off India, a former Paterson dye worker wrote his union mates back home. Private Carmen Iozzio, now stationed with the Army Quartermaster Corps in India, found to his surprise that the quaint American slang and even choice non-King's English, has been absorbed by India's native tots. In addition, cigarettes appear almost as urgent for native adults as they do for Americans, Iozzio reported, while children will beg for anything including empty ration cans and boxes.

"Iozzio wrote his observations to Dyers' Local 1733 of Paterson to which he belonged while working in the Royal division of the Associated Dye and Print Company. "One of the main GI expressions is "Hubba Hubba" and to say that it rates with "Baksheesh Sahib" well proves its popularity." Iozzio wrote. "I know of one character who recently had occasion to ride in a gharry (comparable to an English Victorian chariot, horsedrawn). After painful tutoring on the GI's part, the driver was able to stand, slap his hossie and sing out "Hi, Ho, Silver!" Guess you might call that progressive education.

"It is a common practice, Iozzio reported, for Indians to mix ancient and modern customs in their dress and rituals, as well as racial stock. "This is especially true of the Anglo-Indians, those of mixed English and Indian blood. Others have Portuguese, Spanish and Middle East strains, and the result is some mighty pretty girls. "I know of a fellow who was recently riding one of the local versions of trains and happened to get into a conversation with two apparently white girls. One offered

the fact she was born in England, so the soldier asked the other if she were also English-born. "No" she replied "I'm a Bitsa." A bit puzzled, he asked explanation. "Oh" she replied "just a bitsa this and bitsa that."

"The potency of Indian brews made a sharp impression on young Iozzio. "I have learned time and again to abstain from Indian "potions." he wrote. "including the camouflaged arsenic that's passed off as gin. I know two characters who partook of this gin one night then retired to their trundle beds. By sheer coincidence both felt the light touch of an Indian woman awakening them from their slumbers then both thought they heard angels fluttering about their tent. One "saw" the Indian woman sitting atop the tentpole therefore climbed up and broke the whole damned tent down. The pair went out of the tent like mad and refused to return. After a lapse of time they compromised and re-entered their tent but refused to sleep in their beds. Instead they slept on the floor under piles of their clothing and their mattresses. They awoke in the morning to find they had evaded the seraphic influence. After seeing that I have taken the pledge--almost."

In addition to occasional trips into Karachi, the Army provided Carmen, and his fellow soldiers organized activities to fill his off-duty time. He and his fellow GIs visited the beautiful sandy beach at Hawke's Bay for swimming and sun. Hawke's Bay is located about twelve and one-half miles southwest of Karachi. This beach is named after Bladen Wilmer Hawke, who owned a beach house there in the 1930s. On base were weekly movie nights, inter-league baseball games at Mosolium Field, and semi-monthly dances with Polish refugees whose settlement camp was adjacent to Carmen's base.

After the Soviet Union invaded eastern Poland in 1939, it exiled many Poles to prison camps in Siberia. As the war dragged on, Soviet authorities expelled these exiles, who then traveled through Siberia, Iran, and finally to Karachi, where the British Army established two camps for them. Between August 1942 and December 1944, 28,000 Polish refugees were housed in the camps. Approximately 7,000 lived in the camp near Carmen. The camps were the antithesis of Siberian gulags. They were well-run and provided the refugees with schools, canteens, medical facilities, theatres, an orchestra, post office, churches, and organized sports. Carmen and the other GIs would make joint trips to Hawke's Bay with the Polish occupants. Dances for the soldiers and Polish ladies were frequently held at the refugee camp and the U.S. depot. Both groups enjoyed each other's company as described in the 185th Unit Journal on June 27, 1944:

> *"Sunday was night of Organization big second anniversary dinner-dance. 40 polish refugees gave us a 'gal for every man and oodles of fun all around.' Monday some of the men attended a dance at the refugee camp and Tuesday was movie night. 'Made for 3 busy nights in a row.' A swim to Hawks Bay, brought out a truck load of Polish refugees."*

While Carmen was granted liberty to experience the Indian civilization, most of his time was spent supporting the mission to drive the Imperial Japanese Army off the Asian continent. By this time, the Allies were steadily pushing the Japanese from Burma, planes were regularly flying supplies over "the Hump," and an overland route to Chinese forces had been established. His mechanical skills were needed to keep the trucks rolling across those dangerous roads, delivering to Generalissimo Chiang Kai-shek the supplies his army needed to defeat the Japanese. Since arriving in India, Carmen worked in the Depot's Motor Transportation area, keeping the overused trucks running.

Upon receiving his orders, Carmen fully expected to move across the depot into the 185th's Motor Transportation Section, where he would continue to work on the trucks. However, the Company's new Commanding Officer, Lt. John J Buckley, had other plans for PFC Iozzio.

As men and supplies poured into India, the demand for more replacement depots grew. By the end of 1943, in addition to the original one at Malir, depots were established in Camp Angus (No. 2) and Camp Kancheapara (No. 3) to support supplies entering Calcutta.

On January 1, 1944, India's third port in Bombay officially opened to U.S. traffic. Up until this time, it was primarily used by the British Army. Initially, U.S. forces relied on British staging areas to move troops and supplies. They met delays in unloading troops and equipment because of a lack of rolling stock and poor timing of trains. A month after operations began, war planners decided to build a U.S.-run replacement depot at Lake Beale, a main trans-India railway connection 125 miles north of Bombay. Construction began in May and was completed in July. Replacement Depot No. 4 officially opened on June 1. Twenty officers and fifty men were initially stationed there, but the Army needed another two hundred. The 185th was tasked to supply forty-seven enlisted men. Nine left for Lake Beale on July 28, and another fifteen followed on August 1. Lt. Buckley selected PFC Iozzio to be one of those transferred in the final group of twenty-three.

On August 23, PFC Iozzio and twenty-two other enlisted personnel from his new unit embarked on an 802-mile journey to Replacement Depot #4, heading first down the coast to Bombay and then east to Lake Beale. The ride from Bombay was through desolate land with inhabitants living in small farming villages. The depot was just as desolate. It sat next to a beautiful lake along rail lines. But it was far removed from any urban areas. Though newly constructed, the buildings were crudely built for temporary use. Like his CCC camps or other Army posts, he was assigned to spartan barracks with limited amenities.

For the next two months, Carmen drove trucks moving supplies from Bombay to the depot, where they were staged until they could be loaded on trains that transported them to troops on the front lines. In October, the British provided the U.S. Forces with a section of Camp Kalyan in Bombay to use as a staging area for supplies. Since it was close to the port and rail lines, it eliminated the need to move supplies out to Lake Beale. The depot was reassigned to the Replacement Service to be used exclusively as a staging area for troops arriving in the CBI. It temporarily housed transient soldiers awaiting assignment or movement to their forward-deployed units in the CBI or on their way to the Persian Gulf. Carmen continued to drive trucks, but now he transported people instead of supplies.

Off the Islands of Palau, Pacific Ocean
September 1944

At the same time and across the International Date Line, Seaman First Class Steffens was finally sailing in harm's way. It had been four months since he reported on board Intrepid. For two days, the ship's planes prepared Palau and its neighboring islands for an assault by the Marines. It bombed and strafed the Japanese garrison, concentrating on airfields, antiaircraft, and coastal gun positions. The next day, the Intrepid fast carrier task force steamed west toward the island of Mindanao in the Philippines for two days of bombing airfields that otherwise could support Palau's defenders. It then moved to the Visayan Sea, where it attacked island bases from September 12 to 14. This preparation allowed for the invasion of the Palau island group on September 15.

Eskew found the aircraft carrier in wartime to be an amazing ship that stirred a range of emotions from awe to sheer panic--there was activity everywhere. The flight deck was longer than a football field and filled with constant activity, noise, and all the elements man could conjure in the middle of an ocean. Eskew found planes were either taking off or landing in a manner that scared even the bravest sailor. When planes were not flying, the ship's crew serviced and taxied them for the next mission. He had to watch for hazards everywhere on the flight deck, such as walking into a propeller, getting blown over the side of the ship by propeller wash, or getting run over by a plane in tow. Massive elevators, moving fighters and bombers between the flight and hangar decks, added to the deafening noise.

The carrier could be in the cross-hairs of an enemy plane, submarine, or warship at any time. Thus, teams of men stood watch around the ship, searching for any danger with binoculars, radar, and communications equipment. If Eskew wanted to find some quiet to absorb his world, he was unsuccessful. Everywhere he went was the noise of revving engines, bells, whistles, the 1MC blasting out orders, and the sounds of the ship's machinery. Solitude and silence were fleeting privileges he learned to enjoy when they came his way.

Eskew thought about how fast his life could be taken from this planet. As he walked across the flight deck or hangar bay, he eyed all the high explosives packed into this compact "artificial island." Everywhere Eskew looked, he saw bombs, torpedoes, depth charges, and rockets. He smelled high-octane gasoline stored throughout the ship. When Eskew boarded the ship, he was told that the carrier was the number one target in the case of an enemy attack. Eskew thought he was young and indestructible, but he was also relieved that his will was in order.

Eskew and the Intrepid crew next took part in the bloody Battle of Peleliu, which saw the highest casualty rate of any amphibious assault in American military history. The Army's 81st Infantry Division assaulted and quickly secured the islands of Angaur and Ulithi while the First Marine Division was assigned to capture Peleliu. Major General William Rupertus, the 1st Marine Division commander, predicted the island would be secured within four days. It took over two long bloody months.

After days of massive naval bombardment and carrier-based aircraft strafing and bombing Japanese emplacements, the Marines landed on the island's southwest corner. Unlike previous amphibious assaults, the Japanese adjusted to the U.S. tactics. The island defenders built a series of connected caves that allowed them to avoid destruction from naval bombardment. As they secured the island's southern part, the Marines faced unexpected fanatical opposition from the defenders in hillside caves and mangrove swamps.

The withering assault on the Marines required Intrepid and her task force to divert her airpower to the island for the next week, starting on September 17. With the support of Intrepid and other ships, the Marines advanced on the rest of the island while facing heavy artillery fire and a fusillade of small arms from Japanese forces occupying caves dug into the rocky surface of Umurbrogol Mountain. Fighting was so fierce that U.S. troops sustained 40% casualties.

When the fighting was reduced to Marines clearing the defenders one cave at a time, and aerial bombardment became ineffective, Intrepid and the other carriers were ordered back to the Philippines.

After the Intrepid left, Japanese troops continued to zealously hold their ground. Army units reinforced the Marines. Finally, after two months of bloodshed, the defenders, corralled around Umurbrogol Mountain, were virtually all killed. The island was secured on November 25. Of the 28,000 Marines and Army troops involved, 1,800 were killed in action and 8,000 wounded, for a total of 9,800 casualties.

Cloyes-sur-le-Loir, France
September 6, 1944

As XII Corps liberated Pont-à-Mousson, the 267th continued its convoy, 360 miles behind them, toward Sens. Fair weather and good roads allowed it to cover 250 miles in two days. It bivouacked in an area near Cloyes-sur-le-Loir that night and then finished the remaining 117 miles the following day. The Battalion arrived at the Third Army Concentration Area near Sens that evening. Upon arrival, Major Collins received orders officially attaching the 267th to XII Corps' 410th Field Artillery Group with instructions to move the Battalion 174 miles to Moutrot, where it should expect combat operations.

The night of September 7 was tense. The artillerymen were quiet and reflective as they made last-minute preparations on their howitzers and other equipment. The flashes and noise of explosions on the horizon further weighed on the men.

The following day, while convoying toward Moutrot, the 267th received orders over the radio to halt and remain in place for further instruction. After a few hours, MPs in a jeep pulled up to the command vehicle and handed Major Collins new orders to detach from XII Corps and the 410th Field Artillery Group and attach to XV Corps and the 144th Field Artillery Group. The message further directed the Battalion to reroute and bivouac in Saint-Dizier, 152 miles away. The Battalion was still going to war, just in a different place.

Since July, XV Corps had been in continuous combat bridging the Seine River, passing through Paris, and now seeking to push an entrenched and desperate Wehrmacht over the Rhine River back into its homeland. It was ordered to the Lorraine area and transferred to General Patton's command. Since the Third Army pushed out of Normandy, it had been advancing with an exposed southern flank, so XV Corps was ordered to move south of General Patton's main army and protect it. However, before taking on that critical mission, it increased its fighting strength by adding more units, including more powerful artillery to dislodge dug-in Nazi troops. The 267th was selected for that task.

On September 11, as XV Corps began to drive the Wehrmacht toward the Moselle River, Major Collins and headquarters staff left to reconnoiter positions in the vicinity of Diarville. XV Corps personnel informed the Major that the XVth would attempt to cross the Moselle River the next day and needed his big guns to destroy the enemy's defenses. After locating firing positions for the three batteries, Major Collins directed the Battalion to make the 132-mile trip to their designated areas. The weather cooperated during the convoy, and the batteries worked late into the night, emplacing their howitzers in plumb orchards divided by wire fences.

Many enemy planes flew over the 267th during the night. The Luftwaffe was actively searching for the big howitzers and their light and unarmed spotter planes. The collocated 975th Field Artillery Battalion's observation planes were just attacked by enemy fighters, with one shot down. To combat the menace from above, the 456th Anti-Aircraft Automatic Weapons Battalion was assigned to protect the 267th. Its assignment was to shoot down any low-flying enemy planes that attempted to bomb or strafe the 267th's artillery positions or attack its spotter aircraft. For this purpose, the 456th was armed with quadruple .50 caliber machine guns and rapid-fire 37mm cannons attached to revolving turrets. These electrically operated turrets were mounted on armored half-tracks, vehicles equipped with two rubber-tired wheels in front and tank-type tracks in the rear. Half-tracks were fast, extremely mobile, and offered tremendous firepower. They were the same type of vehicle that Charles trained on at Tank Destroyer School on Fort Hood.

At 4:30 in the morning, the 456th rolled up to the big guns. It had just completed a grueling sixty-six-mile convoy that took eleven-and-one-half-hours! It convoyed with the 675th Field Artillery Battalion, which suffered several wrecked vehicles and two 155mm howitzers sliding into ditches due to poor visibility and weather. Upon arrival, Major Collins briefed the 456th's officers that: *"There is some enemy air activity in the vicinity. In the event that our liaison planes are attacked, our planes will dive directly at anti-aircraft guns to give warning. Be on the lookout for fighters on their tail."*

Later that morning, the 267th fired its cannons in anger for the first time and continued firing them for the next seven days. Its six howitzers provided harassing and interdictory fires--as called in by the Battalion's forward observers--on the towns of Mirecourt and Bettoncourt, both less than seven miles away. Over the next two days, the 79th Infantry Division pushed out the German defenders and secured both towns. The powerful 360-pound shells launched seven miles by Charles and his fellow artillerymen obliterated Wehrmacht observation posts, troop concentrations, and vehicles.

Even though the artillerymen had fired their howitzers in practice, they were stunned by the continuously deafening sounds of the big guns in combat. It was not just the "boom" of the 240mms that impacted them, but the concussion from the explosion in the barrel and all the associated noise as the cannon absorbed that impact. Added to that was the whine of spinning brass safety rings that flew off the shells right after they left the gun muzzles. The shells were disarmed by these rings for normal handling but were armed and ready to explode after the rings flew off. Troops of the 456th said the continuous slamming of heavy artillery sounded *"like giant doors slamming in an empty house."*

However, Charles and the artillerymen were unable to bring to bear the full fury of their guns. Ammunition supply points were virtually devoid of artillery ammunition and fuses. All firing was rationed to absolute need and use of the minimum number of projectiles. Throughout September, the Third Army and the 267th had to limit operations because of fuel and artillery ammunition shortages.

They also got their first glimpse of German artillery in action. Enemy artillery focused not only on front-line targets but also behind the lines, where artillery units emplaced, by sending interdiction fires on roads and command posts. One artillery spotter plane was destroyed on its landing strip. Added to artillery attacks were Luftwaffe planes bombing and strafing outfits within view of the 267th and five German soldiers walking into Battery B's encampment to surrender. Charles and the other artillerymen were new to combat, but they felt like they were on the front lines, and it turned out they were right. There is a saying in combat: *"the fog of war."* Because of the chaos of combat, it is hard to know the battlefield's complete picture. Several days into the battle, the 267th learned that when it moved into Diarville, it cut directly in front of an entire German armored division and set its guns up only 2.7 miles from it. That "small pocket of resistance" they kept hearing about across the hill was not so small, after all.

As Charles sat around smoking cigarettes and shooting the bull with his buddies in Bude, they rehashed the war's progress reported in the military newspaper, *Stars and Stripes,* or across *Armed Forces Radio.* Since D-Day, the Allies had been making steady advances, and the positive reporting by military media gave credence to the belief that the war would be won before the 267th got to Europe. They griped that two years of training might have been for naught if they continued to sit in Bude! But any lingering thoughts of missing the war were dispelled on the third day in combat.

The 267th awoke to the news that German forces were counterattacking the 80th Infantry Division's bridgehead on the Moselle River's far side. Full-scale assaults threatened to push Allied troops back across the river, and the beachhead was only saved after massive artillery and reinforcements poured into the area. The battle hit home to the artillerymen. The Germans overran a position manned by a sound and flash detachment of the 14th Field Artillery Observation Battalion. The unit, which provided fire direction for the 267th, fought as infantry with massive artillery supporting it for six hours while holding its ground against withering assaults. They were finally relieved as the entire offensive was eventually broken up and repelled. Fourteen German tanks were destroyed or disabled by division artillery fire. Charles and his fellow artillerymen learned that as the Wehrmacht's backs came closer to their homeland, the more vicious it fought.

The next three days were spent firing in support of XV Corps as it launched additional units across the Moselle River. The Third Army captured the important border city of Nancy, and an hour-and-a-half south, Vittel fell. In Vittel, soldiers repatriated 2,087 Allied Nationals who were interned for four years in hotels surrounded by wire barricades. Included were 361 Americans and 1,160 British nationals, with the remainder from 29 other nationalities. On September 18, the 79th Infantry successfully attacked and drove across the river near Bayon.   Major Collins and his staff left on reconnaissance for the Battalion's next position near Froville and Landécourt, eight miles behind the advancing infantry divisions' next target, Lunéville.

All the while, the 267th was assaulted by both the weather and Germans. The artillerymen kept up their firing despite near-constant cloudy, rainy, and cold conditions.   September 17 began with German bombers passing overhead after midnight and dropping their bombs just east of the artillerymen. They heard one plane crash after being hit by Allied 90mm anti-aircraft rounds. Then mid-afternoon, the Germans jammed the 267th radio communications and commenced a counterattack. Charles's battery found itself taking the brunt of the assault. Because Battery "C" seemed to be the usual location that the Germans attacked, the men of the 267th and the 456th labeled it "Snake Pit Charlie."

On a rainy Tuesday, September 19, the Battalion packed up its guns and equipment and slogged through thirty miles of muddy roads northeast across the Moselle River to Landécourt in two separate moves. The roads were rutted mud and clogged with retreating civilians, making it difficult to transport the heavy guns. Because the 240mm howitzer fired at targets over the horizon, Charles did not see his shells impact their targets. The "eyes" of the 267th were First Lieutenant James Pollard, who-- along with one of two pilots, First Lieutenants George Lawrence or Hunter Harbinson--flew in the Battalion's light observation airplane over the battlefield. Calls from Lt. Pollard and forward observers of the 14th Field Artillery Observation Battalion would direct the 267th fire and report its results.

When the Battalion moved to forward positions, its men saw the destructive power of their weapons. As they convoyed to Landécourt, Charles was struck by the devastation he saw and the overpowering smell of death. The smell was so strong that First Lieutenants Lawrence and Harbinson reported the stench affecting them hundreds of feet in the air. On the ground, destruction and putrefying animal and human bodies strewed the fields adjacent to the road. Everything was covered with flies and blue bottles. In the hot sun, the cattle appeared as masses of crawling maggots even though they had been killed only days before. Unburied Germans, swollen to elephantine grossness by the hot sun inflating the gasses in their stomach, laid with their blackened faces in grotesque positions. In the heaviest bombarded areas, fragments of bodies hung in the trees. Driving was slow as some roads were nearly impassable due to the congestion caused by burnt-out trucks, dead horses, smashed tanks, and large craters. The scene Charles saw would be the basis of nightmares for the rest of his life.

The Germans, no stranger to fierce warfare, were also awestruck by the effect of American artillery fire. A German prisoner told his XII Corps captives:

> *"The incredibly heavy artillery and mortar fire of the enemy is something new for seasoned veterans as much as for the new arrivals from reinforcement units. The assembly of troops is spotted immediately by enemy reconnaissance aircraft and smashed by bombs and artillery directed from the air; and if, nevertheless, the attacking troops go forward, they become involved in such dense artillery and mortar fire that heavy casualties ensue and the attack peters out in the first few hundred meters. The losses suffered by the infantry are then so heavy that the impetus necessary to renew the attack is spent. Our soldiers enter the battle so low in spirits at the thought of the enemy's enormous superiority of material. The feeling of helplessness against enemy aircraft operating without hindrance has a paralyzing effect; and during the barrage the effect on the inexperienced men is literally soul shattering. The best results have been obtained by platoon and section commanders leaping forward uttering a good old-fashioned yell. We have also revived the practice of Bugle calls."*

The German Army estimated that over 50% of their casualties were due to artillery in the battle for France.

Upon arrival in the Landécourt area, the Battalion reassembled their howitzers and set up firing positions, launching supportive fires into

Lunéville and Hériménil. That evening, the big guns fired at targets three miles away in the town of Xermaménil, coming to the aid of the 313th Infantry Regiment, which ran into a bitter fight with the Germans. After a few hours, the Germans retreated, and the town was secure. For the next three days, the 267th Battalion's guns pounded away at entrenched defenses. The Wehrmacht was determined not to give up Lunéville without subjecting the XV Corps to bloody urban combat. Finally, after several days of battle, XV Corps liberated the city on September 22.

But there was no rest for the XV Corps' 79th Infantry, the 2nd French Armored Divisions, and the artillery units supporting them. Immediately following the capture of Lunéville, the Divisions were ordered to attack the thickly-wooded Forêt de Parroy. This attack was set for September 25 after Allied planes and artillery softened up the enemy defenses.

On September 23, the 267th moved into position to support the assault, with Battery A establishing a fire position near Hériménil, followed shortly by the other two batteries who emplaced their howitzers near Lunéville. Once operational, they began to rain their rounds on the forest.

Convoying through the town and Battery C's motor shop in Lunéville, France, sometime between September 24 and October 14, 1944.

The Wehrmacht turned the dense forest into a natural fortress, using the woods' thick cover and extensive pre-war defensive fortifications. It established command posts and firing positions with commanding views of the terrain. The American troops had not yet fought in dense forests, and this spot was important to the Germans because Adolf Hitler fought there as a corporal in World War I. Rumors spread among the Allies that Hitler ordered it held at all costs.

Several days of poor weather and another critical gasoline shortage postponed the attack, allowing the 79th to patrol enemy defenses aggressively. All patrols reported strong resistance from well dug-in positions on the forest's edge. This intelligence was fed back to their artillery and air support. Before the assault, XV Corps artillery destroyed several enemy tanks and provided counter-battery fire against more than thirty enemy artillery positions.

On September 25, the original date of the assault, the 267th and other XV Corps artillery shifted their fire toward the town of Flin, about ten miles southeast of the 267th positions. The Germans opened a counterattack with heavy artillery fire on Allied infantry troops holding the town and engineers building bridgeworks over the Meurthe River. Exposed to fire, the engineers on the bridge withdrew to cover with their equipment. Corps artillery fired twenty-three counterbattery missions, destroying enemy guns and considerably reducing the German artillery fire. The artillery halted the assault and allowed Allied forces to regain the bridgeworks.

The assault on Forêt de Parroy finally occurred after three days of weather delays. It did so despite continued poor weather, which significantly reduced the effectiveness of Allied air bombardment on the Wehrmacht's defenses. The 79th was able to overrun stubborn German outer defenses and fought its way into the forest, not knowing that it would take fourteen days of constant combat before they would emerge from the other side.

As the Third Battalion of the 313th Regiment charged into the forest, it was forced to call for artillery support when the Wehrmacht counterattacked and rained artillery on their advanced elements, which caused heavy casualties and endangered the assault. Division artillery immediately went into action, silencing the German artillery pieces and inflicting terrific casualties on the enemy. The heavy bombardment allowed the 313th to continue its advance.

At month's end, the 267th and Third Army leaders reflected on September as they drew up their monthly after-action summary. The 267th was integrated into a very different war plan for the Third Army than the one that existed during the first thirty-one days of European action. The breakout from Normandy and the fast pace of the Army's August advance were slowed, requiring General Patton to revise his plan of attack. As the 267th arrived on France's shores, an acute gasoline shortage seriously impaired the Third Army's mobility. Subsequently, other supply shortages emerged, such as artillery ammunition, and there was an enemy buildup and steadily worsening weather conditions. By late September, the Third Army had gone from an offensive to a defensive status, allowing the Wehrmacht to turn around in front of the German border and fortify the Moselle River line. There the enemy fought desperately to prevent crossings of the Moselle and Meurthe Rivers with intense counterattacks. The Germans rushed to build hurried field fortifications along the front, especially along the Moselle River's east bank. Manning these fortifications were hastily assembled units consisting of stragglers, untrained recruits, some convalescents, and students from the Officer Candidate School at Metz. Also, forced civilian labor, Hitler Youth organizations, and newly formed Army units frantically repaired and strengthened the Siegfried Line's defensive works, constructing successive lines of defense between Moselle and the German border.

Despite stiffened enemy resistance, the Third Army's tank, infantry, and air assaults--aided by the intensive use of artillery--had pushed the enemy successively across the Moselle, Meurthe, and Vezouze Rivers by the end of September. The Germans were now pushed into the thick forests of the Forêt de Parroy. As the Third Army crossed the French rivers, terrific tank battles raged along the bridgeheads. While their equipment was new, the bulk of the Wehrmacht's armored and infantry divisions were manned with troops that only had two or three weeks of training. Thus, Panzer brigades became less effective and suffered increasing losses.

Third Army artillery faced many challenges over September, including a prolonged scarcity of ammunition and poor weather limiting air and forward artillery observation. German artillery also suffered from the effects of weather and a high proportion of duds.

Despite all its challenges, the Third Army ultimately proved to be a deadly force advancing toward the German homeland. As it assumed air superiority, it sharply curtailed German air activity. Only 128 raids by 287 aircraft occurred in September compared to August's 1,117 raids by 3,213 aircraft. Anti-aircraft artillery claimed twenty-eight planes destroyed and fifteen probables destroyed. Overall, German casualties were estimated at 32,000 killed, 96,500 wounded, and nearly 30,000 captured. The Third Army captured or destroyed 607 enemy tanks, 663 artillery pieces, and 1,735 vehicles. Allied casualties for the month were 2,130 killed, 12,307 wounded, 4,100 missing, and 390 deserted. The German war machine could not sustain these losses.

While the 267th was embroiled in near-daily combat operations, the Army did provide temporary respite to the soldiers. Off-duty soldiers from the 267th and 456th were occasionally allowed to travel into Lunéville or Charmes, where the USO provided short breaks from war's misery. For example, on September 20, Bing Crosby and Bob Hope put on a show in Charmes. The daily log of the 456th described the show:

> *"An uneventful morning, but how different an afternoon! Bing Crosby scheduled to appear in Charmes, so Lt Miller led two trucks and a Jeep full of "A" Battery men toward that battered town, through which we passed on yesterday's move. At Einvaux about 2 miles from the site of our Battery Hq, we saw a suspiciously large crowd of GIs and an inquiry found that Bing was staging a performance there too. We stopped took the rest of it in, and followed the show on to Charmes, where a special staging was given for the XVth Corps in a slightly damaged airplane factory. The Bing was great, as usual, only more so, and was ably backed up by a strong supporting troupe of USO singers, dancers, musicians and comedians...Bing sang 8 of his*

very best which deserves listing: "San Fernando Valley,"
"Aloha," "Blue Hawaii," "Sweet La Lanne," "Easter Parade,"
"If I had it My Way," "White Christmas," "Swingin on a Star."
About 4,000 men jammed into the building, everybody from Gen.
Haislip on down. Things like this are what makes this war worth
fighting, and men like Crosby and [Bob] Hope are more than
home front soldiers. In our excitement we forgot to say that we
had pancakes this morning."

Despite having to dodge occasional German 88mm artillery bombardment, troops in Lunéville found "Red Cross Girls" passing out coffee and donuts, and the theater showing movies such as "Lady in the Dark" with Ginger Rogers and Ray Milland, and Susan Hayward in "Hit Parade of 1943." The 456th log recorded: *We were a year late, but it was still good.* The end of the month was payday, which brought the usual cracks from the men as they signed for their pay about this being discharge papers or the army of occupation documents. Payday also brought showers and a chance to be mud-free, at least temporarily. Catholic mass was held at the Battalion Headquarters once a week. These temporary breaks from the war were essential for the men's sanity.

By October 1, the 79th cleared approximately one-third of the Forêt de Parroy. The Germans now frantically reinforced their lines with additional troops, tanks, and assault guns to hold their ground. The battlefield was marked by a steady stream of artillery duels crisscrossing the contested forest areas. At night German artillery and mortar fire fell, causing trees to explode from the bursts forcing Allied troops to crouch low in their foxholes. Tree bursts occurred when artillery shells were fused to explode before impacting the ground. The shells hit treetops and detonated, showering everything below with shrapnel and wood splinters. The next three days were filled with attacks and counterattacks--the Germans made the Allies pay with blood for every inch of territory they ceded.

The Third Army quickly addressed a brewing shortage of cigarettes and other tobacco products that could significantly impact morale. Loss of their smokes was unacceptable to the men and the Army command. Thus, Third Army Supply sped up the delivery of a ten-day allotment of tobacco components to ensure that frontline troops would not be deprived of their smokes.

While the battle for the forest persisted, the entire XV Corps, including the 267th, was transferred from General Patton's Third Army to the U.S. Seventh Army commanded by General Alexander Patch. The Seventh Army had sailed from Italy to land at the port of Marseille in southern France, then fought its way northward to join the right flank of the Third Army. The 267th was attached to the Seventh Army for eleven days until it was reattached to the Third Army and the 40th Field Artillery Group on October 14.

A crucial attack on the German lines was scheduled for 7:00 a.m. on October 4. In preparation for the battle, Charles's Battery C was moved across the Meurthe River into a cleared area of the forest in Forêt de Mondon near Moncel. As the Allies prepared to attack, the Germans counterattacked with armor, mortars, and infantry. The attack caused the 79th to suffer heavy casualties, put a gap in its lines, and halted the Allied assault.

There was a lull in activity for the next three days as both sides reinforced their positions. Charles and the other troops were grateful for the break that allowed them to listen to the St. Louis Cardinals play the St. Louis Browns in the World Series. For six nights at 8:00 p.m., the men of the 267th gathered around short-wave radios and listened to the games while bets consumed the money in their pockets from the previous payday! On October 9, the Cardinals won the last series game three to one, clinching the title four games to two.

At 6:30 a.m. on the same day, the Cardinals won the Series, the Allies resumed their advance against heavy fire from dug-in German tanks and machine guns. Finally, at approximately 3:30 p.m., they captured the Wehrmacht's main supply crossroads, causing the German defensive lines to collapse and forcing the Wehrmacht to retreat from the woods into the hills behind it. German planes responded that night to the 267th's guns by dropping anti-personnel bombs around them.

The 79th pursued the Germans into the hills east of the Forêt de Parroy for another twelve days of intense fighting. On October 12, the 267th Battalion's Battery A joined Battery C in the Forêt de Mondon, providing fire support for the pursuers. That same day, the 456th was relieved from protecting the 267th and replaced by the 398th Anti-Aircraft, Automatic Weapons Battalion. Richard S. Funk was a member of the 398th and wrote the following about his experience guarding the 267th and watching the firepower of Third Army artillery:

> *"A week later the re-united Battery was back in Charmes for three days protecting the bridge there before returning to Lunéville to guard the 267th Field Artillery and their gigantic 240mm howitzers. The shells for these guns were almost 10 inches in diameter and the noise was almost overpowering when they were fired. After three days, the Platoons were re-attached to the 961st again, now on the east side of Lunéville near Croismare. Here the 79th Infantry was engaged in a bitter battle to take the Forest of Parroy. This turned out to be the biggest artillery duel we had ever seen...Later in the morning, a really breathtaking event occurred. All of the artillery in the area was programmed for a Timed-On-Target exercise -- and there was a lot of artillery. The objective was to carpet the area above the forest with air bursts of artillery shells, all of which would arrive on target at the same time. This meant that the 155mm Long Toms located up to 10 miles away would fire several minutes before the 105mm howitzers, which were only a few hundred yards from the forest, and the other gun sizes in between would be scheduled to fire at appropriate times. At 11 o'clock we could hear the whine of the long-distance shells coming our way just as the near-by 105mm howitzers fired. The area over the forest lit up like a malevolent Christmas tree as about 100 shells burst at once a little bit above treetop level. The noise of the airbursts was deafening. The leaves on the tops of the trees were shredded as the shrapnel rained down to the forest floor below. Then it became eerily quiet."*

The battle for the Forêt de Parroy was extremely costly for the 79th. While it defeated some of Germany's best troops, the Division suffered more than two thousand casualties in less than a month, more than it had seen in any other single battle.

Also, on October 12, General Patton issued an operational directive ordering the Third Army to move into a defensive posture to prepare for an upcoming offensive. Troops were to be rested, trained, and given time to perform maintenance on their equipment. This lull would allow a buildup of supplies for the forthcoming operation. He also directed his units to conduct aggressive patrolling and cover all avenues of tank approach. To address shortages, artillery staff integrated captured artillery pieces and ammunition into Allied lines, including Russian 76.2mm guns, German 88mm, 105mm howitzers, 150mm guns, and Schneider 155 howitzers. Ammunition for the Schneider howitzer was also successfully employed in the American 155mm M-1 howitzer.

The effect of General Patton's directive trickled down to the 267th, which had either been continuously on the move or in combat since leaving Bude, England, on August 28. Along with orders detaching the Battalion from XV Corps and back to the Third Army, XII Corps, and the 40th Field Artillery Group, Major Collins was notified that the Battalion would be moved off the front line for two weeks of well-deserved rest and relaxation (R&R).

Second Gun Section of Battery C somewhere in France

Philippine Sea
September 1944

Combat was also intensifying 10,330 miles away. For the next month, Eskew witnessed history when the Intrepid turned to its next mission: preparing the Philippines for General MacArthur's return. From September 21 to 24, the ship focused its air might on shipping and air installations in and around Manila and in the waters south of the Island of Luzon. On the 24th, Intrepid and other carrier planes sunk five cargo vessels and set fire to three others.

After weeks of constant General Quarters and combat operations, Eskew and the crew looked forward to a short break from combat, stopping on September 28 in Saipan to replenish and rearm the ship. Saipan was captured from the Japanese two months prior. Eskew could only see destruction from the ship's anchorage as all buildings and much of the island's vegetation were leveled in battle. The ship then steamed to Ulithi in the western Caroline Islands for additional supplies. Beginning October 2, Eskew learned what it was like to ride out a typhoon in a ship for two days. Though there was no significant damage to the ship, she pulled back into Ulithi to allow the battered crew to recuperate from being tossed around and seasick.

On October 6, Intrepid and her accompanying ships sailed northwest, heading back into combat. Arriving south of Okinawa on October 10, her planes participated in raids that wiped out picket boats off that island. She was off Formosa and Okinawa for the next four days, neutralizing enemy airfields. Attacks on Formosa included the Shinchiku Airfield, the Rising Sun Petroleum Company facilities, and a military seaplane base.

Next, Eskew and the crew of Intrepid participated in the Battle of Leyte Gulf, one of the most famous and definitive sea battles in the Pacific campaign.

The Intrepid spent October 21 supporting Sixth Army troops battling on Leyte to hold their tenuous beachhead. Two days later, U.S. submarines operating off Borneo, Palawan, and Manila reported multiple Japanese fleets converging on Leyte. It turned out that the remaining combatant strength of the Japanese Navy was steaming to dislodge the Army from

Leyte in a desperate attempt to hold the Philippines. U.S. ships and planes met the oncoming Japanese fleets in four major sea battles, collectively called the "Battle of Leyte Gulf."

On the 24th, American search planes reported contact with a Japanese force that included one large carrier, three light carriers, two battleships, five cruisers, and six destroyers off Luzon's northeastern tip. An Intrepid spotter plane identified one battleship as Admiral Kurita's flagship, the Yamato. Two hours later, planes from Intrepid's first wave pierced withering antiaircraft fire to attack the Japanese fleet. Intrepid and her sister carriers spent the entire day launching waves of planes that dropped their deadly ordinance. As Intrepid retrieved her planes at sunset, the impact on the Japanese was devastating: the battleship Musashi with her massive 18-inch guns was sent to the bottom of the ocean, and her sister ship, the Yamato, battleships Nagato and Haruna, and the heavy cruiser Myōkō were damaged. That evening the "medical alcohol," scotch, flowed in the pilot ready rooms on the Intrepid as they learned the results of their warfighting. However, the exhausted pilots and crew had little time to recuperate from the intense air operations.

That night Admiral Halsey redirected Intrepid and the rest of the fleet north to intercept Japan's Northern Force. Dawn brought another full day of combat air operations against a fleet off Cape Engaño. Joining planes from other carriers, an Intrepid pilot scored a direct hit on the light carrier Zuihō. Another Intrepid pilot put a torpedo into the hull of the large carrier Zuikaku, knocking out her communications and hampering her steering. By the end of the day, Intrepid and her sister ships had delivered a decisive blow against the Japanese forces off Cape Engaño by sinking four enemy carriers and a destroyer.

On October 26, Intrepid and her task force turned south to launch her planes against another Japanese task force retreating to Japan. Her planes met that force passing through the Sibuyan Sea west of Panay Island and inflicted extensive damage on the fleeing ships.

The Battle of Leyte Gulf was a decisive victory for the Allied forces. It allowed General MacArthur's force to move inland and eventually recapture the Philippines. The damage inflicted on the remaining

Japanese ships was so significant that it eliminated the Japanese Navy as an effective fighting force.

Third Army Assembly Area near Gerbéviller and Framboise France
October 14, 1944

The scattered batteries of the 267th packed up their gear and reunited at a Third Army Assembly area. There the muddy and tired soldiers arranged their convoy to move forty-seven miles behind the front lines.

Since the Allies' breakout from Normandy, their armies had been rapidly advancing in all directions, and the rapid expansion of the front outpaced the fragile supply lines. All the supplies needed to keep the armies on the offensive were shipped into Europe through the Normandy Beaches and trucked to the far-flung front lines. The port facilities at Utah Beach and a limited number of trucks assigned to supply runs could only meet a fraction of the troops' material needs.

Since Charles arrived, the Army experienced shortages of all types of materials. Tents, personal gear, ammunition, and food were all scarce. Bakers were using captured German flour to make bread. Troops were issued German rations, including tins of fish, sauerkraut, and beef. Of particular concern to Charles and his fellow artillerymen was the shortage of artillery ammunition. Shells were rationed, and fire missions were given to other types of support, such as tanks or tank destroyers, not because they were better suited but because they had more ammunition. According to Third Army instructions, the 267th resorted to modifying captured German ordnance to work in their guns.

The most severe shortage with the most significant impact was gasoline. The "reverse blitzkrieg" required massive amounts of petrol that the supply system could not provide, so tanks and other offensive vehicles became fixed defensive emplacements when their fuel tanks emptied. As a result, Patton was forced to curtail his advance on the Germans and move into a defensive posture.

Near the end of September, General Eisenhower prioritized fuel and other supplies toward General Montgomery's 21st Army Group as it drove toward Antwerp. The Allies had to capture that deep-water port for another major supply hub. Once Antwerp's port was in the Allies' hands, General Eisenhower figured enough supplies could be brought in for all the armies to restart driving the Wehrmacht back to Berlin. The new plan forced General Patton's Army to delay its offensive from mid-October until early November. A relative calm fell on the Third Army line, and the Germans were happy to oblige. Both sides used the period to resupply units with troops and materials and give war-weary soldiers some R&R.

Charles and other Third Army soldiers were suspicious about General Eisenhower's plan to hold back fuel to the Third Army. They believed that if the fuel and supplies had been directed to General Patton, he would have driven his Army straight into Berlin and ended the war sooner. Charles and his fellow soldiers talked about how coalition politics and fear of a rogue General Patton led the other generals to use fuel to keep him in check.

With the pause in operations on September 29, the Third Army Headquarters established a policy to rotate the front line and reserve battalions, providing all troops with some rest and maintenance time before the future offensive. On October 15, the 267th began a ten-day rest in Foug.

Upon arrival in the war-torn town, the troops were quartered in buildings and provided indoor space to perform maintenance on their guns and equipment. Charles and the mud-covered artillerymen were very appreciative to have shelter from the elements, even if temporary. The Lorraine area received higher than average rainfall during the fall of 1944 (for example, Nancy received a total of 7.2 inches of rain in November, which was more than twice the standard three inches.) Soldiers did their job under steady rain, grey and overcast skies, and constant raw cold.   The rain was accompanied by declining temperatures and a shortage of winter uniforms, jackets, sleeping bags, waterproof groundsheets, raincoats, and rubber overshoes, making for a miserable operating environment. These effects were amplified for the artillerymen who had to set up emplacements in muddy fields with little protection from the cold wind and rain.

In addition to shelter, Charles was issued clean clothes and trucked to a leave center in Nancy for a bath and movie. Instead of C-rations, he feasted on fresh bread, freshly roasted coffee, and beef captured from German warehouses. He was also treated to coffee and donuts served by volunteers from an American Red Cross clubmobile. Like his CCC days, Charles loved playing baseball and participated in softball games organized in the muddy fields around the town. Charles was also treated to a USO show featuring film star and entertainer Marlene Dietrich. She performed a nine-week tour along the front lines starting on October 17.

Charles and his fellow artillerymen looked forward to sleeping in a bed, but he also relished the thought of working on his equipment in dry indoor quarters without standing in knee-high mud. The ten days allowed the Battalion to perform maintenance on their howitzers, vehicles, and personal gear, put off the past several weeks in combat. Personnel also participated in training, including a refresher on the Articles of War.

Unfortunately for the Allies, the German Army was doing the same: building up supplies and resting their troops. They were also fortifying their defensive lines by massing artillery and antitank companies in weak points, improving positions by digging trenches, laying mines, and constructing fortifications.

While both sides took advantage of the lull in operations, intense planning occurred for a major offensive. On October 15, General Eisenhower and Lt. General Jacob Devers visited Third Army Headquarters to review General Patton's plan for a resumption of the offensive. The following day, General Patton issued a memorandum titled "Outline Plans for Resumption of the Offensive" that laid out the battle plan for the Lorraine Campaign. The plan called for the Third Army to envelop Metz's defensive works from the north and south and advance northeast to seize Mainz, Frankfurt, and Darmstadt. XII Corps (26th, 35th, and 80th Infantry Divisions, the 4th and 6th Armored Divisions, and support troops, including the 267th) would advance northeast toward Pont-à-Mousson and seize rail and road facilities in the vicinity of Falkenberg. In conjunction with XX Corps, they would destroy enemy forces withdrawing from Metz; they would then advance northeast to establish a bridgehead east of the Rhine River between

Oppenheim and Mannheim and seize Darmstadt. The Germans were not expecting this offensive to start until the Spring, as the weather was projected to worsen with the onset of winter.

On October 25, Major Collins was back on the front, near Bratte, reconnoitering areas to emplace the 267th's powerful howitzers. Sergeant Potter spent the morning inspecting the gun section's sleeping quarters and workspace to ensure they were clean and acceptable to new occupants. Once all this was done, the Battalion loaded up its convoy and left the relative comfort of Foug for muddy fields in the Bratte and Faulx area.

The 267th did not have any major fire missions for the next twelve days along the relatively quiet front. But this did not stop casualties among the troops. Even though the soldiers were issued new wet and cold weather clothing, the cold rains remained constant, and trench foot became a deadlier enemy than the Germans. It soon incapacitated more Third Army soldiers than battle injuries.

On November 2, the Number 1 gun of Battery "B" fired on enemy troops at a crossroads. On the 5th, Lieutenant Pollard and his pilot aboard the Battalion's light observation airplane took enemy antiaircraft fire without any casualties.

The officers who flew these light planes over the battlefield risked their lives daily, directing fire. Many air observers lost their lives flying in treacherous weather while under fire from enemy positions. A Third Army after-action report thirteen days after Lieutenant Pollard was fired upon describes the dangers faced by these men:

> *"XV Corps experienced adverse weather conditions including heavy rains, poor visibility and high winds as it continued to drive German forces back toward the Siegfried Line. Adverse weather was seriously hampering the operation of Corps Air Ops. In addition to six planes lost because of flood waters, one vanished when a sudden localized snow flurry reduced visibility to zero, two were torn from their moorings by high winds and were turned over and two crashed in attempting to take off because frost formed on their wings."*

While Charles battled to stay warm and dry, General Patton finalized his offensive plans to begin on November 8. The month hiatus worked to resupply his Army with men and gear--he now had approximately a quarter-million men under his command, including thirty-eight field artillery battalions. Supplies were back up to a four-day reserve of food and five days of fuel. The only shortage was white phosphorous shells for 105 and 155mm howitzers. Otherwise, all other ammunition was in plenty of supply.

Morale was high among the 267th. Ten days in the rear rejuvenated them. But they knew an offensive was coming, and the scuttlebutt was that this would be the war's final push. Another telltale sign of impending combat was the 267th being augmented with an eight-inch howitzer from Battery C of the 243rd Field Artillery Battalion. The eight-inch was another massive gun with the longest range of any American Army field artillery weapon in World War II.

The artillerymen felt that General Patton would push the Germans back into Germany, where its Army would collapse. Many Second Gun Section members were betting that the war would end by Christmas.

Gulf of Leyte
October 29, 1943

As Allied forces encircled Japan and neutralized its overseas forces, the military government in Tokyo devised a suicide plan for its troops. It ordered its service members to turn the remainder of its planes, small submarines, and even warships into suicide weapons, hoping they would inflict such pain on Allied forces that they would sue for peace. The most menacing suicide weapon was the kamikazes, planes loaded with fuel and bombs piloted directly into Allied ships. Nothing brought more terror to Eskew and the other sailors serving in the later Pacific Campaign than to hear "*incoming bogies*" over the ships 1MC.

With Intrepid at General Quarters, Eskew and the other sailors prepared the ship for the worst: a Japanese plane flown by a suicidal pilot crashing into her. On deck, all guns were manned and ready, damage control teams were in position, and lookouts scanned the sky. Below the flight deck where Eskew worked, hatches were battened down, and ventilation was shut off, causing temperatures to rise to 130 degrees in some spaces. Every sailor had a job, including pilots who sat in their ready rooms or plane cockpits, Airedales standing by their planes, cooks preparing battle-ration sandwiches, and even musicians were standing by with damage control gear or stretchers. Sailors did their jobs and depended on the 1MC to know when enemy aircraft were approaching and the status of the battle. Eskew could hear gunfire and explosions from near misses, and he could feel the ship shudder when a kamikaze found its mark. General Quarters could last for hours or even days, depending on the operation.

Sunday, October 29, found Eskew at his battle station when the 1MC blared *"incoming bogies."* The ship was in the Gulf of Leyte conducting multiple strikes against Japanese aircraft on Clark Field and ships in Manila Harbor. Also manning their battle stations was the crew of Gun Tub Ten. Black sailors manned this 20mm gun station.

During World War II, black sailors were not initially accepted for combat duty and typically worked as cooks or waiters in a mess. Like the Army, the Navy was segregated, so on Intrepid, black sailors manned their own battle station designated Gun Tub Ten. Around noon, a lone Japanese Zero fighter approached Intrepid on the starboard side, causing her antiaircraft guns to open fire. Pulling high above, the pilot rolled the plane over and dove straight for the flight deck. The six 20mm cannons of Gun Tub Ten shredded the left wing and most of the incoming aircraft's tail. The Japanese pilot lost control and veered away from the flight deck, but instead of crashing into the sea, the pilot slammed his disintegrating plane directly into the still-firing gun tub. Ten sailors were killed, and several others were badly burned.

The Gun Captain for Gun Tub 10 was Gunners Mate Third Class Alfanso Chavarrias. He survived the sinking of the USS Lexington (CV-2) during the Battle of the Coral Sea. Even after it became apparent that the plane was heading for the gun tub, Alfanso remained at his station, directing fire from the guns until the plane struck. He was posthumously awarded the Navy Cross.

Eskew felt a thundering explosion rock the ship, smelled the smoke, felt the heat, and responded to the fire and destruction as a damage control team member. Eventually, the fire was contained, and flight operations resumed. They were all relieved when the 1MC advised the crew that hostilities had ceased and to secure from battle stations. At that point, all hatches opened, fresh air was pumped back into the ship, and the crew left their battle stations. All over, Intrepid crewmen headed for breakfast. Chow lines snaked through the cavernous hangar deck between the ship's vehicles and ordnance carts. Ship stewards slapped powdered eggs, tomato juice, coffee, toast, and apples on steel trays. Eskew and the crew felt sad and relieved--until the next operation.

Commencing on November 5 and lasting two days, Intrepid's planes attacked Southern Luzon to support General MacArthur's advancing army. On November 7, she headed to Ulithi, where Eskew and the crew worked day and night under intense heat for five days, provisioning the ship with food, ammunition, and supplies. The tedium of continuous working parties was only broken up for a few hours one day when Admiral William "Bull" Halsey came aboard Intrepid to inspect its damage. On the 14th, she was ready to return to the firing line in the Philippines.

On November 19, Intrepid was back off the Philippines, conducting flight operations in support of the Army. These air assaults continued until Friday, November 24, when Intrepid pulled back from Luzon to allow the crew to celebrate Thanksgiving (being on the other side of the International Date Line, it was Thursday in the U.S.). Eskew started the day with a church service and enjoyed his last dinner of turkey with all the trimmings, cherry pie, and cigars. He reflected on the Thanksgiving prayer printed behind the ship's menu:

> *"This day we render thanks, O God, for the many blessings and gifts received. To us, Thou hast entrusted a great and mighty nation in which we enjoy the inalienable rights of life, liberty and the pursuit of happiness. Grant us, O loving Father, the daily strength of body and soul to preserve these rights, to overcome our enemies and to honor thee ever in justice and charity. Amen"*

Since the kamikaze attack twenty-six days prior, other planes tried to plunge into Intrepid, but none could reach it. The fleet's defensive aircraft and antiaircraft batteries successfully stopped the suicidal planes. Eskew thought as he ate his meal, *"We have been too lucky...how long before it runs out?"* After dinner, he slipped away to an unused catwalk that was aft under the flight deck, where he could find some time alone. He enjoyed a cigar and thought about Paterson, his mom, sisters, and his fiancé, Roseann. Like he did every day he could find the time, he wrote a letter to Roseann. He dreamed about seeing her and his family again--this dream would never come true.

The next day, Saturday, November 25, was the darkest day in that grand ship's history. Intrepid resumed offensive operations against the Philippines. According to the Ship's Deck Log, she began her day steaming at twenty-four knots as a member of Task Force 38.2. Other ships in the Task Force were the aircraft carriers John Hancock, Independence, and Cabot, battleships New Jersey and Iowa, cruisers Miami and Vincennes, and destroyers Tingey, Miller, Brown, Cowell, Capps, Boyd, Colahan, Marshall, Hickox, The Sullivans, Stephen Potter, Taylor, Henley, and Lewis Hancock. The last three destroyers were stationed on picket duty to warn and screen the fleet against kamikaze attacks. The fleet had been steaming in zigzag patterns, making it difficult for Japanese submarines to lock torpedoes onto them. At 5:55 a.m., the Intrepid went to its first General Quarters of the day. Between 6:22 and 7:05 a.m., she launched aircraft and spent the remainder of the morning either zigzagging or launching and recovering aircraft.

Simultaneously, a formation of approximately 150 kamikaze planes was preparing to take off from that same island chain. The pilots performed the traditional kamikaze ceremony, drinking a cup of sake while facing the Emperor's palace's direction. Each pilot then took off, intending to plunge their plane, bomb, and remaining fuel into a U.S. flattop. Many knew they would never get close to the carriers or any American ship, as their planes were thick around the fleet. However, two pilots would find their mark on the USS Intrepid. Suehiro Ikeda's plane would penetrate Intrepid's flight deck and cause extensive fires in the hangar deck. Four minutes later, Kohichi Nunoda's aircraft would also plunge into Intrepid.

Around 12:04 p.m., the ship commenced zigzagging on a course of 200 degrees as its radar picked up the Japanese formation heading toward the fleet. The combat air patrol encircling the fleet shot down most of them, but approximately ten to fifteen made it over the American ships. At 12:15, Eskew--like the rest of the Intrepid crew--was eating lunch when he heard the familiar gong and announcement of *"General Quarters, General Quarters: All hands man your battle stations"* over the 1MC for the fifth time that day. With that command, Eskew and the ship's thousands of sailors streamed in an orderly manner up and forward on the starboard side and down and aft on the port side, just as he had done hundreds of times since reporting on board the ship. Thirteen minutes into battle stations, Eskew heard the announcement, *"incoming bogeys,"* as three single-engine dive bombers headed for the carriers in the center of the mighty fleet. They attempted to plunge into the Intrepid's sister carriers, but gunners crashed them into the Philippine Sea.

At 12:52, Intrepid's radarmen contacted what appeared to be two Zeroes at 8,000 feet and eight miles out bearing down on Intrepid. A minute later, Eskew heard, *"All hands topside take cover."* Suddenly, the five-inch guns commenced firing, quickly followed by the 40mm, and then the 20mm guns. He knew that the 20mm's firing meant the enemy was close. The ship's after-batteries fired furiously at two Zeroes heading toward its stern. The gunners found their mark when the port side plane exploded just above the water 1,500 yards astern. Eskew then heard the 1MC direct the crew to fire quarters.

But Suehiro Ikeda's plane kept coming. Eskew could feel the deck angle and shimmy beneath his feet as the ship conducted a series of sharp evasive turns. Starboard 40mm and 20mm guns trained their sights on the second Zero sweeping in low toward the stern. Ikeda dodged a U.S. Hellcat fighter and dove through flak from the after guns. At 1,000 yards out, he climbed to 400 feet, went into a power stall, and did a wingover, diving right into the center of the flight deck. Eskew heard the plane impact the flight deck. He looked at the clock--it was

12:55. Then the ship shuddered as the bomb Ikeda carried penetrated the flight deck and blew apart a pilots' ready room.

A cloud of smoke rose from the hole in the flight deck thousands of feet into the sky. Flames shot through the entire length of the hangar deck, igniting anything that could burn. Trying to recover from the blasts, Eskew was tossed against a bulkhead as the ship made tight right turns to drain water and flaming gasoline over the port side, away from critical systems in the island structure on the starboard side.

There is nothing more dangerous on a ship than a fire, and every sailor in the Navy is trained to be a firefighter. Firefighting teams, including one with Eskew, launched into action. One team fought smoke and flames toward the site of the bomb blast. Fortunately, the pilot ready room that received the Japanese bomb was empty. Not so fortunate were thirty-two sailors in the adjoining Ready Room Four, twenty-six of whom were radarmen standing by to relieve those manning the radars in the ship's Combat Information Center. The firefighting team opened the Ready Room Four hatch and did not find flames or billowing smoke. Inside were the bodies of the room's thirty-two occupants without any burns or marks. The only signs of injury were small amounts of blood near some of their ears and mouths. This was a telltale sign that the concussion from the bomb, exploding in the next compartment, had instantly killed them all. The team members found it hard to believe they were dead. They called for corpsmen and stretcher-bearers, then moved on to battle the flames, as there was nothing more they could do for their fallen shipmates.

Eskew's firefighting team immediately responded to the raging fires in the hangar deck. It was a scene of unimaginable devastation filled with dismembered bodies, burning planes, and wounded men. The team put water and foam on burning planes as they were met with a hail of exploding fifty-caliber and 20mm ammunition.

Eskew heard explosions, ordnance whizzing past him, and the screams of wounded men as Captain Bolger took to the 1MC to request more volunteers to fight fires in the hangar deck. Above deck, the ship's gunners continued their firing at orbiting attackers. Two minutes after the first impact, two more suicidal Zeroes were spotted flying about 100 feet from the surface. Smoke pouring out of the ship was billowing across the flight deck and over the ship's stern, obscuring the view of all starboard and after gunners. Kohichi Nunoda followed the blinding smoke. Undetected, he came in low over the water as if he was making a carrier landing. He climbed into a power stall while riddled with antiaircraft rounds and set afire, but it was too late. Just above the flight deck, with his plane being torn apart around him, he released his 500-pound bomb and opened fire with his machine guns. Nunoda's plane smashed into the flight deck belly first and slid across the deck. Much of the plane and his body came to rest on the forward part of the ship. However, the bomb Nunoda carried pierced the flight deck, passed through the gallery deck, and into the hangar bay. Eskew heard the earsplitting sound and looked up as the bomb punctured the hangar bay overhead. He saw it hit the armored deck near the Number 3 aircraft elevator, bounce up, hit the deck again, and skid toward him and the other firefighting team members. It exploded when it reached them, and Eskew's twenty-three-year life ended. This ship's clock read 12:59 p.m.

It took the crew three terror-filled hours to bring the roaring gasoline fires under control. Six officers and fifty-nine enlisted men were killed that day. With her flight deck torn apart and her mangled hangar deck strewn with wreckage, the Intrepid--one of four carriers hit that day--withdrew from the firing line.

On November 26, all crew not on watch mustered on the hangar deck. Eskew and fifty-five of his shipmates were each placed in a canvas bag, along with a five-inch shell to weigh them down. (The bodies of the other nine sailors were either never found or could not be identified.) The canvas bags were laid out on the deck. At 1:59 p.m., two chaplains said a prayer, sailors bowed their heads, and a bugler played taps. Then the Marine detachment raised their rifles and fired a salute. With that, Eskew and his shipmates' bodies were slid into the ocean under the Stars and Stripes from the port side opening of the hangar bay. Navy tradition dictates that the burial at sea location is noted in the ship's log. Thus, Lieutenant Junior Grade R. Carter recorded Eskew and his fellow fallen sailors' burial site in the Intrepid's log at latitude 14-47-12 North and longitude 131-25-00 East.

On Thursday, November 30, Roseann was spending the day with her cousins Josephine and Carmela when the phone rang. She answered and, after a brief pause, gasped and began to sob. Josephine hugged her, instinctively knowing what the call was about, and they both cried together. On the other end was Blanche, who had just received the following Western Union telegram:

"MR. AND MRS. WILLIAM STEFFENS
22 WEST BROADWAY, PATERSON NJ

"THE NAVY DEPARTMENT DEEPLY REGRETS TO INFORM YOU THAT YOUR SON ESKEW RAY STEFFENS SEAMAN FIRST CLASS USNR WAS KILLED IN ACTION IN THE PERFORMANCE OF HIS DUTY AND IN THE SERVICE OF HIS COUNTRY. THE DEPARTMENT EXTENDS TO YOU ITS SINCEREST SYMPATHY IN YOUR GREAT LOSS. ON ACCOUNT OF EXISTING CONDITIONS BURIAL AT SEA WAS NECESSARY. TO PREVENT POSSIBLE AID TO OUR ENEMIES PLEASE DO NOT DIVULGE THE NAME OF HIS SHIP OR STATION.

REAR ADMIRAL JACOBS THE CHIEF OF NAVAL PERSONNEL."

For his service, Eskew was awarded a: Purple Heart, Navy Good Conduct Medal, Asiatic-Pacific Campaign Medal, Philippine Liberation Medal, American Campaign Medal, and a World War II Victory Medal. A grave marker for him is located at the Manila American Cemetery and Memorial in Manila, Philippines. His name is also etched on a bronze plaque, mounted on a five-foot-tall granite monument dedicated to ninety employees of Picatinny Arsenal who lost their lives during the war. The monument is near the Arsenal entrance at the intersection of Parker Road and Route 15 in Dover.

Gun barrel, tank, and crane (plenty of mud) and first snowfall on November 8 while the 267th was in firing positions near Bratte France

Bratte France
November 7, 1944

General Patton issued the code words "Play Ball," which meant the offensive would commence the following morning at 6:00 a.m. or H-Hour. A top-secret letter, "Target Data," covering air support and targets for the attack, was issued to corps commanders. XII Corps was ordered to advance northeast to Falkenberg, France, and destroy the forces withdrawing from Metz. It was also to advance as rapidly as possible to the northeast, establish a bridgehead east of the Rhine River, and seize the area around Darmstadt, Germany.

At 5:00 a.m. on November 8, the wet and cold men of the 267th were called upon to do their job. A steady cold rain fell all night, and dawn revealed more rain, fog, deep mudded fields, and rivers swollen to flood stages. As the temperature plunged, the rain turned to sleet, then snow, and that weather pattern lasted the next four days. These bitter conditions allowed General Patton's offensive to achieve a tactical surprise over the unsuspecting enemy.

A couple of days prior, the 267th ammunition pit was uncharacteristically filled to capacity. Before first light, the 267th began firing rounds, and within an hour, eighteen other battalions--many augmented with their captured German artillery and ammunition--participated in an intense, coordinated three-and-one-half bombardment from H-Hour minus 60 minutes to H-Hour plus 147 minutes. After the first half-hour, divisional artillery was released for "on-call" missions and targets of opportunity in close support of the advancing divisions.

The massive bombardment destroyed the Wehrmacht's frontline positions, disrupted its communications, and stifled its artillery. Specifically, XII Corps fired the following artillery concentrations:

- ninety on towns;
- thirteen on defiles;
- 190 on enemy artillery locations;
- forty on enemy command posts;
- thirty-one on enemy anti-aircraft artillery locations;
- fourteen on assembly areas;
- one on a strongpoint; and
- one on a farm building.

The heaviest bombardment was a six-battalion, two-volley concentration on the town of Oriocourt. Upon completion of the prearranged shelling, Corps Artillery, including the 267th, continued to maintain intense neutralization fires on enemy forces until noon, after which heavy fires were delivered as called upon by the advancing infantry and armored troops. This heavy artillery support prevented any aggressive German artillery reaction to the attack. There were only fifteen reports of enemy shelling over the entire Corps front, and all were small concentrations of less than twenty rounds each. Also, the destruction of command and communication posts severely disrupted German communications. Since the weather hampered air support, it was up to the artillery to back the assaulting troops.

At H Hour, one hour after the guns began their fire, the armored and infantry divisions of XII Corps attacked along the entire front. The objective was to capture thirty miles of territory up to the Saar River. Following General Patton's order, the 80th, 35th, and 26th Infantry Divisions and the 6th and 4th Armored Divisions launched their attack.

Throughout the month-long campaign, the 267th supported all divisions except the 26th.

For three days, the 267th continuously fired its massive guns on occupied towns, heavy German batteries, and command posts, intensifying its shelling at night. It barraged the town of Luppy and fired in front of the 35th Division as it advanced on Laneuveville-en-Saulnois. It also assisted the 316th Infantry, which faced stiff resistance as it crossed the Seille River. The river was swollen from rain and heavily defended by German infantry and artillery. They eventually crossed and secured the town of Éply.

Much of the 267th's firepower was directed at Delme Ridge. This 1,300-foot-high four-mile-long ridge blocked the 80th from its ultimate objective: Saarland, Germany. Though heavily shelled by the 267th and other Corps artillery, the Germans fiercely defended the ridge from well dug-in positions. Between the massive bombardment and General Patton's decision to assault the ridge from its flanks instead of head-on, it eventually fell with significant loss of life on both sides. As Allied troops poured onto the ridge, the 267th redirected its fire on the retreating German soldiers and their relief columns.

The XIXth Tactical Air Command provided air support for the Third Army. Its pilots fearlessly flew combat support, bombing enemy emplacements and formations. On November 9, even as it rained and snowed, the XIXth's pilots took to the air to support the ground troops. Charles had previously watched them neutralize enemy positions, but on this day, he saw the face of a pilot who had lost his life. A U.S. Army Air Force P-51 fighter plane was hit by enemy fire and crashed near the 267th position near Malleloy. They ran to aid the down pilot, but it was too late for him. The Battalion's Service Battery placed a guard on the crashed aircraft until his body was removed from the wreck.

Fighting intensified on November 11, Armistice Day, as snow continued to fall. The Battalion supported elements of the 35th and 4th Armored Divisions who entered the heavily forested area of Forêt de Château-Salins the previous day. It also fired several volleys into the town of Bois de Château-Bréhain. The Battalion's air observer reported German armored and infantry units withdrawing in disorder after the concentrations were laid down. German artillery covered the withdrawal of their retreating soldiers by firing on the advancing Allies. Along with other artillery units, the co-located 243rd platoon fired four rounds from its eight-inch gun in a ten-minute barrage on the town of Béchy at 7:00 a.m. This bombardment of obstacles and dug-in German riflemen aided an Allied combat team in entering the town.

During the day, Major Collins and his Operation Chief made a reconnaissance for forward emplacement in the vicinity of Donjeux, Liocourt, Delme, and Puzieux. At 10:30 p.m., he ordered the Battalion to pack up their weapons and prepare to move their position twelve-and-a-half miles forward to the vicinity of Puzieux. The move began at 9:30 the following morning and took them half a day as they averaged one mile an hour. This was extremely taxing on Charles and the other exhausted artillerymen. It was cold and overcast, and the roads were full of thick mud and rutted from continuous rain and traffic. The Battalion crawled along the hacked-up roads congested with all types of support units, trying to keep up with the advancing infantry and armored units.

Despite the bitter cold and slow pace, the 267th completed their transverse and emplaced their weapons right behind the infantry--they had to because the Commanding Officer of XII Corps Artillery was General John Max Lentz, a crusty combat field artilleryman from World War I. He said that in the first war, he never saw a general officer in the batteries. He vowed that this war would be different. General Lentz visited two or three fighting battalions and numerous firing batteries every day in combat. Not only did the General command from the front, but he pushed his batteries closer to the front line than any other Corps. As a result, the 267th learned to operate on the front lines since its first action in Diarville, which helped give XII Corps artillery a reputation for staying right with the infantry and armored units.

General Patton pushed his infantry and armored divisions to move quickly and strike hard. General Lentz's artillery followed the same philosophy. If an armored division found entrenched German opposition in a town, they knew General Lentz would quickly have multiple battalions of artillery blasting the Germans. While subject to enemy air and counterbattery attacks, no Corps artillery was ever lost.

The infantry and armor appreciated the big gun support right behind them, making conditions harder for Charles and the 267th. Frequent moves, enemy attacks, and continuous operations on the war's front lines took their toll on the men as it did that night.

From their new position in Delme, the 267th was able to fire on German positions in the Delme and Chenois vicinity to support XII Corps' advance through the region. On November 12, XII Corps met stubborn resistance in Bazancourt and along the road from Han-sur-Nied to Herny. Floods continued to hamper bridging operations, a situation upon which the Germans capitalized with intense artillery firing into Allied bridge sites. Artillery pilots advised XII Corps Artillery of a large enemy troop concentration in Bois de Château Salins's northern portion. Eight-inch guns and 240mm howitzers fired into the area for twenty minutes causing the Wehrmacht's armored and infantry elements to flee in confusion. Charles's Battery also fired rounds into the town of Morhange to soften resistance against a planned assault by the 80th the following day. The crossroads of Morhange served as a hub for the German Army operating in Lorraine. It had to be taken.

Meanwhile, the trench foot epidemic continued to spread, and artillerymen were frequent victims since firing positions were emplaced in flooded and muddy fields. Major Collins directed the Battalion's medical personnel to train the troops on trench foot preventive measures. Charles and the other artillerymen were instructed to massage their feet and keep them dry by changing into clean socks issued daily with their rations.

As the sun rose on the 13th, columns of the Combat Command B (CCB) of the 4th Armored Division began a two-day assault on Morhange and surrounding villages. For those two days, the 267th's guns battered the villages of Achain, Villers-sur-Neid, Marthille, Destry, and then Morhange ahead of the armor columns. As the villages fell one by one, the 134th Infantry moved on the outskirts of Morhange. The weather, unfortunately, favored the Germans. As the Allies were about to enter Morhange, heavy rains resumed and turned to snow and bitter cold after sunset. These conditions slowed the armored advancement and made the situation more miserable for the exposed Allies. Despite the inclement conditions, the troops pressed on. In addition to twelve rounds fired in a thirty-minute morning assault by the 267th, the town was pelted with shells from other 155mm and 8-inch batteries the entire day of the 14th. On the morning of November 15, the Wehrmacht abandoned Morhange, leaving only minefields and blown bridges behind.

Third Army Headquarters ordered all XII Corps Artillery--except those supporting the 26th Infantry Division--to displace forward during the day. The 267th advanced eight and a half miles to Chenois, France, in the freezing wet pre-dawn hours of November 15th, keeping right against the forward-moving divisions. The following day, November 16, after advancing twelve hard-fought miles in eight days, the 35th Division finally halted to rest and await new orders.

On November 17, quiet fell on the entire XII Corps front as its three infantry and two armored divisions consolidated and prepared for the next round of assaults. Charles and the 267th spent the next two days performing equipment maintenance and targeting their guns on the next objectives. They also looked forward to drying out their uniforms and enjoying a few hot meals as the rain and snow cleared, ushering in three days of cold weather with good visibility.

The clear skies allowed the XIXth Tactical Air Command to bombard the enemy from the air. As the men of the 267th prepared their weapons for a full day of firing on the morning of the 18th, they smiled as they looked up to see the sky darken from American planes with shiny wings and emboldened white stars. These winged warriors flew in large formations toward the German lines. The XII Corps' infantry divisions also restarted their advance on these German lines with the Saar River as their goal. The lull was over, and the Allied juggernaut continued its forward march.

From its positions in Chenois, the 267th coordinated its bombardment with the XIXth's fighter bombers, causing projectiles to assault the Germans from air and land. The 267th fired rounds in support of the 6th Armored and 80th Infantry Divisions on Faulquemont, Lelling, Virming, Fontpierre, Hemmering, Maxstedt, Saint-Avold, and Puttelange. Charles's Battery also fired into Grostenquin, Bérig-Vintrange, Bistroff, and Lanning, France. The barrage on Grostenquin supported the 6th

Armored Division, which ran into heavy resistance from dug-in units along the Morhange-Grostenquin Road. The 267th guns, eighteen other field artillery battalions, and fighter-bombers from the XIXth pounded the village, which was then followed by white phosphorus shells setting it ablaze. The following day, the 6th entered Grostenquin and reported that the survivors were "*quaking with fear*" and surrendered without a fight.

The 267th also participated in an assault on hundreds of German trains traveling in the Rhine area, exposed by the clear skies. U.S. P-47 and P-51 aircraft, flying hundreds of sorties and heavy artillery from other units, joined the 267th in attacking railways and trains. As it helped aim the 240mm guns, the Battalion's aircraft was fired upon but not shot down. Under enemy fire, the light plane redirected the heavy guns on four enemy railroad guns with one direct hit. Though Allied intelligence did not know it then, these trains were transporting troops, vehicles, tanks, and artillery to participate in a massive German offensive to be known as the "Battle of the Bulge."

The following day, the 267th focused their fire on heavy enemy activity in St. Avold while the Battalion Commander and his Operations Chief scouted out the next firing position twelve miles southeast near Racrange, which had fallen to the Allies on the 15th.

On November 19th, the 80th and 35th Infantry Divisions encountered intense enemy artillery opposition as they pressed their attack to the east. The 80th Infantry artillery and its supporting Corps artillery battalions, including the 267th, conducted an effective counterbattery resulting in enemy artillery rounds declining and becoming negligible after dark. XII Corps Artillery fired 284 240mm howitzer shells in the last seven days.

November 20th saw both the 267th and the German Army moving east, as the 267th took up positions in Racrange and the Wehrmacht withdrew the bulk of their forces toward the Saar River, leaving only a skeleton force along the XII Corps front. As they convoyed to Racrange, the surrounding scenes weighed on the artillerymen. All the towns they passed through provided horrific testimony to the brutal fighting that had taken place in front of them. Villages were burnt rubble; dead horses, cattle, and German soldiers littered fields and roads all along the route. Upon arrival in Racrange, the 267th--along with the organic artillery of the two divisions and three other Corps artillery battalions--supported the 35th and 6th Armored Divisions' attack to the east with a forty-two-minute artillery preparation.

For two days, the 267th targeted the retreating Germans attempting to regroup their forces in the towns of St. Avold and Sarralbe. Major Collins ordered that at noon of November 22, the Battalion follow the front line and move seven miles north to Bistroff in the vicinity of Grostenquin.

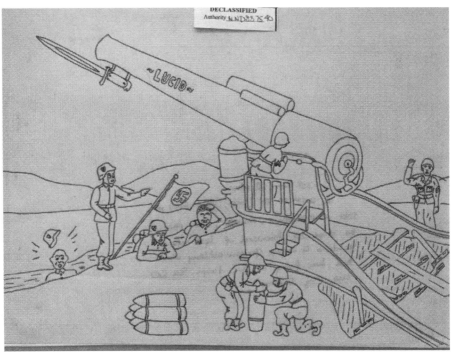

The caption on this cartoon, located in the National Archives, is, *"3rd Army XII Corps - The 267th FA BN (Lucid) (240mm how) just east of Morhange, France, Nov 1944. Bn emplaced forward of light arty. positions to engage German artillery which had been firing on our troops. BN CO was Maj Collins."*

The Battalion experienced four days of intense combat in Bistroff, supporting the XII Corps' advance. Though common along the front, artillery duels were especially intense in this area. On November 22, the 320th Infantry of the 35th Division attempted to advance on the town of Gréning but was pinned down by German artillery in the town of

Hellimer, less than fourteen miles from the 267th's positions. Two days of Allied artillery fire on Hellimer and German positions in Gréning had little impact on the Germans' resolve.

On the 23rd, the Germans counterattacked against the 35th. American infantry, supported by intense artillery fires, repulsed the threat and inflicted heavy losses, allowing the 320th to enter Gréning, at which point the Wehrmacht retreated. The 267th also came under enemy artillery fire. On the evenings of November 22 and 23, Battery B was subject to heavy counterbattery fire from a German gun believed to be larger than 88mm.

Amid the firing and receiving incoming rounds from the Germans, the men of the 267th celebrated Thanksgiving on a cold and cloudy Thursday, November 23. Thanksgiving snuck up on the troops because, in combat, there is little awareness of the calendar. Long days of firing roll into the next, and weekdays are no different from weekends. Time and date are meaningless except when planning your next mission. However, they woke up on Thursday morning looking forward to a good meal. General Patton was adamant that the Army make every attempt to provide all soldiers with a traditional Thanksgiving dinner. Turkeys and all that goes with the meal were shipped to cooks who spent the night preparing them for the troops across liberated Europe. Officers arranged to serve the meals wherever the troops could savor the treat. Troops were brought into barns, bombed-out buildings, or anyplace they could take some cover from the cold, mud, and rain.

All day, chow trucks laden with Thanksgiving dinners, complete with all the trimmings, made runs to the troops on the line. Major Collins found barns and a few buildings for his artillerymen to eat in shifts. Along with turkey, they were served raisin bread, mashed potatoes, and all the trimmings, including cigarettes and cigars. Some of Charles's fellow troops "liberated" some wine from a French house that perfectly matched the meal. All the artillerymen ate until they were sick but happy. On the chow trucks were sacks of mail so the troops could read letters from their wives, girlfriends, and others as they filled their bellies. It was a welcome break from the endless grind of warfare, even though it was short-lived, as their guns were needed to assist troops advancing that day.

For the next three days, the Battalion supported the 6th Armored Division as it advanced on towns around Puttelange. When the Wehrmacht made a stand in the village of Hilsprich, the 267th and other artillery units nearly pulverized the town. It also supported the 80th Division as it moved on emplacements in the old Maginot Line, spanning the French/German border. As the advance approached the Saar River, the volume of enemy artillery fire increased throughout the Third Army area. Forward observers reported medium caliber fire coming from new areas, indicating that the Germans were bringing up additional artillery to defend the River. The two divisions were hampered by stiff German resistance, mines, artillery attacks, and poor roads turned nearly impassable because of thick mud. Finally, on November 25, the 80th took the town of Falkenberg, an important mining town. It then advanced on the main works of the Maginot line after an intense five-minute artillery concentration. By midday, nearly all the German defenders had either surrendered or been killed.

Amid all the chaos of battle and the miserable cold and wet conditions, Charles remembered that he needed to mail a card to Bertha and Karoly if it was to arrive in time for them to read it on Christmas day. So, he took one of the cards issued to the troops and found a quiet spot where he penned the following:

> *"Dear Mother and Father, I am hoping this card finds you and dad in the best of health. I also received your letter you wrote Nov 8th. I received Mary and Mr. Glowa packages and I am going to write to them letting them know it. I am feeling fine and I didn't have time to write you sooner. Give my best regards to everybody at home and please do not worry about me. Love Son Charlie"*

He put the card into the outgoing mail and returned to his job on the 240mm.

On the morning of Sunday, November 26, the 80th continued its advance. In front of it, rear elements of the Wehrmacht covered its main Army's retreat. Upon the sixth counterattack by one of those rear-guard elements on a battalion of the 318th Infantry, the 267^{th,} and eight other field artillery battalions were called into action. The German force was decimated. As the 80th advanced on St. Avold, the former German Army headquarters and a coal center for its war machine, the German defenders withdrew from the town's back end. It was a busy day, with the 267th firing ninety rounds on enemy troops and strong points, including harassing fire on Sarreguemines, France. In addition, it successfully neutralized an enemy artillery piece camouflaged inside a house and an exposed enemy battery.

The German Army continued its retreat toward the defenses of the Maginot Line. While the former French positions were old and unkempt, they provided cover for the retreating Germans as they reorganized their defenses. The 267th, like the rest of the Allied Army, stayed right behind the retreating Germans. The 267th convoy traveled a little over six miles on rutted and deep mud roads that were nearly impassable to the vicinity of Diffembach, France.

The winter of 1944 saw the Lorraine area of France receive record rainfall and cold weather. Troops were bogged down by thick mud on the roads. It was even more challenging for the 267th as they transported their heavy artillery. Here they are traveling on Muddy Roads in the Lorraine area.

Excitement ran through the Battalion as Charles and his fellow artillerymen looked at their orders and maps. It hit them that they would be close enough to the border that German towns would be within range. They were ready to stop destroying their French allies' land and concentrate their guns' destructive power on the Reich itself.

In Diffembach, Charles and the Second Gun Section pulled a projectile out of its case and painted it with the word "FAE." This was the name of one of Charles's fellow artilleryman's wife. They loaded it into the breech of their 240mm and launched their first round into Germany proper.

Left: Second Gun Section first round fired into Germany. One of the boys put his wife's name on it (FAE). Fired approximately November 27, 1944, while in Diffembach, France. Right: Fred Ackley in his tent.

The 267th spent the next six days in this emplacement, continuously firing on German positions in and behind the Maginot Line fortifications. Their job was to dispel any notion that German troops were safe in the aging Line's bunkers. The 240mm battalions were organized and brought to Europe specifically to utilize their long-range and massive firepower to punch holes in the Maginot Line. Nevertheless, while these were aging defenses, they were still the most formidable fortifications the 267th ever faced. In addition to shelling the occupied French border towns of Liplingen, Sarreinsming, Frauenberg, Forbach, Sarreguemines, and Wittring, the 267th unleashed harassing fire into the German towns of Saarbrucken, Großblittersdorfer, and Kleinblittersdorf. The Wehrmacht must have felt trapped in the Maginot Line with powerful shells falling on them as well as in the towns in front and behind them. Nowhere seemed safe!

On Thursday, November 30, the 267th suffered its only combat casualty in Europe while operating as an artillery unit. His name was Private Fred Albert Ackley, from Battery C, and he was Charles's best friend.

Fred was a Native-American citizen born into the Ojibbeway tribe in Indiana on March 4, 1922. While he was young, his family moved to the Mole Lake Band of Chippewas Reservation in Wisconsin, where their father raised him, his three brothers, and one sister. For a few years, he attended grammar school, then--like most men back then--went to work to help support his family.

While Charles was at Camp Hood, Texas, Fred received a notice drafting him into the U.S. Army. On December 1, 1942, at five feet, six inches, and 121 pounds, Fred walked into the Army enlistment office in Milwaukee, Wisconsin, and took the oath that made him a soldier.

Assigned to the 267th while at Camp Shelby, Charles and Fred were bunkmates and ultimately best friends. They spent their liberty time together, exploring the sites of Hattiesburg and other places around the base. Many hours of "hurry up and wait time" were spent trading stories of growing up in a New York City suburb or a Wisconsin Indian reservation. The closest friends a person can have in life are war buddies. War builds a bond between military personnel that cannot be replicated nor adequately described to a civilian.

On that Thursday, in an area outside of Diffembach, Battery C's artillerymen heard the familiar sound of the chow truck pulling up with well-earned meals. As it drove into a location covered by trees and brush, the artillerymen hunted for their mess kits, wondering what the Army would feed them. It was a busy day, with the 267th firing 93 rounds, more than any previous day, and the backbreaking work had the troops hungry and exhausted.

General Lentz had the 267th right up on the front line. Battery B reported seeing the muzzle flashes of German artillery that day, so snipers kept Charles and his fellow soldiers under cover. As they lined up for chow, Sergeant Potter reminded them to stay covered because of snipers. The chow line snaked along the trees leading up to the truck. Charles would move up to the next tree, closer to the chow truck, as the man in front made his way closer. Overhead came the familiar sound of incoming rounds, and as he hunched down behind the tree, he heard loud explosions impacting nearby. When the rounds stopped, Charles looked back and saw Fred on the ground, wounded and bleeding. He ran over and helped the medics care for his best friend. That was the last time Charles saw his closest buddy, and he would spend the rest of his life wondering what had happened to him while being too afraid to find out.

Unbeknownst to Charles, Fred recovered from his wounds and, on November 4, 1945, was discharged from the Army with a Purple Heart. He returned to Wisconsin, but the war haunted him for the rest of his life. Two days before Christmas in 1973, Fred was killed in a car accident. He was just 51 years old.

During the six days that the 267th fired from its positions in Diffembach, it assisted the Allied infantry and armored units in making significant advances all along the line. On the 27th, the 80th completely liberated St. Avold after massed artillery fires repulsed four enemy counterattacks. From there, XII Corps assaulted the Maginot Line and reinforced German defenses along the Saar River. Third Army Intelligence reported that the Wehrmacht was adding mobile weapons to its heavy artillery to increase its defense of the Saar River against an Allied crossing.

As the sun set on November 30, each Third Army unit's headquarters began to compile their unit summaries for the month. They wrote that November opened with the Germans continuing to use defensive tactics and hoping for a winter stalemate that would allow them to rest, refit, and reorganize their battered divisions. German Army units concentrated on the defensive reorganization of the terrain between the front lines and the Siegfried Line, constructing anti-tank ditches, communication lines, fire trenches, pillboxes, and minefields. Barbed wire was strung extensively, and POWs told Allied interrogators that they winter-proofed dugouts and foxholes. On November 8, the Third Army opened the Lorraine Campaign, which upset the enemy's hopes for a winter breathing spell. XII Corps delivered the attack, preceded by a devastating artillery preparation that disrupted German communications and curtailed their artillery employment. The Seille and Moselle Rivers, both at flood stage because of unusually heavy autumn rains, imposed unforeseen obstacles on the Third Army. Bridgeheads had to be won and maintained only by the utmost effort. Throughout the entire month, lousy weather significantly hampered

Third Army operations, limiting air support and largely confining armor and tank destroyers to the roads.

The Germans took advantage of the defensive opportunities offered by the weather. They fought delaying actions from one critical terrain feature to the next. Practically every village was turned into a defensive strongpoint, and maximum use was made of their limited amount of artillery. In the Metz area, the Germans' attempt to make a fortress stand, hinged upon the elaborate system of forts, was shattered between November 15 and 20. By the end of the month, the Wehrmacht was forced into the Siegfried Line, where they massed the greatest concentration of artillery yet to confront the Third Army.

As mentioned earlier, trench foot constituted a serious problem due to constant exposure of feet to water and cold. The Third Army experienced 4,587 cases admitted to division clearing stations, with 95% of cases determined to be of no further value for combat duty during the winter months. The Third Army suffered an average of 702 casualties a day, or 21,059 for the month, while it captured 200 towns. The Germans lost 374 artillery pieces 75mm or greater, and the Third Army lost eight.

Saarbrücken, Germany, was the major troop and supply hub supporting German forces seeking to halt the Third Army advance. An analysis by Third Army Intelligence of the enemy railroad movement indicated that the major portion of rail traffic between November 17 and December 2 was toward the Saarbrücken and Eifel areas. On November 17, 300 trains were observed by tactical reconnaissance, and marshaling yards were particularly active. Reports indicated that eighty-four trains moved into the same area over the next two days, with many trains stationary in marshaling yards or on routes heading north. On November 26, forty-six trains were observed. Finally, on December 2, the rail movement analysis indicated a definite buildup of enemy troops and supplies in that area. While its guns could reach parts of the city, the 267th was given orders to advance closer so their 240mm's full power could rain on those railyards. Thus, at 9:00 a.m. on December 2, the Battalion departed for Biding and Marienthal-Barst, France. By noon, it completed the eight-mile transit with Charles's Battery emplacing in Marienthal-Barst.

With their guns registered on Saarbrücken, the 267th began a bombardment of the city that lasted the next five days. Its mission was to disrupt further German supply lines by shelling railroads and railyards in and around the city. This was part of a larger XII Corps artillery effort where light and medium artillery continued harassing and interdicting fires on thirty-nine towns while heavy, long-range weapons attacked Saarbrücken, Sarreguemines, and Forbach. In response, German artillery shelled small towns behind Allied lines to disrupt unit command posts and shelters.

The Allies failed to realize that the 267th was actually fighting the next battle as they pummeled German trains loaded with troops, armor, artillery, and other supplies. These trains were not headed to the Lorraine campaign but towards the Ardennes area in preparation for the Battle of the Bulge.

The Battalion also supported the 80th Division and the 6th Armored Division as they drove through Diebling and the towns in Lorraine en route to capture the area's largest border city, Sarreguemines. On December 4, the 267th joined other artillery units in a sixty-minute bombardment of Farébersviller, ten-and-a-half miles from Sarreguemines. The targets were German artillery positions, towns, command posts, and supply points. When the shelling halted, the 80th liberated the town and hills to its northeast, causing the Germans to withdraw into the Siegfried Line.

Sarreguemines is a major shipping depot located at the confluence of the Blies and Saar Rivers. It has a contentious history between the French and Germans. Originally French territory, it was transferred to Germany in 1871 with the Treaty of Frankfurt that followed the Franco-Prussian War. With Germany's defeat in World War I, the French reclaimed it until Hitler's army seized it in 1940. The French wanted it back, and on December 9, that wish came true.

Left: Battery C gun pit, tents, and ammunition. Right: Charles Asztalos' pup tent and foxhole

On December 7, the third anniversary of the Pearl Harbor attack, the 267th again packed up their howitzers to convoy eight-and-a-half miles east toward the German border to Guebenhouse, France. As the convoy made its way through the smoking ruins of Puttelange, Charles thought to himself, *"Boy, we really did a job on this town."*

In Guebenhouse, the 267th spent the next four days opening holes in the German defenses for XII Corps to advance.   From this location, the Battalion's powerful guns could lob shells deep into Germany, hitting the towns of Sankt Ingbert, Sulzbach, Bliesransbach, Fechingen, and Bischmisheim.

On December 9 and 10, the Battalion participated in one of the greatest artillery advances of World War II. In World War I and World War II up to this point, both sides lacked a reliable fuse to deliver airburst explosions.   These types of blasts were used for anti-personnel bombardment. The Army formed a dedicated team of researchers and electrical engineers to tackle the problem, and the result was the Pozit fuse or variable time (VT) fuse. This new Top-Secret fuse was a device that exploded automatically by magnetic attraction when it came within approximately 30 feet of either the ground or metal objects. With the new fuse ready to enter battle, the Third Army set up a demonstration for its top brass and artillery leadership. One 240mm gun from Battery A was given the honor to demonstrate the Pozit. It traveled 155 miles south to Audincourt, France, near the Swiss border. There the 267th artillerymen, along with others from the 313th, 974th (155mm howitzers), and 741st (8-inch howitzers) field artillery battalions, demonstrated the new device. All batteries were registered and fired several rounds with Pozit fuses. The results were successful, with very few early bursts occurring--the percentage of effective rounds were 89% for the 105mms, 80% for the 155mms, 92% for the 8 inches, and 100% for the 240mm from the 267th.

The December 9 demonstration for XII Corps' leadership included General Patton, who mentioned the Pozit in his private diary, referring to it as *"that funny fuse."* A second demonstration was conducted on December 10 for artillery personnel with XX Corps.

When the Germans launched the Ardennes Offensive eight days later, General Eisenhower quickly distributed the new fuses to his troops. It was put into use at a time of great need, assisting in the Allied counterattack. Its accuracy and reliability made the Pozit fuse one of World War II's great technological achievements and a device that the U.S. Field Artillery continued to use up through the Iraqi and Afghanistan Wars.

For seven miles between Sarreguemines and Saarbrücken, the Saar River serves as the border between France and Germany. The 267th spent December 10 and 11 supporting infantry units to establish toeholds on the river's German side, the XII Corps' first incursions into the Third Reich's homeland. December 10 was a historic day for the Third Army. It conducted its first flag-raising ceremony in Germany in the town of Eft-Hellendorf. Townspeople were assembled outside the military government office for the reading of the proclamation and raising of the American flag.

On December 11, the Battalion convoyed eight-and-a-half miles to Neufgrange, a small village just south of Sarreguemines. From this position, the batteries spent the next seven days firing deep into Germany, concentrating fire on the towns of Bliesransbach, Blieskastel,

Webenheim, Nu Wurzbach, and Sankt Ingbert. Additionally, the attached eight-inch gun shelled Deux Ponts and Kirkel, Germany.

The Wehrmacht intensified combat operations as it now fought to defend the homeland. As XII Corps units steadily advanced, the 267th's long-range guns were increasingly called upon to neutralize enemy infantry, armor, and artillery. The big guns were clearly affecting the enemy because the Germans were increasingly targeting them. On December 13, the 267th batteries and spotter aircraft came under heavy enemy fire.

For the next five days, artillerymen responded to the attack with greater ferocity. Despite a steady rain and a thick fog, it struck an ammunition or gasoline dump in the town of Walsheim, Germany, setting off explosions, which the Battalion's air observer described as "*looking like a Fourth of July celebration.*" On the 16th, the Battalion fired 117 rounds, destroying two enemy batteries and an ammunition storage area. During the night of December 17 and the day of the 18th, the Battalion launched 310 projectiles. It was its heaviest concentration of fire and the last time the 267th guns would fire in World War II.

In September and October, as the Allies raced across France, liberating new towns each day, Charles and his fellow soldiers were sure the war would be won by Christmas. November tempered that prediction, as that month's campaign through Lorraine only saw a thirty-mile advancement, or approximately a mile a day. But Charles and the men of the 267th were still hopeful in mid-December that victory was around the corner. While they were still 450 miles from Berlin, XII Corps punched through the Maginot Line and drove the Wehrmacht back into its country.

Everything changed at 6:30 on the dark and foggy Saturday morning of December 16. German heavy artillery opened up along a sixty-mile front in the Ardennes Forest, north of Charles. The firing intensified, and by 9:00 a.m., patrols were piercing the U.S. First Army lines. By noon, it appeared the entire German Army was pouring through a fifty-mile gap in the line. Two American divisions and an armored command crumbled before the advancing Nazis. The large bulge in their lines inspired the Americans to name it the Battle of the Bulge.

Camouflaged 240mm howitzer of the 267th and mud

Seventy-one hours after the attack began, General Lentz drove through the bitter cold to Third Army Headquarters in Nancy for a meeting of all corps commanders, including their artillery and operations officers. General Patton confirmed the rumors of a major breach in Allied lines to the north and that the Germans were decimating U.S. forces. He informed them of a tentative plan to put the surviving forces under his command, thin out the Third Army line, and rush available forces, including XII Corps, into the Ardennes.

It is said that soldiers in World War II lived on chow, tobacco, and rumors. The Army's rumor mill had a way of reaching every GI in every fighting hole, including the Second Gun Crew of Battery C camouflaged in a field near Neufgrange, France. Like the rest of the troops, they were confused and apprehensive in those initial days after the attack. *"How could the Nazis, so close to defeat, seize the initiative like that?"* Guards were doubled with rumors of Germans, in American uniforms and speaking perfect English, parachuting deep behind American lines. All GIs were challenged and re-challenged as they approached sentries. Other rumors of German-armored convoys on our side of the line made the artillerymen jump for their rifles with the sound of approaching vehicles.

On Sunday, December 17, outside Malmedy, Belgium, Waffen-SS troops murdered eighty-one American soldiers from Battery B of the 285th Field Artillery Observation Battalion. Because they had surrendered and were murdered in cold blood, it became known as the Massacre at Malmedy and galvanized American resolve to crush the German war machine.

One hundred and thirty-eight miles to the south, Charles, and the rest of the 267th were told they would soon be removed from the front line in Lorraine. Their Battalion would be relieved from XII Corps and placed on special duty with the Third Army's Provost Marshal. The co-located platoon from Battery C of the 243rd Field Artillery Battalion would be detached from the 267th. Throughout the Corps, troops packed their gear and loaded vehicles for redeployment to the Ardennes area.

Through the night of the 17th and into the morning of the 18th, the Battalion fired 193 rounds at the Germans. The gun tube was so hot from the continuous firing that Charles and the other artillerymen were lighting their cigarettes on its sides. The artillerymen expended their supply of ammunition before 6:00 a.m. They then spent the remainder of the day cleaning and securing their guns for transit one last time. The following day, the 267th joined an exodus of units heading northwest as it convoyed thirty-one miles to a former Nazi POW Camp near Niedervisse, France. After months of constant movement east toward Germany, it struck Charles as odd to be heading away from the front. While it was some comfort to be moving away from Germany, the convoy was extremely difficult. The artillerymen rode in open vehicles, subject to bitter cold and cloudy weather. Vehicles heading to different locations jammed the roads--some were lost, ran off the road, or suffered mechanical problems due to the extreme cold. These vehicles slowed the long-mechanized columns behind them. The roads also hindered progress as rutted mud holes trapped unsuspecting vehicles. Occasional enemy fighters harassed the columns, sending troops diving into the muddy and ice-caked road banks. Charles was happy to pull into Niedervisse, where he disembarked and was assigned a building to sleep.

After a night's rest, Major Collins mustered his troops and read them their new orders. He described a major shuffle of artillery units as the Third Army regrouped its corps to attack the southern flank of the enemy's Ardennes incursion. While the other units either remained in Lorraine or headed north with the bulk of the Third Army, the 267th shifted into a new role. According to Troop Assignment No. A-75, 17 Dec 44, the Battalion's new mission was guarding rear areas and administering and evacuating POWs in the Third Army area. Battery C was ordered to Nancy to guard the Third Army's Rear Command Post. Battery B was assigned to Pont-à-Mousson, France, to guard bridges. The remainder of the Battalion stayed at the captured POW Camp in Boulay, which the Third Army overran on December 1, administering the Camp and evacuating the prisoners to the rear.

In his less than two-and-a-half years in the Army, Charles was given his fifth new job, which he first learned in boot camp. Charles was assigned the primary job of every soldier--a rifleman--and he knew a rifleman's job was to shoot German riflemen.

Shifting troops to security behind the front became a rising priority, even before the Ardennes offensive. Earlier in the month, Third Army intelligence reported that the Germans used definite routes for infiltrating and returning agents through Third Army lines. Enemy agents traveled through Sainte-Marie-aux-Chênes, Thionville, St. Avold, Nancy, and Hagenau. The Provost Marshal increased security and established roadblocks along the routes. The movement north toward the Ardennes further exacerbated the need for more MPs.

Major Collins explained that General Patton ordered his Army to disengage from combat, pivot north, and attack the Germans, who did not anticipate nor plan for a counterattack of this magnitude from the south. The entire XII Corps pulled back from the line, with most of it heading for combat in Luxembourg and Belgium. It was a brilliant operation that only General Patton could pull off.

Third Army MPs and soldiers involved with transportation were confronted with the most complex troop movement of the campaign. The Corps deployed MPs along every passable road and moved 100,000 troops with all their material and transport about 150 miles during two days of miserable weather. A constant traffic flow of more than 11,200 vehicles was directed north over four routes. All available personnel were concentrated on traffic duty, and special officer couriers were dispatched to each MP battalion along the four major troop movement routes. General Patton ordered all unessential personnel to be pulled from support units, like the 267th, and attached to military police or infantry units to augment the operation.

As Charles prepared for his new mission, he got his first up-close look at the Nazi extermination machine. The camp he bivouacked in was a liberated German POW camp for Soviet soldiers. Adjacent to it was the Johannis Bannberg Hospital, which the Reich used to exterminate those deemed "undesirable." Charles shook his head as he watched medical personnel from the U.S. Army 7th Field Hospital, which arrived simultaneously with 267th, care for 2,393 recovered Allied POWs. They were primarily Russian, with some Italians and Yugoslavs. In wretched condition, they suffered from malnutrition, tuberculosis, and other diseases. Also in the camp were mass graves containing about 22,000 victims.

Niedervisse was not a pleasant place, and it would only worsen for the men of the 267th. The Germans sought to finish the job of eliminating its former prisoners, so it incessantly shelled the former camp and the American troops occupying it. Once their artillery and other equipment were secured, Charles and Battery C's men traveled fifty-five miles south to Nancy and assumed their mission to guard the Third Army Rear Command Post. Battery B convoyed thirty-nine miles in the same direction to Pont-à-Mousson. It, along with soldiers from the 4405 Quartermaster Service Company (an all-black unit), the First and Third Companies, 151st French Infantry Regiment, 31st French Gendarmes from the Tenth Legion Gendarmes, and the Fourth and Eighth Squadrons of the Fourth Regiment, French Republican Guards guarded seven railway tunnels, twenty-seven railway bridges, one highway overpass, and fourteen highway bridges in the Pont-à-Mousson area.

The remainder of the Battalion (Headquarters, Service, Medical, and A Batteries) remained in Niedervisse to finish evacuating the liberated prisoners. On December 28, the repatriated prisoners were evacuated from the bombardment to Toul, France. The last 267th artillerymen left the following day, traveling thirty-seven miles northeast to Hayange, France, where the Battalion established its headquarters.

Upon the 267th's arrival in Hayange, most enlisted members were dispatched to guard critical areas within the Third Army perimeter. The officers were tasked with a high-level security mission: conducting a reconnaissance of all railway lines within the Third Army area and determine locations of important bridges and tunnels that were unguarded or inadequately guarded. After several weeks of scouting the French, Belgium, and Luxembourg countrysides, they returned to Headquarters with a detailed report on their findings.

Charles had mixed emotions as the convoy carrying Battery C departed Niedervisse en route to Nancy. As he heard the artillery shells falling on the camp in the distance, he felt for his fellow artillerymen who stayed behind. However, Charles relished pleasant thoughts of his last visit to Nancy. There on R&R last September, he enjoyed his first hot meal, bath, and a night's sleep in a bed in over a month. He even got to see Marlene Dietrich in a USO show--and what a show it was!

The Third Army had captured Nancy on September 15, while the 267th was twenty-three miles south in Diarville. On October 5, the Third Army Rear Echelon Headquarters moved to Nancy. General Patton co-located his rear and forward headquarters in the town for the next few months.

As the convoy pulled up to the Rear Echelon Headquarters, Charles looked at the large buildings that made up the Headquarters complex. The 190 officers and 500 enlisted troops with 242 vehicles that made up the headquarters occupied one of three "casernes" (large groups of stone barracks) named Caserne Landremont. Other headquarter units used Caserne Blandan and Caserne Molitor.

Inside Caserne Landremont, Charles ate a hot meal at a table in a large chow hall and completed the check-in procedures. Even though the cavernous building suffered damage from fighting, he was impressed by it. It was named after General Charles-Hyacinthe Leclerc Landremont, who joined the French Army in 1759 at the start of the Seven Years War. He served through the French Revolution and retired in 1796. Caserne Landremont and the other two casernes were originally built and occupied by the French Regular Army, then German troops occupied them in 1940 when they captured the town. Because Nancy is centrally located in an arch that made up the Third Army's front lines, General Patton pressed the mammoth buildings into service as his headquarters.

The 267th soldiers quartered in buildings around the casernes. Sergeant Potter directed Charles and a few other Second Gun Section members to an adjacent private residence where he shared a small room on the second floor with another soldier. His window overlooked a large courtyard with stables and a wooden garage. On the far corner was a large stone church. The room was nicely furnished with a comfortable bed, and a wood stove heated the house. It had been quite some time since he lived in a shelter that provided more protection from the elements than one gets from a piece of canvas! Charles slept well that first night.

Charles Asztalos: "A view from our quarters in Nancy, France."

The Battery's mission was to provide security in and around the headquarters and guard the stockade that housed deserters and other GIs who violated Army regulations. It was a busy time for the Headquarters' staff. Not only were they doing all the planning and support to move the Third Army into the Ardennes area, but they were in the process of moving themselves. On December 20, the Forward Echelon Headquarters shut down its operation in Nancy and proceeded ninety miles to a new location in Luxembourg. The following day, Third Army units fanned out across Luxembourg to assume the defense of the city of Luxembourg, the steel mill at Differdange, and the radio station at Junglinster.

German forces continued to advance in the VIII Corps zone, surrounding the city of Bastogne, which the 101st Airborne Division defended. After establishing a defensive perimeter in Luxembourg, the Third Army prepared to attack the enemy protrusion's southern flank. As Rear Echelon staff coordinated the Army's movement, it began preparations for its move by conducting reconnaissance for a new northern location. Five sites were considered, with Esch-sur-Alzette, Luxembourg, selected on December 29. An advance party began preparing the site on New Year's Day, 1945.

As the Third Army advanced, streams of civilian refugees, including Germans, moved through its rear area. Soldiers were pulled to assist MP units in removing unnecessary civilian traffic from all major roads. The Provost Marshal attempted to control the exodus by organizing transportation and bivouacking of German civilians. MPs evacuated more than 3,000 German civilians and approximately 2,500 scattered villagers from the Saar River area. They were moved to holding areas behind regimental lines for military security and to simplify control problems. Despite these efforts, Nazi agents continued to disrupt Allied supply and communications in the rear areas.

Charles and his fellow MP's' job became more intense as concerns about rear area security continued to grow exponentially during the last part of December. On December 22, Charles and the other battery members received a briefing detailing German tactics to disrupt operations behind Allied lines by donning American uniforms and equipment. On Christmas Day, German agents sabotaged the tracks in five separate places along the rail line between Longwy, France, and Arlon, Luxembourg, delaying the delivery of supplies to III Corps. Three days later, Charles and the other security personnel were directed to watch for unusual pigeon activity or people handling pigeons after receiving reports of enemy agents using pigeons to communicate across lines into Germany.

While Charles spent much of his time on duty, he still managed to enjoy the benefits of being stationed in Nancy. Near Headquarters was a rest center for the troops, thermal baths, and a swimming pool. Also close by was a Red Cross Club, and next to it were the Empire and Garrison Theaters with daily movies and USO shows. When Charles arrived, the show was "Five Pips and a Drip," followed by big-league baseball players Mel Ott, "Dutch" Leonard, Frank Frisch, and "Bucky" Walters, who arrived on Christmas Eve. On Christmas Day, Joe McKenna's "Keep Em Rollin" USO Camp Show played to 2,000 troops at the Club.

On New Year's Day, 1945, Charles got to earn more money when he was promoted from Buck Private to Private First Class, and his pay jumped from $50.00 to $54.00 per month. Since he arrived in Normandy, he was paid in "flag ticket" Francs, a currency issued by the U.S. Military to its troops and civilians in Allied-occupied France. They were called "flag tickets" because of the French flag printed on the back of these small square bills, which came in two, five, and ten Franc denominations. When Charles got to Luxembourg and Belgium, he was paid in Belgium Francs.

As soon as Charles fell into a routine of work and some time to feel human, Sergeant Potter put out the word to prepare to move out. Over three days from January 7 to 9, Charles helped the other Rear Echelon Headquarters staff pack up and load convoys. They moved sixty-nine miles north to Esch-sur-Alzette, in the southwest of the country, just over the French border. It is Luxemburg's second-largest population center after the City of Luxembourg.

Charles stayed in Nancy until the casernes were emptied and turned over to local authorities. Then on January 11, he and the remaining security team convoyed to the new location. When he arrived, he found the headquarters fully operational, supporting the Ardennes Offensive. It was in three large schools--one housed operations, and two were barracks. Troops also worked out of a nearby office building and numerous stores and apartments. One small hotel was commandeered for overnight guests. Officers were billeted with private families after the city and steel plant officials conducted a door-to-door survey of available rooms. Due to a lack of garage space, vehicles and motor transport maintenance areas were in open lots. An officer's mess for 245 and one enlisted mess for 850 were established in the Supply Group building. While the town did not offer Nancy's amenities, Charles was happy to have a cot indoors. He was also glad to see some old friends as his convoy rolled into the town. The USO moved its operation from Nancy to the Klwines Theater near his barracks.

As Charles was traveling to Esch-sur-Alzette, the Nazi Ardennes Offensive was crumbling. Their mid and late-December success was aided by rain and low clouds, which hampered Allied air support and some ground operations. General Patton needed clear weather to beat the Germans, so in late December, he directed his Chaplain to put forth the following prayer:

> *"Almighty and most merciful Father, we humbly beseech Thee, of Thy great goodness, to restrain these immoderate rains with which we have had to contend. Grant us fair weather for battle. Graciously harken to us as soldiers who call upon Thee that armed with Thy power, we may advance from victory to victory, and crush the oppression and wickedness of our enemies, and establish Thy justice among men and nations. Amen."*

General Patton's prayer for fair weather was followed a few days later by a break in the clouds. The clear weather allowed Allied forces to halt the enemy's Ardennes penetration and drive it back toward Germany.

While Charles and Battery C guarded the Rear Headquarters and the 267th officers were conducting their assessment of security for all railway lines, bridges, and tunnels, the remainder of the Battalion--along with troops from 4405 Quartermaster Service Company, the 734th Field Artillery Battalion, and the First and Third Companies of the French 151st Infantry Regiment--were guarding key areas in France, Luxembourg, and Belgium. These units provided security for thirty-six railway bridges, seven railway tunnels, twenty-five highway bridges, and one highway overpass. They also guarded the Twelfth Army Group Communications Center, Third Army Radio Center, and the Post Telegraph and Telephone Building in Luxembourg City, the SHAEF Radio north in Sandweiler, Luxembourg, the Post Telegraph and Telephone Building in Metz, France, the SHAEF Radio west in Longwy, France, and the Repeater Station located in Aubange, Belgium. "SHAEF" was an acronym for Supreme Headquarters Allied Expeditionary Force which was the headquarters for General Eisenhower, the Commander of Allied Forces in Northwest Europe.

On Tuesday, February 6, Sergeant Potter put out the order to pack up their gear and load it onto trucks. Nine days prior, the Third Army and other Allied Forces repelled the German Army back to the Sigfried Line and recovered all territory lost in the Ardennes Offensive. From that point on, the German Army was in steady retreat, with its command and control crumbling as it collapsed upon itself. The Headquarters staff were breathing easier with the Army now on the offensive against a disorganized foe. For two days, Charles and the other security personnel assisted staff in moving their operation twelve miles from Esch-sur-Alzette to join the Forward Echelon in the city of Luxembourg. The new headquarters occupied two office buildings, three schools, several residences, stores, and five hotels.

With the situation stabilized in the Low Countries, the Third Army made plans to turn security over to the Belgium and Luxembourg armies and shift more troops back to the French border and into Germany. The 11th Belgian Fusilier Battalion began training to assume the guard duties currently performed by the American units, including the 267th. On February 1, a detachment from Battery C was sent to the French city of Metz to relieve the 734th Field Artillery Battalion from guarding the Post Telegraph and Telephone Buildings. With their training complete, local troops took over guarding the Third Army Rear Echelon Headquarters on February 11. Charles and the rest of Battery C were relieved of guard duty in Luxembourg, less ten enlisted men left to guard prisoners in the stockade.

Left: Charles on guard duty with a G.I. and French soldier. Right: troops from several nations guarding a bridge

Charles was reassigned to Belgium to work with Belgium units to guard bridges, tunnels, and the Third Army Repeater Station in Aubange. He would eventually reunite with other members from his Battalion whom he had not seen since his convoy pulled out of Niedervisse in mid-December. Under the command of the Battalion's Executive Officer, Major Heenan, Battery A was soon given a new mission to run the Third Army Prisoner of War Enclosure Number 13 in the nearby town of Arlon.

Enclosure Number 13 held several thousand German POWs, with hundreds arriving and being transported to the rear daily. These enclosures were temporary primitive holding areas established near the front to collect prisoners from frontline units, perform initial interrogations and registration, then ship them out to permanent camps.

POW enclosure duty was onerous and wrapped in controversy to this day. In 1989, James Bacque published a book titled, "Other Losses," which argues that General Eisenhower, as head of the American occupation of Germany in 1945, may have deliberately starved over one million German POWs to death. His allegations set off a series of documentaries and scholarly debates culminating in a conference on the subject at the Eisenhower Center of the University of New Orleans. It was attended by World War II and post-war-Germany historians and experts from the U.S., Canada, Britain, Germany, and Austria. The participants included the famous World War II historian and Director of the Eisenhower Center, Stephen Ambrose, who wrote a paper titled "Ike and the Disappearing Atrocities," which rebuts many of the allegations in "Other Losses."

The experts at the conference agreed on several points and disagreed on others. What they did agree to, according to Stephen Ambrose, is that there was:

> "widespread mistreatment of German prisoners in the spring and summer of 1945. Men were beaten, denied water, forced to live in open camps without shelter, and given inadequate food rations and medical care. Their mail was withheld. In some cases, hunger drove prisoners to make 'soup' out of water and grass. Men did die needlessly and inexcusably."

Rations for the POWs were generally between 1,000 and 1,550 calories per day, which cannot sustain the human body over time.

However, scholars disagreed with Mr. Bacque on the scope and the reasons for the inhumanity. Mr. Bacque argued that General Eisenhower oversaw a process that systematically starved over one million German POWs to punish them for the war. Mr. Ambrose argued that the reason for small rations was not to starve former German soldiers; instead, the Army had to feed millions of civilians and soldiers fleeing to American zones, many in advance of the Soviet Army. In addition to five million German prisoners, the American military had to feed millions of civilians, including thirteen million displaced German civilians, civilians of the liberated nations, and two million liberated slave laborers in Germany. All of them were generally fed a diet of 1,500 calories a day. Mr. Ambrose also challenged the claim that up to one million German POWs died, arguing that the total death, by all causes, could not have been greater than 56,000.

Despite disagreement over the extent of camp conditions, we know life was harsh for the prisoners and the guards overseeing them. The camps were extremely overcrowded. War-weary prisoners mostly slept without shelter, exposed to the elements with meager rations and little or no access to clean drinking water. Some died of exposure and diseases. Guards had to provide for men in the uniform that killed and wounded their comrades in battle, administered the barbaric concentration camps, and inflicted other atrocities on civilians and unarmed Allied soldiers.

Guards also had to sort out the prisoners for interrogation and determine initial levels of guilt for Nazi atrocities. SS soldiers were separated and given harsher treatment because of their fanatical allegiance to Nazism--many SS soldiers switched into Wehrmacht uniforms or civilian clothes and denied their identity. In 2001, Charles was with a group of veterans of the Ardennes Offensive, and in a rare moment of open discussion about their war days, they spoke about how they beat the SS soldiers to death with their shovels. *We did not waste our bullets on them*," one of the veterans said, and they all fell silent, shaking their heads.

Guards also had to assess the next steps for captured members of the Volkssturm or "the People's Militia." The Volkssturm was made up of older men--mainly World War I veterans up to age sixty--and boys sixteen years or younger. The guards and camp authorities often directed the old men to go home and take care of their grandchildren, and the boys to return to school.

On February 9, the Third Army established Prisoner of War Enclosure Number 13 in Arlon, Belgium. It was administered by artillerymen from the 734th Field Artillery Battalion who--like the 267th--were pulled from their artillery mission to help with rear area security and manage the flow of prisoners. At 3:15 p.m. the following day, Major Heenan entered the headquarters of the 734th in Esch-sur-Alzette for a briefing from Battalion leadership on the operation of the POW enclosure. The 734th field artillery unit fired "Long Tom" 155 howitzers before guarding prisoners. The "Long Tom" was a heavy field gun known for its accuracy when hurling its 100-pound shell a maximum range of 13.7 miles. The Third Army was looking for additional artillery and reuniting the 734th with its Long Toms was under consideration. The battalion was originally activated the same month as the 267th (March 1943) and landed on Utah Beach on August 18, 1944. It supported XX Corps until September 21, then joined the 267th in support of the 80th and 35th Infantry Divisions during the Lorraine Campaign. It was transferred to the Provost Marshal around the same time as the 267th. The Major got a briefing that lasted over three hours on receiving, classifying, guarding, sustaining, and moving out enemy prisoners. He left the briefing with mixed feelings.

On the one hand, he was happy for the men of the 734th because they were returning to do what they did best: fire big guns. On the other hand, he regretted it was not the 267th heading back to its guns. Nevertheless, the Major was a soldier and followed orders regardless of his feelings.

On February 22, Major Heenan returned to Third Army Headquarters to participate in a Provost Marshal POW Subsection conference on replacing the 734th Headquarters and Service Batteries at the Third Army Prisoner of War Enclosure. The 734th was preparing to withdraw from its guard duties as it developed plans to marry up with its artillery pieces and conduct refresher training for its artillerymen. The Provost Marshal developed a plan that generally called for substituting the 631st Tank Destroyer Battalion's Headquarters Company for the Headquarters and Service Batteries of the 734th. Because the 631st did not have the manpower or equipment of the 734th, it was necessary to augment its Headquarters Company with a detachment from the 267th and co-located Army Military Police Escort Guard companies.

On February 24, the 734th received orders relieving it from tactical guarding of all installations in the Third Army area and was reassigned to its primary mission: firing its 155mm Long Tom guns to support the infantry. At the time, the 734th guarded several installations in addition to Enclosure Number 13. Along with the 267th, 631st, and the 1st and 3rd Companies of the French 151st Infantry Regiment, it guarded thirty-five railway bridges and tunnels, sixteen highway bridges, the Repeater Station at Aubange, Belgium, the Twelfth Army Group Radio in Romain, France, the Twelfth Army Group Radio of Kapellenberg, Germany, the Third Army Radio Center, Luxembourg, and the Post Telegraph and Telephone Buildings located in the Luxembourg towns of Bettembourg, Dudelange, Kayl, Differdange, Bascharage, and two other locations.

The following day, the 734th turned over command of Enclosure Number 13, with its 1,000 POWs, to Major Heenan. Officers and enlisted men of the 267th and the 631st came under his command as planned in the conference two days earlier. After a brief training period, the 734th supported multiple infantry and armored divisions through Germany until the middle of April, when it returned to guard duty.

With Belgium and Luxembourg completely back in Allied control, the Third Army turned rear area security in those countries over to Belgian units. The 11th Belgian Fusilier Battalion assumed guarding installations in the Duchy of Luxembourg and Belgium, exclusive of the City of Luxembourg, whose security remained with two companies from the 631st. The French government did not permit Belgian Battalions to guard installations in France. Thus, the 267th took over guarding installations in occupied France. It shifted most of its troops, who had gone north during the Ardennes Campaign, back to France. In the last week of February, Charles, and the remaining Battery C troops in Belgium joined the Battery's main body in Metz. Of the 443 men of the Battalion, 342 were now in France. Only 101 personnel from Battery B remained in Belgium with Major Heenan. The Headquarters and Service Batteries and the Medical Detachment remained in Hayange. Battery A was working out of Cons La Grandville, France.

Major Heenan and his detachment operated Enclosure 13 until it was closed one month after it opened, on March 9. During February, it received 6,763 POWs and evacuated 5,727 to more permanent camps. In the nine days it operated in March, the Enclosure received 4,248 prisoners and evacuated 5,331.

Turning the calendar from February to March was a welcome event for Charles and all the soldiers on the line. The historically cold and wet winter of 1944-45 was coming to an end, and the European war's cessation was in sight. Charles and his fellow soldiers now turned more attention to *Stars and Stripes'* reporting of the Pacific Campaign. As the German Army was meeting defeat with delaying actions and large-scale surrenders, the Japanese military chose another course to meet that same fate. Instead of capitulating, it intensified its fanatical campaign to launch waves of suicidal troops and military hardware against the American juggernaut, hoping to make unconditional surrender too costly. Like the one that killed Eskew, kamikaze attacks were now daily, if not hourly, events for the troops encircling the Nippon homeland.

Soldiers of the 267th got nervous as they read reports coming out of the small island of Iwo Jima in the Pacific. Since mid-February, three divisions of Marines tried to occupy the eight square-mile island. It took almost all of March before the island was finally declared secure. Nearly all the 21,000 Japanese defenders fought to the death, inflicting 26,040 casualties (6,821 killed and 19,217 wounded) on the invading Marines. Charles feared that the end of the Nazi regime might not end the war for him.

March saw the Third Army drive out of France, Belgium, and Luxembourg into Germany's heart, where it systematically destroyed two German armies in front of it. It started the month by capturing German territory up to the Rhine River. It then destroyed German forces in the southern part of its zone by an outflanking movement across the Moselle River that cut them off from their homeland and supply lines. During the latter part of the month, the Third Army crossed the Rhine River, further driving back German forces and penetrating industrial, communications, and defensive areas in the heart of Germany.

While it made steady advances, Third Army elements met stubborn resistance from some German commanders attempting to obey their delusional Fuhrer's orders, who still believed that Germany could turn the tide of war to victory. German generals also expended forces to delay the western armies' advance, giving German soldiers and civilians time to escape the Soviet Army's onslaught and position themselves to surrender to western forces. Word traveled through the German military and civilian populations about large-scale systematic murder, rape, and other atrocities committed by the Red Army--this was evident by the large numbers of soldiers and civilians coming over to the western forces. During March, the Third Army took a countless stream of civilian refugees and a record number of 142,000 German POWs--an average of 4,580 POWs per day.

As the Third Army moved into Germany, the 267th continued to guard critical areas behind the front lines under the Provost Marshal Security

Subsection. With the rapid movement of the infantry and armored units, pockets of German soldiers and sympathetic civilians fought behind American lines. Thus, security details had to conduct combat against the enemy, which created greater demand for additional rear area security forces.

The 267th was scattered in France at the beginning of March, except for Battery B, which, after closing Enclosure Number 13, was still in Virton, Belgium, as part of a force guarding sixty-nine railway bridges and tunnels, forty-five highway bridges, eight highway checkpoints, and the Twelfth Army Group Radio in Romain, France. However, Headquarters was making plans to move the Battalion into Germany. Two companies, the 1st and 4th of the French 30th Battalion Chasseurs were integrated into the security forces and assumed from the 267th and 631st guarding installations in France and Luxembourg. The Belgian 10th and 11th Fusilier Battalions also assumed security for sites in Belgium and Luxembourg, including the SHAEF Mission and radio installation in the City of Luxembourg, the Repeater Station in Aubange, Belgium, and Post Telegraph and Telephone Buildings located in in the Luxembourg towns of Bettembourg, Dudelange, Kayl, Belvaux, Differdange, Bascharage, Rodange, Pétange, and the City of Luxembourg. Charles knew what was next for him when he and his Battery were shown the film titled "Subject: Germany," which addressed the Army's non-fraternization policies with German noncombatants.

Lake Beale, India
January 27, 1945

At 6:00 p.m. PFC Iozzio walked into the Depot Hospital with a 102-degree temperature and a three-day-old sore throat. Second Lieutenant Freeman admitted him for acute tonsilitis. After three days in the hospital, Carmen was released back to duty. While doctors released him back to drive trucks, India continued to be hard on Carmen's health. Since arriving, he suffered from headaches, congestion, and digestive issues.

The CBI's harsh climate and foreign environment also wore down the health of the other American soldiers. Thirteen months prior, Carmen and the other soldiers who stood on the deck of their troopship knew their bodies would be challenged as they looked out at the foreignness of Bombay. Even the booklet he was given called "Welcome to Bombay – a Guide Provided to Newly Arriving Soldiers" warned:

> *"Avoid Exposure to your head to sun before 4 p.m.; eating over-ripe fruit or fruits not protected by skin; drink water from a street fountain; walking barefooted; drinking intoxicating drinks during the day, especially spirits; soft drinks from marble-stoppered bottles; patronizing beggars, mendicants, fortune-tellers and curio dealers.*

> *"Swimming Baths*

> *"It is dangerous to swim in the sea during the months of June to September."*

Nevertheless, the assault on the American GI's bodies went beyond the nuisances in the booklet. In 1943, 120 soldiers became ill for every allied soldier wounded in the Burma Campaign. The malarial rate was 84% of all the soldiers in that area. Like the soldiers in Burma, troops in India were issued daily medication to protect them against malaria and scrub typhus. Exhaustion, malnutrition, amoebic dysentery, and accidents kept a steady stream of troops rotating through mobile hospitals.

The hot, dry climate, which then drenched troops during the monsoon season, also caused skin issues. Prickly heat and fungus were endemic. Water was rationed, and vermin, such as poisonous snakes, scorpions, and jackals, roamed the depot. It was common for the 185th to have several soldiers admitted or discharged from depot hospitals each month.

As the Allied armies continued to push the Japanese forces east, back toward the Pacific Ocean, the 185th also moved east. On December 15, 1944, the 185th received orders reassigning it to Base General Depot #2 in Calcutta. Five days later, the 185th's main body headed toward Calcutta. Left behind were:

- A Depot Headquarters Section with nineteen enlisted men and one officer in Bombay;
- One storage section with thirty-three enlisted men and one officer in Karachi;
- 1st Platoon with forty-two enlisted men, including PFC Iozzio, at the Replacement Depot in Lake Beale;
- Four enlisted men in New Delhi; and
- Two enlisted men in Kharagpur, India.

The main body arrived in Calcutta on January 1, 1945, where First Lieutenant Franklin A Mead took command from Captain John J Buckley, and its soldiers took up their new assignment.

Replacement Depot #4 processed many thousands of troops in its short existence. However, the depot was no longer necessary by March of 1945, as the Allies continued to weaken the Japanese Army, and port operations shifted from Bombay to Calcutta. With its closing, the staff of the 181st General Hospital that treated Carmen for his tonsillitis moved to Malabar. The remainder of the men stationed on the depot, including the 185th's Storage Platoon, consisting of one Officer and twenty-seven enlisted men, including Carmen, were transferred to Calcutta. They augmented the 35th Replacement Depot Company working the Budge Budge and Northbrook warehouse sections of the city. PFC Iozzio was assigned as a pump operator at the cold storage plant on Hyde Road in Calcutta. The plant consisted of 134,790 cubic feet of freezer space and 6,570 cubic feet of chiller space to store frozen meat for Allied Forces in the CBI Theater.

Trier Germany
March 17, 1945

Charles and the other 97 men of Battery C were the first Battalion members to enter Germany after traveling sixty-eight miles to take up positions in Trier. The other batteries were also moving north and east, with Battery A's 101 personnel in Schieren, Luxembourg, and the 100 Battery B troops in Arlon, Belgium. Only the headquarters elements remained in Hayange, France.

By the end of the month, the 267th Headquarters--consisting of the Headquarters and Service Batteries, along with the Medical Detachment--repositioned itself 126 miles deep into the heart of Germany at Bad Kreuznach. The "Bad" in Bad Kreuznach literally means "Bath" because it was famous for its health spas and resorts. On March 16, the day before Charles entered Germany, Lieutenant Colonel Johann Kaup, the commander of the German forces defending that heavily bombed town, surrendered his men to Third Army forces with no resistance. With the Headquarters' movement, nearly all of the Battalion was operating in Germany. Battery A was in Bekond, and Battery C remained in Trier. Battery B regrouped in Thionville, France, and prepared to enter Germany. Upon entering Germany, the 267th and the 631st immediately went to work guarding the Third Army Radio Center in Strassen, the Twelfth Army Group Radio in Kapellenberg, and the storage room for rare books in Nürburg. Battery C was responsible for security at the electric power plant in Trier.

As in all wars, the rear area is not far from the frontlines. One evening, Charles was assigned to take part in a reconnaissance patrol deep into enemy territory. Their mission was to travel eight miles behind German lines. Because it was night in rough and unfamiliar terrain, the patrol became lost and finally emerged back into U.S. lines way off course. It entered a zone occupied by a unit of black American soldiers. Because no white American soldiers were operating in this area, the defending GIs assumed the wayward patrol members to be German spies and hogtied them. They were kept prisoners until the following day when an officer arrived and interrogated the men. Upon confirming their identities, they were untied and returned to the 267th.

Sunday, April 1, came much as March did. The news in Germany was positive as the German war machine continued to collapse, with its high command slipping away or into underground bunkers. Like March, all eyes were on another Japanese-held island where an eighty-two-day hellish grind to occupy it began that morning. The island, this time, was Okinawa. It became one of the bloodiest battles in the Pacific War, with approximately 135,000 to 160,000 casualties on both sides and the loss of nearly 150,000 local Okinawans. Okinawa sealed it for Charles, just about every other soldier, and the War Department that the Japanese would not surrender and victory in the Pacific could only be achieved by an invasion of the Japanese mainland--that invasion would need troops currently in Europe.

Once the Third Army crossed the Rhine, it entered the final phase of the European War. It now faced spotty and ineffective resistance from German troops under a collapsed command and control structure. It also encountered isolated pockets of fierce resistance from fanatical SS troops following the suicidal orders of Hitler. But a growing problem from the German Army's disintegration was the continued mass surrendering of troops, including entire German units peacefully capitulating. This changing battlefield required the Third Army to scale back its combat functions and redesignate entire combat units to occupation, prisoner control, and mopping up operations.

After swiftly moving across western Germany, the Third Army was ordered to cease advancing east as part of an arrangement with the oncoming Soviet Army. Over General Patton's objections, the Army leadership slowed the Allied advance to allow the Soviets to capture Berlin. Instead of advancing east toward the city, the Third Army was ordered to concentrate forces south and prevent Germany's ability to create a "national redoubt," where forces would make a last stand. A "national redoubt" refers to a plan where a nation, on the edge of defeat, withdraws its remaining forces to a region chosen for geography that favors defensive operations, such as a mountainous area. Germany's national redoubt plan called the "Alpenfestung," or "Alpine Fortress," was developed by Heinrich Himmler and called for the Third Reich's government and armed forces to regroup in an area from "southern Bavaria across western Austria to northern Italy." While General Eisenhower took the plan seriously, the German leadership did little to implement it.

By April 8, all 447 personnel of the 267th were in Germany when Battery B joined Batteries A and C in Trier. The headquarters' elements were still in Bad Kreuznach. With the shifting emphasis on occupation duties, the Third Army augmented the 267th, 631st, and 10th and 11th Belgian Fusilier Battalions with the 195th Field Artillery Group, the 174th and 270th Field Artillery Battalions, the 13th Armored Division, and the 70th Infantry Division, which was subsequently given responsibility for security in the rear areas.

Together, these units guarded fifty railway bridges and tunnels, 144 highway bridges, and thirty-three signal installations. They also guarded the SHAEF Mission in Luxembourg, the Storage Room for Rare Books located in a castle in Nürburg, the Trier's electric power plant, a lens factory in Bad Kreuznach, and the 14th Liaison Air Strip. They also provided security for Counter Intelligence Corps, Naval Archives, and Military Police Interpreter teams.

Because the Third Army was operating in hostile territory with pockets of German soldiers and civilian saboteurs in rear areas, security forces faced sporadic combat and had to remain vigilant. One night, Charles and the other 267th members were guarding a road into town. Out of the quiet darkness came a noise that sounded like the entire German Army descending on them, so they opened up with machine guns and every weapon that could launch a round out of its barrel. Once the gunfire subsided, there was only stillness, and the guards had to wait until morning to see the results of their defensive action. They laid there the rest of the night, peering into the darkness and listening for any sound. When the sun came up, in front of them was a pile of dead horses. The town was not assaulted by Germans but by a stampede of doomed animals. Charles thought, *"What a waste of beautiful animals."* However, he had seen so much death and destruction; it was just part of daily life.

April 13 saw the entire Battalion, now in Trier, wake up to bad news. Armed Forces Radio announced that President Roosevelt had passed away. Charles remembered Franklin Roosevelt speaking to him and his family through the radio when he was a young boy. His fond memories included the President's encouraging words guiding Americans through the depths of the Great Depression, the expansion of totalitarianism in Europe and Asia, and fighting through World War II. When times appeared their bleakest, the President was counted on for reassuring words and policies aimed to help ordinary people and preserve American society. The battle-hardened men of the 267th openly wept at the news.

Now events were moving even quicker in Germany to conclude the war. One day after Adolf Hitler's fifty-sixth birthday on April 20, the Soviet Army commenced the Battle of Berlin. The 267th continued to move east through southern Germany, with Battery A advancing to Bamberg, Battery C to Zeil, and Battery B shifting to Haßfurt along with the Battalion Headquarters. On April 25th, 200 miles east of Charles, forces from the U.S. First Army's 69th Infantry Division linked up with troops from the Soviet 58th Guards Rifle Division of the 5th Guards Army. This linking of the eastern and western fronts occurred along the Elbe River at the town of Torgau. Four days later, the 697th Field Artillery Battalion, the last 240mm unit in an artillery support role in Europe, fired the last 240mm round against the German army near Munich. The following day, April 30, the Battle for Berlin culminated with the suicide of Adolph Hitler and his wife, Eva Braun. Admiral Karl Dönitz assumed control of the German government and made preparations to surrender the Reich.

Between the death of Adolf Hitler and a formal surrender on May 8, Charles and the rest of the troops watched chaos emanating from the remains of the Nazi government. Some of Hitler's lieutenants attempted to make peace with the western allies, while others went into hiding or committed suicide. Admiral Dönitz cobbled a government together in northern Germany whose goal was surrendering the Reich in a way to save as many of his soldiers and civilians from the Soviet war machine.

Among the pandemonium, Charles and the rest of the 267th still had a job to do. With much of the rear area turned over to the 70th and its accompanying units, the Security Subsection's zone became much smaller. The 267th, 631st, and 174th guarded thirty-one highway bridges, eight railway bridges, eight signal bridges, the Third Army Command Post, and the 14th Liaison Squadron airstrip. In addition, they continued to provide security for the Counter Intelligence Corps Interrogation Team in Bamberg and the Naval Archives in Tambach. Continuing to move south, nearly all of the 267th was now operating in the Nuremberg area. Battery B was in Furth, Charles, and Battery C in Herzogenaurach, and the Headquarters was set up in Schwabach. Battery A remained thirty-four miles north in Bamberg, Germany.

With German military units surrendering *en masse* and no organized military structure, Admiral Dönitz authorized the Chief of the Operations Staff of the Armed Forces High Command Alfred Jodl to meet with the Allies in Reims, France, to sign an instrument of unconditional surrender. In the early morning of May 7, General Jodl signed the terms of surrender, directing, "*All forces under German control to cease active operations at 23:01 hours Central European Time on 8 May 1945.*" At which point, the war in Europe officially ended.

It was time for Charles and the other troops to enjoy the victory. Troops were given about three days of liberal duty to celebrate. However, with all they had been through and what might come next, it was a celebration with trepidation as the Japanese shadow loomed over them. The officers posted a letter from General Patton commending the Third Army on the war's conclusion. It stated:

> "*...During the 281 days of incessant and victorious combat, your penetrations have advanced farther in less time than any other army in history. You have fought your way across 24 major rivers and innumerable lesser streams. You have liberated or conquered more than 82,000 square miles of territory, including 1,500 cities and towns and some 12,000 inhabited places. Prior to the termination of active hostilities, you had captured in battle 956,000 enemy soldiers and killed or wounded at least 500,000 others. France, Belgium, Luxembourg, Germany, Austria, and Czechoslovakia bear witness to your exploits.*
>
> "*All men and women of the six corps and 39 divisions that have at different times been members of this Army have done their duty. Each deserves credit....*"

However, the General's letter ended with a reminder that World War II was not over. He concludes, "*The termination of fighting in Europe does not remove the opportunities for other outstanding and equally difficult achievements in the days which are to come.*" That line hit Charles and the other men of Battery C. Nevertheless, Charles learned in combat that you focus on what is in front of you today and not worry about tomorrow until it comes. It was time to celebrate until tomorrow comes.

After celebrating, Charles and his brothers-in-arms talked aloud that not everyone would be needed for the Pacific War--some would go home. They discussed how they helped bring about the fall of Berlin and the formal surrender of the Nazi regime, so they had only one question: *"When can we go home?"* A few days after the Reich's surrender, Major Collins assembled the Battalion to answer their question by announcing the Army's point system for its enlisted personnel's demobilization and discharge.

He said that the goal is to demobilize two million soldiers over the next twelve months, with half coming from European forces and the remainder from Pacific and American-based units. After he addressed the troops, the directive was posted along with a points chart. Soldiers who earned eighty-five or more points were eligible to demobilize as soon as transport back to the U.S. was available. Soldiers received one point for each month of military service and an additional point for each month of overseas service. Each combat award earned five points, and twelve points were given for each dependent child, up to a maximum of three children. Charles took out a pencil and calculated his points based on a chart attached to the directive. He added up fifty-two points: twenty-two months of service, ten months of overseas service, and four combat awards. He was short thirty-three points, and Garfield still looked pretty distant!

As General Jodl was signing the surrender documents, Third Army planners were shifting unit roles to address their biggest problem in the immediate postwar Europe: the daunting task of sorting out the population of Europe from wartime to peacetime roles. Allied POWs had to be repatriated, nursed back to health, and returned to their respective countries. Former forced laborers, concentration camp survivors, and other refugees from many countries had to be returned home or to new homes. German civilians and military personnel had to be sorted between war criminals, those who needed to be sent home to civilian jobs, and others who would be part of a de-Nazified post-war government.   The Third Army, like other Allied units, was overwhelmed by these populations, especially with the unanticipated human wave escaping from the Red Army.

It fell on former artillery units to assume the hands-on job of sorting, sustaining and directing this mass displaced populous in the Third Army zone. On May 7, the Third Army issued a Letter of Instruction assigning responsibility to the 33rd Field Artillery Brigade *"to collect, protect, supply, administer, and evacuate all Allied POWs and civilian internees."* Additionally, it was responsible for "*collecting, guarding, and protecting all other displaced persons.*" The 33rd's 3,000-plus men would have to establish and administer Allied POW installations and civilian internment camps to meet this need. As part of this massive task, the 267th and the 174th were relieved from their guard duties by the 36th Anti-Aircraft Artillery Brigade and assigned to the Prisoner of War Subsection.

The day the war ended, the Third Army guarded 91,714 prisoners, with another 174 admitted to Allied hospitals. Additionally, it was responsible for 12,904 wounded soldiers and civilians who were patients in overrun German military hospitals. A constant stream of other displaced civilians and repatriated prisoners of the Reich added to this.

The Prisoner of War Subsection directed the 267th to reform as a battalion in Auerbach, which was 119 miles northeast of Nuremberg near the German-Czechoslovakian border. The idyllic small town had about 8,900 residents at the time and is embedded into the beautiful hilly landscape between the Jurassic mountains and the Veldenstein Forest of Bavaria. It is in the heart of the territory that some believed would have been Germany's National Redoubt.

Within two weeks of the War's end, all the batteries had turned their guard responsibilities over to the 36th and assembled in the town. Of the 545 men reporting, Headquarters and the Headquarters Battery had 111 personnel: Battery A had 129, Battery B had 128, Battery C had 128, the Service Battery had 37, and the Medical Detachment had 12. The Battalion would administer a POW camp established on the grounds of a former German Army training center. Like other camps within the American sector in Germany, the flood of prisoners arriving soon caused it to swell beyond capacity. Initially filled with whole German units, its population grew as military stragglers--those escaping the Soviet sector and soldiers who tried to disguise themselves in civilian clothing--were apprehended. Interrogation and sorting the POWs was time-consuming, while the 267th had to do their best to house the growing number of detainees.

By early June, the camp housed 20,000 German POWs in areas around four former German Army barracks. The men of the 267th separated the prisoners into four separate "cages" or confined areas: one held 5,000 men with some role in the German war machine; another had 5,000 Hungarians who served alongside the German Army, including the SS; a third contained an assortment of German military men; the last one held 1,200 women who served the Army in non-combat roles.

Like the Third Army Prisoner of War Enclosure Number 13 near Arlon, life was hard for the prisoners and the guards in Auerbach. Initially, many prisoners were in areas with little to no protection from the environment--open latrines spilled over when it rained, and it was usually raining. Troops coming to the camp told Charles they knew they were getting close because they could smell the camp five miles downwind. Many prisoners were suffering from lice and the effects of constant exposure to the elements. Typhus was an epidemic. Because food and medical supplies were allocated first to the thousands of displaced persons--especially those liberated from the concentration camps--rations were never enough, leaving the POWs always hungry. Duty for the camp staff was also challenging. The camp guard staff was undermanned for the population, including a large group of battle-hardened prisoners who had little to do but forage for necessities and find things to distract them from their boredom. The pressure was put on the staff to quickly interrogate and sort prisoners for final action, be it to a war crimes tribunal or sent back into society. Working hours were long with diminishing staff as troops hit their eighty-five points and were sent home.

As the camp moved into the summer months, conditions began to improve. Third Army engineers supervised prisoners as they built tentage and other temporary buildings, giving all the POWs some protection from the elements. POW Interrogation Teams and Military

Intelligence Investigation Teams worked feverishly to interrogate and discharge soldiers found to be unwanted or no threat to security. Once deemed safe to discharge, former POWs were given a Discharge Control Form D-2 and allowed to go home. By relieving the overcrowding, rations and morale improved. The black market and infractions by the prisoners also sharply declined.

Charles and the men of the 267th faced many issues when dealing with their prisoners. Foremost were the conflicting emotions from housing SS troops who committed unspeakable atrocities against the Allies, civilians, and even the German people. When Allied soldiers liberated the concentration camps or found the mass bodies of civilians executed or massacred, their reactions varied from shock and horror to disturbed and angry. The masses of dead bodies and the unrepentant combativeness of many German SS troops and guards were unfathomable. Execution was too good for them; rooting out and sending SS troops to their punishment were major functions of the staff. In July, the POW interrogation teams were directed to find the SS troops who massacred the ninety-eight artillery observation soldiers in Malmedy during the Battle of the Bulge. The teams identified five SS troops in the camp as participants, and it took every bit of strength for Charles to maintain his military bearing when dealing with such despicable human beings.

The women prisoners also presented unique problems. Some were pregnant when apprehended and gave birth in the camp. In addition to obstetrical care, the babies needed milk and baby food, which were difficult to find. Arrangements were made with the local populous to help feed and care for the mothers and their babies.

Lastly, the Hungarian soldiers' status was somewhat unsettled between Displaced Persons and POWs. In many areas, they were disarmed and allowed to remain unguarded in their camps. Other units brought them into the POW camp system and arranged for transport back to Hungry. Even though they participated in atrocities committed by their German allies, many were left to their own and allowed to go home. Charles could not help but wonder how many of these prisoners were relatives or from Veľké Kapušany.

Charles in Paris (last on the right in the back row)

But not all of Charles's time was spent on guard duty. USO shows and movies flowed into the occupation area, providing relief to the homesick troops. Traveling shows and temporary movie theaters also found the small town of Auerbach. Eventually, military trains and planes were allocated to accommodate weekend passes to exciting locations. Troops were given three days, plus travel time, passes to the French Riviera, London, or Paris for the lucky ones like Charles. Because the city avoided street fighting and the people were determined to return to everyday life quickly, Charles found Paris was as far away from the war remnants as you could get in Europe. The trains were packed. The nightlife was wild. Charles and the other soldiers were happy to spend money, and Parisians were happy to take it. Champagne flowed, and everyone enjoyed their time. Soldiers who had not interacted with women for months could relearn how to be with the opposite sex.

Another task that occupied Charles and the 267th's time was training to sharpen their artillery skills for a potential role in the Japanese Home Islands invasion. Ranges were established so artillerymen, such as Charles, could fire cannons that he had not operated since before the Ardennes Campaign. Charles said goodbye to friends in other units, relieved of their postwar duties, and moved to Marseilles or LeHavre for "Direct Redeployment" or "Indirect Redeployment" to the Pacific.

The Pacific War was becoming more real as rumors of redeployment ran rampant, and in July, the Army made the 267th's fate official. The Army published a directive classifying European-based units into four categories: Category I units, consisting of 337,000 personnel, would remain as an occupying force in Germany; Category III units were to be reorganized, retrained, and await further orders; Category IV units, which made up more than two-thirds of the force, were to return to the U.S. to be deactivated and personnel discharged.

The last category that the 267th fell into was Category II--those units to re-deploy to the Pacific. About one million soldiers received orders to the Pacific, including thirteen infantry and two armored divisions. Nearly 400,000 soldiers were to transit directly to the Pacific for arrival between September 1945 and January 1946. Another 400,000 would receive eight weeks of retraining in the U.S. and then ship out to the Pacific to arrive by April 1946.

Since Japan lost Guadalcanal in February 1943, U.S. forces had systematically captured Japanese-occupied islands, encircling a noose around her Home Islands. By March 1945, U.S. forces were assaulting Japanese sovereign territory, including Iwo Jima and Okinawa. Taking both islands came with significant loss of life as Japanese air, naval, and ground forces defended the territory with suicidal ferocity.

These fanatical tactics led U.S. military planners to seek surrender from Japan without invading its four main islands: Hokkaido, Honshu, Shikoku, and Kyushu. The Navy mined Japanese ports and shipping routes. It shelled and blockaded the coast, destroying any vessel attempting to bring food or resources into the besieged country. The Army Air Corps sought to bomb Japan into submission. It conducted massive bombing raids with hundreds of planes using conventional and napalm ordinances, some killing tens of thousands of Japanese at a time.

The American industrial might was now laser-focused on defeating Japan. Its shipbuilding program swelled the U.S. Navy to 6,768 ships in mid-1945 (compared to 475 ships comprising the 2024 Navy). This included 23 battleships, 28 fleet aircraft carriers, and 2,547 amphibious craft.

Bombing Japan's cities required a heavy long-range bomber, and the aircraft industry met that need with the B-29 Superfortress. A massive bomber with an astounding combat range of 3,250 miles was rushed into production and mass-produced, with nearly 4,000 delivered in the latter part of the war.

In Paterson, Roseann and the Wright Aeronautical workers also did their part to crush the Japanese military. Roseann helped design parts for the R-3350 Cyclone engine that powered these massive war machines. It was an ongoing project for the Paterson plant, as early models were beset with dangerous reliability problems. Eventually, testing and trial and error allowed this engine to evolve into a trusty workhorse for the B-29.

Roseann spent long hours at the plant, traveling to and from work only when it was dark, but it was for a purpose. Helping to get the B-29 engine right was personal for her. The parts she helped design would be used against the people who ended her fiancé's life. She found meaning in her work.

The War Department planners were determined to fully use these massive military and industrial resources to bring the Japanese Empire to its knees. Despite Japan's population being starved and bombed, it refused to surrender. Instead, its military turned whatever men and weaponry it still possessed into suicide machines. kamikaze pilots and large numbers of troops prepared the islands for an invasion and vowed to defend them to the death, as their fellow soldiers did on Iwo Jima and Okinawa.

With Japan's refusal to surrender, the U.S. Joint Chiefs of Staff drew up an invasion plan called "Operation Downfall." It consisted of two phases: "Olympic" was a November 1945 invasion of the southern island of Kyushu, and "Coronet" was an assault on Honshu in March 1946. GIs would be transported with an invasion armada this planet had never seen. Already assembling in Pacific island ports, the plan called for 1,371 transport, cargo, landing, and evacuation ships that could carry 539,290 men along with 61,190 tanks and vehicles. General McArthur estimated involving about 681,000 military personnel for the landing on Kyushu. Once Kyushu came under Allied control, phase two would commence the final battle of World War II. Up to forty divisions--over one-and-a-half million men--would be tasked to seize the Kanto Plain, including Tokyo and Yokohama, and then carry out any additional operations necessary to break Japanese resistance. The one million troops and their equipment redeployed from the European Theater of Operation would participate in the "Coronet" operation.

European-based troops and equipment were to be transported to the Philippines via the Panama Canal. Others would sail to the east coast of the U.S. and be transported to the west coast by train before shipping out to the Philippines. Some soldiers would remain in the States to receive specialized training before joining their fellow GIs in the Pacific.

Reconnaissance photos studied by Army war planners revealed the Japanese erecting formidable fortifications along its beaches. The Army's solution was to develop a mobile weapon capable of firing a shell that penetrates reinforced bunkers five feet before exploding. The weapon called the T-92 was a 240mm howitzer mounted on a Pershing tank chassis--it was a mobile version of the gun that the 267th fired in Europe. The Army ordered 216 of these behemoths. T-92 battalions were planned to land with the invading troops and drive their sixty-nine-ton weapons alongside them, destroying enemy emplacements in their path.

Within the European Theater of Operation were fifteen battalions that operated the 240mm howitzer whose troops were either idle or doing other jobs. They would be an experienced pool of troops to man and operate the T-92s. In late July 1945, while conducting POW operations in Auerbach, the 267th received Shipment #R4085-HH, directing the Battalion to prepare for movement to the South West Pacific Area for the invasion of Japan.

With orders to participate in Japan's invasion, Charles, and the artillerymen of the 267th intently followed developments in the Pacific. He still had not entirely accepted that President Roosevelt had passed away, but President Roosevelt died four months earlier. Since that day, the voice guiding America into the final phases of victory did not have that distinct Roosevelt northeastern accent. Instead, it was a softer midwestern drawl from a man as determined as his predecessor to vanquish the aggressors as quickly as possible. That man was Harry S. Truman, and he was now President.

On August 6, as Charles and the 267th were guarding prisoners and training for their redeployment to the Pacific, Armed Forces Radio announced the President would address the country on a major development. All troops not on duty gathered around radios to hear the President give a short three-and-a-half-minute speech. In it, the President announced the dropping of a massive new bomb "*on Hiroshima, an important Japanese Army base.*" He went on to describe this "atomic bomb" and provide a history of its development. Then he warned Japan:

> "*We are now prepared to obliterate more rapidly and completely every productive enterprise the Japanese have above ground in any city. We shall destroy their docks, their factories, and their communications. Let there be no mistake; we shall completely destroy Japan's power to make war.*"

"*Maybe,*" Charles thought, "*this will end the war, and I can head home to Garfield instead of Japan.*"

Three days passed, and while Army scuttlebutt was rampant with rumors of surrender, Tokyo did not respond to the President's decision to drop the bomb and his threat to obliterate Japan. Truman broke the silence with another threat to drop additional bombs until "*we completely destroy Japan's ability to make war.*" Later that day, a B-29 bomber dropped a second atomic bomb. This time it detonated over the shipbuilding city of Nagasaki and killed between 60,000 and 80,000 people.

Still, there was only silence from the embattled island. While the men of the 267th nervously awaited their fate, the final acts of the war played out in private. In the U.S., the Manhattan Project team prepared another atom bomb for use against Japan on August 17 or 18. Across the Pacific, Emperor Hirohito finally directed his divided War Council to accept unconditional surrender by declaring that *"continuing the war can only result in the annihilation of the Japanese people...."*

Between August 10 and 14, fragmented communications took place in Washington and Tokyo on terms of ending the war. With each report from Armed Forces Radio, the spirits of the artillerymen grew. They were hopeful that Washington and Tokyo's communication to draw this brutal conflict to a close was now occurring. Finally, on Saturday, August 14, Tokyo cabled Washington that it accepted the terms of surrender of the Potsdam Declaration, issued by the Allies on July 26, 1945. The following day, Americans confirmed this by eavesdropping on Japanese radio, who overheard the Emperor announce Japan's surrender to his subjects. For most listeners, it was the first time that they had heard the Emperor's voice. He said, *"the war situation has developed not necessarily to Japan's advantage,"* and *"the enemy has begun to employ a new and most cruel bomb."* With that news came spontaneous celebrations from Allied troops across Europe and the world.

The men of the 267th stayed up late into Saturday night, ears glued to the radio, waiting for an official announcement. Finally, in the early morning of the 15th, Armed Forces Radio reported that the President had made it official: Japan surrendered. For Charles, some initial celebration was followed by quiet relief. All at once, the fear of facing fanatical Japanese warriors and perhaps dying on a far-off island in the Pacific disappeared. His dream to return to Garfield and resume his life with his friends and family was now a reality.

New York City, New York
August 14, 1945

It was Saturday afternoon, and Americans, sensing the end of the war, began to gather spontaneously across the country. Times Square in New York City, with its history of attracting large crowds, was no exception--those streets had never seen a crowd like the one that descended on it to celebrate what would become Victory over Japan Day (V-J Day).

Like other congregating spots across the U.S., it started that afternoon as New Yorkers began to gather in Times Square to await the announcement they had been hoping to hear for nearly four years. An anxious crowd, swelling to over 200,000 people by mid-afternoon, closely followed updated news bulletins scrolling across the news ticker at One Times Square.

Reporters broadcasting from Times Square gave radio listeners around the country first-hand reports of the growing crowd. Roseann and the other musketeers had been going from house to house, celebrating with neighbors, and catching parts of radio broadcasts. Finally, Roseann and her musketeers decided they needed to be in the middle of the crowd and headed to Times Square. They caught a bus to Paterson's Train Station, then a train into New York City. With her eyes welling up, Roseann walked across the same train platform where she kissed Eskew goodbye. She then thought about her brother Carmen, who was still serving in India. The thought overcame her sadness that Carmen would be coming home.

The trains and buses were crowded for a Saturday, but the trio finally made it into a mass of people swarming the Times Square area. By evening, the crowd grew to 750,000 people bustling with anticipation. Finally, at 7:03 p.m., a headline on the zipper news ticker at One Times Square read, "*** *OFFICIAL -- TRUMAN ANNOUNCES JAPANESE SURRENDER* ***" Three-quarters of a million people burst out in a collective outpouring of euphoria.

While rejoicing, the three musketeers and hundreds of thousands of strangers began to hug, cry, and laugh together. Two strangers in a sailor's and a nurse's uniform embraced in a kiss that Life Magazine photographer Alfred Eisenstaedt captured. Eisenstaedt's legendary picture, "V-J Day in Times Square," caught the country's mood at that moment and is recognized as one of the greatest "kissing" pictures of all time.

Roseann made her way through the crowd of people who were cheering, crying, dancing, and hugging. Music came from every open window and door. She waded through ankle-deep piles of streamers made from rags, ticker tape, and toilet paper falling like snow from high-rise windows. So many people flooded into the Square that by 10:00 p.m., the crowd was over two million. The celebration lasted into the night, and people only left when they were too physically or mentally exhausted to continue.

On Monday, Roseann returned to her job at Wright Aeronautical and found a different environment. Gone was the stress that hung over the workplace, producing complicated equipment at lightning pace. Lifted was the fear that you had to work fast to produce more and that American servicemen would lose their lives if you made a mistake. Co-workers joked and laughed, but just below the surface, everyone wondered now that their services were no longer needed, what happens next?

Roseann thought about how she had worked at the plant for over two years. She was proud to help win the war and financially support her elderly parents. The war was expected to last another year; however, dropping two atomic bombs by planes she had a small part in the design resulted in the unexpected early end to the war and her job.

The downside of victory was that all the major U.S. airplane producers, including Wright Aeronautical, suffered massive contract cancellations. Operations at the plant abruptly slowed to a trickle, leading to layoffs for most workers, including Roseann. What few jobs remained were given to returning veterans. The scaled-down plant remained open until 1948, when Wright Aeronautical decided to cease operations in Paterson and sell the properties. Roseann was out of a job that she loved, and if she wanted to remain in the workforce, she would have to look for a more "traditional female job."

PFC Carmen Iozzio (center rear) and his fellow soldiers.

Calcutta India
September 2, 1945

By September, all 185th personnel were at work in Calcutta, shipping out and disposing of excess war supplies and materials. The Company also began the process of shedding men back to the U.S., leaving the remaining soldiers to take on the jobs of their departing quartermasters. PFC Iozzio's warehouse continued to store and ship meat to the remaining troops while transferring surplus stores to local Indian merchants. The days were long, and the men of the 185th looked forward to Sundays when they could enjoy a day of relaxation, which included sleeping late.

However, Sunday, September 2, was not a day anyone in the Army slept late. With the mess hall open especially early serving coffee, Carmen and his fellow soldiers rose long before sunrise to find a radio and gather around it. At 5:30 a.m., they intently listened to a radio announcer, broadcasting from the Veranda Deck of the USS Missouri, describe an event taking place in Tokyo Bay, 3,200 miles away.

The announcer described the scene where more than 250 Allied warships lay at anchor within the mist that covered Tokyo Bay. Planes flew overhead in the cloud-filled sky. Above the USS Missouri fluttered the flags of the U.S., Britain, Soviet Union, and China. Packed on every inch of its deck were people in uniform, there to witness the formal surrender of the Empire of Japan to the Allied Powers. The ceremony began at 9:00 a.m. Tokyo time with a brief explanation of the Instrument of Surrender by General Douglas MacArthur. The announcer described in detail the arrival and signing of the documents by Japanese Foreign Minister Mamoru Shigemitsu and General Yoshijiro Umezu.

General MacArthur, in his role as Supreme Commander, next signed then expressed the desire of all that, "*It is my earnest hope and indeed the hope of all mankind that from this solemn occasion a better world shall emerge out of the blood and carnage of the past.*" Next to pen the documents were representatives of the U.S., China, Britain, the Soviet Union, Australia, Canada, France, the Netherlands, and New Zealand. Then the twenty-minute ceremony concluded, ending the most destructive war in human history. The announcer remarked that near the ceremony's conclusion, the sun finally shone through the low-hanging clouds. Carmen and the men of the 185th wept and cheered. They were also ready to go home.

Later that day, the men of the 185th celebrated the promotion of their Commanding Officer, Lieutenant Franklin A. Mead to Captain. Because of the day, it was truly one of the happiest and most celebrated promotion ceremonies in the history of the Company.

The Army began a demobilization process immediately following V-E Day, but the demand to accelerate the pace greatly intensified with that day's surrender ceremony. Pressure from families, legislators, and the troops themselves forced military leaders to develop a plan that greatly sped up demobilization. Four days after the surrender ceremony, Fleet Admiral Ernest J. King authorized combat ships to carry American troops home. Named Operation Magic Carpet, battleships, aircraft carriers, smaller warships, and merchant vessels were tasked to carry hundreds of thousands of soldiers to the U.S. The operation would run through September 1946.

The Operation Magic Carpet plan included reactivating the port at Karachi for CBI personnel heading home. Troops were initially required to take a long, taxing train ride from Burma, but as planes were freed up for troop transport, evacuees were airlifted across India. The men were billeted at the Replacement Depot in Malir, where they were processed and awaited space aboard a ship. Before the month's end, the first transport carrying 3,000 servicemen departed Karachi.

Because Carmen was coming up on his fifth anniversary in the Army and his second year overseas, he had more points than many of his fellow 185th soldiers. On September 22, sixteen days after Admiral King launched Operation Magic Carpet, PFC Iozzio received orders transferring him to the Replacement Service, which began his journey home. Joining Carmen were:

- Master Sergeant Issaic Poss;
- Staff Sergeant Phillipp Shutt;
- Staff Sergeant Francis Demitrovich;
- Staff Sergeant Colon Brock;
- Sergeant Russell Jenkins;
- Sergeant Peter Faraccio; and
- Technician 4th Class Hubert Woolman.

The eight enlisted soldiers were placed on a troop train to Karachi. They spent six uncomfortable and aggravating days traveling through the blazing heat of the Sind Desert. They watched Indian hitchhikers hanging on to the outside of the train, ate rations they brought with them, and sometimes walked alongside the slow-moving train to alleviate boredom.

The group arrived in Karachi at the beginning of October. They were shuttled to Camp Malir, which shortly grew to 30,000 Americans awaiting passage homeward. The eight said goodbye to each other as they separated into groups based on their destination in the U.S. Carmen was at home back at the depot where his India service began. However, he and his fellow quartermasters would not have to wait long. Evacuation operations peaked in Karachi that month with 26,350 troops loaded on eight transports. The harbor would eventually sendoff over

80,000 personnel before the Army closed port operations in January 1946.

One of those eight transports was the USS General Harry Taylor (AP-145), named in honor of Brigadier General Harry Taylor, who graduated from the U. S. Military Academy in 1884 and was commissioned a Second Lieutenant in the U.S. Army Corps of Engineers. General Taylor engaged in extensive river and harbor work for the Army and served in World War I as the Chief Engineer Officer for the American Expeditionary Force in France. He went on to become the Army's Chief of Engineers. The ship displaced 9,950 tons, had a length of 552 feet, a beam of 71.6 feet, and a draft of 24 feet. It could make sixteen knots and carried a complement of 356 crew and troop capacity for 3,224 GIs. The transport was relatively new. Its keel was laid under a Maritime Commission contract on February 22, 1943, at Richmond, California by Kaiser Co., Inc., Yard 3. The ship was launched on October 10, 1943, and acquired by the Navy on March 29, 1944. After some additional yard work to prepare her for transport service, she was commissioned on May 8, 1944.   After V-E Day, the General Harry Taylor made two "Magic Carpet" voyages between Marseilles, France, and New York City.

Both PFC Iozzio and the USS General Harry Taylor began their journey to Karachi on the same day. On September 22, Carmen detached from the 185th, and the General Harry Taylor sailed out of New York Harbor eastward toward the Mediterranean Sea, Suez Canal, and the Arabian Sea. Upon docking in Karachi's port, Captain James L. Wyatt began preparations for a return voyage to New York City as he welcomed 3,188 troops aboard. They included the following units: Headquarters and Headquarter Detachments of the 39th Quartermaster Group Headquarters and 21st Quartermaster Regiment. In addition, Groups 3305th, 3306th, 3307th, 3308th, 3309th, 3310th, 3311th, 3301st, 3302nd, 3303rd, and 3304th Quartermaster Truck Companies; Headquarters and Headquarter Detachments of the 108th and 36th Quartermaster Battalions and the 445th Signal Heavy Construction Battalion.

Carmen and the other troops settled into their berthing for two days while the crew prepared the ship for sailing. At noon on October 16, Carmen stood on a crowded deck to watch the ship's dock lines pulled from the pier and India slowly move over the horizon. The ship took the reverse route of his 1943 voyage. Three days after setting sail, the General Harry Taylor passed Aden and entered the Red Sea. Five days later, she entered Port Said, Egypt, for refueling, then into the Mediterranean Sea.

Like Carmen, some of the soldiers on board the General Harry Taylor were passengers of the bloody eastbound convoy that suffered the sinking of the HMS Rhona. When the westbound transport passed the area where the Rhona was bombed, soldiers bared their heads and held a memorial service. After five days in the Mediterranean, the ship passed the familiar Rock of Gibraltar and transited into the Atlantic Ocean.

Roderick Nordell described his time on an earlier voyage on board the General Harry Taylor. In his story, published in 1995, he writes:

"I wish you could see the workings of a United States troopship. This is the USS General Harry Taylor, an Army ship, operated by the Navy, transporting marines and Seabees. Yet it rivals a land station in efficiency. We're crowded in our four-deck bunks, but we're allowed on deck at practically all times. Ice cream and candy are available. The ship's band plays afternoon concerts, and a public-address system gives out with good records at other times. The Red Cross has furnished us with stationery, as you can see, and books and sundries, all in little drawstring bags. I'm actually reading 'Ellery Queen' and enjoying it. Right now, though, I'm on 'A Tree Grows in Brooklyn.' Amazingly, they feed us three good meals a day with neatness and dispatch. All activities are integrated by the PA system or 'squawk box,' as they call it. ...I continue to sleep in the casual intimacy of compartment 8. Reveille awakens me, momentarily, at 0530. My day begins about 0630 when I crawl out of the sack, drop about seven feet to the deck, wend a tortuous series of ladders - Navy for stairways - and become part of the mess formation. I relax after the formation for about 45 minutes - unless I have guard duty (now every other day) - storing energy for the day's exertions of going on deck and moving as the sweepers come by. There I read weighty tomes like 'Lost Horizon' and 'The Chinese

Orange Mystery,' indulge in intellectual exercise (crossword puzzles and a game called 'Battleship'), and observe the skies and the scenery, which up until recently has been of an endless variety - big waves, little waves, etc. ....."

After nine days crossing the stormy Atlantic Ocean, word traveled through the massive ship that land was in sight. Troops rushed on deck, and Carmen could make out the large guns of Fort Hancock protecting the entrance to New York Harbor. He cleaned the same guns as a recruit five years earlier! The USS General Harry Taylor joined eight other troopships pulling into the harbor on November 6, 1945, to discharge 14,143 returning veterans.

PFC Iozzio was bussed to the Separation Center at Fort Dix, where he began his out-processing by the Army on Friday, November 9. He was examined by a dentist who found his teeth in good shape. He next reported to Captain J.W. Peterson, Medical Corps, for a physical. The Captain found Carmen to be 62 inches tall and 114 lbs., all examinations were normal, and there were no wounds, syphilis, dysentery, or malaria. Since Carmen did not serve in battles or campaigns, he did not have combat wounds. Once completing his examination, Captain Peterson signed off that PFC Iozzio met the physical and mental standards for discharge.

The following day, PFC Iozzio continued his discharge process. A clerk documented his military career. Over his five years, he spent one-and-one-half months as a Private in Basic Training (MOS 521), twelve months as a Private, Postal Clerk (MOS 056), twelve months as a Private, Truck Driver, Light (MOS 345), twelve months as a Technician 5th Class, Automotive Mechanic (MOS 014), and three months as a Private First Class, Pump Operator (MOS 220). His highest rank was Technician 4th Class, and he served two years, ten months, and eight days in the continental U.S. and two years, one month, and three days overseas.

Dressed in a new, freshly pressed uniform, Carmen was awarded the following medals: American Defense Service Medal, Asiatic-Pacific Campaign Medal, American Service Medal, European-African-Middle Eastern Service Medal, and a Good Conduct Medal. In addition, he was given a World War II victory lapel button and an Honorable Discharge from Major J.H. Gunter. Colonel J. Harris provided a check for $61.81 and $50.00 in cash for his trip home. Carmen joined seventy-five Passaic-Bergen County men and women discharged from the Army at Fort Dix on November 10. Fourteen were from Carmen's hometown of Paterson. They were all put on a bus for one final mission…to report home.

At the end of 1945, the 185th Quartermaster Depot Company was awarded a Meritorious Unit Commendation for its contribution to the war effort from December 9, 1944, to September 30, 1945. The men of the 185th held their final formation in Calcutta, India, when the Company was inactivated on April 22, 1946.

The General Harry Taylor would commence a second-round trip to Karachi, then continue transport service for the Navy, Air Force, then back to the Navy until 1983. The ship was renamed the General Hoyt S. Vandenberg in 1963 in honor of the former Air Force Chief of Staff. On May 27, 2009, the ship was sunk off Key West, Florida, to complete her final mission of serving as the second-largest artificial reef in the world.

Auerbach Germany
Mid-August 1945

With many German POWs and Displaced Persons released to home or other areas, the camp population was significantly reduced, and operations were winding down. The 267th was directed to place the remaining prisoners--primarily SS troops--on parole to military units and responsible civilians to work as laborers on infrastructure repair projects. By September, Charles had accumulated enough points to go home before the projected departure of the 267th. To make that happen, Major Collins transferred him to a unit scheduled to ship back to the States. The 695th Armored Field Artillery Battalion was identified, and orders were cut to transfer Charles on September 18.

The 695th was reorganized on August 26, 1943, as an "Armored" Field Artillery Battalion. August, two years later, found the Battalion providing security in Fulda, Germany, which contained four Displaced Persons camps. On August 20, the Battalion was relieved of its guard duties by the 3rd Battalion, 7th Infantry Regiment. By the end of the month, it turned in its equipment, including tractors, tanks, and half-tracks. It then convoyed 350 miles to Camp Baltimore, twenty-five miles southeast of Reims, France, where it would await transportation back to the U.S.

Camp Baltimore was a sprawling tent encampment that was one of the Army's redeployment camps around Reims. Other camps in that area were also named after American cities. These camps originally held troops awaiting movement to the war's front lines; now, they served a reverse role, staging troops awaiting movement out of Europe.

The 695th was preparing for a late October departure when the Army changed its plans for Charles. Just before the 695th left Europe, he was transferred to the 302nd Military Police Escort Guard Company, reporting in on October 14. The 302nd came ashore on the beaches of Normandy late in the afternoon of D-Day, June 6, 1944, and followed the front-line troops through France, the low countries, and Germany. It was recently relieved of its stockade responsibility by 1st Infantry Division MPs and was awaiting transportation to the U.S. While this seemed like a short delay for Charles, it would put him on an arduous ocean crossing that would make movie theater newsreels and delay his homecoming by more than a month. He said goodbye to his new friends in the 695th, boarded transportation to his new unit, and so his odyssey home began.

In November, Charles, and the men of the 302nd got word that it was their turn to ship out. Charles packed his gear and, along with his unit, moved into transient quarters in Marseilles to await a ship to take him home. There they received classes on how to integrate back into civilian society, and on November 6, the medics took advantage of a final chance to put needles in Charles's arm as it was time for additional vaccinations. The Company was scheduled to return to the U.S. on the Liberty ship, S.S William Few. However, the ship suffered engine problems before sailing, and the Army put the Company back on the list for another ship. Two weeks later came word that another ship was available.

On Sunday, November 18, 1945, Charles's two-month wait for a ride home ended when he, along with 540 other MPs, climbed the S.S. Henry Ward Beecher's gangplank. The Beecher was one of the 2,710 Liberty ships built during World War II. On August 4, 1942, her keel was laid by the California Shipbuilding Corp in Terminal Island, California. Launched a month later, on September 11, with hull number 642, she was operated by the Union Sulphur Company.

Beecher was 10,000 tons, just over 441 feet long and 57 feet wide. She had a 2,500-horsepower steam engine with a cruising speed of 11 knots, just over one-third of the Queen Mary's speed. This meant the ride home would be much slower than the one over. Her five cargo holds, three forward of the engine room and two aft, were reconfigured to carry a maximum of 550 troops.

When war broke out in Europe, President Roosevelt initiated the emergency fleet program to quickly build a large merchant fleet. "Liberty ships" were mass-produced cheaply and quickly using assembly-line methods and standardized parts. The Beecher is a classic example, being built in just thirty-nine days. Because of their rudimentary design and primitive outfitting, Liberty ships were built for a five-year lifespan--they were considered expendable.

That also meant primitive conditions on board with minimal accommodation for passenger comfort. Life in the transport holds was crowded with any available space filled with bunks stacked five high from the deck to the overhead. For many, there was not even enough room to turn around in their sleep. The heads consisted of a row of back-to-back toilets down the center of the room, with no dividers for privacy. Constant seagoing missions with limited port and yard time resulted in some parts of the ship in disrepair. Bad weather caused passengers to be confined below deck for much of the voyage, where the air reeked of oil, and there was constant engine noise. However, the Transportation Corps officials did their best to accommodate the battle-hardened troops with as much comfort as possible. They told the boarding troops that the Beecher would be a "break" for them since they were permitted more freedom of the ship and reconfigured the berthing area to give them more living space.

In addition to the 302nd Military Police Escort Guard Company, the 542nd and 544th Ordinance Heavy Maintenance Companies also came on board.

When the ship sailed out into the open sea, the passengers were assembled, told the voyage would last twelve days, and they were scheduled to dock in Hampton Roads, VA, on Thursday, November 29. Charles figured he would be home for Christmas after out-processing, but Thanksgiving would be aboard a ship in the middle of the Atlantic Ocean. They were also ordered to head down to their gear and bring any war booty on deck to be tossed overboard. Over the fantail went German helmets, uniforms, and every imaginable weapon, including lugers, SS daggers, and rifles. Charles tossed a luger over the side but kept a Nazi flag, Wehrmacht belt buckle, rifle cleaning kit, and coins from European counties.

Charles knew the voyage home on a Liberty ship would be harsh, but he had no idea how challenging it would be! The 1945 Atlantic hurricane season that "officially" ended on October 31 was very active, with six of the eleven tropical cyclones occurring in September and October. Storms continued to churn the North Atlantic throughout the rest of the year, and the Beecher was heading right into them.

The Beecher encountered turbulent weather soon after departing Marseille. On November 22, it passed the Rock of Gibraltar and entered the Atlantic Ocean, where it ran head-on into a series of storms that pounded the ship. With engines running at capacity, the Beecher bucked the wind, rain, and heavy seas for two days. During one twenty-four-hour period, waves and headwinds prevented the ship from making any forward progress, even though it's one propeller churned at full speed. Finally, the Captain decided that Beecher would cease fighting the storm and change its course to the southeast. However, the course change proved futile as the troopship ran into another storm southeast of the Canary Islands. At this point, the Captain reversed course again and resumed plowing through the heavy seas in Hampton Roads' direction.

The turbulent ocean made conditions below decks even more dreadful. Liberty ships did not have stabilizers, and their hull shape forced passengers to feel the sea's every motion. Seasickness became rampant. Many toilets overflowed, resulting in excrement covering the deck. Charles and the other troops confined to the dark spaces below became further nauseous from the smell of oil, vomit, and feces.

Adding to the seasickness was a water system plagued by contamination and poor-quality food served in the galley. The food could only be described as just edible. Meals were made from canned and dehydrated foods with few appealing flavors. Dishes produced from powdered eggs and milk were served in mass quantities. Most of the troops survived on O'Henry Bars and Ritz Crackers from the ship's store --until the supplies ran out.

Garfield, N.J.
December 4, 1945

Back in Garfield, it was a typical Tuesday afternoon with Karoly working in the shoemaker shop and Bertha preparing dinner when a few neighbors ran into the store out of breath. At the same time, the phone started ringing and did not stop. They showed Karoly and Bertha the newspaper and said Charles was in a front-page story. Over the past four years, the last thing a parent of a GI wanted to hear was that their son was in the newspaper, which was filled with bad news about troops killed, missing, or wounded and battles fought. An initial panic set in as Karoly read the Herald News article out loud:

> *"Relief Speeds to Stricken Transport*
>
> *"New York (AP) – A seagoing tug and possibly other ships sped today from Bermuda to the aid of the Liberty Ship Henry Ward Beecher, carrying 541 homeward bound American troops, which earlier radioed for assistance after losing its propeller about 340 miles northeast of Bermuda.*
>
> *"{The Associate Press reported there are sixteen New Jerseymen aboard the Henry Ward Beecher. Two from this area are listed: PFC Charles A. Aszialos, (sic) of Garfield and T/5 Vincent A. Bruck, of Paterson. No street addresses were given.}*

"Third Naval District officials here said the Navy tug Restorer was on its way to the stalled vessel, which was not believed in serious danger, within two hours after the first distress call at 2:26 A.M. EST.

"The Henry Ward Beecher, bound for Newport News, VA, from Marseilles, France, was reported in a well-traveled sea lane. Her first call for help was heard by other ships in the area and it was believed at least some of them also were on their way to give assistance.

"Weather was reported moderate in the area.

"Units aboard the Beecher are the 302nd Military Police Escort Guard Company and the 542nd and 544th Ordinance Heavy Maintenance Companies, according to personnel rosters released by the Army."

This story was printed in hundreds of newspapers across the country. Over the next several days, newspapers and radio newscasters reported on the ship's saga while Karoly's shop and Bertha's kitchen were transformed into vigil sites for neighbors, friends, and family members.

North Atlantic Ocean
December 3, 1945

Back in the Atlantic Ocean, the story transpired as follows: On Monday, December 3, the Beecher finally found calm seas and was making the best speed of the voyage. Approximately 510 miles north-northeast of Bermuda, the Captain pushed his ship to make up for the lost time. While traveling at maximum speed, a giant swell lifted the ship out of the water, shearing off her propeller shaft and, with it, her only propeller. At 2:26 a.m. on December 4, the Beecher put out a distress call incorrectly stating her position to be 340 miles northeast of Bermuda. The Navy responded by dispatching a Navy salvage vessel, the USS Restorer (ARS-17), which departed Port Royal Bay, Bermuda, within two hours of Beecher's distress call. Packed with extra food and supplies for the stricken ship, the Restorer raced to Beecher's reported position at her maximum fifteen knots speed. The Beecher was in a well-traveled sea lane. Because the Navy told Beecher that Restorer would be there the following afternoon, its Captain refused offers of assistance from a multitude of passing ships that responded to her call.

On Wednesday, the Navy determined that the Beecher was not 340 miles northeast of Bermuda but 510 miles north-northeast, or 170 miles further away. The Restorer was given the correct position and estimated that it would not arrive until late in the day. Over the first twenty-four-hour period, the ship drifted thirty-five miles south toward a storm. She began to experience thirty-three-knot winds and heavy seas, causing her to wallow and list heavily from port to starboard. Morale on the ship deteriorated. Because the ship was supposed to dock in Hampton Roads on Monday, December 3 at the latest, her supplies were nearly exhausted. She put out a call for food stores, especially meat. Charles and his fellow soldiers watched a destroyer escort attempt to resupply the ship, but heavy seas prevented any transfer. The soldiers also picked up U.S. radio broadcasts reporting on the Beecher's saga. News outlets reported that aid was in the area. So, Charles and the others grumbled when all the ships that came within sight kept sailing past her, not knowing that the Captain was waving them off. Just before 6:00 p.m., the Beecher crew finally smiled that the harrowing forty-hour wait was coming to an end as they spotted the Restorer navigating mountainous waves toward her. Since darkness was setting in and the seas were heavy, the Beecher requested to delay towing operations until the morning, and Restorer came alongside Beecher for the night.

December 5, 1945, was a busy day for the U.S. Navy in the Atlantic. In addition to the Beecher, the Navy responded to two other troopships' distress calls. First, the Greek registered Navarchos Koundouriotis left Antwerp, Belgium for New York on November 17 with twenty-eight U.S. troops on board. On Saturday, December 1, a storm sheared off her propeller 260 miles north of Bermuda and 320 miles southeast of New York City. The Navy rescue tug USS Alsea (AT-97) rendezvoused with the crippled ship that night and proceeded to tow it to New York Harbor. The second ship, the S.S. George W McCrary developed boiler trouble 900 miles off Bermuda beginning on Nov 28. Carrying 586 homebound soldiers, she left Antwerp on November 18, the same day as Beecher. Navy Patrol Craft 1209 was dispatched by Naval

Operations Base, Bermuda, to take her in tow if necessary. The patrol craft hovered close to the McCrary, still underway on reduced power and heading toward Bermuda. The two vessels were estimated to arrive in Bermuda on Saturday, December 8.

There were other casualties of treacherous conditions in the North Atlantic. Two days after Beecher departed Marseilles, her radioman picked up a transmission that another Liberty ship, the S.S. Charles C. Glover struck a wayward mine and sank. On December 8, a rumor spread through the troops that radio signals were picked up reporting a Victory ship with a regiment of the 36th Infantry Division also sailing from Marseilles--broke up and sank. Later that month, the S.S. John B. Hood, with 566 members of the 3225th and 4203rd Quartermaster Service Companies, left Marseille on the same course as the Beecher. She also lost her propeller early on the morning of New Year's Day, about 300 miles southwest of the Azores. The aircraft carrier, USS Enterprise, rescued her passengers.

At the same time and sixteen hundred miles southeast of the stricken Beecher, a squadron of five U.S. Navy Avenger torpedo-bombers took off from the Ft. Lauderdale Naval Air Station in Florida on a routine three-hour training mission.

Two hours into the mission, Lieutenant Charles Carroll Taylor, the flight leader, reported that his compass and backup compass were not working, and his position was unknown. The other planes reported similar instrument malfunctions. The Navy could not get a position on the squadron and spent two more hours attempting to assist the confused flyers with little success. Finally, with darkness and deteriorating weather upon them, a garbled radio transmission from Lieutenant Taylor was picked up, directing his pilots to ditch their planes as they exhausted their fuel.

In addition to losing five Avengers, a search and rescue Martin PBM Mariner flying boat with thirteen men aboard mysteriously vanished without any wreckage. Despite stormy conditions, the Navy led one of the most extensive air and sea searches ever conducted. Hundreds of ships and aircraft combed thousands of square miles of the Atlantic Ocean, the Gulf of Mexico, and remote locations within Florida's interior. They found no trace of bodies or aircraft. The mysterious disappearances of six aircraft and 27 airmen on December 5 serves as the origin of the "Bermuda Triangle" legend.

Wednesday night and early Thursday morning brought worsening weather that mercilessly battered the drifting Beecher with waves and wind. She had been rolling in heavy seas since Tuesday, but the increased pummeling sent terror through the helpless troops. *"We tossed about for five days...It was a rough sea and for a few days we didn't think we were going to hold together"* said Technician Fifth Grade Joseph McCormack. The ship often listed between 35 and 40 degrees, and Charles thought he would never get home. All Charles and the other tossed-about soldiers could do was play cards, pray, and complain to each other. When the sun rose, Restorer relieved Beecher's food shortage by transferring food over and reported back to Bermuda that the food situation was "*in hand*." At 7:53 a.m., the Restorer set about rigging a towline. While connecting the cable to Beecher, a seaman on the Restorer was injured and swept off the smaller ship's deck. Beecher sent over its only medical officer who remained on Restorer for the remainder of the voyage. Finally, after battling heavy seas, the Restorer secured a line and began towing the stricken ship. It estimated arrival into Bermuda at 5:00 a.m. on Sunday, December 9.

Meanwhile, Americans closely followed the saga unfolding on Beecher and McCrary. The Army vowed to get the 1,127 stranded war heroes to Bermuda, then whisk them home to be with their families for Christmas. Bertha and her sisters prayed for this to come true. Major General Clarence H. Kells, the Commanding General of the New York Port of Embarkation, knew he had to act quickly to meet that promise. In port was the 27,000-ton U.S. Army Hospital Ship Frances Y. Slanger (WDGO-41). Recently commissioned on May 23, 1945, she was named after the first American nurse to die in action in Europe. She first sailed as a hospital ship on June 30 and was preparing to commence her fifth mission to transport patients between Cherbourg, France, Southampton, England, and New York when she was told to stand by for new orders. General Kells devised a plan to quickly decommission the Slanger as a hospital ship and immediately recommission her as the S.S. Saturnia, a troop transport with 1,200 berths. With that change, he ordered the ship to get underway to Bermuda at 4:00 p.m. and collect the troops from the two stricken transports. General Kells told Captain Oscar Trevisan, *"Bring the men back in time for Christmas."*

Mountainous waves and forty to fifty-knot headwinds thwarted Restorer's nineteen-hour attempt to tow the larger Beecher. According to Sergeant Quinton Griffith, a Beecher passenger, *"The tug was too small, and we soon found we were pulling the tug."* At 4:30 a.m. After snapping two cables, Restorer abandoned the tow and informed Beecher that it could only stand by until calmer weather. Floundering again in heavy seas and determining that the small tug could not complete the tow, Beecher put out another call for help.

While transiting the Atlantic on a cargo run, the S.S. Cecil N. Bean responded to the Beecher's distress call. A new challenge was added to Beecher's list of misfortunes--military bureaucracy. Cecil Bean stood by while Beecher and the Army debated whether she should transfer food or tow the ship. Regulations did not allow it to tow the Beecher, and they had to wait nine hours for permission from higher command. Finally, at 4:30 p.m., the Cecil Bean was permitted to tow Beecher to just outside Bermuda's harbor. Because of the setting sun, Cecil Bean decided to postpone towing until Saturday morning.

Passengers on the two other disabled troopships got better news. The Navarchos Koundouriotis limped into New York Harbor with the Navy tug's aid, and twenty-eight battered and seasick soldiers were bussed to Fort Hamilton for a steak dinner. The McCrary was sixty miles north of Bermuda and making slow but steady progress. It was waiting for storms to abate to make its final run into Bermuda.

On Saturday morning, the Cecil Bean successfully rigged a towline to Beecher, which spent the last thirty hours wallowing in heavy swells 240 miles off Bermuda. Unfortunately, the situation on the stricken ship continued to deteriorate. The ship again was running out of food. Charles and the others were placed on reduced rations, adding hunger to seasickness. The ship's radio was failing, and Cecil Bean had to relay messages to the U.S. Despite these conditions, the Cecil Bean got underway with Beecher in tow and the Restorer standing by if further assistance was required. The small armada estimated a three-day trek to Bermuda.

Meanwhile, other vessels continued to converge on Bermuda. The McCrary limped into St George on its own power that morning. As the ship pulled into the harbor, the weary and seasick troops lined the rails and chanted, "*We wanna be home by Christmas.*" Her Captain, Allan Covy, from Daphne, Alabama, described their harrowing twenty-one-day voyage. Captain Covy said, "*It was a nightmarish experience.*" He described how the ship experienced boiler problems as soon as it left Antwerp. It was also lightly loaded with ballast. He said, "*I disliked taking the ship out in the first place because she was in damaged condition and loaded light. That's a dangerous combination for sailing.*" He also stated that taking twenty-one days for what should have been a fourteen-day transit were fog in the English Channel, a hydraulic steering casualty, and blown boiler tubes. As the voyage dragged on, conditions deteriorated on board the ship. Yesterday, McCrary took a forty-five-degree roll that Captain Covy thought would be her last. She also ran out of food, serving the last morsels to the troops at noon before docking. Turbulent seas, seasickness, and nine days of half rations had a dismal effect on the troops.

The USS Cherokee (ATF-66) was steaming from Guantanamo Bay, Cuba, to the Naval Operational Base, Bermuda. The Cherokee was a fast fleet tug with greater towing capability than the smaller Restorer. At 8:00 p.m., she received orders to alter course toward Beecher to take over the tow. Later that night, the Saturnia dropped anchor in Murray's Anchorage two miles outside St George Harbor. A heavy storm delayed it. On Sunday morning, 586 grimy troops happily departed the McCrary to take up berthing on the Saturnia. The ship's staff, including the nurses and other medical personnel, did their best to welcome the troops with the best food and comfortable conditions they could offer. The McCrary passengers would enjoy the food and comfort of Saturnia until the Beecher reached port and unloaded her passengers.

On Monday, the Cecil Bean continued to make steady progress toward Bermuda as the small armada grew. At 3:00 a.m., the Cherokee joined the Cecil Bean and Restorer. Later that day, Navy Patrol Craft 1209, which escorted the McCrary, also attached itself to the flotilla. Naval aircraft out of Bermuda were now flying regularly over the ships collecting newsreel footage that was rushed for showing in theaters across the U.S. Charles's tension was starting to ease as he and the other troops flocked on deck, as weather permitted, to view all the activity.

Sunrise Tuesday found Beecher just a few miles off Bermuda. Because of bad weather, Cecil Bean did not tow Beecher into the harbor but was directed to proceed to Five Fathom Hole, an anchorage about two miles northeast of St. George. Scattered morning showers intensified in the afternoon to steady rain, low visibility, and wind gusts as high as thirty knots, making for slow going and delaying arrival until mid-afternoon. Once safely at anchor, the Cecil Bean dropped the tow cable and attempted to transfer it to Cherokee, who had orders to tow Beecher on its final leg around St. George to Murray's Anchorage, where Saturnia was awaiting its passengers. However, Cherokee became the third tow vessel to encounter difficulties connecting a cable to Beecher. The Cherokee finally took the Beecher in tow just before 5:00 p.m. Like the previous two towing operations, the Navy decided to wait until morning because of impending darkness, choppy seas, and dangerous reefs.

Beecher stood offshore one last night. Food stocks were nearly exhausted; gone were bread, milk, and sugar. Last night they were served soup, which contained the last remnants of food for dinner. Tonight, it was emergency K-rations, which they knew all too well from their days in combat. As Charles ate his meal, he thought it tasted like these K-rations must have been the first ones packed. But the food was not what occupied his mind. He was seasick, tired, and could see land. Thus, he knew that home was the next leg of his trip.

Wednesday, December 12, 1945, had relatively mild weather for Bermuda this time of year. The temperature started at fifty-nine degrees and rose to sixty-five. The sun was out with only scattered light showers. After a relatively calm night, Charles felt the ship moving first thing in the morning. By 9:17 a.m., the Cherokee had completed its tow, and the crippled ship moored at Murray's Anchorage, within a few hundred yards of the Saturnia. Though her white paint was chipped and faded, she looked beautiful to Charles. With the Beecher's anchor set, and all the troops lined up along her rails, tugboats pulled alongside her. The crew rigged up a "Jacob's Ladder," and at 11:15, one-by-one soldiers descended off the stricken vessel and onto the tugs. As each tug filled, the men were transported to the white ship.

Charles and the other seasick and weary soldiers were overjoyed when they transferred to the Saturnia, which the press had labeled the "Christmas sleigh." Private Woodrow Bense of St Louis was the first to board the Saturnia. He said, "*this ship looks like Santa Claus to me. A real Christmas present.*" As he entered the ship's hatch, Charles thought, "*he died and went to heaven.*" The Saturnia was a former transoceanic passenger ship of the same name, which was seized from the Italian government in late 1943. She could make 19 knots and care for 1,628 patients while in service as a hospital ship. The ship's luxurious attributes were removed, covered with plywood, or obscured by military grey paint; however, within her decks, Charles found comfortable berthing, lots of space, including promenade decks, excellent food, and nurses. He did not miss the elegance!

Once all the 1,127 stranded troops were safely on board, the Saturnia initiated "Operation Santa Claus" and commenced a course to arrive in New York Harbor by Friday. About 400 medical personnel, including sixty nurses, made up the 235th Hospital Ship Complement that staffed the great ship. Colonel Gilbert Saynes, a surgeon from the University of Pittsburgh, commanded the complement and warmly welcomed the stranded passengers. That evening the McCrary and Beecher passengers were treated to a turkey dinner with all the trimmings. Since the crew spent much of the early part of the year stationed at Camp Kilmer, while waiting for the ship's conversion or were from the New York/New Jersey area, Charles devoted much of the voyage to catching up on local news.

Finally, on Friday, December 14, twenty-seven days after leaving France, Charles's ship, which he described as "*paradise*," sailed past the Statue of Liberty into New York Harbor. Despite being twenty degrees and windy, all hands ascended on deck to view her. Battle-hardened soldiers wept, some prayed, and all were thrilled to be home. As they transited up the Hudson River, an Army boat with a band and Miss America on board unfurled a banner reading "*Welcome Home.*" Earlier in the morning, WOR Radio Paul Killiam boarded the Saturnia to conduct a radio interview with the soldiers. At 2:00 p.m., civilians lined the shore, and news cameras captured the ship sailing upriver and docking pier side. As Charles descended the gangplank, he looked back on the great ship and vowed never to return to Europe or sea on a ship. He kept the first promise and did not break the second one until late in his retirement years.

On December 21, the Beecher was towed to Baltimore, where she was repaired and went on to serve a long career as a merchant ship, finally meeting the scrapper in 1969. The Saturnia remained a transport ship for a brief period. Then, in late 1946, she was returned to the Italian government, which converted the ship to her former role as a transoceanic passenger liner until 1965, when she was retired and scrapped.

Port of New York
December 14, 1945

Most of the troops were from Texas and California. They were whisked away to special troop trains waiting to take them to separation centers near their homes. Centers were told to process the troops rapidly and return them for Christmas. Since Charles was local, he could stroll off the Saturnia. Charles walked through a crowd of well-wishers with a duffle bag over his shoulder. Women hugged and thanked him, and men saluted. A group of women provided him with a cup of hot coffee and a piece of apple pie, his first food in the U.S. in a year and a half.

It was a joyous day for Charles with one dark spot. While he was at sea, Charles learned that his beloved General, George Patton was severely injured and fighting for his life. On December 9, General Patton's 1939 Cadillac crashed into an Army truck belonging to the Quartermasters Corps. The General was the only injury when he was thrown forward and then hurled back. He had cuts on his head and appeared paralyzed. After arriving at the 130th Station Hospital in Heidelberg, surgeons found the General suffered a fractured cervical spine and paralysis from the neck down. He was fighting for his life. One week after Charles arrived back in the U.S., he heard a news broadcast that General Patton had taken his last breath. On December 19, 1945, the General developed difficulty breathing and increased pressure in his spinal cord. He struggled for two days, then succumbed to acute heart failure. Before dying, he confided to his brother-in-law, *"this is a hell of a way for a soldier to die."*

Charles was transported to Camp Kilmer, the same place where his voyage to Europe began. The camp was packed with returning troops. On Victory over Europe (V-E) Day, the U.S. had more than twelve million men and women in uniform, of which three million were serving in the European Theater. The New York/New Jersey area was the receiving point for many of these troops coming home via the Atlantic Ocean--and they were rapidly coming home.

The U.S. military discharged one million GIs in December 1945 alone! Charles was caught in the logjam between the Port of New York pushing out arriving troops to keep piers open for convoys of troop-laden ships and overworked separation centers clogged with GIs anxious to head home. After a brief stay in Camp Kilmer, Charles transferred to the Separation Center at Fort Monmouth, N.J.

On December 16, Charles and a throng of other troops arrived at the Separation Center to complete the Center's eight steps for demobilization to civilian life. Open twenty-four hours a day, seven days a week, clerks processed troops at all hours, but nobody complained about the unorthodox schedule if it would get them home sooner. The first stop for Charles and his group was a snack bar where they got coffee, milk, donuts, and sandwiches before assembling to be briefed on the separation procedure. They completed the first in a series of forms and then proceeded to the "Initial Clothing Shakedown," where Center GIs evaluated the returning group's uniforms' condition and relieved them of all unauthorized government clothing, equipment, and war trophies. Since Charles had already tossed his prize war trophies over Beecher's side, he quickly cleared this station.

Stripped of any unauthorized gear, Charles and his group were assigned to a processing company, Group NYK, 1020-47. A Roster Leader trained in separation procedures ensured Charles and the other men ate, slept, and navigated their way through the Separation Center. He also conducted an "Orientation Lecture," giving the details about separations, information regarding the camp facilities, and a pitch to re-enlist, which fell on Charles's deaf ears!

On Monday, December 17, Charles began his day with his "Final Physical Examination." First Lieutenant A.L. Cooper, with the Medical Processing Branch, gave Charles a thorough examination and reviewed his medical history to make it a matter of record for future follow-up by the Veterans Administration. He also conducted a psychiatric evaluation. Finding no issues and all his test results normal, Dr. Cooper signed him off as "fit for discharge."

Having passed his physical examination, Charles entered the fifth separation stage, "Counseling." Here he was given tips on transitioning to civilian life, told his rights and benefits as a veteran, and offered vocational and educational guidance. Charles sat through the lectures, but at this point, he did not want anything more from the Army. Instead, his mind was on restoring his civilian life and putting his service behind him.

The next step was "Outgoing Records," where it was time to get all his records in order. Though it did not seem important at the time, one of the essential functions performed at the Separation Center was accurate documentation of the soldier's service. These records were critical when Charles would apply for Veterans benefits later in life. His records were reviewed, and all mistakes and discrepancies were corrected. His thumbprints were placed on his discharge forms, and all the documents, ribbons, and medals were assembled for his final discharge ceremony.

It was now time to get paid. "Finance" staff deciphered Charles's incomplete pay records and, after much checking and calculating, determined that he was entitled to leave the Army with a $185.57 check issued by Major H.M. Fix.

The day was long, but before heading to his "Departure Ceremony," he had one last stop back at the clothing issue warehouse to ensure he had a proper uniform that fit well. His health and service records were up to date. He had been paid and dressed in proper uniform. Now the last step was a presentation of his discharge certificate.

Charles donned an inspection-ready uniform and joined the other men of Group NYK, 1020-47, for their final formation as soldiers in the U.S. Army. They assembled for their "Departure Ceremony." An officer expressed the War Department's gratitude for their service and sought to instill pride in them for serving their country. Military and religious significance was given to the occasion by having both a field grade officer and a chaplain in charge. The chaplain opened with an invocation then an officer provided a few pointers about returning to civilian life. The men of the 1020-47th were praised for their loyal service to the Army and given a pep talk on being good Americans when they became civilians again. Once the speeches concluded, decorations were issued. For his thirty-eight months of service with fourteen overseas, Charles was awarded five medals, including an American Campaign Medal, European Campaign Medal with four Bronze Stars, World War II Victory Medal, Occupation Medal with a Germany Clasp, and a Good Conduct Medal. He was also issued a World War II Victory Lapel Pin. Once Charles and the other troops received their awards, they filed past the officer in charge to receive their discharge certificates signed by D.C. Weaver, Major, Field Artillery. The separation process was now complete. Charles headed out the door to catch a bus that would take him back to Garfield and civilian life.

On February 11, 1946, the 267th Field Artillery Battalion's main body arrived in New York Harbor. The next day, it was inactivated. It was authorized four battle streamers, Northern France, Rhineland, Ardennes-Alsace, and Central Europe. Three officers received Air Medals. Four officers and forty-eight enlisted men received Bronze Star Medals, and two enlisted men received Purple Heart Medals. On March 7, 1955, the 267th was reactivated, armed with 155mm self-propelled howitzers, and re-designated as an Armored Field Artillery Battalion at Fort Sill, Oklahoma. The unit deployed to Germany the following year and was again inactivated on December 1, 1957. The unit has remained inactive to this day.

Chapter 9
Post-War and the Future

Broach of Charles in uniform that Bertha wore throughout the war.

Garfield New Jersey
December 17, 1945

Charles returned to a very different Garfield from the one he left three-and-a-half years earlier or even the one he visited before shipping out to Europe. Not only did Charles demilitarize, but so did Garfield and the rest of the country. Karoly gave up his white helmet and armband of an Air Raid Warden. Bertha took off the broach she wore each day, containing the picture of Charles in his uniform. She no longer sewed uniforms for troops, and all the neighbors who worked in the factories along the Passaic River producing war goods were no longer needed.

Early 1946 saw an economy in tremendous flux. Each day thousands of men were pouring back into the country and the civilian economy. Government contracts for war supplies were abruptly canceled, transforming factories from running three shifts to standing idle. Massive layoffs of the wartime workforce were occurring, and the elimination of wartime economic controls allowed prices and, thus, inflation to rise. Charles heard predictions by economists that the country was about to reenter a depression as steep as the one that occurred after the 1929 stock market crash. Like other veterans, he did not go to war, only to return to a country ensconced in despair as he experienced as a child. This is not the America he fought for in the fields of Europe, and he was not going to relive those desperate years with his current and any future family.

Fortunately for Charles and the other returning GIs, the nay-saying economists were wrong. Many wartime workers voluntarily left the labor force to further their education or return to their prewar roles as housewives. Others, like Roseann, remained in the workforce but moved into traditionally female jobs. Charles found work as a carpenter.

The economy made a rapid transformation from war material to consumer production. After four-plus years of deprivation and sacrifice, Americans wanted better food, houses, cars, appliances, and other luxuries. Additionally, most of the industrial world's production was destroyed in the war, creating a great international demand for American consumer goods. American factories quickly retooled to meet the enormous demand. By the end of 1946, more than ten million demobilized veterans and millions of wartime workers found employment in the fastest and most massive transformation any nation ever made from war to peace.

Price controls expired, and prices rose moderately, allowing businesses to make more money. This incentivized those businesses to flow more products into the market and increase workers' wages. As a result, the average worker saw a 10% wage increase in 1946, further fueling demand for consumer goods and services.

Americans entered a well-deserved period of prosperity and enjoyment after enduring a depression and world war. In addition to splurging, Americans wanted to have fun!

Charles's generation grew up in desperate poverty and went on to forgo luxuries to win the war. They also endured the loss of friends and family members. But, with the surrender of the Axis powers, it was time to enjoy life, so nightlife flourished.

Jazz musicians and big bands uplifted morale during World War II, and many musicians served in the military and toured with USO troupes overseas and across the U.S. However, veterans of the military and war plants were looking for new types of music. Swing, popular during the war, was giving way to less danceable music, such as bebop. As a result, many great swing bands broke up, and new performers emerged to meet the changing tastes. The dance halls were full on Friday and Saturday nights, but the sounds were diverse and changing. And that is where Charles and Roseann met.

Left: Roseann dressed for work. Right: The "Paterson Girls."

Roseann was nineteen years old and moved from her wartime job to office work in the Ming Toy Dyeing Company, an affiliate of the silk dye factory where Pietro was employed. There she would help manage the busy plant's books. On weekends, she and about five of her friends would spend evenings at one of the dance clubs in Paterson or several miles away in the surrounding towns. Affectionately called the "Paterson Girls," they would all meet at one of their houses then-- because nobody had a car--take a bus to a dance hall for that night. Dances would go from 7:00 to 11:00 p.m.

The scene was the same regardless of the location. The men congregated on one side of the room, and the ladies on the opposite side. The men would come over when the music started and ask the ladies to dance. If you liked the person asking, the couple headed out on the dancefloor. Those ladies who were not asked ran into the ladies' room until they could hear the start of the next song--it was better to hide than stand on the sidelines of the dance floor with everyone else able to see that the askers skipped over you!

The Paterson Girls had a pact that if a boy offered a ride to one, he had to take them all home. So, that unexpecting boy would have up to six girls pile into his car to ride back to Paterson. Most were good about taking the group home. The last bus to Paterson would leave at 11:30 p.m., a half-hour after the dance finished. Therefore, if a ride did not appear, then it was time to hustle to the bus stop to catch the last bus home.

At a dance in 1946, Charles approached the Paterson Girls and asked Roseann to dance. She was moved by his deep blue eyes but only rated him a fair dancer. His friends were better dancers, so Roseann preferred to dance with them. After seeing each other at several dances, Charles asked Roseann on a date, to which she replied, "no." In fact, she did not say "yes" until his third ask--not because she did not like him, but because she did not want to miss dances with Paterson Girls.

Their first date was a New Year's Eve dinner dance with about sixteen of Charles's friends. They had a great time, and at midnight everyone kissed their dates, but Charles was embarrassed and hesitated. Roseann told him it was okay, and they had their first kiss. On their second date,

Charles came to East 18th Street to meet Pietro and Giuseppina. He walked into the house with a big Valentine's box of chocolates and won over Roseann's mother.

For the next two years, Charles and Roseann dated. In the beginning, the dates were meeting at dances. Roseann and Charles would dance with their friends for the first half of the dance, but after intermission, they would spend the rest of the night dancing together. Charles would then drive Roseann and the other Paterson Girls home. She was always impressed by how thoughtful he was and how he could make her laugh. They fell in love.

One day a coworker at the silk dye factory asked Roseann on a date. They had been friendly, and the guy finally summoned the courage to ask her out. She declined the offer telling him she was *"kind of going steady."* When the Paterson Girls heard the story, they chastised Roseann for saying no. They said she was foolish because Charles had not committed to her. So that weekend, Roseann worked up the nerve to ask Charles if they were going steady or not. He said, *"Of course,"* and that was that.

In early 1948, after two years of dating, Charles drove Roseann home after a dance. They were sitting in his car and said *"goodnight"* to one another. After she left the car, he came running after her and said in a really soft voice, *"Will you marry me?"* Tears streamed down Roseann's face as she said, *"Yes."*

Soon after Charles proposed, Pietro gathered family and friends to his house for a big party. When everyone assembled, he announced that his youngest daughter would marry Charles. Money was tight for both Charles's and Roseann's parents, so it was up to the couple to shoulder much of the wedding and reception cost. To save money, one of the Paterson Girls, Margaret, offered to make a wedding dress--she graduated from a fashion academy in Pittsburg. Margaret and Roseann found off-white heavy satin material and a beautiful pattern for a wedding dress. The dress came together with a sweetheart neckline, a lace-over-satin top, long sleeves, and tiny buttons from the neck to the waist. It had a satin skirt. Roseann went on a crash diet to fit into the dress, dropping her weight to 107 pounds. She felt awkward that her collar bones were protruding but happy to fit in the gown.

Roseann worried as the wedding approached because it had been raining for several days. Then on October 9, 1948, the sun came out, and the weather was beautiful. Charles and his parents came over to Roseann's house, and the two families went to an 8:00 a.m. Catholic mass at St. Joseph's Church. They then returned to East 18th Street to decorate the house for the wedding reception. They placed streamers along the ceiling and flowers throughout the house. After lunch, Josephine Foti styled Roseann's hair and helped her with the gown. They took pictures, and then it was time to leave for the 4:00 p.m. ceremony.

One of Charles's friends offered to drive them to the service in his black Buick. He put a white curtain in the rear window to make it even more special. (The picture of Charles and Roseann looking out that window is at the beginning of this book.) Because Charles was not Catholic, the service could not be held in the main church but rather in the rectory, which is the building that houses the priests. The service was conducted in the rectory's small parlor, which could only accommodate two people in the wedding party and the immediate family. Charles wore a black tuxedo with a white bowtie, while Roseann wore her full-length silk wedding dress with a lace veil. Father Darrick presided over a small and simple ceremony, but this did not seem to matter to the smiling couple. With the Best Man, Tony Belle, and Josephine Foti as the Maid of Honor, Charles and Roseann said, "*I do.*"

The rest of the family and friends met them in Pietro and Giuseppina's third-floor apartment for a simple reception with ham and cheese sandwiches, soda, beer, and wine. At 10:00 p.m., Charles and Roseann left for a night in a New York City hotel.

After their short honeymoon, Charles and Roseann began their new life together. They depended on their two families and communities' support structure to start a life and eventually exited the societies that shaped them. When Pietro came to the U.S. in 1905, he dreamed of putting his homeland behind him and building an American family. That dream also drove Karoly to make the arduous journey from

Hungary back to the U.S. Those dreams would become a reality for Pietro and Karoly as they watched their children's marriage.

Josephine Foti helps Roseann get ready for her marriage. Back from their one-night honeymoon, Charles and Roseann read about their wedding in the Herald News.

Charles and Roseann moved into the apartment above Karoly's shoemaker shop. Charles worked in the mills around Garfield while Roseann prepared to be a mother. Nine months after their marriage, Kenneth Charles was born. The date was July 19, 1949. Four years later, on June 2, 1953, their second son, Richard Alexander, was born. The family outgrew the small apartment, and it was time to buy their own home.

Both Charles and Roseann were fond of Garfield. It was more suburban than inner-city Paterson, but they chose not to settle in the town's Hungarian section. In the 1950s, Garfield was ethnically divided, with most Italians living in a section called the "Heights" because it was on a hill, Hungarians living on the western part of town, and those of Polish and German descent residing in the "Valley" on the east side of town. In the Valley was a small circular dirt road that encircled a tree and grassy area--the residents called it "*the island*." Around the island were fourteen three-story houses with high-pitched roofs, asbestos shingles, and yards between one-half to one acre. The street was developed in the 1920s to house immigrants from Germany who worked at the giant Forstmann wool mill. The immigrants who inhabited these houses were recruited from Germany to work as foremen in the factory. Since they were management, these were nice houses for that time. While most of the original German residents moved away with World War II, a handful of German families still lived on the street. Moving into a German neighborhood gave Charles an uneasy feeling, still suffering nightmares from the war, but the price of the house was too good to pass up. Additionally, it was within walking distance to a ball field, Catholic Church, school, and grocery stores. Thus, the family of four became members of a neighborhood that was foreign to any of their roots.

In April 1955, Charles and Roseann became homeowners when they signed a mortgage to purchase 21 Louise Street from Mr. and Mrs. Rudolph Orlando. During the war, the Orlando's daughter, Elsie, was engaged to marry Second Lieutenant Steve Luka. Like Roseann, Elsie lost her fiancé to fighting in the Pacific Theater when his plane was shot down over Hainan, China, on March 6, 1945. Charles got a job maintaining machinery at a plastic bag factory called Standard Packaging in nearby Clifton, while Roseann alternated between being a stay-at-home mom for newborn children and working in a bank when they were old enough to attend grammar school. She worked at Garfield Trust Company and then Spencer Savings and Loan, both on Outwater Lane in Garfield, and enjoyed the one-mile walk to and from Louise Street each day. Roseann worked in the two banks for over 30 years until she retired in 1982.

Once Kenneth and Richard were old enough for school, Roseann enrolled them in Saint Stanislaus Koska Catholic School. It was a luxury that required her to work, but a Catholic upbringing was important to her, and she made the sacrifice. With Kenneth and Richard in school, Charles and Roseann continued to expand their family. I was born on March 13, 1959, and on November 27, 1962, Roseann got her wish to have a daughter with Patricia's birth.

Merry Christmas
— and a
Happy New Year

1963 Christmas card with Asztalos children taken on the side of the house and 21 Louise Street in 2018

Values for me and my siblings blended my immigrant family traditions and those from the melting pot that was Garfield and America in general. Most Sundays were dedicated to family, with a traditional Italian meal that consumed the entire afternoon with aunts, uncles, and cousins. A traditional Italian meal of pasta, sauce, meatballs, braciola, or Italian sausage was served with salad, nuts, and Italian cookies or pastries. Occasionally, Sunday was spent around Hungarian delicacies with Charles's relatives. Surrounding the food were the adults' discussions about politics, entertainment, and any other subject that could spark a lively conversation. We kids just played outside. Enjoying Italian or Hungarian culture was important to Charles and Roseann, but they never imposed old-world heritage on us. In fact, stories told to the children were not about life in the old world but focused on growing up in the 1920s and during the Great Depression. Talk about World War II was rare to nonexistent.

The extended family experience is not always pleasant. Now and then, feuds broke out between siblings or cousins, and hard feelings would set into the Sunday conversations until the feud passed. The longest feud was between Charles and Roseann's uncle, Joseph Blondin, which lasted more than a decade. It started before I was born; nobody remembers how it began, but the two would nearly come to blows when they saw each other for years. Over time, it fell into a stalemate where they simply ignored one another, even though Joseph and Margaret lived two houses from us. It was always odd for us kids that we were not supposed to talk to him though he was our "Uncle Joe." Finally, when I was still a young boy, my dad walked over to Uncle Joe, and they shook hands. I wonder if they even remembered why they did not speak all those years. A few years later, in 1968, Joseph died. Charles and Roseann went to his funeral, and although Charles never said it, I bet he was glad he extended his hand to him.

Garfield exposed my brothers and me to different cultures, making us part of a fabric very different from Charles and Roseann, who were raised in neighborhoods of a single heritage. Five days a week, we attended classes at the Polish school, then before meeting the relatives on Sunday, it was back to the same building for Polish mass. At Saint Stanislaus Koska, we learned the Polish language and history. The Asztalos family was more likely to celebrate Polish over Italian holidays and attend Polish festivals--it was rare that we attended the traditional Italian Feast of San Gennaro. However, we could always be found at the annual church picnic honoring General Kazimierz Pulaski, a Polish immigrant who valiantly fought against the British in the American Revolutionary War, even saving George Washington's life. Kazimierz Pulaski was eventually promoted to General in the Continental Army and awarded honorary U.S. citizenship. He is a hero to Polish Americans.

We grew up in a typical American household of the 1950s and 1960s. Except for an occasional phrase from our aunts and uncles, or conversations between grandparents, Italian or Hungarian were not spoken--only English was spoken at 21 Louise Street. When it came time to learn a foreign language, Polish was taught in grammar school and Spanish in high school. Except for Sunday dinner, our meals were classic Americana. Roseann had to learn to cook American meals because that cooking was foreign in Giuseppina's household. Early on, Roseann saw a recipe for "Heavenly Hot Dogs" in the newspaper. She thought, "*What a treat to serve my family of young children!*" However, she did not realize that she had to cook the hot dogs before putting them under the broiler with cheese on top, so the creation was burnt cheese atop raw hot dogs. American cooking was an art that she had to learn. When frozen meals called "TV dinners" became the rage, Roseann stocked the freezer and served them as a treat to the family.

A central tenet of the American dream is to create a life where your children are better off than you and that education is the pathway to that better life. Giuseppina and Pietro were raised in a culture of child labor and struggled to ensure that Roseann graduated with a high school diploma. Charles and Roseann prodded us to attend college and scraped together a fund that provided us with that opportunity. My siblings and I all went on to earn some level of college education.

Another aspect of the American dream was to earn and enjoy leisure time. Despite hard financial times, Charles and Roseann found money to provide a summer vacation every year. Usually, it was a week at the New Jersey Shore. Never campers, Charles and Roseann loved the beach and lived for vacations filled with eight-plus hour beach days. Every few years, when money was saved, summer vacation was a bus trip to Florida or the Catskill Mountains in New York. One year we all spent a week in Hawaii, and another, at my insistence, in Niagara Falls. Wherever the trip, Charles was adamant that the family would take a week's vacation each year and enjoy each other's company.

Our upbringing did include several "old world" values, a primary one being good Catholics. Pietro and Giuseppina ensured their children were baptized and received the sacraments, but they did not consistently practice their faith because they did not have money for the collection plate or nice clothes for mass.

When Roseann was eight or ten years old, her friend Ann convinced her to attend mass with her family. Roseann enjoyed the experience, setting up a life of devotion to her Catholic faith. Throughout her adult life, Roseann ensured her family attended Sunday mass. On many days she attended daily mass or joined a group reciting the rosary. Charles, who was brought up in the Hungarian Reform faith, was so moved by Roseann's faith that he converted to Catholicism on May 20, 1966. Wherever they lived, Roseann would find a Catholic Church and become an active member. As Roseann entered the final chapter of her life, she refused to give up driving her automobile, even though she knew she should. The reason she kept driving was to attend daily mass and to deliver the Eucharist to those who were in the hospital or homebound.

Another immigrant value she instilled in us was the importance of family--not just our immediate family but our extended family. Even though Roseann's children scattered to the country's farthest corners, she encouraged us to call one another and visit. She was extremely close to her cousins--especially Josephine--and confessed she regretted that we were not close with our cousins.

To Charles and Roseann, family extended beyond those who share your blood.   Special people who greatly impacted their lives found themselves in my parents' family sphere. Though Charles never met Eskew, as he died four years before Charles and Roseann were married, his memory lived with them.   Charles and Roseann stayed close to Eskew's mother and sisters throughout their lives. As a child, our family regularly visited Eskew's sister and mother, Margaret, and Blanche Steffens, at their New Jersey lake house. We thought of them as a cousin and an aunt.   Our parents never told us about Eskew or their war experiences, generally. Only once, when I was in the Navy, and my ship was in the Philadelphia Navy Yard, my mother and I drove past the mothballed USS Intrepid. In passing, she told me that she had a fiancé killed on that ship--she never said anything more about it, and I, regretfully, never asked her. Thus, we never knew our relationship with the Steffens family until after our parents died. All we knew was that the Steffens were part of our lives, and they made the best fried chicken!

A plaque dedicated to Charles, Roseann, and Eskew is mounted on a "Seat of Honor" in the Allison & Howard Lutnick Theater on board the USS Intrepid, now the Intrepid Sea, Air & Space Museum Complex docked in New York City.

Staying friends with Eskew's family was one way for Charles and Roseann to ease the war's trauma; however, it would stay with them their entire lives. While Charles did not suffer physical disability from the war, it never left him. Roseann learned early in their marriage how to take care of him when he had nightmares. The dreams he--like other veterans-- experienced were very different from other dreams. Post-war dreams involve all your senses. In his dreams, Charles not only relived combat but would feel his uniform on his skin, smell gunpowder and the stench of death, taste grit in his mouth, and his ears would ring from the boom of the artillery. Many nights, he would wake in a cold sweat crying. Charles did not have to sleep for the dreams to come upon him. Sometimes he would sit awake and look down to see his uniform on his arms, and he would hear, feel, and smell battle. Sweat would immediately appear, and he would cry out and then leave his trance. Over the years, the dreams lessened, but they never ended.

Garfield New Jersey
1960's

As they raised their children, Charles and Roseann also cared for their aging parents. Karoly retired from his shoe repair shop in 1961 and died of throat cancer on May 30, 1964, at the age of 66. Like many of his generation, he was a heavy smoker and usually had an unfiltered Camel cigarette hanging from his lips. In the final stage of his life, Karoly would take the bus to and from Saint Mary's Hospital to receive radiation treatments, a new and experimental cancer treatment. When he would return home from the treatments, he would light up a cigarette. Four months before Karoly passed away, the U.S. Surgeon General released the first Report of the Surgeon General's Advisory Committee on Smoking and Health announcing to the American people that cigarette smoking causes lung cancer, laryngeal cancer, and chronic bronchitis. Unfortunately, the news came too late for Karoly.

Bertha lived on Dewey Street until she could not keep up with that large house. She moved into a senior citizen apartment building until she passed away in 1986 at the age of 84. Charles regularly visited his mom and cared for her needs the entire time she lived alone.

Pietro and Giuseppina moved in with their daughter Anna and her husband, Walter Fedishen, on Ryerson Avenue in Paterson when it became a challenge for them to maintain their East 18th Street residence. There Roseann and her siblings spent many weekends gathered with their aging parents. Though up in age, their nature remained the same. Pietro remained easygoing, and Giuseppina remained in charge. As a child, I remember sitting by Pietro as he relaxed in his chair on those Sunday afternoons. Giuseppina would stand over him and, in Italian, give him orders. He would look down and smile at me as he turned his hearing aid off. That act kept their marriage secure as she continued with her orders and he with a smile derived from silence. After sixty years of marriage, Pietro died of a heart attack in 1970, and Giuseppina followed him two years later.

As Charles and Roseann's parents moved on, so did their children. By the mid-1980s, we all had moved out of Louise Street and begun our own families. Kenneth earned a degree from East Stroudsburg State College in the Pocono Mountains of Pennsylvania in 1972 and had a successful career in the trucking and railroad business. He married a schoolmate, Donna Eshelman, and they had two children, Benjamin and Joanne. After separating from Donna, he married Kim Jones, and they reside in Brookings, Oregon. Richard graduated from Boston College and is a retired Behavior Specialist from the Boston Public School System. He married Patrice Anzalone, and together they have three children: Julie, Andrew, and Corey. All reside in the greater Boston area. Patricia moved to South Florida, where she manages hotels. She married Francisco Reyes Molina in 1994, and they had two children, Christopher and Nicholas. Patricia and Francisco divorced, and she married Mark Osit; they live in Pembroke Pines, Florida. I met Phyllis Calderella, and we married in 1985 and have one daughter named Courtney. We live in Tallahassee, Florida, where I work in government.

Charles and Roseann lived the American Dream up until the end of their lives. During his late 40's and early 50's, Charles suffered a series of heart attacks. Finally, in 1978, at age 55, Charles underwent pioneering quadruple heart bypass surgery in New York City. Since it was experimental surgery, the doctors provided him a prognosis of five more years, but American medicine gave him another thirty-one. However, his condition forced early retirement. Roseann worked a few more years, then retired from the bank. They moved to Toms River on the New Jersey Shore, then to Florida in 1998. They settled in Zephyrhills outside of Tampa, where they lived out their lives as many northern retirees do.

They moved two doors down from Richard and Maria Lazar. Charles's cousin Richard was Frank and Margaret (Kovacs) Lazer's son and was born exactly ten years after Charles. Because neither had a male sibling, they treated each other like brothers. They were also Army veterans.

In March 1953, Richard enlisted in the U.S. Army as the Korean War raged in Asia. He went to boot camp at Fort Dix and was stationed in Germany for occupation duty with Company L of the 18th Infantry Regiment. There Richard attended radar school and played on the company's baseball and basketball teams. He also met a beautiful seventeen-year-old German girl from Aschaffenburg. The first time Richard laid eyes on Maria, he knew he would marry her, and he did. In February 1955, as Corporal Lazar's enlistment ended, Maria boarded a Trans World Airlines flight from Frankfort, Germany, to New York to join the ranks of 20,000 German "war brides" and begin her new life in Garfield.

Charles and Richard shared a love of sports, especially baseball. Richard umpired baseball games from professional spring training to minor leagues to local school teams. Charles especially enjoyed joining Richard when he umpired the New York Yankees spring training games in Tampa. Like all brothers, their relationship had its ups and downs. Although cousins, they were the brothers to each other that they never had.

Roseann outlived her siblings and said goodbye to them one by one. Anna's marriage to Thomas Baeli ended when he left her in September 1951. In December 1953, she divorced him and three months later married Walter Fedishen. Walter was a handsome man with a painful past. Born in Poland, he fought against the German Army when it invaded his country. He was captured by the Germans and held in a Prisoner of War camp. After the war, he was liberated by the Russian Army, who then incarcerated him in a Soviet gulag. In 1949 he made his way to Paterson and became an American citizen on April 14, 1955. In 1964, he suffered an accident while working as a roll tender for the Royal Textile Company when four fingers on his left hand were crushed in the roller of a plastic machine. His fingers had to be amputated. His life experiences left him bitter, and he died on August 29, 1986, after

Alzheimer's Disease robbed him of his memory. Four days after her 70th birthday, Anna died on January 22, 1988.

The following year, Roseann's brother Anthony died while residing in New Port Richie, Florida. His wife, Carmella, would live in isolation in Florida until 2003 when she finally joined Anthony.

Carmen was always small framed and became frail with age. Maybe, due to his rugged life in the Army and CCC, he suffered health issues for the remainder of his life. In the late 1940s, Carmen suffered from dental issues aggravated by his military service. He also battled diabetes. In 1976, his diabetes began to rob his eyesight and forced him to quit his $5,000 per year watchman job at Beattie Rugs in Little Falls, NJ. For health reasons, he and Lillian moved to the Florida Panhandle and eventually to Spring, TX, near Houston.

Life never gave Carmen a break. After the war, until he retired, he moved through a series of jobs. But he always felt his future was in Florida. In the early 1950s, he got caught up in a land scam when he bought what was essentially swampland in central Florida. Realizing he was taken, he put the worthless deeds in a drawer and wrote off his loss. Several years later, he received a call from someone interested in purchasing the land, albeit at a cheap price. Deciding something is better than nothing, he sold the land deeds. The buyer was The Walt Disney Company.

Somewhere when I was a child, Anna and Roseann drifted apart from Carmen and Lillian. I do not think the former bride and bridesmaid got along very well. I know Roseann deeply missed her brother. In March 1986, Charles and Roseann visited Carmen and Lillian in Florida and reconciled their differences. After that, she was at peace that she and her brother were on good terms again.

In January 1998, Carmen became bedridden from Type One Diabetes and a year of advancing Alzheimer's Disease. He was admitted to a nursing home, Mariner Health Care of Northwest Houston, and passed away on June 20, 1998, at age 85. Lillian lived another thirteen years, passing away on June 16, 2011. They are both buried in the South Florida National Cemetery located in Lake Worth, Florida.

Eventually, age would catch up with Charles. He suffered a stroke and, after a series of trying years, passed away, surrounded by family, on May 20, 2009. His pallbearers were our cousin Richard, my two brothers, and me. He is buried alongside his military brothers and sisters at the Florida National Cemetery in Bushnell, Florida.

Roseann continued to live in their "Driftwood" condominium after Charles passed away and remained active until her death. Along with friends from the community and church, Richard and Maria helped fill some of the void from life without Charles. She was a Eucharistic Minister and attended mass every day at St. Joseph Catholic Church in Zephyrhills. She also volunteered at the local hospital, participated in Driftwood community events, and loved traveling to visit her children and grandchildren.

Roseann always dreamed of visiting Santa Croce Camerina and seeing firsthand the land of her parents. However, Charles kept true to his word that he never set foot in Europe again. It was not until 2014, the year before Mom would pass away, that she and my sister, Patricia, took a European cruise that stopped in Catania, Sicily, where they met our Sicilian relatives. Even though she did not visit Santa Croce Camerina, meeting her relatives on Sicilian soil was a dream come true. When I was in the Navy stationed on an aircraft carrier in 1980, I took a week's leave from Naples and visited our Sicilian relatives. I sent detailed letters and pictures each day describing the experience. After Mom passed away, I found a box in her closet where she saved those letters and pictures. I am happy she got to walk on Sicilian soil before she left this world.

In September 2014, not long after her trip to Europe, Roseann became ill. Her condition deteriorated in the latter part of 2014, but she was determined to see 2015. Gravely ill, her last spoken words were a whispered "Happy New Year" on January 1, 2015. Ten days later, she passed away in her bed at Springtree Health & Rehabilitation Center in Sunrise, Florida. Her body lies next to Charles in Bushnell.

Roseann, Carmen, and Charles reunion in Florida, March 1986

History is really a collection of stories about the individuals who make up a society. My ancestors' stories are weaved together with others, and together they make up the history of our great country. They suffered and persevered as the country went through economic hardship and enjoyed times of prosperity. When our society was threatened, they responded to the call and did their part in defeating our nation's enemies.

Karoly, Pietro, Bertha, Giuseppina, Charles, and Roseann shared a collective dream to build an American family and ensure their offspring would benefit from our nation's bounty. They each did their part to perpetuate the American dream by focusing inward on raising their children. Their story…my story…is America's story.

Acknowledgments

After my mother passed away, I was cleaning her apartment and found a journal she had been writing in over the last few years of her life. Every couple of weeks, she would write a page describing some aspect of her and Dad's lives. I shared it with my siblings, and we all realized that there was much of our parents' lives that we did not know. My mother and father--or, for that matter, many World War II generation members--rarely discussed their experiences, and to our fault we did not ask the right questions. As I pieced their lives together from archives and the few stories from them that I remember, I realized their life is a microcosm of our nation's history. The work in front of you is an accurate record of their lives based on written and verbal records. This book is as factually accurate as possible to the extent that archives and memories are filled with contradictory and illegible records. However, some of the experiences attributed to my ancestors were really from those who were with them or in similar situations and documented their experiences. To the extent those experiences are supported by the archival record--I took the liberty of making them the thoughts and actions of my ancestors.

I want to acknowledge my wife Phyllis, who was an active partner in the search for information and let me travel to archives and historical sites and spend many hours in online archives. To my daughter, Courtney, thank you for all your help with graphics and improving the photos in the book.

The following books and websites provided insight into my ancestors' experiences, and I wish to acknowledge and thank their authors for saving our history.

- For information used in multiple chapters
    - Ancestry.com was a primary source of research and its archives provided invaluable information in this book.
    - FamilySearch.org
    - Fold3.com for original military reports
    - Life Magazine issues during WWII

- National Archives and Records Administration provided original information on military and Depression work programs. Their team in the College Park, MD archives was incredibly helpful.

- Newspapers.com provided access to newspapers of the day that gave first-hand information and helped put that information in the context of other events.

- Public Papers of the Presidents, National Archives and Records Administration, https://www.archives.gov/federal-register/publications/presidential-papers.html

- U.S. Department of Veterans Affairs provided original records.

- Wikipedia was a great starting point for research.

- **Chapter 1 We Came to America**

  - Susan M. Papp, "Hungarian Americans and Their Communities of Cleveland" Cleveland State University, https://pressbooks.ulib.csuohio.edu/hungarian-americans-and-their-communities-of-cleveland/front-matter/cleveland-ethnic-heritage-studies-cleveland-state-university/

  - "Passenger lists and emigrant ships from Norway Heritage" Norway Heritage Collection, http://www.norwayheritage.com/gallery/gallery.asp?action=viewimage&categoryid=30&text=&imageid=1568&box=&shownew=,

  - "Historical Ephemeral Collections 1880s-1950s" Gjenvick-Gjønvik Archives https://www.gjenvick.com/

  - "The horror of emigration ships" Heritage Ezine 2016 http://www.italyheritage.com/magazine/articles/history/emigration-the-ships.htm

- o   Dr. Allan McLaughlin, U. S. Public Health and Marine Hospital Service, "How Immigrants Are Inspected at Ellis Island circa 1903," The Popular Science Monthly, February 1905, Volume 66, Pages 357-361. https://www.gjenvick.com/Immigration/EllisIsland/1905-02-HowImmigrantsAreInspected.html

- o   Linda Alchin, "Ellis Island Immigration Process," http://www.american-historama.org/1881-1913-maturation-era/ellis-island-immigration-process.htm

- **Chapter 2 The First World War**

  - o   John R. Schindler, "Fall of the Double Eagle The Battle for Galicia and the Demise of Austria-Hungary" Potomack Books, 2015

  - o   William W. Scott, "History of Passaic and Its Environs" Lewis Historical Publishing Company Inc New York and Chicago, 1922

- **Chapter 3 The Roaring Twenties**

  - o   Howard D Lanza, "Images of America Garfield" Arcadia Publishing, Charleston, South Carolina, 2002

  - o   "Model T" History.com Editors, Updated May 2, 2019, Original April 26, 2010, https://www.history.com/topics/inventions/model-t

  - o   Adams James Truslow, The Epic of America, Greenwood Press, 1931

- **Chapter 4 The Great Depression in the Hoover Years**

  - o   Arthur Guarino, "Time of Despair, Time of Hope, New Jersey in the Great Depression," June 24, 2014, https://gardenstatelegacy.com/files/Time_of_Despair_Time_of_Hope_Guarino_GSL24.pdf

- **Chapter 5 The Great Depression and the New Deal**

  - "Franklin D. Roosevelt, Papers as President: The President's Secretary's File (PSF), 1933-1945" Franklin D. Roosevelt Presidential Library & Museum, http://www.fdrlibrary.marist.edu/archives/collections/franklin/?p=collections/findingaid&id=502

  - Elizabeth M. Smith "History of the Boise National Forest 1905-1976" Idaho State Historical Society 1983 https://www.fs.usda.gov/Internet/FSE_DOCUMENTS/fsbdev3_042206.pdf

  - Kathleen Duxbury, "The Boys of Bergen" 1912 Duxbury Media Inc, Ridgewood, New Jersey

- **Chapter 6 The Second World War During Neutrality**

  - New York Times Article Archive, https://archive.nytimes.com/www.nytimes.com/ref/membercenter/nytarchive.html

  - Adam Foreman and Dalya Meyer, "American Nazism and Madison Square Garden," April 14, 2021, **https://www.nationalww2museum.org/war/articles/american-nazism-and-madison-square-garden**

  - "Franklin D. Roosevelt, Papers as President: The President's Secretary's File (PSF), 1933-1945" Franklin D. Roosevelt Presidential Library & Museum, http://www.fdrlibrary.marist.edu/archives/collections/franklin/?p=collections/findingaid&id=502

  - Coast Artillery Journal, 1941–42 editions, Coast Artillery Training Center, Fort Monroe, VA

- **Chapter 7 The Second World War and Fortress America**

  - "Franklin D. Roosevelt, Papers as President: The President's Secretary's File (PSF), 1933-1945" Franklin D. Roosevelt Presidential Library & Museum, http://www.fdrlibrary.marist.edu/archives/collections/franklin/?p=collections/findingaid&id=502

- LT Col George Dyer "XII Corps: Spearhead of Patton's Third Army" 1947 "History of the Second Army" a transcript
- Coast Artillery Journal, 1942 editions, Coast Artillery Training Center, Monroe, VA,
- "Tank Destroyers of the USA" www.tankdestroyer.net
- "Hood Panther," the newspaper of Fort Hood, Tx. 1943 editions, www.tankdestroyer.net
- "A Handbook for Air Raid Wardens, 1943," Digital Maryland, https://collections.digitalmaryland.org/digital/collection/mdww/id/121
- Howard D Lanza, "Images of America Garfield," Arcadia Publishing, Charleston, South Carolina, 2002
- "Convoy Web, The Website for Merchant Ships during WW2" http://www.convoyweb.org.uk/
- Staff Sergeant Robert Tessmer, Company 1, 397th Infantry Regiment, "Life Aboard a Troop Transport" by https://100thww2.org/anecd/TRANSPORT.html
- Roland W. Charles, "Troopships of World War II" 1947
- Geoffrey F.X. O'Connell, "The Mystery of the 364th," Gambit Weekly, April 30, 2001
- CHINA - BURMA – INDIA, Remembering the Forgotten Theater of World War II, www.cbi-theater.com
- Carlton Jackson "Allied Secret: The Sinking of HMT Rohna" University of Oklahoma Press, 1997
- Levant, Admiralty War Diary 1943, http://naval-history.net/xDKWD-Levant1943d.htm
- A Pocket Guide to India - CBI Theater of World War II, http://www.cbi-theater.com/booklet/guide-to-india.html
- Raymond T. Stone, Radarman 2/c, "My Ship! The USS Intrepid" G.P. Books, 2003

- **Chapter 8 The Second World War and the American Offensive**

  o Raymond T. Stone, Radarman 2/c, "My Ship! The USS Intrepid" G.P. Books, 2003
  o "A History of the USS INTREPID CV-11 (16 August 1943 - 22 March 1946)" by the Ships Data Section, Office of Public Information, Department of the Navy
  o Charles M. Province, "Patton's Third Army: A Chronology of the Third Army Advance, August 1944 to May 1945" Hippocrane Books, 1992
  o LT Col George Dyer "XII Corps: Spearhead of Patton's Third Army" 1947
  o "After action report: Third US Army, 1 August 1944 - 9 May 1945. Vol I, the operations," Ike Skelton Combined Arms Research Library Digital Library, https://cgsc.contentdm.oclc.org/digital/collection/p4013 coll8/id/2199
  o Gary Funk "My War in Europe: 1944-1947, a memoir" A blog, https://14tharmoreddivision.blogspot.com/2009/
  o Patricia Kollander and John O'Sullivan, "I Must be a Part of this War: A German American's Fight Against Hitler and Nazism," 2005
  o Robert P. Bowers, "The War Years 1942 – 1945," an autobiography by Robert P. Bowers prepared in June 1994
  o "The World War 2 Letters of Private Melvin W Johnson" 2016 http://www.worldwar2letters.com/?cat=1
  o Hugh M Cole, "The Lorraine Campaign" Center of Military History, United States Army, 1993
  o Major Hermon E. Smith, "An Informal History of the 697th Field Artillery Battalion," Merriam Press, 2015
  o Colin Fraser, "The Notorious Rheinwiesenlager – Thousands of Germans Died in American-Run POW Camps In Germany in 1945," War History Online, https://www.warhistoryonline.com/instant-articles/was-

it-a-war-crime-thousands-of-germans-died-in-american-pow-camps-in1945-m.html
- o Stephen Ambrose, "Ike and the Disappearing Atrocities" https://archive.nytimes.com/www.nytimes.com/books/98/11/22/specials/ambrose-atrocities.html, February 24, 1991
- o "Welcome to Bombay – a Guide Provided to Newly Arriving Soldiers" https://cbi-theater.com/menu/cbi_home.html
- o Thomas Bl Allen and Norman Polmar, "Codename Downfall" 1995
- o Walter Jackson Brantley, "WWII Recollections" https://www.witnesstowar.org
- o John C. Sparrow Major, Quartermaster Corps United States Army, "History of Personnel Demobilization in the United States Army" Department of the Army Pamphlet No. 20 -210, July 1952
- o Roderick Nordell, "Letter Home: Life as an Enlistee," Christian Science Monitor, September 12, 1995, https://www.csmonitor.com/1995/0912/12161.html
- o Video of the Henry Ward Beecher Rescue, Getty Images, Grinberg, Paramount, Pathe Newsreels, https://www.gettyimages.com
  - ▪ Video of the S.S. HENRY WARD BEECHER's rescue and the FRANCES Y. SLANGER'S docking in New York include:
  - ▪ "Returning GIs temporarily stranded in Atlantic Ocean as their Liberty ship 'Henry Ward Beecher' is towed to Bermuda. WS Liberty ship S.S. Cecil N. Bean tows crippled S.S. Henry Ward Beecher, escort ships follow" "Army transport ship USAT Saturnia, former luxury ship, at anchor off Bermuda shore, as ship convoy crosses in distance" "Saturnia aft section" "VS tow ship pulls Beecher" "Beecher at anchor" "CU Beecher bow" "POV around Beecher stern, hundreds of GIs lined up along ship's rail, tug

boats at her side."
http://www.gettyimages.com/detail/video/liberty
-ship-ss-cecil-n-bean-tows-crippled-ss-henry-
ward-news-footage/802912860

- "Crippled Liberty ship S.S. Henry Ward Beecher is towed to Bermuda by S.S. Cecil N. Bean. Aerials: VS S.S. Cecil N. Bean tows S.S. Henry Ward Beecher in Atlantic Ocean" "Circle around Army transport ship USAT Saturnia anchored near Bermuda to rescue troops aboard the Beecher" "Pilot boat leaves Saturnia side" "VS Saturnia gets under way" "Circle over Bean towing Beecher."
http://www.gettyimages.com/license/802941326

- "Crippled Liberty ship S.S. Henry Ward Beecher is towed to Bermuda by S.S. Cecil N. Bean after troops it was carrying removed to ship USAT Saturnia Aerials S.S. Cecil N. Bean tows S.S. Henry Ward Beecher in Atlantic Ocean" VS aboard vacated Beecher, life rafts stacked on deck" "Airplane wing as it flies over ocean and USAT Saturnia" "Fly around Saturnia."
http://www.gettyimages.com/detail/video/aerials
-ss-cecil-n-bean-tows-ss-henry-ward-beecher-
in-news-footage/802929604

- "Returning GIs temporarily stranded in Atlantic Ocean are rescued by Army transport ship USAT Saturnia" "VS soldiers lined up along ship's rail" "Soldiers climb over rail and down 'Jacob's Ladder' to tug boat alongside the S.S. Henry Ward Beecher" "Soldiers at ship's rail lean over it to watch those leaving ship"
http://www.gettyimages.com/license/802897212

- **Chapter 9 Post-War and the Future**

  - "The Economic Report of the President to the Congress," January 8, 1947, https://www.presidency.ucsb.edu/sites/default/files/boo ks/presidential-documents-archive-guidebook/the-economic-report-of-the-president-truman-1947-obama-2017/1947.pdf

Made in the USA
Columbia, SC
23 December 2024

60625d87-b59c-477c-af06-f36e8a4029b7R01